Mickleover Born & Bred

Book Three: 1954 - 1968

By Peter Brown

Cover Illustrations: The author aged 22; Derby Evening Telegraph aerial photograph showing the new school in Vicarage Road; St John's Church; Mickleover railway line.

Other Titles by the same author:
Peter's School, Littleover, St Peter's Church School, Littleover 1845-1945.
Mickleover Born & Bred (Book One: 1066-1937)
Mickleover Born & Bred (Book Two: 1938-1953)

© Peter Brown
First Edition 2009

All rights reserved. No part of this publication may be reproduced, in any form or by any means, without prior consent of the author.

ISBN 0-9547637-3-4

Further copies can be obtained from the author.

Published by:
    Peter Brown,
    17 Gisborne Close,
    Mickleover, Derby DE3 9LU.
Printed by Tranters, Chandos Pole Street, Derby.

This book is dedicated to Simon Peter Brown (1968-1991) and Neve Lily Rose Fewkes, my youngest grandchild.

ACKNOWLEDGMENTS

I am indebted to the help I have received over the last three years from local people who have played their part in making this volume a comprehensive history of Mickleover.

Lifelong friend, Ken Guy particularly, has given me a good deal of his time and knowledge of the village.

My wife Ann whose help and patience in researching records and newspapers, followed by continuously reading a mountain of proofs, and to neighbours and friends Pat and Colin White for their time in correcting my grammatical errors, deserve my deepest thanks. Graham Nutt and other volunteers at The Magic Attic Archive in Swadlincote who have allowed me to scan local newspapers from their catalogue. Thanks also to the *Derby Evening Telegraph* for allowing me to publish a number of their photographs, both scanned and original. The help and advice from the staff at Mickleover Library, Derby Local Study Library, Derby Museum, and Dr Margaret O'Sullivan at the County Records Office in Matlock whose help has been invaluable.

I am grateful to the governors and headteacher, at Vicarage Road Primary School, for allowing me to visit the school to further study the Log Books of both the earlier Infants' and Junior Schools in the village. Thanks also to David Cooper, the former head, for helping to arrange the study of Ravensdale Junior School Log Books which are held at the County Records Office.

Thanks also to: Peter Arnold, Joyce (née Warner) Baker, Don Barnes, Michael Bowden, Allan Bradshaw, Doctor John Charlton, Ann (née Taylor) Colville, David Craddock, Pat Crockett and her daughters, Ann and Finella, Stella (née Nichols) Derrick, Catherine and John Dicken, Frances (née Sherratt) Eaton, Ann Ellis, Vic Evans, Nancy (née Watson) Flint, Pauline Gallear, Harry Matthew Gaskill, Linda (née Gibson) Lodge, Peggy (née Langley) Goodwin, Peter Hallam, Barry Hanson, June (née Nadin) Harrison, Sheila (née Brown) Harrison, Colin Haxell, Cecile Hales, Elaine (née Purdy) Hawksworth, David Hayton, Charles & the late Geraldine Hodgson, Margaret Huckle, Charlie Kenderdine, Linda (née Gibson) Lodge, Pamela McCahey, John Morley, Bill Nadin, Chris Nixon, Mick Nordemann, Marjorie (née Hinton) Vickers, Jean & Frank Parry, Molly (née Peake) Horton, Pauline (née Taylor) Phillips, Sylvia Phillips, David Purdy, Kathleen Ratcliff, Jean Slack, Ann (née Follows) Smith, Tom Titterton, Dr E J Walker, Wilf Warren, Alan Woodcock.

I thank those school pupils who now live far and wide. They are acknowledged in the narrative. All the illustrations given, loaned or copied, are acknowledged on the page they appear.

CONTENTS

Acknowledgments	i
Introduction	iii
Chapter One: Progress is the Aim! (1954)	1
Chapter Two: The Creeping Giant! (1955)	20
Chapter Three: School Becomes Hospital! (1956)	39
Chapter Four: Petrol on Ration (1957)	59
Chapter Five: Secondary Education in Mickleover? (1958)	81
Chapter Six: The Driest Summer for 200 Years (1959)	100
Chapter Seven: Public Swimming Pool? (1960)	120
Chapter Eight: Ravensdale Remembered (1961)	144
Chapter Nine: "Goodbye Green Field" (1962)	164
Chapter Ten: Everyone's Convenience (1963)	186
Chapter Eleven: Royal Visitor (1964)	207
Chapter Twelve: The No! Campaign (1965)	230
Chapter Thirteen: Pastures Hospital Modernised (1966)	251
Chapter Fourteen: Supermarket in Brisbane Road? (1967)	272
Chapter Fifteen: Parish Council's Farewell (1968)	293
Chapter Sixteen: Conclusion (onwards)	314
References & Bibliography	323
Index	324

Photos courtesy of Peggy Goodwin

This photograph of Personal Service Garage on Uttoxeter Road is thought to have been taken in the late 1940s or early 1950s when the garage belonged to Ossie Ashford. He and his family emigrated to Australia. The garage building has been demolished but the shop adjoining is now Ilkeston Co-op Travel

INTRODUCTION

After the Dissolution in the 16th century, and the fall of Burton Abbey, Mickleover prospered and expansion began with the building of the Derbyshire Pauper Lunatic Asylum and the extension of the Great Northern Railway.

In 1962 Rosemary Meynell mentioned in her *Derbyshire Advertiser* column, "A Derbyshire Woman's Diary" that in a document of Sheriff's Tourn for Derbyshire, for the year 1606, Mickleover is referred to as Magna Over and Littleover as Parva Over.

The document was sold at Sotherby's in the first week of August 1962 to a private collector for £90, and was donated to Derbyshire Record Office in March 2005.

Such documents are rare and in fact none survive for this period in the National Archives. It contains evidence of the sheriff's tourn or circuit which he undertook twice a year. It describes criminal offences, obstruction of highways and watercourses and cases of trespass etc. It also carries important evidence of how local communities managed their environment and all manner of regulations.

At the time of the expansion the population had risen to 1555 and the Local Government Act of 1894 brought in different ways of running the village. Local people became more involved with politics, none more so than Tom Radford who became the first clerk to the parish council and went on to serve the parish for some sixty years. When he died in 1945, just after VE Day, he was in his 88th year, he had been chairman of Mickleover Parish Council for fifteen years and had served on various committees on Repton Rural District Council.

Tom had overseen the changes in the sewage system, the cleaning up of the water supply and the installation of street lighting in 1932. He was obviously not on his own in working tirelessly for Mickleover. Other local businessmen such as Charles Ayre and Ernest Nadin were long serving members of the parish council, and in fact it was Ernest who followed Tom Radford as the chairman.

The Second World War had ended almost ten years before this book begins and the council faced new challenges, particularly in the building of new houses and encouraging business enterprises.

After publishing Book One the same pattern emerged from Book Two. Information came forth from an additional number of people who lived through the 1940s.

Jim Caborn was born in 1920 at Common End, now Park Road, and was a pupil at Mickleover County School when Thomas Hewitt was the headmaster. He recalled all the children being taken into the playground to see the R100 airship flying over Mickleover.

Photo courtesy of Michael Bowden

The volunteer Fire Service in 1941 with the Daimler car behind them. Members of the Brigade, left to right: Alice Walters, Ted Woolley, Sam Brown, Ossie Ashford, Rita Allsop, ? Horobin.

Photo courtesy of Jim Caborn

Volunteer fireman Jim Caborn with his girlfriend Eva Sharp.

At the age of 19 Jim volunteered to join the Mickleover Fire Service alongside Ossie Ashford, Sam Brown, ? Horobin and Ted Woolley.

The small brigade were stationed at Ashford's garage on the corner of Limes Avenue and Uttoxeter Road. The owner, Tom Ashford, Ossie's father, was a huge man weighing over 24 stones and he drove to work in an Austin Seven which had only two wide doors. To gain extra space he had removed the back seat to accommodate the driver's seat.

The brigade was supplied with two cars to pull fire pumps. The first, a Daimler, was constantly needing maintenance but the second, a French Citroen, was driven by Jim to pull a 120gpm pump.

Jim was a plumber during the day and a fireman in the evenings, Friday being an all-night shift. One call Jim brings to mind was to Burnaston airfield when incendiary bombs fell, one through a roof of one of the hangers, setting fire on a bed. Their remaining duties that night were to shovel soil onto the remaining incendiary bombs.

In May 1941 Jim Caborn was called up to join the army. He was stationed

Photo courtesy of Charles & Geraldine Hodgson

In 1940 an LDV unit (later to be named the Home Guard) was formed at the County Mental [Pastures] Hospital.

with the 5th Wiltshires in the south of England working on experimental landing craft which were being water proofed.

Eventually he was to fight in France, arriving days after the D-Day landings. In taking Caen aerodrome he was severely wounded by a mortar bomb at hill 112 which brought an end to his military service. His final convalescence was spent at Ashe Hall, near Etwall. On being demobbed he married Eva Sharp and they set up home in Quorn Street, Jim worked as a joiner for the remainder of his career.

I had occasion to meet Molly (née Peake) Horton who added to my knowledge of those Mickleover men who were killed during World War II.

Edwin Charles Peake obtained the position of Company Secretary at Royal Crown Derby and brought his family, (wife, two sons and two daughters) from a

Photo courtesy of Molly (née Peake) Horton
Sergeant Air Gunner, Ken Edwin Peake. This photograph was taken in February 1944, three weeks before he died.

v

Photos courtesy of Pat Crockett (above) and Frank & Jean Parry (below)

A children's party in the Memorial Hut organised by the Mickleover Royal British Legion. Could it have been taken for the VE Celebrations at the end of the Second World War?

Photo courtesy of Dr E J Walker

The Mickleover County School Staff photographed in the school playground in 1947. From left to right, top row: Olive Mary Plumpton, Ronald Bagguley, Gladys Ravensdale, Robert Charles Walker, Mabel Wibberley, Ken Parkin. Bottom row: Edith Mary Wedd, Mrs M E Henchliffe, John Walter Jacquest, Sheila Adams, Mrs Mary J Jacquest.

position in the Potteries to live in Western Road in 1941. The eldest son, Ken Edwin, was aged fifteen when war broke out but as soon as he reached the age of eighteen, volunteered to join the RAF and became a Sergeant Air Gunner, serving on a Lancaster bomber. In March 1944 he was reported missing on a bombing raid on Stuttgart. It was later discovered that the plane in which he was flying over Lake Constant in Switzerland, came down in the Black Forest in unknown circumstances. Seven of the crew are buried in a communal cemetery in the small French village of Villars Le Pautel. An eighth grave, an "irregular member" of the crew was on his first sortie over Europe. Ken's younger brother, Frank was eight years old when the family arrived in Mickleover and was a pupil at Mickleover County School. His sister Molly told me that Frank once threw an ink well at his teacher Miss Wedd and was made to stay in school all day – he never really enjoyed going to school! Frank played for Mickleover Football Club in the 1950s. Father, Edwin eventually became Production Director at Royal Crown Derby.

The children who were pupils at Mickleover County School after the war were now pre-secondary school age. Despite the transfer of children to

Photo courtesy of Frank & Jean Parry

This photograph gives a glimpse of the return of the carnival band from All Saints' Church in August 1948. The picture in Book Two, p166 showed the Carnival Queen, Barbara Carr on her decorated lorry on her journey through the village.

Littleover County Secondary School and Grammar Schools at the age of 11 years, the roll on the registers since 1946 grew from 256 to 324 in early 1954. This led to additional teaching spaces being provided, increasing the total number of classrooms to nine.

The lavatory block was completely extended in 1951 and a new playground for juniors was laid in the following year. Gardens had been provided with every class being allocated a piece of ground for use in practical nature study or gardening and a small field within the new boundary had been levelled.

In the autumn of 2006, and quite unannounced, Dr E J Walker, the son of Robert Charles Walker, a teacher in Mickleover County School from 1947 to 1951, left a large envelope for my attention at the Community Hall. It contained photographs and programmes of school concerts and a single photograph of the staff.

Unfortunately I was not able to speak to Dr Walker. He left a small note which informed me that he lived in Bristol. His father had undertaken the emergency training scheme at a college in Manchester after serving in the RAF during the Second World War.

Photo courtesy of Pat Crockett

Pat Crockett with her husband, Reverend B S W (Ben) in the Vicarage garden, October 1949.

"My father kept bees and a 'gentle' hive was moved into the school," writes Dr Walker. "Classes were then allowed to see the hive opened up and the queen identified. They were told to stand still and not to wave their arms about – no one got stung and at the end of the lesson they all took home a small pot of honey."

When Robert Walker left the school he moved to teach in a school in Malta. He died in 1968 but Mrs Walker stayed in Rykneld Way until she moved into Ivy House on The Green in Mickleover.

I made the decision, with the help of my wife and friend Ken Guy, to stage an Exhibition of the material presented by Dr Walker in the old school building. This brought forth a number of new photographs and memories to help in the production of this book.

Photo courtesy of Jean Parry

Jean Parry photographed in her garden at Western Road as a dragonfly in Princess Ju-Ju, "First time treading the boards." The costume was made by Miss Plumpton from what is thought to be packets of gauze used in war-time First Aid.

Photo courtesy of Dr E J Walker

The full cast of Princess Ju-Ju *performed at the school in March 1948. The whole of the proceeds of this concert was given to the Save the Children Fund formed by the United Nations. Its aim was to help the starving children in the countries devastated by war.*

Photo courtesy of Dr E J Walker

The Charcoal Burner's Son, *one of the productions in the County School's Christmas Concert in 1950. Standing (top): Soldier, unknown; King, David Bird; Ogre, Eric Ward; Second Soldier, Alan Rodgers; Soldier, Eric Taylor; First Soldier, Paul Graves; Princess, Julia Sutton; Sheila Cottington; Queen, Patricia Cottrell; Soldier, Alan Bullars. Kneeling: Soldiers, Dave Craddock, John Ratcliff; Dragon, Michael Harkins; Soldiers, unknown; Gordon Nuttall.*

Photo courtesy of the Derby Evening Telegraph

A Mickleover Royal British Legion members day trip to Ladybower in the early 1950s, (2) Arthur Thornhill, (5) George Young, (9) Edwin Peake, (10) Frank Grimshaw, (15) Ted Allsop, (19) George Finney, (24) Sam Cooper, (27) Harry Stiles, (32) Frank Wall, (35) Walter Sharpe, (40) Edgar Stubbs, (44) Arthur Johnson, (51) Charlie Lichfield, (52) Bill Hughes.

Peter Arnold arrived with a box file of photos taken by his father Ernest Richard Arnold, always known as "Dick". He was a well known figure in the area and his family were very much involved in both All Saints' and St John's churches and the Royal British Legion. Dick became the chief photographer at the *Derby Evening Telegraph* after beginning his career there at the age of seventeen. He remained at the *Telegraph* until he died in 1977. His photographs, many published, are now scattered around this book.

Another visitor at the Exhibition was Mick Nordemann who became a pupil at the County School in 1950 and he recalls that he was the first child to wear the school uniform introduced into the school by the new headmaster, Mr J W (Jimmy) Best. The blazer and badge were made by Mick's mother but by the time other children came to school in the "official" uniform Mick began to

Photo courtesy of Peter Arnold

The Reverend Ben Crockett leads the church choir outside the Vicarage at Christmas 1950?. From left to right Rev Crockett, (Females): Unknown, Unknown, Joyce Storer, Audrey Robinson, June Nadin, Vi Purcell, Pamela Tatford, Cynthia ('Pat') Purcell. The two boy choristers are Chris Moseley and Colin White.

Photo courtesy of Peter Arnold

The choristers under the direction of William H J Gibbs the choirmaster and organist who arrived in 1950?. The Reverend Ben Crockett joins in the singing. The choristers, left to right are ? Burton, Eric Taylor, Richard Morley, Peter Goodman, Peter Morley, Michael Bowden, Brian Henderson, Richard Harris and Barry Turner.

feel ashamed that his mother's very worthwhile attempt did not, according to Mick, match up to those supplied by Ranbys in Derby.

David Purdy, was also a pupil at the County School and he became one of the first batch of children to attend the new Junior School at Vicarage Road. He was appointed Treasurer of Mickleover Sports Club in the 1970s and had the foresight to retain some of its invoices from as early as 1950 which now make interesting reading.

Harry Matthew Gaskill worked at Holly Cottage Farm on Radbourne Lane before the Second World War. It has now been developed into Linden House. The farm was only small, with just twelve cows but it was the start of Harry's career

Photos courtesy of Frank Parry

A Mickleover County School sports day held on Vicarage Road Playing Fields in 1950. The junior boy sprinters are, left to right: Brian Wall, Unknown, Pat Burns, Frank Parry, Tony Blood, Ernest Turner, David Jackson.

Photo courtesy of Mick Nordemann

An infant boys race at the same sports day as above, left to right: Mick Nordemann, Peter Hill, Barry Hanson, Graham Hulland, Billy Carnell, Unknown,

Photo courtesy of Peter Arnold
Young Peter Arnold pulling his sledge in The Crescent, Station Road in the early 1950s.

in agriculture. It was when he was working at a farm at Smalley that a telegram boy delivered his call-up papers in 1939.

He was stationed in Siddals Road, Derby, at the RAMC unit. The accommodation was sparse with Harry and his comrades having to sleep on wooden floors. Their training, such as it was, took place in the fields behind Derby Railway Station. The only pieces of equipment in their possession was a stretcher and a "Thomas' Splint", a relic from the First World War, with which they were able to practice.

Harry didn't have to experience the lack of comfort for too long as he was soon discharged and told to return to farming to help bring in the harvest.

Little time passed before he joined the RAF, having made himself redundant. He became a ground crew wireless operator and served in Egypt and Italy.

This story will be new to hundreds of people who came to know Harry in a very different occupation. After the war ended his wish to purchase a farm could not be achieved owing to a lack of capital. He opted instead for education and began his two years training at college in 1948. Eight years later he was appointed as deputy headmaster at Mickleover County School. Harry was married at the time and he and Avis raised a family of four sons and one daughter. Harry and his wife still live in Mickleover.

Another highly respected teacher, Mr W J (Wilf) Warren, arrived in Mickleover while his school, Ravensdale was being built.

Before the Second World War Wilf was a civil servant, working in the Employment Exchange at Matlock but joined the Army in December 1939 and served in North Africa and Italy during his six years service.

When he returned to the Civil Service he found it dull and boring. Having spoken to his Department Manager, who insisted on calling him "Laddie", he took the opportunity of covering a colleague in Wirksworth for two weeks. However he found he was hardly allowed to complete any duties with the staff insisting, "it was their job." It was even impossible for him to open the post!

Deciding to occupy his time clearing out a cupboard of documents he reached for the top shelf and a pamphlet fell out and hit his foot. It was headed "Take up Teaching as a Career".

All the information in the leaflet seemed to apply to him so he immediately wrote a letter, on Ministry of Labour paper, which he trimmed and posted.

He and his wife, he had married Irene in 1942 before he went to North Africa, were very much in favour of him changing his career.

He was accepted under the Emergency Teaching Scheme and went to Wymondham, Norfolk in 1947 where an old American camp had been turned into a college for teachers.

Photo courtesy of Kath (née Blackham) Ratcliff

The two boys, Roger and Richard Blackham were boarding pupils at the Manor School from 1927 to 1931. The red caps were embroided with a capital "M".

After thirteen months he obtained his first teaching post at a church school in South Darley where he taught from 1948 to 1954. He then moved to Bakewell Methodist School. where he stayed until applying for the headship of the Ashbourne Methodist School. He began at the summer term of 1957 and taught there until 1961 when Ravensdale School was being built.

I must confess that the first two books had little detail of the Manor School which was situated in the old Manor House next to the church. I am not aware of any material being deposited at Derby Study Library or the County Record Office in Matlock. I did come across one ex-pupil during my research but none connected with the teaching staff or the administration.

XV

Photo courtesy of Edna (née Lemmon) Beadsmoore

The girls from Mickleover County School are dancing round the maypole at the Royal British Legion ground. They were part of the celebrations for the Festival of Britain. The two girls in the foreground are Gillian Hannah (left) and Edna Lemmon.

Photo courtesy of Ann (née Follows) Smith

"Peter Rabbit", performed at Mickleover County School in 1953. Left to right, back row: Unknown, David Hackett, Geoffrey Willis, ?John Bull, Roger Allsopp, Charles Hodgson, Peter Hammond. Second row: unknown, unknown, Anne Willis, unknown, Sandra Yates, Ann Follows, Gillian Allsopp, Sandra Shaw, Deanna Ball, Rosemary Heathcote, Ann Brierley, ?Pearl Eastap, Janice Kniveton, Valerie Athill, Helen Taylor. Third row: David Frost, Roy Johnson, Chris Brown, unknown, unknown, Linda Hodgkinson, Janet Edwards, Joan Chambers. Front row: Neil Gunn, Jean Jeffreys, David Samuel, Margaret Hinton, Fenella Crockett, Anna Bussell, Glynn Moseley, Graham Webster, Jennifer Tomlinson.

Having read other documents covering a variety of subjects my interest was drawn to the meeting of the Housing Town Planning and Plans Committee of Repton Rural District Council (referred to in future text as the RDC), who had received a letter from Sheffield Regional Hospital Board, proposing a change of use of the Manor School to the Woodlands Hospital.

"The Minister of Health is about to purchase the Manor School, Mickleover. The school at some future time, will be used to house some 70 mental patients. The school, as you are aware, is situate in close proximity to the Pastures Hospital, Mickleover, and I should be glad if your Council would give favourable consideration to this Change of User."

This letter arrived only days after the school had placed an advertisement in the *Derby Evening Telegraph* stating that the school was recognised "as efficient by the Minister of Education."

In November the Manor School announced that it was to be closed at Christmas 1952. The private boys' school for day pupils and borders had forty-two pupils aged between eight and fourteen years. It was opened in 1922 and the headmaster Mr J N Charlton had been there for ten years.

Mr Charlton said that the school was being closed because of "economic reasons." He continued that private schools, especially those such as The Manor, with extensive grounds and buildings, had heavy overhead expenses.

The parents of the children at the school arranged for them to go to other private schools.

In January 1953 the auctioneers, Allen and Farquar advertised surplus school equipment under the supervision of the headmaster, Mr Charlton. The Electoral Register published in the same year named ten residents at the school, including the headmaster and his family.

My friend, Jim Nixon, has a younger brother, Chris, and following the previous pattern of children living in Jackson Avenue he became a pupil at a school in Littleover, in his case, the new school in Carlisle Avenue.

His abiding memory of the school is one of misery. So miserable in fact that his mother persuaded the Derbyshire Education Authority to transfer Chris to Mickleover County School.

Chris remembers that "Mickleover was a better place by far and there was no smell of new paint. The teachers were, on the whole, quite humane with cuddly names like Miss Wibberley, Miss Plumpton and Mr Peach."

He added: "I was only there a matter of days when, as the morning break hand-bell sounded, Miss Wibberley asked, 'Who would like to to stay behind and show Chris how to tidy his desk?'"

Chris thought: "What's wrong with my desk? How can you see through this lid?" A couple of his classmates pointed him in the right direction. "Like the rest of the world, I knew nothing about the 'scruffy gene' back then," reports Chris. He was one of the last pupils to attend the County School up to eleven-years-of-age. At the beginning of 1958 a new Junior School opened in Vicarage Road and the old school was to continue as an Infant School.

One of the most remarkable photographs to appear in this book is on the Contents page. It has been supplied by Peggy Goodwin who was the daughter of the landlord at the Masons Arms, Charlie and Mabel Langley. Thought lost, Peggy came across the smallest of photographs when attempting to compile an album for her grandchildren.

Book Two ended on a high note with the nation celebrating the climbing of Everest and the crowning of Queen Elizabeth II. Mickleover was now at the beginning of dramatic changes with housing stock rising to unheard of figures.

Book Three covers these changes when residents old and new were becoming aware of Derby Borough Corporation's desire to extend their boundary. Throughout the period of the books on Mickleover the unfolding story has emerged under its old parish boundary (see a section left).

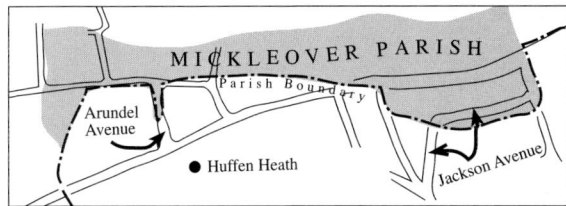

From the end of the nineteenth century until Chapter 15 of this book Mickleover was administered by its parish council within those boundaries and confusion has arisen, and still does, in understanding where these lay as the postal authorities termed parts of Littleover as Mickleover.

Much of the confusion regarding the parish boundary lay to the east of Cavendish Way. Arundel Avenue was cut in half, as was Jackson Avenue and a large slice of Uttoxeter Road was in fact in the Littleover parish. Administrative difficulties, such as lighting and bus routes had to be settled diplomatically by Mickleover and Littleover Parish Councils.

Matters became easier when the Borough Extension was finalised. The traditional parish boundary of Mickleover was swallowed up into a large area administered by Derby.

I have included a final chapter which highlights some photographs and information after 1968. It is from this period that Mickleover achieved the unwanted title of becoming the largest suburb in Europe!

The narrative of the books is more anecdotal than academic and I have

Photo courtesy of Stuart Barker

One of the largest families in Mickleover in the period of the three "Mickleover Born & Bred" books were the Barkers'. The ten sons of George Henry Barker and his wife Harriet Ann lived in The Green. They were, and still are remembered in the village, many becoming tradesmen. Dennis was a plasterer and worked as a sub-contractor to local builders. The best known of the sons was Bill. He became Sexton at All Saints' Church and is mentioned in the following chapters. Standing: Derick, Raymond, Bill, Charles, Bernard. Front Row: Robert, Donald, Dennis, Roy, Stuart. Father George is photographed (right) at the family home, 6 The Green. When reaching their teenage years a few of the boys went into service at the big houses in the village.

again been guided by my maternal grandfather, Lewis Straw, who had the foresight to keep diaries and record some of the changes.

I moved to two new addresses in the period of this book, both in Mickleover. In the second my wife Ann and I still maintain Gisborne Close which we have owned since our marriage in 1965. Our son Simon was born when this book ends, December 1968, our daughter Julia followed in 1971.

Peter Brown

CHAPTER ONE
PROGRESS IS THE AIM!
1954

My grandfather, Lewis Straw's three great interests were his love of writing, his garden, which he planned meticulously every winter in order to purchase his seeds, and walking. His hikes in the Derbyshire Peak were arranged down to the finest detail. Along with all this he walked regularly from his home, 22 Station Road, around Mickleover, the village he had grown to love.

The combination of all these activities led him to keep a daily diary in which he recorded his experiences and more importantly, for the readers of *Mickleover Born & Bred*, noted the changes he was seeing in the village

January 1st 1954 was a fine day and after completing his "household chores", he walked towards Mickleover Station. On reaching the junction of Station Road with Radbourne Lane he turned towards Radbourne village. He noted that Soldier's Cottage, at the corner of the lane to Kirk Langley was being demolished.

The highlight of my first days of 1954 was to visit the cinema with my friend Jim Nixon to see *God's own Country*. On January 2nd, I, along with some school friends, supported Derby County who were playing Bristol Rovers at the Baseball Ground. The Rams had been relegated

Lewis Straw (right) with his two sons, Tom (left) and Lewis Jr, in his garden at 22 Station Road, Mickleover. Left: his youngest daughter, Hilda Straw.

1

from the old Division I, and Bristol had achieved promotion from Division III (south) – the Rams lost 0-1!

Football has been a life interest with Derby County being the focus. At a cost of 6d per week, I looked forward to the magazine *Soccer Star* dropping through the letter-box. Edited by former Rams star Raich Carter, this was quite a new way of reporting football and I collected them from the first issue.

Boys played out their own football fixtures with "Subbutteo", a table top game with cardboard players moved round on a green marked cloth.

In the summer, tennis became my favourite game, inspired by the gifted Australian players, Lew Hoad and Ken Rosewall, whom we looked forward to watching play at Wimbledon on television. Jim Nixon and I walked regularly from our homes in Jackson Avenue to the public shale courts at the Rowditch. We often managed to persuade the court keeper to let us play all afternoon, having only paid for an hour.

Life for youngsters was just a total game, we played various activities non-stop, often inventing our own. Things like eating or sleeping were a necessity, but having your hair cut was an irritation (still is for me), to having a good time playing cricket or football. We did have regular tasks such as walking down to the Co-op grocers and butchers (now Totel Ltd) near Manor Road. I can still recall our Co-op Dividend number (60950), and receiving the change after our money had travelled in cylinders which ran on an overhead system driven by compressed air.

My sister Sheila had left school in 1952 and had begun to train as a Nursery Nurse.

On January 9th grandfather records, "The Soldier's Cottage has now completely disappeared. Thus vanishes another landmark." The last occupants were

I was still attending Derby County's home matches with my school friends and four of us are captured in this programme photograph taken on the "Pop" Side of the Baseball Ground. (1) Peter Brown, (2) Tony Taylor, (3) Brian Tye, (4) Roger Maskrey.

Photo courtesy of John Morley

Soldier's Cottage was the home of the Morleys on their seven-and-a-half acre smallholding which they rented from the Radbourne Estate. Behind the cottage was a four cow shed cover for pigs and an outside toilet. Left: John, Freddy and Joe Morley.

Frank and Nellie Morley and their three sons John, Joe and Fred. All three had to walk a mile to the County School in Uttoxeter Road when they lived in the cottage. "Even during the bad winter in 1947," recalls John, the eldest son.

The family moved to a sixty acre farm halfway down Walkers Hill on the Radbourne Estate only weeks before the cottage was demolished.

Now aged fifteen, I was thinking about the important change in my life, leaving school and beginning a career. I had by that time attended an interview at the printers, Bemrose. The available position was in the art department and although I passed the general knowledge exam, my skills in art were a little limited.

The general trend was for boys to follow in their father's trade, but my father was not insistent on my taking up an apprenticeship at Rolls Royce. Not entirely sure where my future lay, I knew that transport would be a part of the economics, so I opted to purchase a new, reliable cycle, to transport me to wherever I was destined to go.

On January 30th, grandfather wrote: "Peter came to show me his new bike." I had paid a deposit on a new blue Phillips cycle, at Currys in East Street, the remainder to be paid on "Hire Purchase". It proved to be a lucky move, for on Friday February 5th I went for my entrance examination as an apprentice compositor at the *Derbyshire Advertiser,* accompanied by my father. Having proved to be successful I began my career on February 8th. This had been arranged by Geoff Critchlow, the deputy head and careers master at Littleover Secondary Modern School, Pastures Hill, Littleover.

A major event was taking place in the village on the following day. A large company assembled for the opening of Mickleover Methodist Sunday School. A new building that consisted of a hall to seat 250 people, with a kitchen and classrooms, at a cost of £9,000.

A plaque was unveiled to commemorate the laying of bricks in May 1953, and contained the names of ten people who had assisted in the scheme, started in the early "twenties", to erect a school hall.

The amount was raised by a donation from the Joseph Rank Benevolent Trust £4,000; Methodist Chapel Committee £900; proceeds of the sale of former Methodist property in Derby £512; donations from friends not members of Mickleover Methodist Church £2,921 and £520 from the proceeds of the official opening ceremony.

The Reverend Ben Crockett had been the incumbent at All Saints' Church for the last nine years. Married, with three daughters, he became a supporter of Derby County but his address to the Parochial Church Council in February concerned the repairs to the battlements and pinnacles of the church tower which had been completed.

He suggested that as the church was so cold in the winter the choir might rehearse either in the church room in Limes Avenue or at the Vicarage, and remarked that it would be a good idea to form a choirboys' club, using either venue for the headquarters.

The cold winters in the early 1950s were not made any warmer by people using coal to heat their premises. The newly nationalised industry was facing constant financial problems as the Treasury pressed for increased coal production for export. This left a shortage of supply for the householder. On February 16th grandfather wrote: "We are entirely without coal, we have retired more or

Photo courtesy of Derby Evening Telegraph

Harry Pett's building plot (A) in Station Road. This Derby Evening Telegraph air photograph shows Mickleover before Hope Avenue (bottom), Edale Avenue (right) and all the developments at Chestnut Avenue, Devonshire Drive and Brisbane Road. The building of the Mackworth Estate is shown at the top left.

Maps courtesy of Derby Local Study Library

less to [the] back kitchen, as it is more economical on electric. We even transferred there in the evening." The coalman called three days later, "left six bags, resumed fire-making."

Mickleover Parish Council was asked by the County Surveyor for their observations on a "Private" notice erected on a footpath off Station Road (see map above).

Local electrician, Harry Petts had received planning permission in 1952 to build a detached house and garage on the west side of Station Road. His plot was on the field (OS 106) which he had purchased from William Hardy Watson, the Corn Merchant in Vicarage Road.

Mr Petts had objected to the path adjacent to his plot being used as a public footpath as it had been sold to him as a private road. The previous owner confirmed that there had been a farm gate at the Station Road entrance up to March 1953.

However, the council informed him at the February meeting that although the path was not marked on any maps, it had been used by the public for more than sixty years. It had also been claimed in 1951 as one of eighteen rights of way.

Jim Holloway, chairman, commented that he had never known anyone to be refused entry to the pathway in about forty years.

Although it was generally agreed that the path had been used by the public, Harry Petts was allowed to build his house and although investigation led to the path being designated its own number of GR308351 by the County Council it soon became swallowed by the increased house building. Other plots on the field mentioned were sold resulting in house numbers 142 to 156 Station Road being built.

Residents living at the southern end of Station Road were also beginning to see changes around them in early 1954.

A serious case of "misconduct" was the discussion at the February meeting of Mickleover Sports Club. A member of the football team had declined to play in the position selected for him which led to the difficulty of fielding a team. He also failed to report to the committee and had no reasonable excuse to offer. The committee took into account a written apology and admission of misconduct and decided, with the full backing of the Derbyshire Football Association, that the player would be suspended from playing football during the month of February and that similar conduct would be dealt with more severely.

There had been a garage business at 16 Station Road since T G Teat was granted a licence to store 500 gallons of petrol in 1937.

Marshall Eric Allsop had left Rolls-Royce in 1952 and set up his own business, servicing cars, in a large shed on the same site with his friend Reg Bagshaw, a fellow worker in Rolls-Royce transport.

Having bought the garden of the house next door Eric cleared the land with the help of a tractor, kindly loaned to him by his friend Ted Moult of Ticknall, who became a famous TV personality.

Two second-hand petrol pumps were bought and a service kiosk erected from scrap angle salvaged from the bottom of the garden. Eric Allsop was a member of the Vintage Sports Car Club and was mainly responsible for the restoration of a 1919 Vauxhall, bringing it back to its original specification.

On March 11th grandfather expressed his view on the expansion. "Two ugly illuminated signs have been erected at garage above. They obtrude as they are meant to do. Progress in capital letters E.S.S.O."

My grandmother had died in 1952 but Uncle Tom who was a window cleaner in the village and his sister Hilda still lived with grandfather at 22 Station

Photo courtesy of Magic Attic Archive, Swadlincote
Eric Allsop with his Vintage Vauxhall.

Road. Grandfather wrote that Tom had "been given a little job on inside windows of Nag's Head Hotel."

The Nag's advertised in the *Derby Evening Telegraph* that they catered for weddings, dinners, parties and coach parties. They announced that the hard tennis courts at the rear had been relaid. It was under the "personal supervision" of Mr and Mrs Alf George.

Grandfather experienced the growth of motor traffic on Easter Monday, April 19th. "This was the first visit to Dove Dale of the children." He was referring to my cousins, Tony and Kathleen, who were part of the family party who made the trip into Derbyshire. "It was thronged with people about the stepping stones. There were two casualties, one needing an ambulance." He continued: "Coming home we ran into two traffic jams, one on the bus to Ashbourne stretching five miles. It took us one and a half hours to get from the Dog and Partridge [Thorpe Cloud] to Ashbourne." A week later he organised a family party to "celebrate twenty-five years' residence in the house."

The headmaster at the County School in Uttoxeter Road, Mr J W (Jimmy) Best, had 127 infant children, arranged in four classes with a new member of staff, Mrs N E Parkin taking over Infant 2.

HM Inspector's report in 1954, the first since 1946, was very complimentary. "The headmaster has considerable organising ability and has in three years effectively re-directed the school towards the fulfilment of the aims of primary

Photo courtesy of Derby Museums and Art Gallery L3337
This interesting photograph of the Nag's Head Hotel on Uttoxeter Road shows a board advertising a miniature golf course. The lady standing on the right is on the junction of Kipling Drive and The Parade. The Total petrol station is now on the left.

Photo courtesy of Michael Bowden
The photograph (right) was taken from 26 Station Road, the home of Michael Bowden. It shows the Nag's Head in the distance and the long wooden fence running to the junction of Uttoxeter Road. On the left is where the ambulance station now stands.

education." He continued: "The teachers are kindly and make considerable effort to ensure that the children are happy and make good general progress."

Pupil Mick Nordemann remembers Mr Best arriving at the school and being very frightened of him.

"One of the boys in the infants playground pushed the caretaker in the back," he says. "Mr Best's office overlooked the playground, the culprit was summoned for six of the best, quite appropriate!"

Headteachers had to maintain a Punishment Book which was supplied by the Authority. It recorded the name of the person who administered the punishment, the name of the offender, and the nature of the offence. There was an insistence that any punishment was not inflicted in the presence of other children. Punishment was only applied on the hands or buttocks on boys, and the hands of girls. This was very exceptional and was only carried out by a woman teacher.

8

Two boys are recorded as receiving one stroke for throwing lettuce at dinner; five boys for throwing coke (residue of coal) in the playground. One of them was Allan Bradshaw who admits to being caught because his hands were still covered in coke dust. Four boys were caned for "shocking and disloyal conduct on 4.50pm bus from Mickleover." Complaints had been received from conductress, driver and two teachers.

On average there were 10 punishments recorded in a year. Although ex-pupils recall little bullying, records in the Punishment Book does make note of a few.

Chris Nixon remembers being summoned to Mr Best's study. "This was always a fearful event – guilty, and therefore punishment was assumed. Happily, he only wanted information. 'What's your father's first name?' he asked. 'I'm not sure sir,' I replied. 'But his mates call him Bill.' "Mr Best laughed. It was the first time I recall making someone laugh, and the first time I realised that a person in authority could have a sense of humour."

In reply to a request for a staff room at the school the Divisional Education Officer stated that it was hoped to provide a new Junior School in the building programme for 1956-57 "in which case this school would be used for infants only, when additional staff accommodation would appear to be unnecessary."

In May 1954 it was announced that there was 26.2% overcrowding at Pastures Hospital where there was accommodation for 1,098 patients. At the end of February there were 1,386 patients and during the year there were 476 admissions and 462 discharges. It was re-named Pastures when the National Health Service began in 1947.

Figures were also revealed that on February 28th there were only 1,912 on the full time staff (1,050 male, 862 female) and 782 (8 male 774 female) part-time staff for a total requirement of 2,982 (1,239 male, 1,743 female) full-time staff in the region. Female student nurses were causing a concern as there were 173 female students for a total requirement of 524.

The *Derby Evening Telegraph* was publishing letters of varying views on the subject of class distinction in hospitals.

An "ex-Nurse" wrote that she had worked for more than four years as a nurse in mental hospitals. "With truth, I can say I've spent some of my happiest working hours there, and found the largest proportion of sisters and staff nurses grand people to work with, unlike some who believe it beneath their dignity and status to find time to explain or show a junior some detail, or to add a kind word of encouragement."

She continued: "I have myself seen colleagues in tears, in linen cupboards.

If these dragons found some victims to vent their wrath on, they could make life unpleasant."

On the question of recruitment for staff for mental hospitals she wrote that the two twelve hour shifts (7.00am to 7.00pm) and (7.00pm to 7.00am) were too long. "If a three-shift system were introduced, as it is in some hospitals, all ranks would be able to spend more time off duty."

Mr J R Riley, secretary of Derby No 3, Hospital Management Committee at the time replied: "It would seem from "Ex-Nurse's" letter that she had not worked in a mental hospital recently. At the Pastures Hospital we have instituted the three-shift system, but the successful operation of the system is, of course, dependent on there being sufficient nurses and – at the present time – we are experiencing a very serious shortage of trained staff."

The Ministry of Health had been advised that they no longer had the power to run or administer farms, this led to the Sheffield Regional Hospital forming a committee to inquire into farming activities. The hospital services in Derbyshire came under the Sheffield Regional Board in 1948.

Grandfather was taken to Derby City Hospital with acute appendicitis on May 4th, the day after he recorded that the field opposite the golf links on Uttoxeter Road was being opened up for house building purposes. (See map p13). After his operation on May 5th he stayed in hospital for seven days. He was then transferred to Etwall Hospital for a further ten days. "I received excellent attention at all times," he wrote.

Photo courtesy of the Derby Evening Telegraph
Florence Ravensdale

A member of a well known Mickleover family, Mrs Florence Ravensdale, who lived at "Mayfield", Burlington Way, had an aptitude for figures which led her to become treasurer of several organisations. In May she was elected Honorary Treasurer of the National Union of Townswomen's Guilds.

She announced to the press that "Women in the Townswomen's Guild movement are encouraged to develop talents which, often, they did not know they had." She continued, "They also have discussions and lectures and widen their outlook." She had been a member of the Townswomen's Guild since 1940. My wife, Ann, is the current treasurer of Mickleover East Townswomen's Guild.

Photo courtesy of the Derby Evening Telegraph

The Derby Evening Telegraph *published a series on local schools in 1954. In July a full page on Mickleover County School was featured. The happy group of pupils above, left to right top row: Rodney Hallam, Peter Hill, John Dutson, Peter Arnold, Chris Brown, unknown, ?Ashley Littlefield, Guy Seddon, second row: unknown, ?Valerie Athill, unknown, Joan Chambers, Helen Taylor, ?Jennifer Tomlinson, third row: Janet Edwards, Deanna Ball, ?Hugh Ford, unknown, unknown, unknown, unknown. Bottom row: unknown, Graham Webster, Michael Dommett, ?Philip Judson, David Frost, Graham Hulland, Glyn Mosley.*

Left: Maypole dancing was a speciality at Mickleover School. [1] *Mavis Bonsall,* [2] *Fenella Crockett,* [3] *Rosemary Heathcote,* [4] *Margaret Hinton,* [5] *Ann Brierley,* [6] *Gillian Allsopp,* [7] *Janice Kniveton,* [8] *Sandra Shaw,* [9] *Maxine Lane,* [10] *Anne Willis,* [11] *Ann Follows,* [12] *Mary Jeffreys,* [13] *Pauline Brown (face hidden),* [14] *Janet Millward* [15[*Betty Salt. Warner Street is in the background.*

11

Florence's husband, Arthur Granville Ravensdale, was the headmaster of Hardwick Junior Boys' School, Derby and co-author, with Tim Ford of *The Mickleover Story* which was published in 1969. The Ravensdales had a daughter Kathleen who was a schoolteacher.

On May 25th the annual meeting of the parish council reported that the Minister of Transport had refused to grant permission for the building of a public convenience in Mickleover Square.

A letter from the County Council stated that permission had been refused on the grounds that the convenience would obstruct the vision of road users. It was decided to ask George Brown MP to take up the matter with the Minister.

Councillor Joe Nadin told the council: "I feel that we have got to dig our toes in really hard over this. The proposed site is lengthwise like the [wartime] air raid shelter was and as that was not regarded as detrimental I do not see how this can be. I would like this council to press this matter further." The discussions about a public convenience had been taking place for four years when it was first suggested that the grounds of the Nag's Head Hotel might be suitable.

Information had also been received from the RDC that they were at last prepared to install a number of bus shelters in Mickleover so the parish council's opinions were sought as to the type of shelter they required.

In a *Letter from the Vicar* in the June church magazine the Reverend Ben Crockett hoped that the services of an Assistant Curate would be obtained in the near future at All Saints' Church.

"He must be adequately housed and paid a living wage", he said. "The benefit to a Parish Priest, and congregation and to the parish generally would be great. This is the 'long term' policy as it were. But the matter cannot be postponed for more than two years at the most."

His wife, Patricia Crockett, wrote a *Woman's Page* in the church magazine offering advice and recipes. In the current issue she wrote: "To ease and quiet a screaming child, stoop down beside him and whisper a few simple words. It is a curious fact that this often puts a stop to screams due to fear or temper." Was she speaking from experience with three young daughters, Elizabeth, Ann and Finella?

Fred and Cecile Hayles purchased a plot at the corner of Arundel Avenue and Uttoxeter Road in the Littleover parish but were unable to convert the existing cottage into a habitable house. However Fred decided to demolish the building himself, enabling him to build a new house alongside. The large cottage was once an Inn (The Plough) which had been closed during the nineteenth century.

Most of the yard was cobbled and during the excavations the Hales found

The sketch on the left was created by Fred Hayles after he had seen a painting of "The Plough" inn in an antique shop. The old sign was at the front of the building and just beyond it was a mounting stone, used for getting off and on horses. It could well have been a coaching inn as the stables are shown at the rear of the building.

<small>Drawing and illustration, courtesy of Cecile Hales</small>

The photograph of the old inn, below, was taken before Fred Hales dismantled it in 1954. It was on the junction of Arundel Avenue and Uttoxeter Road.

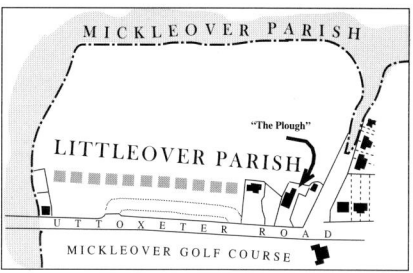

many interesting articles including Roman coins which were presented to Derby Museum. On a ledge in an old fireplace was a crumbling fabric bag of clay marbles, obviously placed there by children to harden after being baked. Cecile remembers seeing two young girls on a garden swing in the grounds when she was a young girl.

North of the plot, which bordered Arundel Avenue, were the remains of a slaughter house which was pulled down to accommodate a garage. Their former house has now been transformed into a large detached residence.

Mrs Wilson, who lived two doors away, was the owner of the field which stretched from Arundel Avenue to the two cottages which are still situated on Uttoxeter Road near the junction with Cavendish Way. The whole field was sold as building plots and my Uncle Eric Mangham and Aunt Gladys (née Brown) purchased one of the plots where they had a house built to their design.

Meat rationing came to an end on July 3rd 1954 and a representative of one big company said "Retail prices looked like soaring to ridiculous heights- rump steak may be as much as 6s.6d or 7s.6d a pound, but, if people hold off buying, prices may easily drop again, even before the end of the week." The *Derby Evening Telegraph* wrote that "From tomorrow, ration books – everyman's key to the nation's cupboards for more than 14 years – will possess only historical interest, except for children entitled to cheap milk."

The RDC Sanitary Inspector had stated in January that the government had not announced their intentions regarding the regulations of slaughter houses when the decontrol of meat and livestock was to take place.

This did not prevent him from granting licences to four applicants in Mickleover: Harold Barker, Staker Lane (knacker's yard); Frank Charnley, Uttoxeter Road (butcher), Pastures Hospital, and Arthur Platts, 55 Station Road (butcher).

The Inspector was of the opinion that the private slaughter houses would again have to be brought into use. The local meat traders also thought that their own premises were preferable to the establishment of one or more central points. Any fears were unfounded, for the resumption of private slaughter houses also came into operation on July 3rd.

I was entering into one of the most pleasurable periods of my teenage years. Jim Nixon had introduced me to some of his Ashbourne Grammar School friends who were attending the youth section of the Mickleover Methodist Guild. Ken Guy was among them and we were to become two of the diminishing numbers of people supporting Derby County. Ann Bakewell was previously a pupil of St Peter's Church School, Littleover, my old school, and along with Peter Hallam, Gillian (Gill) Hannah and Edna Lemmon we became very close friends.

Apart from being regular attenders at the Guild most of our evenings or weekends were spent together, either walking from Littleover via Jackson Avenue, or escorting the two girls, Ann and Gill back to their homes in Littleover. We also entertained ourselves by playing tennis on the playing fields and walking to Markeaton Park to have a round of golf on the small 'pitch and put' course.

The clerk to the RDC, Fred Bailey MBE, and Surveyor attended the July meeting of the All Saints' Parish Church Council and said that land would be required for a new graveyard owing to the increasing population in Mickleover.

Repton RDC suggested 1.19 acres be acquired. "The owner [Arthur Morley from New House Farm] was willing to sell," said Mr Bailey. They estimated the cost would be in the region of £500, which should include fencing, cost of land and water supply.

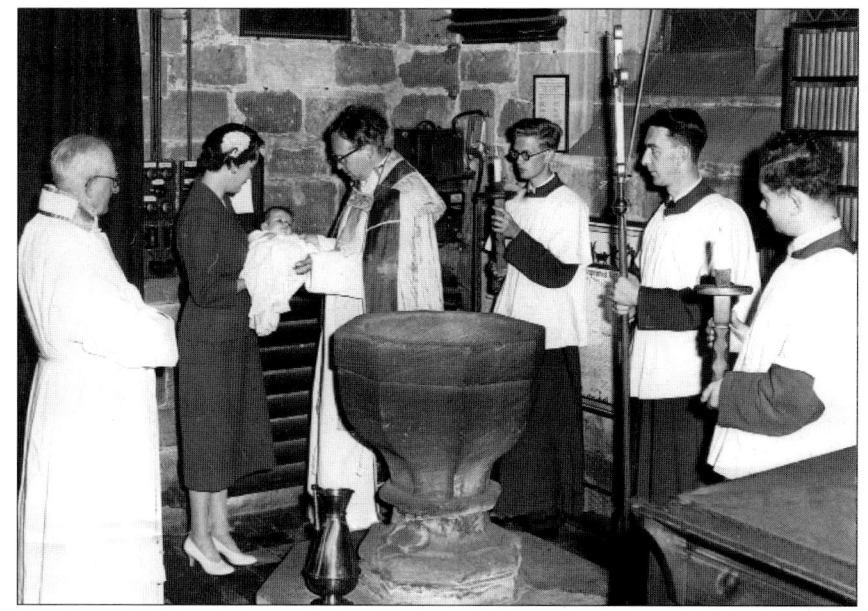

Photo courtesy of Peter Arnold

The date of this christening is thought to be 1954. Reverend Crockett, centre, conducts the service, in the centre. Behind him is Colin White and Michael Bowden is on the extreme right.

Mr Bailey explained "That wherever possible the RDC liked to arrange that the churchyard was extended and kept as a graveyard instead of being made a cemetery, which of course happens immediately the RDC take over."

Local farmer, Arthur Morley, said that if it remained a graveyard he would donate the land.

Harry Rudkin, the treasurer, said the PCC "Had not got the money to do it", Mr Bailey asked if the Methodists had been approached to see if they would contribute.

When the estimate was received at the end of the year the Vicar said that the council remembered the figures quoted by Mr Bailey but it now amounted to £1,800.

The treasurer, said that "this PCC regret it cannot take the responsibility of providing an extension to the churchyard, and there is no alternative but to refer the matter back to the RDC."

Holiday makers in Derby and district refused to be intimidated by the weather at the end of July. The temperature was no more than 56 degrees when eighty five Trent coaches left Derby bus station before 9.00am for the sea and countryside. Some were also leaving Derby by air. Three seven-seater passenger

Photo courtesy of Maureen (née Robinson) Cain

The 1954 Pastures Hospital Bowls team. The three players standing are unknown.
Kneeling, left to right: Albert Wain, George Tate, Alan Taylor, unknown, Sid Robinson,
Paul Taylor, Charlie Lamb, unknown, Charlie Thomson.

aircraft left Derby Airport at Burnaston for Jersey and two more left on the following day.

The RDC formed a Mickleover Sub Committee to discuss the village's future development. A meeting was held at The Limes in August and the Mickleover representatives, Charles Ayre and Joe Nadin were in attendance.

The considered opinion of the Area Planning Authority was that at the time, the population was 3,500 (not including Pastures Hospital), and with added building applications now flooding into the district council, particularly for the north side of Uttoxeter Road, the ultimate population would increase to 8,000.

What concerned the Mickleover Committee was the overloading of both the Bunkers sewage works and those at Findern. It was their opinion that the RDC should give consideration to the extension of the Findern works with the eventual abandonment of the Bunkers works.

The construction of Willington Power Station was underway on August 20th. The first section was operational by the end of 1956 and the £20 million station was completed in 1958. In the same month the United Kingdom Atomic Energy Authority was founded, following the first "breeder" nuclear reactor coming into operation at Harwell in February. Locally Rolls-Royce announced that it had developed a prototype vertical take-off plane, named "The Flying Bedstead".

Grandfather took a stroll down Station Road on August 27th and noted that "House building is taking place and soon all the land will be built up to the station." He must have been referring to the remaining open space between West Drive and "Brass Button Row". The numbers 212 to 222 were listed as occupied in the 1956 Electoral Register.

Mickleover was following the national trend in the mid 1950s with a big push to build new houses and demolish older property as the insanitary conditions were making them uninhabitable. A programme was being considered to pull down houses in Mickleover by the RDC in May 1954 which amounted to two houses in The Green; a block of five in Vicarage Road, and eight at Alma Heights, followed by four in Storer Place, off Vicarage Road, but it took years to fulfil in some cases.

MICKLEOVER COUNTY SCHOOL STAFF - SEPTEMBER 1954
Headmaster: Mr J W Best

	Class	No in Form
Mr S E Peach	J Upper 3	31
Mr J P Roscoe	J3	36
Miss E M Wedd	J2	45
Miss O M Plumpton	J1	45
Mrs M E Henchliffe	I1	40
Miss M Wibberley	I1b	41
Mrs N E Parkin	I2	26
Miss G Ravensdale	I3	21

A Housing Repairs and Rents Bill was at that time before Parliament. In this Bill financial assistance to local authorities would be given to re-house the sitting occupants. In June numbers 2, 3 and 4 in Limes Avenue were to be demolished with the tenant at number 4 being rehoused.

In July the owner of the remaining row of houses in Limes Avenue under consideration had agreed that the properties were "too bad to use." The RDC recommended that orders for the vacation and demolition should proceed.

On The Green number 3 was considered to be in such poor condition that it was recommended that the owner should receive the appropriate notices for its demolition.

Grandfather recorded three interesting events during the month of October: 13th, "They have made a start in building houses in the field next to the playing field, 'Vicarage Park'; 18th, "The poplar tree opposite golf house, a landmark, has been cut down. Mankind on the march"; 21st, "I received news from *Derbyshire Countryside* that they would accept my sonnet 'Repton Park Corner' for publication in their magazine."

Complaints about refuse collection in the Western Road area were discussed at the November parish council meeting. Chairman, Jim Holloway, said he did not think people realised the difficulty there was in getting collectors. "I cannot understand why people have so much refuse. We are asked to burn as much as we can," he said.

The Chief Sanitary Inspector for the RDC reported earlier in the year that "the interruption of the holiday period, together with a certain amount of illness amongst the scavenging [refuse] personnel, has slowed down collections."

It was also stated at the meeting that the council did not mind Vicarage Park housing estate workmen using the water laid on at the playing fields for making tea as long as the supply water to the site was not delayed. However they objected to the lavatory accommodation being used as public conveniences.

Les Miller, clerk, had written to Butterley Co Ltd stating that their workmen were using a short cut across the playing fields and damaging the surface. The company replied that the matters mentioned would be taken up with the site agent immediately.

Harry Rudkin, treasurer of the All Saints' PCC reported at the December meeting that greenhouses had been erected in the yard at the church room in Limes Avenue "and people [visitors] cannot get round to the toilets." He added "That the tenant of the house in the grounds had not had permission to erect these greenhouses."

It was agreed that when Mr Rudkin called for the rent he would ask them to take one down, and if they were unreasonable, a letter should be sent asking them to remove them, as the PCC would not be held responsible for any injury. Harry Rudkin later announced that one of the greenhouses in the Church School yard had been sold.

On December 9th grandfather wrote that "The gates and lodge house of the hall at Etwall have been demolished. A new school is being built." The gates were ascribed to Robert Bakewell, Derby's eighteenth century craftsman, but they were badly damaged during the last year of the war when the hall was occupied by the Army. The last owner of Etwall Hall was Reg Parnell, the famous local racing driver. Derbyshire County Council obtained the site under a Compulsory Purchase Order.

Derby Corporation's proposal to extend the trolley bus service a further three furlongs along Uttoxeter Road to reach the Mickleover - Littleover joint boundary was opposed by the parish council. They asked for "co-operation" from Littleover at the parish meeting.

Henry Ritchie Bower told the council, "there are already three main bus services along this road. We have enough traffic. I don't think people want trolley buses there as well."

"One grouse we would receive is that people could not get decent television," said Tim Ford, local chemist and parish councillor. "I am told that people who live beyond Chain Lane, the present trolley terminus, already get a lot of flashes."

He suggested that, if they found there was a demand for more buses, the council should contact the Trent Traction Company Ltd. An inquiry on the matter was arranged for Spring 1955.

The government announced in 1954 that a new road plan would run from Yorkshire to London and take in three parts of Derbyshire. Work was to start in 1957 and it was thought it would be confined to motor traffic and might even be a toll road!

In November the RDC turned down two applications; the first from Wimpey's who wished to develop 17 acres on the east side of Havenbaulk Lane, and the second by H J Warner who planned to build houses at the rear of property fronting the south side of Uttoxeter Road and east of the Nag's Head Hotel.

However a much larger development was proposed by W G Lee. He had put forward an application to build in three phases, east of Chestnut Avenue and north of the existing Devonshire Drive. The first phase was to cover an area of 30.398 acres, the second and third phases, approximately 23.152 acres. Permission was granted for land use only, subject to detailed layout plans.

Fred Bailey, MBE, the clerk to the RDC, reminded the Health and Public Works Committee meeting that the following developments, with drainage to the Bunkers Sewage Works, had already been approved, namely 350-400 houses, Vicarage Road Development; 179 houses, Western Road Development (George Wimpey); 400 houses, Phase I, east side of Station Road (W G Lee Ltd) and 1000 houses in their Phases II and III. In January 1955 W G Lee Ltd now proposed to proceed with the building of the first phase only, east of Chestnut Avenue. It was understood that the latter phases were still in abeyance. Further more, the sewer would also have to deal with the present Lodge Estate Development (Wade Drive area).

CHAPTER TWO
THE CREEPING GIANT!
1955

At the beginning of the new year Derbyshire County Council confirmed their decision to oppose the trolley bus extensions. The proposed routes included two which affected Mickleover; their main opposition was "because of the depreciation of amenities by the erection of trolley poles and ancillary equipment," They considered that the routes could quite adequately be served by motor vehicles. It was to be decided at an Inquiry in April.

An increase in rabbit population was affecting farm land in the 1950s, but in 1954 a disease called myxomatosis reached Derbyshire, which led to their dying in great numbers.

In mid-1952 myxomatosis had been deliberately introduced into France by a retired physician, who occupied a rabbit infested estate near Paris.

No previous study has alleged the British government was involved in its reaching this country in 1953, but circumstantial evidence indicates that the disease may have been introduced with official blessing.

Bonehill Farm was the closest Mickleover Farm to Egginton, the nearest recorded village to be affected. Although John Dicken recalls that 99% of the rabbits on his farm died, it wasn't heavily populated.

Photo courtesy of the Derby Evening Telegraph
Guests at the Great Northern Hotel darts team dinner.

Photo courtesy of the Derby Evening Telegraph

Alderman A T Neal, of Derby, president of the National Federation of Old Age Pensions Associations, with other guests at the annual Christmas tea of Mickleover Branch at the Methodist Church Hall. Seated from left, are Mrs M J Knott, Alderman Neal, Mrs J Stanton, Mrs S B James.

Nancy Flint and her husband, John, from Manor Farm in Vicarage Road, had a dairy herd. Their land stretched down to the railway line and, as they had public footpaths running through it, a constant flow of people walking the paths kept the rabbit population down.

Its interesting to note that the current rabbit population is probably still half what it was in pre-myxomatosis days.

The parish council agreed on January 18th that the names of fifteen streets in the newly developed parts of the parish should be named after Commonwealth countries. This was suggested by chairman, Tim Ford.

Other suggestions offered by the councillors were that streets should be named after Derbyshire places or rivers, and a rather novel suggestion was that they were named after former Vicars of Mickleover. These did not satisfy the RDC who requested them to reconsider.

The council agreed at the following meeting that the streets on the Vicarage Road Estate should be named after Canadian towns or states with the exception of the main road, which was to be called Vicarage Road. Councillor Thomas Edward (Jim) Whittingham suggested names of towns and cities in Australasia be chosen for the new estate off Western Road being built by George Wimpey

21

Co Ltd, and seven were duly sent to the RDC. The decision was eventually left to the RDC.

On Saturday, February 12th and Monday February 14th 1955, children of Mickleover Methodist Sunday School gave their annual concert in the new hall.

Both sections performed an operetta *Papa Poop and the Pirates* written and composed by Leonard Ashdown, a teacher at Firs Estate Junior School of Derby, who acted as producer. Later in the programme the senior scholars gave an amusing sketch *Great Grandma Speaks*. Arthur G Ravensdale was the MC and the proceeds were for the Sunday School funds.

The East Midlands Electricity Board was making a bid for the title of "Fuel for the Future" in a *Derby Evening Telegraph* article in February.

"It is cheap, it is clean, it is convenient – it is electricity. How is it cheap? Cooking for a family of four costs 4d per day – a budget comparing very favourably with those offered by other fuels."

They maintained that electricity was helping the economy of the nation as the generating stations were using an inferior fuel which could not be utilised by other industries.

"Look how electricity has assisted in the purification of the atmosphere. With the advent of atomic power as the generator of electricity, and the general use of electricity for heating power etc., smog (a blend of smoke and fog) will cease to exist."

The parish council announced in March that changes would soon take place to the library facility in the village. The clerk, Les Miller, read a letter from the County Library Service saying that the WI, which ran the library from 1939 on a part-time basis would be replaced by a permanent librarian. The council were asked to decide whether they wanted the library to continue in the Memorial Hut or move to the Methodist Chapel where it could also be accommodated. They decided unanimously that it should stay in the Hut. The letter said that it was hoped that eventually there would be a new library at Mickleover, but it would not be for a few years . . . . fifty-two actually!

It must be clear to readers of *Mickleover Born & Bred* books that any form of government, be it national, regional or local took a long period to reach any conclusions, if at all.

In 1954 the Minister of Health had informed the Sheffield Regional Hospital Board that he was not prepared to agree to the continuance of farming activities at mental hospitals, "either wholly, or in part."

This led to the Board setting up a committee to investigate and produce their own report.

The first, submitted at the beginning of 1955 stated that the committee was satisfied with 17 out of 20 hospitals visited and that the farms were "fully justified and essential to the interests of patients and hospitals."

On March 25th 1955 questions relating to Pastures Hospital were asked in the House of Commons by Colonel M Stoddart-Smith (Conservative, Ripon).

He asked the Minister of Health what were the duties of the estate manager; how much salary he was paid, who held the appointment and what sums of money had been spent upon alterations, fireplaces, decorating and re-decorating of Grange House since it had been occupied by the estate manager.

What was the salary of the Secretary of the Hospital Management Committee, how many applicants were interviewed for the post when the present secretary was appointed and in which journals the vacancy was advertised.

Mr Ian Mcleod replied: "I am informed that the estate manager is responsible for the management of the farms and gardens belonging to the hospital and his duties include the upkeep and development of the hospital grounds and maintenance of all vehicles."

> **Minister of Health to be questioned on Pastures Hospital**
>
> QUESTIONS about Pastures Hospital, Mickleover, will be asked in the House of Commons on Friday by Colonel M. Stoddart-Scott (Con., Ripon).

The present estate manager, Harry O Hirst, was already in the post at the commencement of the National Health Service, and had chosen to retain the salary and conditions of service to which he was previously entitled. His salary was £849.6s.0d per annum, plus emuluments valued for superannuation purposes at £84.19s.4d.

Re-decoration and the installation of a new range at Grange House before Harry Hirst occupied it in September 1949, cost £250; sums amounting to £450 had been spent on the house since that date.

On the second question Mr Mcleod stated: "I am informed that this officer's salary is £1,350. He was on the staff of the Committee when the previous secretary died in 1951. No other applicants were interviewed for the post and the vacancy was not advertised."

At the March meeting of Mickleover Sports Club one of the founders in 1948, Capt J G Starkey, had to relinquish his presidency of the club through ill health. The treasurer, Jim Mills reported a healthy balance of £103.5s.9d and the committee decided to place £50 into a deposit account.

Mickleover Parish Council was told by its clerk, Les Miller, at their April meeting that there was an obligation on occupiers of land to inform the public health authority of the presence of rats or mice on their property. The council was discussing a complaint that rats had taken goose eggs from the back of Western Road, and other complaints had been received from parishioners in Wade Drive.

Les Miller said he had written to the RDC requesting the piping of the ditch running from the Memorial Hut between Western Road and Hartington Way, on the grounds that it was a breeding place for mosquitoes and flies and was a public nuisance.

Arthur Platts Station Road business, adjoining the hut, which consisted of detached house and butcher's shop, slaughter house, outbuildings, had been sold to Ernie J Beech. Arthur moved to Vicarage Road and his son Peter to Ivy Farm, Scropton.

The Titterton family had been farming at The Oaks, in Western Road since the 1920s. When young Tom married he had houses built further down Western Road. His sister Hilda lived at 156 and Tom and his wife Muriel began farming from 158 which the couple named "Craig-y-don". Unknowingly they had copied the first house named "Craig-y-don" in Mickleover, 1 Western Road, where in 1938 a proposal was made to turn it into shops (see Book Two p5).

In March 1955, Common Farm, just north of Tom's farm, was offered for sale. The auctioneer described it as: "Small brick and tiled Farmhouse. Good cowshed for 17 stabling; Pig sty, etc; 2-bay hay barn. Area 35 acres approximately." Tom Titterton purchased it from John Wilson and it was the neighbouring farm to Rough Heanor Farm which belonged to the Sheffield Regional Hospital Board who were threatened with a cut down of the farming activities. Common Farm was originally owned by the Radbourne Estate. The tenant, Thomas Henry Yates and his family had been offered a farm on the Sudbury Hall estate. (See plan p100.)

Photo courtesy of Tom Titterton

Tom Titterton sits in the family Buick, Oakland, in the 1920s. He admits to driving the car to Mickleover Station when he was fourteen-years of age. The family lived at the farm, The Oaks, Western Road.

In April Tom applied for permission to provide septic tank, drainage, bathroom and re-planning of existing rooms at Common Farm. The estimated cost was £1,155. The Chief Sanitary Inspector reported that it was an isolated farmhouse with no mains, electricity and water supply.

"Excluding the above price, I understand the owner is obtaining these supplies at a cost of £500 for electricity and £350 for water supply," he said.

"The farm is approximately 40 acres and although I have no reason to observe, beyond my own thoughts, I am wondering if this land may subsequently be sold for redevelopment." He requested further instructions.

It was eventually deferred because of the cost of drainage and the possible connection to main drainage on the new Wimpey estate.

The parish council was to take no further action regarding the state of the grass verges along Station Road and the Hollow. Concern had been expressed about the deterioration of the verges because of them being "ploughed up" by people riding horses. The clerk, Les Miller, was instructed to write and ask the riders from Mickleover Riding Stables to keep their mounts off the highways wherever possible.

Irene May Harries, the owner of the stables in Staker Lane, told the councillors that private owners of horses galloped their mounts along Station Road and The Hollow and she was being blamed for it. "We do not tear along like hooligans," she said. "We go on the green in The Hollow because traffic comes tearing round the corner and we do not have a dog's chance."

She had contacted the County Council and was told that there was no law against riding along the verges. The police had no power to stop it.

A complaint about the state in which the building site at Vicarage Park was left, was made by Councillor Anthony Yeomans after huts had been moved to different positions, and it was decided to write to the builder.

An Inquiry at Derby in April opposing Derby Corporation's application to extend the trolley bus service was attended by representatives of local authorities and opposing private residents.

It was the Corporation's intention to extend the service in two ways. One to Cavendish Way and the second along Chain Lane to Burton Road. Their view, they maintained, reflected a tendency of ratepayers to move from the town centre and they were entitled to better transport facilities.

They also believed that trolley buses were more economic than other forms of transport. "We do not accept that the day of the trolley bus is almost over," said F A Stockdale for the Corporation. The position was to change twelve years later.

"There was no interference with television reception by trolley bus equipment, except by the windscreen wipers and bells, which were common to motor vehicles." he said.

Eric Blain, representing the two private operators, said there was no evidence of public demand. He contended that there was no case for taking the trolley bus with its fixed equipment into semi-rural areas that were already well served by motor buses.

He was later backed up by the Minister of Transport and Civil Aviation in July, when he decided not to proceed with the order.

For seasoned Rams supporters such as Ken Guy and myself it was humiliating to read that Derby County had been relegated to the Third Division. George Jule Corbishley wrote in the *Derbyshire Advertiser* that "the fall has been coming. It has been coming for some years, indeed ever since the cup winning days just after the war, when little or no attempt was made to make provision for the future playing staff of the club."

He continued, "Football is a game. If the people of Derby come to recognise it for that, and not look on it as such a grim business, perhaps the fall will not altogether have been in vain." Ken was now joining me in the employed section of the community, beginning with an apprenticeship at International Combustion.

The busy period of house building continued with an application by H J Warner for 24 houses on the corner of Western Road and North Avenue, and also at Avenue Farm on the corner was owned by Tom Titterton, referred to by the RDC as the Titterton Estate.

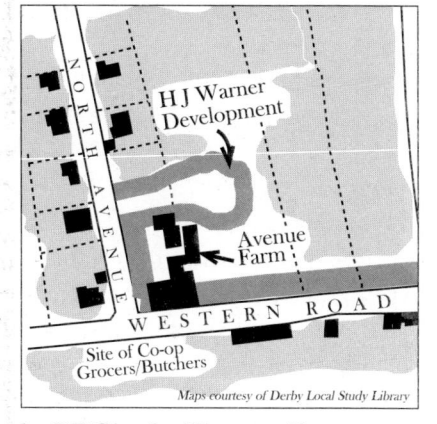

Maps courtesy of Derby Local Study Library

Permission was also requested for development of a public house (The Robin) on the Leeway Estate (W G Lee Ltd). The Area Planning Officer confirmed that this was already on the general development in the area. "Personally I think it is a good site and I have no objections to offer."

At the parish council meeting following the election, the clerk, Les Miller, said he had looked into the deeds of the German Pole Charity and had found that the money could be used for anything that the trustees thought fit. This was an old Mickleover Charity founded in 1682 originally for the provision of tools for apprentices living in the parish. It continued to provide small grants and books for students at University.

At Repton RDC's annual meeting the clerk, Fred Bailey, said that a certain number of wooden type bus shelters, now on order, would be installed when received and with regard to Mickleover said they "would be forwarding details of alternative types to the parish council."

Mickleover representative, Sydney Clarke, complained that while other parishes now had two or three shelters, Mickleover had been making application without success for the past nine years.

Fred Bailey replied that the council had not been considering bus shelters for nine years, and that "nine months would be nearer the mark." As to the type of shelter, he was hoping to communicate with Mr Clarke and other representatives of the parish within a few days.

Councillor Clarke agreed that there had been a difficulty over sites, especially in The Square. They were informed later in the year that a "firm order had been fixed" for the rural type and would be erected as soon as possible.

The new additional housing stock coming into Mickleover was noted by my grandfather on June 1st. "House building commencing on the north side of Western Road [Wimpeys], opposite Arundel Avenue. On the 10th he "walked back by way of new housing estate off Uttoxeter Road."

Miss Frances Emily Newton died in London on June 17th, aged eighty three. She was born at Mickleover Manor, the daughter of Charles Edmund Newton, banker, agriculturalist and one of the family whose most illustrious member was Isaac Newton. For nearly half-a-century she was one of the best known English residents in Palestine.

While in her teens she became interested in the work of the Christian missionaries in the Holy Land, partly through her step-sisters, who, with their father's financial support had established a hospital at Jaffa.

Going out to Palestine when she was 17, she remained there until 1938, the year following the sale of the Manor estate. On her return to England, Miss Newton settled in Cadogan Square in London. She kept open house to visiting Arabs and in 1948 founded a fund to relieve distress among the refugees of Palestine.

On June 21st at All Saints' PCC the Reverend Crockett said he had received correspondence from the RDC about a bus shelter and public conveniences which they proposed to erect on the Vicarage grounds. The Diocese Dilapidations

---

LOCAL ELECTIONS TOOK PLACE IN MAY 1955
Results:
H G FORD	(491)
S A CLARKE	(458)
A G RAVENSDALE	(409)
H W BRICE	(403)
J M BOWER	(383)
A S YEOMANS	(356)
E J GOTHARD	(352)
E W NADIN	(349)
H R BOWER	(337)
J NADIN	(307)
T E WHITTINGHAM	(247)

Not elected:
C H PARKINSON	(233)
G HOLLOWAY	(201)
W WILLIAMS	(154)

Mickleover representatives voted onto the RDC were Charles Ayre, Joe Nadin, Ernest Nadin and Sydney Clarke.

Photo courtesy of the Derby Evening Telegraph

The Derby Evening Telegraph *published this aerial photograph of the expanding housing stock off Western Road.*

Maps courtesy of Derby Local Study Library
MICKLEOVER PARISH
SUMMER 1955

Board turned it down. He suggested the secretary should write to the RDC and remind them of their position of the graveyard which was now serious.

It was agreed that both choirs at the church should be integrated and amalgamated. A full choir practice would now take place on Thursday evenings at 8.00pm. The scheme for the Memorial Chapel was put on hold until the matter was raised again in 1961.

"Work commenced on the field opposite Nag's Head for a petrol station and garage", wrote my Grandfather on July 19th. The building application by P T Smith included petrol filling station, garage, showroom and erection of five petrol pumps plus the proposal of a detached house.

Allegations that new houses on the Vicarage Park Estate were "potential slums" were made at the July parish council meeting when members complained at the size, appearance and particularly the building standards of the houses.

They decided to obtain plans of the two final phases which would complete the estate so that they could see what other houses would look like.

After commenting that he felt the houses already erected were potential slums, the chairman, Tim Ford, said he did not think it was fair on the people who were going to live in the houses. The wiring of the houses was "just plain rubber covered and exposed to the walls." He thought of the results if some young child knocked a nail through the rubber.

"The whole point," he added, "is that if we do not make a shout, we are going to have more of the type built. In 1955 we should not have this, and I think it is a disgrace to the parish council, the Repton Rural District Council, Derbyshire County Council and the Ministry of Housing."

It was decided, on the proposition of Edward J Gothard, to take the matter up with the housing authority, who gave permission for the building, and state that the parish council strongly disapproved.

A letter in the evening newspaper on July 22nd complained: "I read with interest in the *Derby Evening Telegraph* of the references made at a recent meeting of Mickleover Parish Council, to the 'potential slums' which are being erected on the Vicarage Park Estate.

"As one who hopes to occupy a house in this 'potential slum' I would like to register my protest against unwarranted remarks which were made at the meeting.

"I would like to convey to our neighbours-to-be that there is no cause for alarm. The future residents of the 'potential slum' are, no doubt, quite ordinary English folk, with an earnest desire to live decent, happy lives in their new environment. They are quite satisfied with the construction and general layout of the homes they are hoping soon to occupy – and might I add, they are houses they will have to pay for." Signed, "An Englishman."

Grandfather was not aware, until he read it in the newspapers, that an "Official opening of the Ambulance Station" had taken place on July 25th. He had noticed that the station "was open for service on April 9th."

Four women, all of them county Aldermen, opened the Derbyshire County Council's new station. Alderman Mrs E Harrison, chairman of the County Health Committee presided. After paying tribute to the St John Ambulance Brigade and the British Red Cross, who formerly operated the ambulance service, she said it was essential the county should operate an efficient service.

She hoped that in time the county would be able to operate a 24-hour service and it was the provision of the stations such as the one at Mickleover which would make it possible.

After Alderman Mrs D M Sutton performed the official opening she too spoke of the importance of operating a 24-hour service "So that people could have the feeling of security that they could be taken to hospital immediately."

A man completed the ceremony – Dr Ian Mackenzie, who again thanked the St John Ambulance and Red Cross Committee.

W G Lee Ltd had applied for Phase II in the development of Devonshire Drive. This was to include 372 properties and eight shops which would entail the closure or diversion of a public footpath on the northern boundary.

Sir Winston Churchill resigned as Prime Minister in April 1955, and Sir Anthony Eden succeeded him. On May 26th the Conservatives won the General Election with a majority of 59.

One of their first pledges, in early August was issued by Duncan Sandys, Housing Minister. He instructed the local authorities to set up Green Belts similar to London's and other towns and cities. The intention was to stop the unsightly urban area extending across food-producing farmland, and stop the ribbon development of the inter-war years. Where possible, most new urban development was to be "infilling".

As the number of pupils on the County School roll had averaged 301 or more over a period of three years the school had been upgraded from Grade III to Grade IV with a resultant increase in the headteacher's salary.

Miss J G Brown of Matlock applied for the appointment as Assistant Mistress and after an interview it was agreed that she took up her post in August.

Stan Peach was one of the teachers in the juniors and according to one of his pupils, Mick Nordemann he produced some superb chalk drawings which he hung round the walls.

Mick writes of the silver Velocette motorcycle that Mr Peach possessed, along with the white raincoat and white helmet to match.

"One day, when I missed the bus, he gave me a lift to school," says Mick. "I waved to my Mum as we passed, no crash helmets for passengers in those days!"

The appointment of School Managers for three years was confirmed: By Derbyshire Education Committee: Joe Nadin, Arthur Riley. Divisional Executive: Wilf Dutson, Mrs V Gordon. Representing Mickleover Parish Council: Harold W Brice and Arthur G Ravensdale.

Over 40 places at Grammar School were awarded at the County School in 1955. The majority travelled to the Queen Elizabeth Grammar School at Ashbourne with a small number obtaining places in the Borough.

The "Yeoman's Bat" (for boys) and the "Aldred Tennis Racket" (for girls) together with books to the value of £14 were provided from School Funds and presented by the Rt Hon George Brown MP, at the annual prize giving. Anthony S Yeomans had presented an autographed cricket bat in 1954 which was to be awarded annually to the boy displaying the greatest sportsmanship.

Grandfather wrote in August that "houses were being constructed at the Uttoxeter Road end of Cavendish Way and the fence at the corner of Station Road junction with Uttoxeter Road was removed for the construction of Paramount Garage."

In September, on my cousin Tony's thirteenth birthday, Grandfather, Uncle Tom and Auntie Hilda went by train from Mickleover to Cambridge. "We had a comfortable train journey, made more interesting by the comments of the Station Master [Stephen Hemsworth]. He was a fellow traveller, with his wife [Mary] and family."

His job description was not correct as there was no longer a Station Master at Mickleover. There was certainly a young Hemsworth family living in the Station House and Stephen could well have been the Porter/Clerk.

Photos courtesy of Mick Nordemann
Mick Nordemann, right was given a lift to school by his teacher on a Velocette motorcycle similar to the one above.

It was a long day for the trio which they celebrated by drinking "to health and happiness at 12.00am in a glass of home made elderberry wine."

At the September meeting of All Saints' PCC the secretary, Mrs J James, read a letter from the RDC re the burial ground. It stated that they were awaiting the completion of the purchase of the land by the council's solicitors. It was decided that in future the Church Room should now be referred to as the Church Hall.

The Reverend Crockett said that there was never enough money in the "dilapidations fund" to repair the Vicarage and buildings even though the Surveyor suggested work needed to be done after his inspection. The council agreed to explore the possibility of a grant.

It was announced that Edward Kenderdine, the Organist and Choirmaster since 1952 would be finishing his duties on September 25th and

Arthur Parker, the Assistant Organist and "gifted musician" was to take over the choir practice with Terence Bennett as assistant organist.

The Vicar thought a presentation should be made to Mr Kenderdine from the choir and congregation and raised the question of the salary paid to the Organist and Choirmaster. He suggested "that it should be increased to £1 per week at least." It was decided that the matter should wait until the annual meeting.

Mr and Mrs Kenderdine were invited to the last meeting of the year and a presentation was made in the name of the congregation. Mr T W Williams said he considered it a great privilege to make the presentation and hoped they would be very happy in their new surroundings when they moved from Mickleover.

A special meeting was called by the chairman of the parish council, Tim Ford, to discuss the proposed building by Nestlés Ltd of a factory in Mickleover. "So many parishioners had asked me about this new factory which may be built at the northern end of Station Road."

Captain Marshall, the agent for the Radbourne Estate had informed the RDC that he had been approached regarding the sale of land for a factory in July.

Fred Bailey, clerk to the RDC and Mr A P Hancock, Engineer and Surveyor, were asked to attend the meeting. The parish council had heard about the outline plans and had come to agree with the recommendation.

Mr Ford told the meeting: "Nestlés Ltd have put in the application to build this factory in which they want to manufacture chocolates and confectionary and "Parishioners in the affected area have been to me, asking us to oppose it," he said. "They were concerned about the depreciation of their property and the smoke and smells from the factory.

"If the factory is to be built it will create employment for the ever-growing population of Mickleover," Tim Ford went on to say. "I understand there will be employment for 500 people."

Arthur G Ravensdale said the thing that worried him "was that if the factory were erected, more houses would be built in the area." Mr Ravensdale was to be awarded an MBE in November.

Fred Bailey said that the factory would probably be only part built in Mickleover and partly in the parish of Radbourne. "It will not have chimneys or any of the other kind of things one naturally assumes factories to have."

Nestlés anticipated that labour would mostly be drawn from the local female population and "there will be no question of any new houses being built."

Mr Bailey said he understood that sidings would be built into the railway and the main traffic would be mostly by rail. He finally said: "There is nothing you can do about it; there is no machinery for objection. If the plans for the proposed factory are passed by the planning authority, and they conform to building by-laws, the RDC has to approve. They have no choice in the matter."

He said: "However, any individual could make his feelings known to the RDC, and they would be considered!"

The local press reported that the country had faced the longest period of drought for several years grassland was scorched and ponds and wells had run dry. As the water level diminished at Ladybower Reservoir the "lost" village of Derwent re-appeared.

The Earls Court Motor Show opened, with the media announcing that "Britain's cars are second to none." The motor industry, they suggested, had achieved remarkable export targets over the last ten years but it depended on a stable market at home to keep export prices down against foreign competition. However, many publications complained that our roads were so backward in comparison to other countries.

The RDC (acting under delegated powers from the County Council) refused an application by Mr A H Peake to develop Havenbaulk Lane as a housing site.

They based their refusal of the site, situated to the north-east of Havenbaulk Lane, as not being in a designated development area and in addition other land was available. The proposal would also form a damaging incursion into a valuable agricultural holding.

On appeal the Minister of Housing and Local Government agreed with the views of the planning authority and drew attention to its location adjoining other outlying development more than a mile from the centre of Mickleover, also to the isolating effect which the proposed construction of a division of the A38 Trunk Road by the highway authority would have upon it.

He was therefore not satisfied that the neighbourhood appeal site was suitable for more extensive development for the present time. The Minister dismissed the appeal.

Grandfather wrote: "The new filling station [opposite the Nag's Head] was opened today," October 17th. He added: "House building is proceeding at tremendous pace at Mickleover."

"Went a curiosity stroll in the afternoon going up the lane by the old windmill, up which I had never been while at Mickleover." The family moved from Church Gresley in South Derbyshire in 1929.

The Hanson family had farmed at Mill Farm over different periods from 1819. It was Gerald and Dorothy Hanson who moved from Thurvaston to the

Photo (above) courtesy of Derby Museums and Art Gallery L3342
Lewis Straw walked down what is now called Mill Lane, where the stump of the mill still stood. The barns belong to Mill Farm. The photo, left, shows, left to right: Arthur Hanson, Linda Samuel, (258 Station Road) and Barry Hanson with farm dog Peter.

Photo courtesy of Barry Hanson

farm in 1949. Being a typical small mixed farm (about 40 acres), with dairy cattle, poultry, arable and pasture land it was spread where Onslow Road is now situated and across Station Road in the Inglewood Avenue area.

In 1955 there were still a number of farms in the Mickleover parish. The notable few were the Dickens' farm at Bonehill and Arthur Morley's New House Farm on the west. To the south, Brook Fields, the Etches farm and on the east Tom Titterton farmed alongside Rough Heanor Farm. Mill Farm was on the north. We must not forget Manor Farm on Vicarage Road which was the last remaining farm in the centre of the village.

Of all these only Bonehill continues to flourish, the rest have been taken over by house building or the construction of a by-pass.

Mill Farm was typical of the part played by farming more than 50 years ago. Open 365 days a year Dorothy and Gerald Hanson sold eggs and potatotes at the door. They often provided milk and other basics to neighbours when they had run out on a Sunday.

Barry Hanson recalls that during the long summer evenings the Hanson family "organised impromptu games of cricket (sometimes football), in the fields with neighbouring farmers and teenagers from Brass Button Row," the name given by locals to the row of semi-detached houses built in 1933. (See Book One).

Hardly any of the local houses had a telephone and neighbours often asked if "they could use the 'phone". Barry can remember daughters and sons from nearby ringing late at night, asking his mother to inform their parents that they wouldn't be home that night.

Very few houses had garages, so neighbours parked their cars and caravans at the top of the orchard near the mill.

Later on his walk grandfather spotted the building of a new Co-op grocery and butchers shop in Western Road on land that was used as allotments (now Derek Williams bathroom and kitchen business).

John Orme was congratulated on taking 100 wickets during the cricket season at the October meeting of Mickleover Sports Club. A small presentation was made to him. Success had earlier been reported for the men's tennis team at the Management Committee Meeting of the Mickleover Sports Club. They were congratulated on winning all their matches during the season.

The death occurred at a nursing home in Ireland on October 21st of Mr Alexander Preston-Jones. He lived for 18 years at Mickleover House, and was well known for his champion herd of Red Poll cattle, Suffolk sheep and Suffolk horses. In 1930 he went to Milford House, Milford where he lived until 1937.

```
PARAMOUNT
SERVICE STATION
    MICKLEOVER
 (opp. Nag's Head Hotel)
     offer for sale:-
AUSTIN A70 1952 (Nov.) £445
AUSTIN A40 1953 ......... £525
FORD Anglia 1954 ......... £510
HILLMAN Minx 1952 ... £445
AUSTIN A40 1950 ......... £375
MORRIS Minor 1952 ...... £425
HILLMAN Minx 1939 ... £145

H.P. Terms - Part Exchanges

  Open for Petrol and Oil
      8 a.m. to 8 p.m.

   Tel. DERBY 53328
```
Courtesy of Magic Attic Archive, Swadlincote

He left a widow, Isabelle Mary, a son and two daughters. Alexander will always be remembered for donating the Memorial Hut to Mickleover as a permanent reminder to those who lost their lives in the First World War. His son, Donald Preston-Jones was the Managing Director of the family firm, A G Jones and Co Ltd, leather manufacturers of Slack Lane, Derby. His father had been the Chairman. By the early 1960s the factory site had been taken over by Burrows and Sturgess, the soft drinks manufacturers.

Grandfather noted on November 7th: "They are preparing to lay a large water pipe down towards the station." Three days later "I went by way of Station Road, Radbourne Lane to Radbourne village via Silver Hills and thence to Etwall.

A long walk but enjoyable. They are stretching the electric cable on the pylons across the countryside." On November 23rd he wrote that some new houses were now occupied in Vicarage Road. The children from the estate had been admitted to the County School on Uttoxeter Road at the beginning of November.

He had the chimney swept by Archie Warner at a cost of 3s. "Busy cleaning up after sweeps visit. Some job. Wish I could abolish coal fire and substitute something hygienic and as effective." Both the East Midlands Gas Board and the East Midlands Electricity Board were beginning to advertise new ways of home heating.

A rather interesting event took place in Derby in early November which prompted some comment by readers of the local newspapers and the Leader writer of the *Derbyshire Advertiser.*

Derby Town Council authorised the demolition of the air-raid shelters in Markeaton Park. The writer stated "that they may live long enough to regret this."

The Leader continued: "It is well known that defence or form of attack often invites use of another. The type of shelter in 1940 may not offer complete protection from hydrogen bombs (nothing will, if they drop near enough). But the Home Office view is that any kind of underground shelter is better than none."

Allan Bradshaw remembers a corrugated iron "Anderson" air-raid shelter roof being upturned and used as a sledge at Bunkers. This was a popular sledging area, and Alan comments that the so-called sledge "could have caused lethal injuries if you were caught on its downward path."

There was still a reinforced concrete air-raid shelter at the home of Alf and Lillie Walklate on Uttoxeter Road, just above the "boundary" opposite Kings Drive.

Mick Nordemann lived here with his mother and father and remembers it was covered by a rockery. Mick's son lives in his great grandparents house now, the shelter only being demolished about five years ago.

As an infant at the County School Mick was once late for school owing to a chimney fire at home. He recalls helping out, wearing a fireman's helmet. When he arrived at school his teacher, Miss Mabel Wibberley, asked him to tell the class all about it.

The managers of the County School complained of the increasing inadequacy of classroom accommodation and it was reported to the South Derbyshire Divisional Executive. They were told that work on a new junior school was expected to start in April 1956.

The Executive Chairman said: "I hope they will agree that, for the time being, we must look to outside accommodation as a temporary solution.

"Temporary huts would not be available until the next financial year, and by that time they were built, the new school would be well on the way, and the problem half solved. About 600 new houses were to be built at Mickleover, and a site was earmarked for a second new primary school."

The school was soon to be involved in the preparation of its regular Christmas concerts, which teacher Ronald Bagguley was very much involved with. Scenery and costumes from previous productions were stored in the playground.

Elaine (née Purdy) Hawksworth remembers performing in a nativity play as the inkeeper's wife. Miss Wibberley helped her into her costume which she had to wear under her day clothes as she had been suffering from bronchitis. On the big night she had been told to look for her parents in the audience so she knew where they were. In doing so she forgot to say her few words and received a very loud prompt.

Chris Nixon appeared in a school play as a gypsy and can "clearly remember the ladies Sellotaping brass curtain rings to my ear lobes. I have no idea what the play was called but the curtain rings shone more than I did." writes Chris.

When the parish council held their November meeting Henry Bower accused the clerk, Fred Bailey, of the RDC of treating the parish council "like a piece of rubbish."

Councillor Bower was commenting that the clerk had not replied to or even acknowledged a letter from the parish council recommending that a made-up footpath was immediately necessary in front of the council houses on the west side of Havenbaulk Lane.

Les Miller, the parish clerk, had written nine months previously stating that the work was supposed to be put in hand to relieve flooding in Havenbaulk Lane. A verbal promise had been given to residents who attended a parish meeting in December 1954.

John and Charles Etches, farmers of Brook Field Farm were summoned at Derby County Magistrates' on Friday, November 18th, as being the owners of the sheep which were found straying on the road at Mickleover on October 29th.

Police Constable Williams stated that on October 29th he was on duty in Uttoxeter Road when he saw seven sheep straying on the road.

The constable moved the sheep because of the traffic and the following day he reported the matter to Charles Etches who admitted he and his father John were the owners.

Constable Williams then told the magistrates that one sheep had been involved in a collision with a car.

Photo courtesy of Frances (née Sherratt) Eaton

Brook Field Farm photographed in 1935 when Thomas Sherratt was the tenant farmer. It was purchased by the Etches family in 1947 from Charles Ayre. The farmhouse, which oversaw 100 acres was situated at Ordnance Survey No 328. It was demolished with the building of the A38 bypass.

When Charles Etches answered the summons and stood in the witness box the Court were under the impression that he was John Etches.

The name John Etches was on the summons sheet and when Constable Williams was questioned he said that all the time he was conducting enquiries into the matter he thought that Charles Etches was John Etches.

On hearing this the clerk to the Magistrates told Chief Inspector C R Potter, who was prosecuting in the case: "I don't think you have a case because the proper man had not been served the summons."

Inspector Potter replied that if the case was adjourned both Charles and his father, John would then be summoned.

Charles Etches told the court that he and his father ran the farm as a partnership, and so were responsible for the sheep. He added that he did not mind the summons being amended, so that he, as well as his father was accused of the offence.

Ken Guy recalls that he was among a number of local boys who earned pocket money picking potatoes on Etches farm. "We were paid 2s a day, plus midday meal." Cooked potatoes apparently!

Grandfather wrote in December: "Eldest granddaughter [Sheila] engagement at Christmas." To John Taylor.

CHAPTER THREE
SCHOOL BECOMES HOSPITAL!
1956

Grandfather's diary in January 1956 gives an interesting insight to the routines of his daily life along with its costs, the changes that were occurring in Mickleover and his joy and sorrow.

On January 4th he wrote: "Did a bit of shopping – obtained breast of mutton [lamb] for a tanner [6d]." The following day he walked down to the Memorial Hut to view the new Repton Rural District Council valuation lists. "The valuation of my own house up £4."

The RDC rates were payable every six months. People living in the Havenbaulk Lane area were able to go to Peggs', Meadows Farm, to make their payments before the staff moved to the Memorial Hut in the centre of the village.

On January 10th grandfather experienced a strange earth movement. "Just before getting up, I felt a tremor which caused the bed to shake and the pots in the washstand to rattle. It lasted about two seconds." He added: "In the evening paper an earth tremor was reported for the counties of Derby, Nottingham, Leicester and Rutland."

He was thrilled to read in the local papers that his sonnet *Change & Decay* was to be broadcast on BBC radio on Thursday, January 12th. "My Sonnet was recited first in the programme. There was one wistful regret; my wife is not with me to share my joy."

On the following morning he noted: "A remarkable event happened in Mickleover. At long last the dead tree in The Square has been chopped down and the Square is being paved. (See picture opposite).

"Also the wooden fence – rest of it – where the new garage and houses have been erected has been taken down. Thus another eye-sore has gone." He was referring to the long fence at the junction of Station Road and Uttoxeter Road where the Total Filling Station is now situated (see photo p8). In the afternoon of the same day he went a stroll up to Pastures Hospital. "More building taking place there." The modernisation of the hospital is dealt with in Chapters 13 and 14.

After thirty-three applications had been received for the post of Senior Assistant Teacher, at the County School a short list led to interviews on January 5th. Harry Matthew Gaskill of St John's Terrace, Derby, was appointed and agreed to commence after the Easter holidays. He was to replace Ronald Bagguley who had been appointed headmaster at Linton County Junior School in South Derbyshire.

Photo courtesy of Sue Butcher

Mickleover Square in the early 1930s. The Trent Motor Traction Company began a direct service to Mickleover in 1923. The bus on the right stands next to the tree which was planted around the same time as the old pump was erected to commemorate Queen Victoria's Diamond Jubilee. The roof of the "new" Nag's Head is just visible in the background.

The parish council decided to ask the Head Postmaster of Derby to send a representative of the Post Office to discuss the postal and telephone facilities in the village.

Arthur Ravensdale commented that the whole situation regarding post boxes wanted looking into. He said the morning postal delivery at his home had got progressively later.

On one occasion on a Saturday, he said, he had a parcel which was too large to go into a post-box, and he took it to the Post Office at The Square only to find it was closed during the weekend. He made enquiries and was told the situation arose because of a shortage of staff.

Henry Bower said that pensioners had asked him why they could not get their money at the sub-Post Office in Western Road. He added that at times in the morning, those who go to make a withdrawal are asked to go back later as the office had not enough money to pay them. "The Post Office could not pay old age pensions, and old people had to go to Derby for them." he said.

Uncle Tom obtained temporary work at the Post Office delivering post as heavy snow and freezing road conditions had prevented him from continuing his window cleaning round. He began his post delivery at 6.30am and worked for three hours.

He increased his hours after a period delivering football coupons in the

Photos courtesy of Magic Attic Archive, Swadlincote
Pastures Hospital from the air surrounded by fields in its care. On the top right Vicarage Road is visible. The hospital farm at the outbreak of war occupied 289 acres. Left the Nurses home in 1939.

afternoon. Mrs Iris Willis, the Post Mistress, had loaned my grandfather a book on American verse which she had borrowed from the local library.

After meeting a deputation the Postmaster replied that the County Council had been approached to erect a post box at the junction of Burlington Way and Cavendish Way. Other boxes would be considered when development of the parish was completed, he added.

In a statement in Parliament the Minister of Health explained in greater detail that under the National Health Service Act there was no authority to run farms where little or no therapeutic purposes were served. He pressed for action that some, if not all the land at hospitals and all dairy herds should be given up by March 1956.

The Sheffield Regional Hospital Board had now been informed that surplus land should be sold and not leased. This applied to Rough Heanor Farm (Kingsway Hospital) and Pastures Hospital where both dairy herds would have to be dispersed.

The Chairman of the Board said: "We have no farms which are purely and simply farms." He explained that they were mainly used as mental hospitals for a therapeutic purpose. He hoped they could continue to supply hospitals with milk and vegetables and provide some reasonable amenities for the patients.

This indecisive situation had been most unsatisfactory. In doubt had been their cropping programmes and staff were becoming unsettled. Finally he remarked: "I am very disappointed with the Minister's decision, but there it is!"

At Pastures approximately 159 acres (including that allocated for hospital development), were to be retained, the remainder to be disposed of together with the dairy herd.

Land at Kingsway to the east of a specified boundary from the Manor Hospital to the railway on the north was to be retained. The dairy herd together with the Rough Heanor Farm was to be disposed.

The Regional Board asked the Minister if he would permit the retention of The Grange at Pastures Hospital which was the home of the Estate Manager while Harry Hirst was still employed by the hospital.

The British Government brought in Tuberculine Testing on cattle in 1956. This led to Gerald Hanson from Mill Farm selling his herd of Friesians and bringing in a herd of Ayrshires. This is a sturdy breed of dairy cow from Scotland which produces a high butterfat content.

Photo courtesy of the late Bill Short's family

Grandfather observed in March 1956: "The bungalow at the Bakum is vacant and is being altered in some way." It was the property of Arthur Morley from New House Farm and was occupied by his farm workers. It was pulled down in recent times and a new office block now occupies the site, opposite Mickleover Court Hotel.

Licenses were now needed for the delivery of Tuberculin Tested milk. Two were granted in Mickleover, Arthur Morley, 3 The Hollow and Albert Clayton, 72 Western Road.

There were many amusing stories told of notes left for the milkmen. "I've just had a baby. Would you please leave another one each day", or "Please leave an extra pint, but if this note blows away please knock" and "Cancel half pint of cat's milk. Cat now deceased."

"The churchyard at Mickleover will soon be too crowded to accommodate any more graves," said the Vicar at the annual PCC meeting in February. "In view of the increasing population of the village, somewhere else had to be found."

He said the RDC had taken the responsibility of finding another site and had done so, but had not yet purchased the land.

At the next meeting Mrs J James, secretary of the PCC, read a letter from Fred Bailey, clerk of the RDC. It stated that "an agreement had been reached with the Hospital Authorities to acquire a small area of land adjacent to the present graveyard" and it stated that "as soon as the land has been conveyed to the council the consecration formalities will go forward."

The Sheffield Regional Hospital Board had purchased the former Mickleover Manor School in 1952.

The opening of Midland commercial television began on February 17th. The evening focussed on news, variety and *Robin Hood*, the adventure serial starring Richard Greene. Boxing, and a comedy serial *I Love Lucy* with Lucille Ball and Dezi Arnaz, ended the first production day.

Lady Barnett, TV personality, said at Mickleover on March 14th that everyone's main aim in life should be to have a home of their own.

She was opening the showhouse at Vicarage Park, which was being developed by the Butterley Co Ltd, Ripley. She congratulated the company, which had planned for more than two years to achieve the "dream of a reasonable family house within the reach of most people."

Photo courtesy of the Derbyshire Advertiser
With a trick of the camera Lady Barnett sees herself opening the showhouse on Vicarage Park Estate.

The vice-chairman of the Butterley Company, said, "we have tried to recapture some measure of the atmosphere of the village green community. The mortgage payments on our houses cannot compare unfavourably with existing rental values, despite the difficult times in terms of rising interest rates, material costs, transport rates and wage claims."

The parish council in April decided to ask the County Planning Authority what provision had been made for open spaces where land was being developed at Devonshire Drive and Chestnut Avenue. On reviewing any information the council said they would consider the question of playing field facilities being provided in the area.

The Chairman of the County Council, Ald C F White, issued a statement that discussions had been taking place with Derby Corporation about the latest

Photo courtesy of the Derbyshire Advertiser

The Methodist School Hall was full on two evenings when the Youth Choir under the direction of Joyce Wardle, gave the operetta Hong Kong by Harry Maclarin and Charles Jessop. The principal parts were taken by Peter Morley and Pauline Fielden. There were about forty young people in the cast. Two adults, Donald Fawcett and Len Orton also took part.

proposal to extend the boundary. Rural and parish councils had objected in the strongest terms against the proposal since 1929. The Corporation's last attempt was in 1949. Mickleover had been part of the plans but this time it was the area south-west of Mackworth which was chiefly 413 acres of agricultural land.

When asked questions, Ald White declined to comment further. He added: "I should not like to say that negotiations have broken down."

The Council Chambers of the new offices of the Derbyshire County Council at Matlock (formerly Smedley's Hydro) was opened on April 28th. The administration of county affairs was transferred from the County Council offices in St Mary's Gate, Derby.

At a special All Saints' PCC meeting on May 8th, the Reverend Ben Crockett again brought up the question of repairs to the Vicarage. A survey had shown they would cost approximately £545. The Vicar said that there was £170 in hand in the dilapidations fund. Estimates were requested at a later date.

The PCC agreed that they would accept responsibility for the following three items: £545 for immediate repairs; decorations to hall and bathroom; £250 for improvements to the kitchen not exceeding £100. The total expenditure being £895.

There was a condition which stated that the Vicar would be agreeable "to take up a five year loan for any amount not available when payment is due." The PCC would then be prepared to re-imburse this loan and interest to the Vicar. They stated that they were not prepared to accept any further financial commitments until this debt was cleared.

Harry Gaskill, now deputy head at the County School, had previously been teaching at Alvaston and Boulton School. Cycling to Mickleover every day, he was in charge of those children who were about to take the "Classification Examination" which we now call the 11+. His class was situated in the HORSA Hut in the playground, now the home of St John's Model Railway Group.

Although most schools didn't care to admit it, streaming took place and Harry took the "A" Stream. There was indeed a "C" Stream if enough children were on the register.

The "A" Class always had the largest number of children; in one year Mr Gaskill had 48. This presented him with extra responsibilities as all their work had to be marked. One of Harry Gaskill's other tasks was to work out a daily system that would accommodate the 200 children who would be taking school dinners. The school hall was not large enough to take all the children, so four classrooms had to be used in addition. The desks were pushed together to seat eight and they were covered with wipe clean tablecloths covered in flowers. Harry's system worked quite well, which pleased the headmaster.

School dinners prepared by Mrs Gertrude E Warner have been described as "lovely" by Elaine Hawksworth. "The food was good, wholesome and varied. Not lots of choices, like today", says Elaine.

Chris Nixon was one of the children who was entrusted to take the dinner money to the Post Office on the corner of Vicarage Road. "This must have been a considerable sum," says Chris. "Today, I expect the task is performed by Securicor."

Mr Gaskill was his teacher in his final year, and Chris remembers the writing competitions he used to set. However Chris recalls Mr Gaskill's instruction before one of them. "During the competition, Johnson, Cotterill and Nixon, you three can go into the next room, and mix glue for the art class."

Chris admits that his handwriting did not impress any of the staff. "If you are neat, you are neat. If you are not, accept it." writes Chris.

Over the Whitsuntide holiday Mr and Mrs Best, Mr Gaskill and Mrs Brierley spent the four days with some of the senior children at the Litton Mill School Journey Centre. This was a pioneer venture which proved to be an unqualified success.

Photo courtesy of the Derbyshire Advertiser

Living inn signs were and are a rarity, In this photograph published in the Derbyshire Advertiser *The Vine in Uttoxeter Road is seen with a vine growing up the end wall of the building, It had been pruned but the exotic tree soon grew again, covering the whole of the wall with its foliage. Doris Dean was the landlady. The awning covering the shop front shades Wesleys Grocery. On the right is the new Paramount Garage which has now been demolished to construct a new service station.*

The children had previously enjoyed a month's education at Amber Valley Camp but this had ended when a reservoir scheme was developed in parts of the ground (see Book Two).

Jimmy Best, the headmaster at Mickleover County School had expressed his concern to the School Managers at the increasing inadequacy of classroom accommodation caused by the steady influx of pupils from the large-scale housing developments of the parish and adjoining part of the parish of Littleover. He said an additional assistant teacher would be employed after the summer holidays. For additional accommodation The Church Hall in Limes Avenue, the Memorial Hut and the Methodist Schoolroom were under consideration.

The Reverend Ben Crockett announced in the May church magazine that, if any of the villagers wished to speak to him on a particular matter, they should either telephone him beforehand or make an appointment. "People often make fruitless journeys to the Vicarage; most are very understanding but some seem to expect me to be on tap all the time," wrote the Vicar.

Mickleover Sports Club agreed, at their committee meeting in May, to raise questions with the parish council about the facilities at the playing fields. Regarding tennis, they were to ask for additional courts; seating outside and inside and repair of the courts. In regards to cricket they were to request the relaying of the square at the end of the season, better attention to the wicket and the provision of a sight screen. They suggested the possibility of closing the ground on special occasions and offer to split "gate" receipts.

At the parish council meeting at the end of May it was decided to ask local MP, George Brown, to help secure an early starting date for the building of the new school because of overcrowding.

Tim Ford, chairman, said that three years ago the council was told a new school would be started in April 1956, and as far back as 1951 plans were drawn up and passed but the County Council was slow to buy the land.

He said that although there was accommodation for 380 children, the assembly hall was being used as two classrooms. There were 400 children in the school and at least 299 houses would be finished in the village before the end of the year.

"Another 100 children would require accommodation in the junior school by Christmas," he said. It was estimated that the number would be between 450 and 480.

Mr Best was absent from the school from June 11th because of an operation to improve his health. Although only a few weeks into his appointment, the deputy headmaster, Harry Gaskill, took charge of the school.

Arthur Parker, the organist and choirmaster at the parish church, stated "that he would like to see more keenness, ambition and more consistent attendance among the members of the choir." He appealed for more members, particularly women.

He continued to say that the accommodation was far from ideal. The Vicar suggested that if the organ console was moved behind the lectern it might improve the seating.

Grandfather was pleased with the house painters from the Co-op who finished their work two days later. "The major portion of it was done by Horace Titterton, who resides in Mickleover," he wrote. "He was briefly helped by two others. The total cost was £29."

Grandfather was always interested in sport spending some time listening to and watching the Ashes Test Matches in 1956. On July 12th he wrote: "England made a bad start. 3 out for 17 [runs] after [Peter] May and [Cyril] Washbrook made a good stand."

Tables produced by Repton Rural District Council indicated that Mickleover

Photo courtesy of Pat Crockett

The Duchess of Devonshire opened the Mickleover Garden Fete at the Vicarage on June 23rd when £75 was raised for church funds. Attractions at the fete included a Health and Fitness demonstration and a display of Highland dancing by a Derby group.

was the largest village in their area. In July the number of houses listed were 1,431, the next largest being Hartshorne with 928. Mickleover's average rate per house at 16s.4d was £22.1s.0d.

Mickleover's fight to get work started on the promised new junior school was discussed by the South Derbyshire Divisional Executive in July.

The Divisional Education Officer, Roland Heath-Smith, said that additional accommodation had been secured "In very pleasant surroundings" in the Methodist building. The County Education Authority also approved the addition of two classrooms at the existing school.

Mr Heath-Smith said the new school had now reached the sketch plan. He added: "There had been no urgent pressure on school places at Mickleover until there had been a sudden rush of new housing."

The chairman, Ald J W Allitt, said the Mickleover situation was "Just daft." He thought there had been insufficient liaison between various departments.

It was admitted that a credit squeeze had slowed house building programmes, but the chairman said the Mickleover position was quite different. "There had been a lot of private housing there which was not affected so much by the credit squeeze."

Grandfather observed "lots of children attending the new school at Etwall" when he was returning to Mickleover on the bus. Later in the month he called to see my sister, who was now employed at Central Educational bookshop in St Peter's Street, Derby. She had formerly qualified as a Nursery Nurse. However having gained a position at Derby City Hospital maternity department, she became disenchanted with the night shifts. She thoroughly enjoyed her new career looking after the section selling children's books.

George Brown MP wrote a letter to the parish council on the information he had received from the Minister of Education, Sir David Eccles, on the subject of the new school. He began by stating: "It is pretty cold and formal and does not really gives us much to go on."

Sir David Eccles had said: "I do not think there is anything I can do to help the Derbyshire Local Education Authority to bring their new junior school into use more quickly." The Authority had expected to start building in June 1956, using the plans originally drawn in 1951.

Since that time, however, more "economical planning" had been expected in the building of the school. According to the letter it was now expected to start building work at the end of the year.

Mr Brown had discussed the matter with Jack Longland, Director of Education for Derbyshire, and had heard rather more encouraging news. Mr Longland had told him that a new method was to be used to build the school to be ready more or less at the original time. Joseph Peter Roscoe, the teacher of Junior 3, left the school at the end of July.

There was a feeling economic confidence was returning to the country after ten years of austerity. The Queen had laid the foundation stone of the new Coventry Cathedral. Designed by Basil Spence, this very modern building was to incorporate the bombed ruins of the old. Britain's first nuclear power station, (Calder Hall), was the largest plant in the world to come into operation.

With full employment people were planning their annual holidays to further destinations. Many Derby firms, including Rolls-Royce, International Combustion, Royal Crown Derby, closed down favouring the last week in July and the first week in August for the annual summer holiday. Others the fortnight before. The only large employers to opt for staggered holidays were British Celanese and Bemrose, the printers.

My family had opted for the south-west for the last three years travelling overnight on the train, but in more recent times by car. In July 1956, Jim Nixon accompanied us to a camping site near Clovelly in Devon. My strongest memory, apart for the miserable weather, was writing to my friend Gill Hannah, asking her to purchase the next issue of *Soccer Star* as I was miles from any newsagent who may stock it.

Her return letters survive, and she told me that she was not having much success but would keep trying. In her second letter she wrote that the "gang" had been to the Regal Cinema in East Street, to see *Land of the Pharaohs*.

It was described in the local press as a very exciting film, starring Jack Hawkins and Joan Collins. "There is plenty of action and some spectacular scenes."

Gill commented: "I think Jim would have enjoyed it but you are innocent and good aren't you?" I am not sure why she wrote such a statement, and unfortunately I cannot ask her as she died in 1978. Her father, Alec became the clerk to Mickleover School Managers.

By 1956 the teenage mood was beginning to change dramatically. The Teddy boys were appearing on British streets. They were a group of youths who wore a modified style of Edwardian dress which included drainpipe trousers, fluorescent socks and a long jacket with a velvet collar.

Films began to follow a rock and roll theme, with Bill Haley's *Rock Around the Clock* coming to Derby in September 1956. This was also the year when popular music heard an extraordinary new sound. Elvis Presley was embarking on a fantastic career with *Heartbreak Hotel*. Our parents were appalled, they were still listening to and singing the songs of Bing Crosby.

There were not too many Teddy boys in Mickleover, and certainly none among our group of friends who were now in employment. We were still enjoying each other's company finding our own entertainment.

I accepted the offer of a strongly built tandem from a family friend. As it was so low-geared, it took skill and energy to get it on the move. More often than not I was the single rider from Jackson Avenue until I reached Ken Guy's home in Vicarage Road. He was the rear seat rider but to this day I am still not sure if he pedalled all the time. He maintains that the longest journey we took was to Needwood Forest. Apparently we were heading for Charnwood Forest in Leicestershire but took the wimpish decision to turn round at Needwood and head for home. There is no denying that once the heavy beast got underway it could travel at high speeds.

More tourists were flying to their overseas holidays from Burnaston Airport, which had applied earlier in the year to erect large advertising boards announcing: "Fly Derby Aviation to Jersey, Ostend, Isle of Man", but they were turned down by the RDC, as distractions to motorists on the main Burton Road.

Grandfather wrote on August 10th: "Tom has finished with the Post Office job. Unsatisfactory pay and conditions. Round being extended without any compensatory increase in wages." – nothing changes!

Internationally, there were signs that Britain was having diplomatic problems with President Nasser of Egypt. After the Second World War Britain retained a garrison in Egypt to guard the Suez Canal, which was a vital link between Britain and the Far East. However a new chapter had opened when the Russians made an arms deal with Egypt. The last British troops left Suez in June and a month later President Nasser nationalised the Suez Canal Company. This was in reply to the withdrawal by the United States of its offer to finance the High Dam at Ascan.

Prime Minister Anthony Eden told Nasser that Egypt could not have the Suez Canal and imposed an arms embargo on his country. In August Eden said in a television broadcast that Nasser could not be trusted.

Jim Whittingham, parish councillor and teacher at St Peter's Church School, Littleover, circulated a leaflet to 142 householders in the Rykneld Road area. It proposed a pedestrian crossing on Rykneld Road, near Havenbaulk Avenue. He had received 94 replies, all in favour of the crossing.

"Life and safety come before speed" he said. "The movement of traffic may need to become more easy in the country's interest, but we have to be alive to enjoy such abstract thoughts."

The County Council Bridges and Highways Committee turned down the request for the pedestrian crossing. When asked why, the chairman replied that the police were opposed "because of bus stops nearby, which would add to the dangers."

On September 3rd grandfather carried out "a few necessary chores and walked to churchyard with flowers. A new path has been made to the piece [burial ground] just added." He visited my mother, Nellie, at 41 Jackson Avenue on September 10th, and she told him that they (mother and father), were contemplating buying a new house on the Wimpey estate. My sister's fiancé was now living with us, convalescing from the serious effects of glandular fever.

A move was thought to be necessary because of the lack of garage space which a new detached house would provide, plus the benefit of larger living space and a modern kitchen. This would inevitably lead to a longer journey for my father, Fred Edward, who was still travelling daily to his work at the Rolls Royce factory at Mountsorrel in Leicestershire. I too would have further to cycle to the *Derbyshire Advertiser* office in Derby Market Place.

The popularity of television continued to march on, turning into tomorrow's "must". The regular comments that a 14-inch screen "is quite big enough for our house" twelve months previously were rapidly being replaced with 17-inch sets. "The wide-angled cathode ray tube means cabinets of more manageable size."

Demolition Orders were being sent by the RDC to the owners of houses in Mickleover in September 1956, eight at Alma Heights, four at Storer Place and numbers 6 to 10 Vicarage Road. The latter properties were owned by William Hardy Watson. Those at Storer Place were deferred as Watson was willing to carry out improvements when the cottages became vacant. There was no undertaking to relet those in Vicarage Road. These cottages were opposite Manor Farm and the new site of the new Mickleover Library.

At the September meeting of the School Managers it was announced that Miss P A (Ann) Ellis and Miss Pamela M Ratcliffe had been appointed to the school staff with immediate effect. Mr Best, headmaster, commented favourably upon both appointments who would be joining him directly from training college.

He also informed the meeting that the Methodist schoolroom was now in use as an additional classroom. Miss Edith M Wedd with Junior 2 children were the occupants.

The Managers then examined a drawing of the new school which was to be the "Derwent" type of wooden construction, providing 320 places.

They agreed to Mr Best's suggestion that the size of the stock room in the old school be increased and converted into the medical permanent inspection room, instead of a screened space. It could then be used as separate accommodation for the clerical assistant. "This is desirable when the headteacher is conducting personal interviews."

After a meeting of the staff it was decided that a school concert could not be held in 1956 in view of the disruption which would result with the present overcrowding at the school.

An added interest for the young people of Mickleover in the early winter months was the beginning of a drama group. Stella (née Nichols) Green, a young mother with an interest in drama had come to live in Mickleover with her husband Michael and she had offered the Methodist Chapel Guild help in forming a youth drama group. The hall at the chapel gave the opportunity to perform plays for a paying public. However, much work had to be done to form a group of budding actors.

I, along with my friends were fortunate in being offered the chance to try something different, although I had already enjoyed the experience of performing at Littleover Secondary Modern School.

The Greens were kind enough to give up their home on more than one evening a week for a number of us to read through different plays to assess our different skills of performing on stage.

Mickleover Parish Council was told that work on the new Two Form Entry Junior School and playing fields would begin in December and that it was hoped it would be completed in time for the Autumn term in September 1957.

The clerk, Les Miller, read a letter from Jack Longland, Director of Education for Derbyshire, to George Brown MP. The letter said that in the interest of speed the method of construction of the building had been changed. If it was not ready by next September, it should be ready by December 1957.

At the beginning of October grandfather wrote that work had commenced at "Nestlés chocolate factory", and bus shelters had been erected at Western Road and Cavendish Way/Uttoxeter Road junction.

A few days later he went a stroll, and "finished up watching the unloading of a piece of machinery for shifting soil down where they are to erect the chocolate factory. Very interesting."

A rent of £1,000 a year was agreed between the Regional Board and Mr J A Evans of Home Farm, Stapenhill, for Rough Heanor Farm at Kingsway Hospital.

Derby No 3 Hospital Management Committee took control of Rough Heanor Farm to supply Kingsway Hospital in 1943. The farm comprised over 167 acres of land, and a pedigree herd of attested British Friesian cows, which had just been sold.

The Farm Bailiff was Henry Fitch and here with his wife Ursula brought up a young family, Fay and Barry. They continued to farm in later life and Barry now owns a successful butchers shop in Little Eaton. He grew up in the butchery business, delivering meat for Mickleover butcher Frank Charnley and later, in the 1960s, began to learn the art with Rob and Margaret (née Titterton) Shuttlewood at their shop in Western Road.

The Board informed the Minster of Health that there was a grave shortage of hospital beds in the region.

On October 9th Miss Pat Hornsby-Smith, Parliamentary Secretary to the Minister of Health, opened the new developments and extensions at Pastures Hospital.

Among them was The Woodlands, the former Mickleover Manor School which was bought in 1952 and had been converted into a psychogeriatric unit for men. The Woodlands accommodated 73 mental patients over sixty-five

Photo courtesy of the Derbyshire Advertiser

A view of the ring at the sale of attested British Friesian cattle at Rough Heanor Farm. The sale was a stage in the dispersal of the farm decided upon by the Regional Hospital Board. The dairy herd and other live and dead stock sold for £12,445.

years of age and cost, in all, £37,749 to develop.

At Pastures Hospital Miss Hornsby-Smith opened two new 40 bed villas for women; extensions at the admissions hospital and an occupational therapy unit for both men and women. Total costs £81,025.

The Chairman of the Regional Hospital Board said it would cost a quarter of a million pounds to bring Pastures up to the standards of the time.

"Built in 1849, it represents one of the greatest problems in the region." He added: "A mental hospital needed corridors for the

Photo courtesy of Margaret Shuttlewood

Wimpeys were well on the way to completing the first phase off Western Road. The field which Margaret Titterton (right) and her friend sit astride their horses was now Hobart Close. Margaret's family left their farm on Western Road to farm at Burnaston.

proper servicing of wards and that was just what Pastures did not possess to any extent."

Admissions to mental hospitals had increased from 35,000 in 1946 to 78,000 in 1955. "They may appear shocking figures", said Miss Hornsby-Smith. "However it does mean that we have wiped out the stigma of going to mental hospitals."

Repton Rural District Council made an order that two houses in East Avenue be re-numbered. Number one now became number two and number two became number one. Councillor Tim Ford, chairman of the parish council, lived in one of the two houses. He told the October meeting: "There is nothing so ridiculous as this suggestion." (See plan 61).

The clerk, Les Miller, said that a similar order had been made for the re-numbering of Chestnut Avenue and Moorland Road. He read a letter, signed by all the residents in Chestnut Avenue, complaining of "considerable expense and intolerable inconvenience."

The residents said no reason for the order had been given by the RDC but they supposed that the avenue would one day be made to join Moorland Road. They presumed that when the new road was constructed it would be given a new name, so that there was no need to re-number Chestnut Avenue.

Les Miller said that the orders had come into force and technically the residents were liable if they did not conform to it. He added that the present numbering of Chestnut Avenue was "quite illogical, but clear."

He was instructed to write to Fred Bailey, clerk to the RDC, supporting the residents' protests and to ask for notice of any further orders, so objections could be made.

World events were now occupying people's thoughts. On October 23rd insurrection broke out in Budapest against the Soviet Union and began to spread throughout Hungary.

More serious, in the minds of the British, was an Anglo-French offensive which was launched against military targets in Egypt. Israel, always at loggerheads with its Arab neighbours, proposed a plan whereby Israel would attack Egypt giving Britain and France an excuse to intervene and restore order to safeguard the Suez Canal. This was in defiance of the United Nations and the United States. Half of Britain and most of the world protested.

Grandfather was apoplectic, and on October 31st, wrote: "I heard shameful news that our military forces had been used in Egypt for aggressive purposes. These hypocritical statesmen murder for political ends." He continued: "God save us from dishonesty and double dealing." In hindsight, his thoughts are poignant as the public were then not party to the Cabinet Papers which were released in 2006. The press at the time were supportive of the Prime Minister, Anthony Eden, with perhaps the BBC being the main section of the media to retain its integrity by giving a more rounded view.

Still inconsolable on the following day grandfather wrote: "I feel disturbed and depressed about the news. This great country is besmirched and bedraggled by those who should most sustain and help it."

On November 4th there were demonstrations in the streets of London calling for Eden's resignation. Grandfather was "still excited – and disgusted – with the news. As Victor Hugo said, 'Why are we such devils to one another.' " On this day Soviet forces launched an attack on Budapest to crush the uprising in Hungary.

The news did not improve in the next two days. Anglo-French airborne troops landed at Port Said and this was followed by seaborne troops. Brian Henderson of 246 Station Road was serving as an electrical mechanic with the Royal Navy and was on board **HMS** Forth.

Young males, which included myself, were concerned as many of us between the ages of 18 and 26 were still expecting to serve in the armed forces in the near future. We were subject to compulsory service for a period of two years owing to the National Service Act 1948. Those who were exempt were those who worked in the "essential services", which were coal mining, farming and the merchant navy.

Lewis Straw had just reached his seventy second birthday when the Suez war began.

Thankfully Egypt accepted a cease fire on November 7th under United Nations conditions, and a week later an emergency force left Naples for Suez and on arrival found the Suez Canal blocked by forty-nine ships.

All this concern for military action had confined the launch of Premium Savings Bonds to the inside pages of the newspapers. The Bonds went on sale for the first time at the beginning of the month.

On November 17th the first refugees from Hungary arrived in Britain.

The chairman of the parish council, Tim Ford, said at the November meeting that they were willing to receive individual donations for the Lord Mayor of London's Hungarian Relief Fund.

Anthony Eden was said to be suffering from "severe overstrain", due, no doubt, to the strength of world reaction over Suez and the Americans' failure to support him. Further bad news was announced to the British people, highlighted in grandfather's diary "that petrol rationing is to begin in December."

The parish council accepted "with regret", the resignation of Councillor Joe Nadin. In a letter to the council Mr Nadin said that business commitments were making it difficult for him to attend "each and every meeting." He did continue to serve as one of Mickleover's representatives on Repton RDC.

This ended a long political association and commitment to Mickleover for the Nadin family. Joe's father, Ernest William, was still serving on the council after 34 years. The council decided to invite George Holloway of Western Road to fill the vacancy on the council, caused by the resignation of Joe Nadin.

PRIVATE DEVELOPMENT IN MICKLEOVER DECEMBER 1956	No of Properties	Course of Erection	Completed
Wimpey	175	92	79
Butterley			
Phase I	71	-	71
Phase II	163	72	91
Phase III	106	106	-
Leeway Estate (Devonshire Drive)			
Phase I	56	-	56
Phase II	100	24	10
Phase III	210	4	-
H J Warner			
Cavendish Way	12	-	12
off " "	24	-	-
Hartington Way	14	-	14
Titterton Estate	24	-	24
(East Leigh Drive)			

On November 29th the RDC Health and Public Works Committee met to discuss the council's position in relation to petrol rationing on December 17th.

The Ministry had made it clear that essential services such as refuse collection and water supplies would not be restricted "but all possible economy was expected." Supplies had been cut already but the RDC were not prepared to have a less frequent collection than fortnightly. Householders would be asked to burn or compost suitable materials by an advertising slogan "Burn Your Rubbish and Reduce Your Rates!"

Anglo-French forces began to leave Port Said on December 5th and a clearing operation of the Suez Canal was soon to begin by a United Nations salvage fleet.

After Fred Bailey, clerk to the RDC, had given details of other parish's arrangements for cleaning out bus shelters, Mickleover Parish Council decided to approach "old folk" in the village to see if one would take on the job and be paid a maximum of £10 per year.

Mr Bailey admitted that Mickleover presented a slight difficulty with shelters being further apart. The work involved clearing the shelters of rubbish and, as had been done in other parishes, burning it.

Photo courtesy of Harry Matthew Gaskill

Junior Christmas Party at Mickleover County School 1956. This photograph was taken in the main hall, now used by the Mickleover Community Centre by different groups

Tim Ford, chairman, said that difficulty had been encountered in obtaining casual labour in the village. Les Miller, clerk, commented that "the Post Office had had exceeding difficulty in finding OAPs to work for them in Mickleover at 2s.6d an hour."

Grandfather wrote on December 8th: "They have pulled down the stables belonging to Soldier's Cottage at the divide on Radbourne Lane." With some pride and I guess, a glint in his eye, he noted that "we have made an addition to our domestic tools today. We have acquired an ironing board for the first time." The kitchen table had previously been used.

On Christmas Day, "Tom went to football match in the morning, getting a ride with Michael Bowden."

Michael has been of tremendous help to me throughout the writing of these books. His encyclopedic mind has been called upon to recall the well known characters in Mickleover's past.

CHAPTER FOUR
PETROL ON RATION
1957

The future of land adjoining the Great Northern Hotel, belonging to builders, William Walkerdine Limited of Derby, was the subject of a public enquiry at Derby on January 2nd 1957.

The firm's application had been refused by Repton Rural District Council who were acting on behalf of Derbyshire County Council, the local planning authority.

The RDC maintained that there was adequate land available in Mickleover to meet anticipated population requirements. The proposal would also constitute ribbon development along a Class II road and unrestricted access would "not be in the best interests of pedestrians and vehicle traffic safety."

Harold John Walkerdine, joint managing director of the company said the land was close to a new factory being built by Nestlés Limited. "They will require a good number of houses for their work people," he said. "They have already bought one cottage."

When cross-examined Mr Walkerdine said his firm had received many enquiries from people who would like to build there. He added that he had not decided how many houses to build.

Replying to the inspector of the Ministry of Housing and Local Govern-

Photo courtesy of the Derby Evening Telegraph

All Saints Choir Dinner and Social at the Nags Head, January 1957. Standing, left to right: Unknown, Unknown, Unknown, Elizabeth ?, Valerie ?, Peter Arnold, Elizabeth Mitten, Ann Daker, Mr Moseley, Mrs Moseley, John Ratcliff, Eric Taylor, Mrs Daker, Joyce Greenbury, Michael Bowden, Eric Greenbury. Seated: Harold Rudkin, Mr White, Arthur Parker, Pat Crockett, Reverend Ben Crockett, Frances Beavis, George Beavis, Terry Bennett.

59

ment, Mr Walkerdine said that he had not objected at the time of the County Development Plan inquiry to the zoning of the land as "not for development."

The County Development Plan provided for an increase in population of Mickleover in 20 years from 4,300 to nearly 9,000 and for the protection of the settlement by a green belt.

Mr J H Lang, South Derbyshire Planning Officer, said Mr Walkerdine's scheme concerned a "critical open break between rapidly developing units." The Nestlés factory itself, he explained, was a "major departure" from approved plans, and had only been given consent to meet the firm's special needs, and after close consultation with the Minister.

"Mr Walkerdine's scheme was the key to the open door to future development. There had already been an inquiry from a neighbouring owner, who asked for consent if Mr Walkerdine should be successful." The inspector closed the inquiry with a view to visiting the site.

The Walkerdine appeal was turned down in the Spring with the Minister agreeing with the RDC.

At the Sheffield Regional Hospital Board's meeting in January, the Mental Health Sub-Committee recommended that in view of the "detrimental effect" which the entrance lodge had on the Woodlands, the Ministry of Health should be asked

Photo courtesy of Ian Milner

Young Ian Milner with members of his family pictured at the brick-built Lodge in the grounds of the former Mickleover Manor with the main entrance from Etwall Road. (see map p85. Ian recalls that the family left the Lodge in 1959 when Harry Hirst, the estate manager at Pastures became the tenant. Harry later emigrated to Canada to join his two sons who were members of the Royal Mounted Police.

to approve its purchase. Improvements to the drive were carried out along with the repair of the boundary wall.

Grandfather opened his 1957 diary by reporting that "Tutbury and Burton buses have been curtailed owing to petrol shortage." Petrol had been put on ration because of the Suez crisis. On January 9th he wrote that news of Anthony Eden's resignation had been announced on the television in the evening. Harold Macmillan became Prime Minister.

Arthur Ravensdale was appointed as Chairman of the County School Managers at their January meeting when headmaster, Jimmy Best, reported "that the site marks for the new school (Vicarage Road) began during the first week of the new year".

The RDC presented its reason for wishing to re-number the two houses in East Avenue which Mickleover Parish Council decided was "inadequate" in October 1956.

A letter from the RDC clerk, Fred Bailey, stated that further development in the area included the extension of East Avenue by the building of over forty houses.

He wished to conform with the accepted practice in the parish with houses on the left side of the street having odd numbers and those on the right even numbers from the end which is nearest the village centre. In the case of East Avenue the numbering would begin from the junction with Station Road.

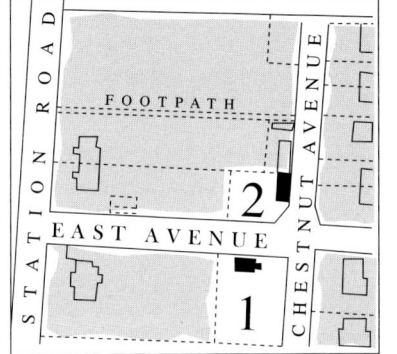

Maps courtesy of Derby Local Study Library
Forthcoming housing developments in 1957 brought changes to house numbers which had been established in 1932. Numbers 1 and 2 in East Avenue were re-numbered, 1 became 2 and 2 became 1.

The parish council was not convinced, by this explanation, as they pointed out to Mr Bailey, many streets in the parish were not numbered in this way and asked him again to bring the matter before the RDC.

Their point of view was a valid one. Two of the oldest thoroughfares in the village were Station Road and Western Road whose house numbering is opposite to Fred Bailey's requirement. When numbering began in 1932 "Rannoch" in Chestnut Avenue was 13, it would now become 64.

Having sold the house where I spent my childhood (41 Jackson Avenue) the family were making final arrangements to move to 39 Brisbane Road in early February. As my future brother-in-law was still living with us after his illness, I had to make the sacrifice of sharing a bedroom until they married in September.

In February grandfather wrote that Miss Shotton, who was seventy-nine years of age, had sold the shop adjoining the Masons Arms, The Square. "It has been empty four or five years."

In March, complaints were being received about the state of the uncultivated land between Cavendish Way and Western Road. Residents of the nearby Mickleover Lodge Estate (Wade Drive) were using the land as the nearest point to the bus services and shopping facilities on Western Road. Joe Nadin, who was still serving on the RDC, suggested the possibility of consent being obtained from the private owner to construct a footpath over parts of the land. The unadopted land under dispute was beyond the pair of police houses on Cavendish Way, now converted to numbers 42 and 44 as residential houses.

At the School Managers meeting in March Jimmy Best expressed his regret that the impending split of the school into Junior and Infants would mean he would lose some of the contact with parents. He and Mr Gaskill had made themselves available for private interviews, a service which a large number of parents had made use of.

The new Methodist Church youth club drama group, under the guidance of Stella Green, in which I was very much involved, was busy in rehearsal for the production of their first play *Murder at the Ministry*. Acting editions were obtainable from the County Library (still available) under the copyright of Samuel French Limited, a company which maintains its branches in many parts of the world. A fee of three guineas (£3.3s.0d) for each performance had to be paid in advance.

The Chancellor of the Exchequer asked the banks to hold down advances during 1956. This credit squeeze amounted to an increase of advances to hire-purchase finance companies. Businesses had no difficulty in getting money by borrowing direct from the public at high rates of interest. The real sufferers were small companies and particularly house builders.

This had led to the Area Planning Officer deferring the development of a school north of Western Road (Ravensdale) until a later date. The RDC had recommended this action owing to the present position regarding development on two phases in Mickleover. Only a few houses had been completed by Butterley at the Vicarage Road Estate, and the first phase at the Leeway Estate (Devonshire Drive) was almost complete, but the next two phases were in abeyance.

Although the RDC were aware that planning permission had been given to Wimpeys for further building north of the site now being completed, they recommended a meeting with the Derbyshire County Council to discuss future development and its implications.

Mickleover County School still had more than 400 children on the register.

Sixty pupils, with four teachers, attended a performance of *Julius Caesar* at the Railway Institute, Derby.

The school had an excellent reputation under Jimmy Best's guidance. One parent once told teacher, Ann Ellis, that he would send his sons to the school even if he had to pay!

Some of the ex pupils have feelings of being well taught and on the whole they enjoyed their time at the school.

There are however some strong memories of discipline by the headmaster and one of the teachers, Edith Wedd. David Purdy recalls "being made to stand out at dinner time for combing my hair, and still not understanding why!" His sister Elaine reports that Miss Wedd "once poked me in the back in assembly and told me to sing. Once she had heard me she soon told me to be quiet."

Mick Nordemann writes that "Miss Wedd took us for gardening. She described me as a 'fly worker'. I assume because I flitted from job to job, without doing anything – nothing changes."

Perhaps the most descriptive of all are the memories of Chris Nixon when he comments that even her name rhymed with dread.

"Now she was not in anyway cosy or welcoming," he writes. "She referred to me as 'Professor' though I'm sure with hindsight, she was being sarcastic. She was remarkable in that the palm of her hand had knuckles in it, or so it felt like when she slapped your ear."

He also notes that he did get better exams the year he was in Miss Wedd's class. "Maybe the Dickensian hand of discipline does bear fruit."

Mickleover dog owners would have been relieved that they would not be forced to keep their pets on leads when walking them through the streets.

After reading a letter from Fred Bailey, clerk to the RDC, at the March parish council meeting, Les Miller, clerk, pointed out that under section 15 of the Road Traffic Act 1956, they could ban dogs from the village streets unless they were on a lead. Arthur Ravensdale commented, "I don't think we need make any order."

He added, "I think it would be very difficult to designate any lengths of road in Mickleover where dogs must be on a lead. We should ask the villagers at the annual parish meeting to enter into the spirit of the Act and keep their dogs on a lead where they think there might be a danger to traffic."

The clerk told the meeting that in 1954 and 1955 something like 2,600 accidents were caused by dogs on roads carrying heavy volumes of traffic.

The Chief Executive Officer of Doncaster Co-operative Society made an interesting comment on shopping in the future at a lecture he gave in Derby on March 13th.

Mr Lees said "that there would be a shortage of male labour in the next ten years and this would bring about a bulk of self-service stores." These would, in his opinion be 'super markets' or 'scramble shops'. "There would be one big shop selling anything that the shop could sell – TV sets or bread and potatoes."

Although 159 acres of land were to be retained at Pastures Hospital the remaining 82.171 acres were to be let on lease from Lady Day (March 25th).

Richardson and Linnell held a sale at Grange Farm on behalf of Derby No 3 Area Hospital Management Committee on March 18th. On offer was the sale of implements including milking machines and dairy equipment.

All schools in Derby and the surrounding areas closed during the afternoon on March 28th for the visit of the Queen and Prince Philip to Derbyshire. The Queen began her tour at Tutbury Castle before travelling to Repton School. She then passed through Mickleover, arriving at Derby Market Place to a Guard of Honour and then moving on to the Leylands Estate off Broadway. Their tour ended at the modern St Philip's Church at Chaddesden which cost £27,000 to build.

The new cemetery at Mickleover was consecrated by the Bishop of Derby, Dr A E J Rawlinson, on Saturday, April 13th. After receiving the petition of consecration from Les Miller, Parish Clerk, the Bishop signed the deed of consecration on the site which adjoins the churchyard.

Mr Miller read a letter from the Trent Motor Traction Company at the parish council meeting which stated that they were reinstating the Sunday morning bus service to Mickleover from Derby on April 21st.

Trent apologised for the inconvenience during the curtailment of the service in the interests of fuel economy. The clerk said a revised time-table for the route composed 26 journeys to Mickleover and 25 from the village.

The council was told of planning proposals for the provision of open spaces in the parish near Devonshire Drive. The Area Planning Officer said in a letter that open spaces would be suitable for children's play areas and for sport.

When considering Wimpeys further development the RDC were concerned that careful consideration should be given in regard to surface water being discharged into Bramble Brook. They were also concerned with the report that other contractors in the area were disbandoning development (Vicarage Road Estate), and there would be a demand for more houses being built by Wimpeys.

Following the disastrous fire in 1956, the Duke of Devonshire re-opened the Playhouse in Sacheveral Street, Derby, on April 25th. Actors returning after the fire were Ralph Broome, Ian Cooper and Anne Kennedy. The newcomers were Peggy Aitcheson, Diana Bishop and Mary Laine. Leslie Twelvetrees was retained as Director of Productions.

As budding amateur actors, Stella Green advised us to see some of the Playhouse productions, enabling us to discover any techniques.

Many of us attended regular performances and walked back to Mickleover along Burton Road and then over Mickleover Golf Course in the dark.

Adult Methodists interested in the formation of a dramatic society met at the Methodist School in April. It was decided to call the new venture the Mickleover Methodist Players and Donald Fawcett was elected chairman with Cyril Dommett as stage manager.

On April 29th grandfather wrote: "We went to churchyard in the evening, and after encountered grandson Peter with others fixing posters about their event on Saturday." Stage nerves were beginning to set in and I was pestering my sister Sheila to listen to my attempts at learning my lines in *Murder at the Ministry*. I was even keeping her up late to go over and over the play.

> **MICKLEOVER METHODIST SCHOOLROOM**
> Friday & Saturday May 4th & 5th 1957
> **"MURDER AT THE MINISTRY"**
> A Play in Three Acts
> By Falkland Cary & A A Thompson
>
> The play takes place in the general duties room in Sir James Reid's special department at the Ministry of Protection. Sir James is shot (twice) at the end of Act I. The first to be accused was Peter Faber a member of the department who was having an affair with Lady Reid. Captain Knowles Parker RN leads an internal investigation, accepting that he too could be accused as he was the last person to be with Sir James. In the final scenes Doctor Irvington is discovered to be a foreign spy. When finally accused by Detective Inspector Richards, he retorts: "No, I don't admit it, I claim it."
>
> (Cast in order of appearance)
> Miss Judd .... JEAN SANDERS
> Miss Wilton .... PAMELA STEVENS
> Lydia Grant .... JANET WHELAN
> Mrs McIntyre .... CYNTHIA PERRY
> Mr Noote .... KENNETH GUY
> Sir James Reid .... COLIN MARK
> Captain Knowles Parker......................... PETER BROWN
> Dr Irvington .... PETER HALLAM
> Peter Faber .... TERRANCE HUTSON
> Lady Reid .... STELLA GREEN
> Detective Inspector Richards................. JAMES NIXON
> Produced by Stella Green

A week later grandfather declared that "we all went to the Methodist Schoolroom to a performance of a play *Murder at the Ministry* given by the Youth Drama Club. Grandson Peter had a leading part to play. He did it very well. The event was well attended and voted a success."

On the following day grandfather attended my cousin Kathleen's Sunday School Anniversary. "The preacher was a bit stodgy" he commented.

At the end of April Mrs Lyn Kendall became a member of the Mickleover County School teaching staff, replacing Mrs Wright. The total number of children on the roll was 459. This led to the school taking over the Methodist Hall to accommodate two classes with Edith Wedd and Pamela Ratcliffe being the teachers.

The Suez Canal reopened for smaller vessels in March and the emergency on petrol rationing came to an end on May 14th. A day later the first British hydrogen bomb was detonated over Christmas Island.

The Planning Authority were interviewed by the RDC Housing and Town

Photos courtesy of Harry Matthew Gaskill

Nineteen children, four teachers and two supply teachers stayed at Litton Mill School Journey Centre. "We walked about 20-25 miles through some of Derbyshire's loveliest scenery," Mr Best recorded.

Planning Committee and it was suggested that there should be a limit to future development. They confirmed that residential development would be confined roughly to the area where consent had been given. This would mean the reservation of four fields for open space uses (behind Onslow Road). The committee regarded the result as satisfying.

All the first housing phases in Mickleover were now complete. Only a small number were left in phase two of the Vicarage Park Estate by Butterley, but 92 were still to be completed out of 105 in phase three. The same applied to the Leeway Estate, off Devonshire Drive, where only 25 houses had been completed out of 100 in phase two and one out of 202 houses and 6 shops in phase three. H J Warner continued with their development between Western Road and Hartington Way and Avenue Farm Estate (North Avenue). None had been commenced in what was termed 'Pan Handle' off Cavendish Way (Hardwick Drive) or on the Station Road/Western Road site (Edale Avenue). It was first suggested that the latter be named Pingle Avenue as the land was once known as The Pingle. Out of 992 new private houses planned for Mickleover, 538 had now been completed.

Seventy nine school children went to the well dressings at Tissington and then to Ladybower Dam on May 30th . "A really lovely day", wrote Jimmy Best, headmaster. He was accompanied by Miss Olive Mary Plumpton, Miss Wedd and Miss Ravensdale. Chris Nixon was informed that he had passed the eleven-plus examinations. He along with three other children went to Ashbourne Grammar School, twelve to John Port Grammar School.

The Reverend Ben Crockett, suggested to All Saints' PCC that repair, redecoration and improvements of the Church Hall should be an aim. Harry Rudkin proposed that they should have a garden party in aid of the repair.

On the question of hire charges for the hall, Mr Rudkin and Mr Williams suggested it should be let for the inclusive rate of 15s with a special concession of 10s a month to the Guides and Brownies.

The Vicar said that Jim Land had been appointed caretaker of the Church Hall which the council endorsed.

Mrs Sherratt proposed a vote of thanks to Mrs Crockett for "letting us have the meeting at the Vicarage for so long." It was agreed that in future the Church Hall should be used.

Jim Mills, treasurer and Norman Hayton, secretary retired from their positions at the Mickleover Sports Club Annual General Meeting. Jim had been a founder member and both were thanked for their work and made life members. Jim Kirby became treasurer and Peter (Charlie) Kenderdine secretary.

```
                    52

          MICKLEOVER SPORTS CLUB

          MEMBERSHIP CARD
                  1957-58
           President—Mr. J. W. Jacquest
         Vice-President—Mr. S. Hobbis
                   Patrons—
   Coun. C. E. Ayre, J.P.     Coun. J. Nadin
   Coun. E. W. Nadin          Dr. M. McCahey
   Coun. A. J. Bussell        Mr. J. H. Thornhill
   Mr. H. G. Ford             Mr. E. C. Peake
   Mr. D. A. Skinner          Dr. D. Harkins
   Dr. E. V. H. Pentreath     Mr. V. Knight
   Mr. P. Bussell             Mr. H. Horner
   Mr. R. Maddocks            Mr. E. J. Gothard
   Mr. H. J. Warner           Mr. F. H. Turner
             Chairman—Mr. G. V. Dunn
         Hon. Secretary—Mr P. C. Kenderdine
           78, Jackson Avenue, Mickleover
          Hon. Treasurer—Mr. J. F. Kirby
           21, Chestnut Avenue, Mickleover
              Telephone Derby 53689
```

On June 8th grandfather and Uncle Tom tramped through the cornfield on the western edge of the playing fields and came across where the farmer had ploughed up the path and sown seed upon it. "Why does he do this?" he moaned.

"The partly built houses on the new estate [Vicarage Park] already look forlorn and derelict," he noted. "They have abandoned completing them owing to restrictions in the government policy on credit.

"What a strand of folly is woven in the government of humanity, and that in spite of experienced education and skilful techniques! Bombs to defend living, but life shut out from being lived."

He ended his memories of this experience on a more positive note: "However the cattle and sheep were in the pastures grazing, quietly and curiously looking as we passed. The railway looked efficient and deserted. We saw no trains. The lane at Radbourne was only troubled by an occasional motor car – we met not a single pedestrian. It was all our own. Tom's solution to this was that TV was the main attraction. Mechanical aids to the rush of unending miles. Two legs with short strides can yet carry one to peace, health and satisfaction."

On the day following Whit Monday he was disappointed to find only "one shop open among those we wanted." His note on Uncle Tom's TV being returned from repairs after $7^1/_2$ weeks on June 11th says much about the service provided in the 1950s.

Percy Pickering started work on decorating the hall and landing at the Vicarage in early July after most of the dilapidations work had been done. At the Parochial Church Council meeting, the Reverend Ben Crockett, said a piano had been presented to the church by Edward and Ruby Chegwidden. He said he would find some way of disposing with the old one.

Could this have been the piano which was carefully transported on the lorry belonging to local coal merchant Sid Millward to Park Cottage on the western edge of Vicarage Playing Fields!

When it reached its destination the recipient, William Barnes, caretaker at the County School, thanked Sid and his helper Ian Milner, but told them that he needn't have taken so much care as he was chopping it up for firewood.

William had previously worked for Arthur Morley at New House Farm. His son Don occupied the cottage after his father with his wife Birdie. They were thinking of leaving when this book was in the final stages of being written. Park Cottage has long forgotten its isolation and is now situated at its modern address in Parkstone Court.

A survey of the All Saints' Church had taken place under the Inspection of Church Measures 1955. Extracts from the reports stated that water had got into the organ and Jack Ivy, the organ firm's representative, had been to inspect it but he said nothing could be done until it dried out. It was thought the ridge tiles were to blame and this, the PCC said, would be acted on.

Discussion led to suggestions that the organ firm be asked for a quote to totally enclose the organ. Reverting to the report, the Vicar said "Canon Hopkins had rung him after having a copy and he said it was a good report which showed the church is being looked after very well." He said that two estimates for treating the woodwork for wood worm had reached him, but thought they were too high. It was agreed to leave this and the repairs needed in the report in the hands of the Standing Committee.

Lydia Mary, the wife of former Mickleover farmer and politician, Tom Radford died in 1956? She made a bequest in her will called the "L M Radford's Trust" which asked for the Radford graves to be cared for.

The PCC said they knew nothing of the Trust but the Vicar reported that the graves were together near the vestry door. Harry Rudkin suggested: "Tom Radford [a younger member of the family], should be approached and asked if he knows which are the graves concerned."

By July the Sexton, Jim Land, found the graves involved and the PCC agreed to implement the full terms of the request and asked the Derby Diocesan Board of Finance to pay over to them the income of the "L M Radford Trust".

The plan for the Development of Mickleover was submitted to a Emergency Meeting of the Town Planning and Plans Committee on July 15th but any decision was deferred, pending the views of the parish council.

Wimpeys plan for their next phases designated 200 properties plus a County Primary School in Phase II and in Phase III, the culminating development, 325 properties plus a Roman Catholic Primary School which would be situated at the north eastern corner of the neighbourhood.

An amended layout of 262 houses and bungalows, 10 shops and a site for a public house, Phases II and III between Devonshire Drive and East Avenue was now put forward by J F Fryer Ltd.

At the July meeting of the School Managers, Arthur Ravensdale understood that work had progressed on the building of the new junior school "to such an extent that two classrooms may be ready for use by the time of October mid-term." The post of headmistress for the Infants' School had been advertised.

The two new schools at Etwall were officially opened by the Archbishop of Canterbury, Dr Geoffrey Fisher, on July 26th. The new schools side by side in the grounds of Etwall Hall (now demolished), were a grammar school (Sir John Port School) and the County Secondary School. Sir John Port was the founder of Repton School 400 years earlier.

Teachers Jimmy Best and Olive Plumpton, with School Manager Arthur Riley, represented Mickleover County School at the ceremony.

Children from the school had given displays of country dancing and recorder playing at All Saints' Church garden party in aid of the repair of the Church Hall.

In August the Methodist Youth Drama Group was in rehearsal for their second production *A Murder Has Been Arranged* by Emlyn Williams. Stella Green had announced to the cast that I was willing to help with the production. My task was to liaise with Derby Playhouse for the loan of props, and writing to Chas Fox Limited for the hire of costumes. My sister Sheila's thoughts were elsewhere, making the final arrangements for her marriage in September.

Photo courtesy of Henry Gaskill

Mickleover County School Staff 1957. Back row, left to right: Mr Peach, Mrs Williams, Miss Wibberley, Miss Ellis, Mrs Kendall, Miss Ratcliffe, Mr Gaskill (Deputy Head). Mrs Murfin (Clerical Assistant), Miss Ravensdale, Miss Plumpton, Mr Best (Head), Mrs Henchliffe, Mrs Parkin, Miss Wedd.

Grandfather's only entry of note in August followed his walk down Station Road. "The chocolate factory is growing apace."

As a result of the passing of the Parish Council Act 1957, parish councils now took on a new importance in local government.

No longer was it necessary to go through so many formalities in the course of carrying out their work. Many things they wanted previously could now be arranged without reference to anyone. Examples of the changes were: "seats can be provided by highways and footpaths but not on special roads; the parish council can now provide, maintain and light public clocks and provide parking space for motor cycles and cycles."

The Act went on to explain that the old Lighting and Watching Act of 1833 was repealed. This allowed the parish councils to change the lighting powers on a simple majority at a parish meeting.

Because of the increase of population in Mickleover, it was decided at a meeting of the parish council to apply to the RDC to increase the number of elected members from 11 to 15. They also decided to seek permission to increase the number of representations on the RDC from 4 to 5.

Tim Ford, chairman, read a letter from a parishioner asking for a "Halt" or "Slow" sign at the junction of Moorland Road and Station Road. There was, he said, the danger of a child cyclists being injured by heavy vehicles coming from the direction of Moorland Road. They decided to put the matter to the County Council.

Ken Guy was the gifted sportsman in our friendship and he was becoming more involved in the cricket section of Mickleover Sports Club. He even persuaded me to make up the numbers in a second team match at Long Eaton. I was out first ball, as last man, and I don't recall getting too involved in fielding the ball when it was our turn to bowl.

With the new football season looming, Mickleover Sports Club was resigned to the first team playing in "B" Section and the second team in the "E" Section.

R E (Dick) Kenderdine was retained as Manager and in his report he said that after 64 games played, Mickleover had scored 367, just over six goals per match. In his message of thanks he paid tribute to team trainer, Jim Mills, and Fred Eastap's work as groundsman. He also thanked the local motorists who had helped out with lifts during the season.

Two players were leaving the club, George Radford to Derby County and Eric Ward to Pastures Hospital football team. In came Albert Wilkinson and the brothers Roome.

At the opening of a new school year there were 429 children on the roll. Miss Patricia Beech from Mackworth began as a teacher, replacing Nancy Parkin. Gordon Parsons of Alvaston commenced as an assistant teacher in the junior section.

At the scouts awards at Mickleover, Mr A L Fenwick, District Commissioner, presented Queen's Scout badges to two members of the 124th Derby (Mickleover) Scout Troop at the Memorial Hut. They were troop leader Eric Taylor and Senior Patrol Leader John Ratcliff who were the first Mickleover scouts to gain the honour.

All Saints' Church choir held their Annual General Meeting on September 19th and it was decided that the head chorister, David Gascoigne, should have more authority over the Choristers "If there was any insubordination he was told to report to Mr Parker, organist and chorister or the Vicar." said the chairman, Ben Crockett.

Signs of the time!

Arthur Parker said that the numbers in the choir were small. "We need more senior tenor, basses and boys. We have a new alto who is joining us shortly." He continued: "Through no fault of their own, some adult members of the choir are not always able to attend the practices." He appealed to everyone to bring in prospective people.

The Memorial Sports Field comprising 5½ acres of land adjoining the Royal British Legion Club was acquired in 1948 as a memorial to the fallen comrades, and for use as playing fields for ex-servicemen. The money had been raised by voluntary effort.

Harry Blow, chairman of the club, expressed gratitude for "the magnificent effort put in by the Gymkhana Committee and other officials who helped to make the event a success."

He went on to say that the policy of the club would be to develop the land as a sports field and he hoped that the younger generation would appreciate it.

My family celebrated the marriage of my sister Sheila at All Saints' Church on September 21st but grandfather wrote that he had been in bed with flu the previous four days.

On Thursday, September 26th he recorded: "Mickleover Methodist Youth Club Drama Group had to abandon their play owing to members being taken ill with flu" (see press article p73). A world-wide influenza epidemic

The Derby Evening Telegraph published a two-page spread on Friday, September 20th 1957. The illustrations are a sample from that issue. The prices of the houses varied from £1,950 for a 3-bedroomed semi-detached "Villa" to £3,295 for a detached house.

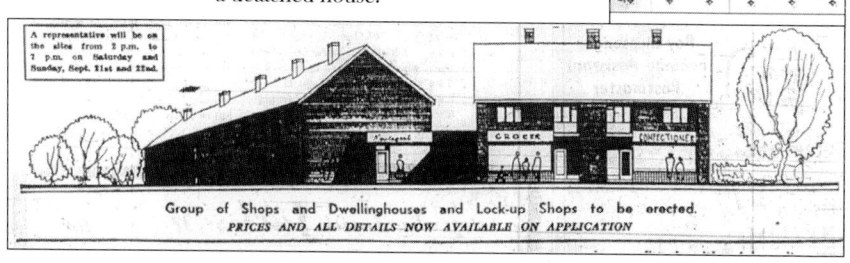

The majority of the cast of A Murder Has Been Arranged *at the Methodist Schoolroom. Left to right (top): Jim Nixon, Colin Mark, Ken Guy, Peter Hallam, Peter Brown. Seated: Stella Green, Cynthia Perry, Anne Bakewell who was too ill with flu to perform.*

DRAMA IN THE DRESSING ROOM
Flu strikes just before "curtain up"

MINUTES before Mickleover Methodist Youth Club Drama Group's production of "A Murder Has Been Arranged," was due to start last night three members of the cast collapsed in the dressing room with suspected Asian flu and the show had to be postponed.

They were Elaine Purdy and Anne Bakewell, two of the principal characters, and the producer Stella Green, who also has a part in the play.

Three other members of the cast, Cynthia Perry, James Nixon and Peter Brown, are also ill.

It is hoped to produce the play to-morrow evening.

threatened Britain throughout the summer and doctors were working overtime in their efforts to keep the malady under control.

The following day he received a postcard from Sheila telling him that they were "having a bad time" on their honeymoon in Scarborough, owing to suffering from heavy colds.

The play *A Murder Has Been Arranged* by Emlyn Williams was performed on Saturday, September 28th. One part was omitted and another was read by Anne Brook.

Grandfather wrote: "Lewis [son] and family to tea and then we all went to grandson Peter's drama at the Methodist School. Good and entertaining."

The fee for performing the play was five guineas (£5.5s.0d) with further productions at four guineas (£4.4s.0d). This was payable in advance and although I believe we performed the play on the following Monday, one day's fee was lost. We also had the problem with the hire of costumes at a cost of £1.1s.0d each as these had to be returned immediately after the final performance to Chas Fox Limited.

The scene of the comic drama is the stage of the St James's Theatre, London. Sir Charles Jasper has hired the theatre (which is closed for cleaning) for his fortieth birthday party, November 26th 1930. All the guests are in fancy dress, "representing ghosts of history".

Sir Charles has amassed thousands of pounds from the sale of his book *The Occult Through the Ages* and there is a hint that the theatre is haunted. If he survives after 11.00pm on the night of the party he will inherit two million pounds left by his uncle. If not it would revert to his only living relative, Maurice Mullins . . . .

The cast who were able to perform (in alphabetical order) were: Anne Brook, Peter Brown, Stella Green, Kenneth Guy, Peter Hallam, Colin Mark, James Nixon and Cynthia Perry. It was produced by Stella Green and Peter Brown and the lighting effects were by Terrance Hutson.

The youth club were not the only group to be interested in drama. There was Mickleover Amateur Dramatic Society and the the newly formed Methodist Players presented *Wishing Well,* a comedy in three acts by E Eynon Evans before Christmas. It was produced by Lorna Aitchison. Members of All Saints' Church Young Wives Drama Group produced two one-act plays at the Memorial Hut.

Many associations were also active in the village. One of the most prominent was the Mickleover Produce Association. They annually encouraged the children at the schools to grow vegetables, presenting prizes to the winners. Regular talks were given to lady members and their annual show always took place around August.

Well known local people acted as officers of the club. These included shopkeeper John T Winspear and headmaster Jimmy Best. There were 225 subscribing members.

Political parties regularly held socials, dances and out-door events, and for charity, people turned out in numbers for various dances at the Nag's Head Hotel.

Mickleover branch of the United Nations Association with Tim Ford as chairman, had an active programme. They made regular representations to Parliament and wrote "deeply regretting H M Government's action" on more than one occasion.

The Royal British Legion Gymkhana Committee announced that as a result of the profit made on the horse leaping show and the gymkhana in June, it would be possible to pay the final installment of an original loan of £1,100.

Members of the parish council met the clerk to the RDC, Fred Bailey, at the site of the new playing fields (Bramble Brook). The council was of the firm opinion that it was not suitable for childrens' recreation. They thought there was excessive dampness and because of the brook-course running through the land it would require constant attention and be a continuing source of trouble.

They asked the RDC to give serious consideration to the site already sug-

Photo courtesy of the Derby Evening Telegraph

A group of guests who attended a dance which was held in aid of troop funds by the 124th Derby (Mickleover) Scout Group at The Hut in September 1957.

gested to them by the Area Planning Officer (OS field numbers 45 and 46) to the north east. This area is now occupied by Murray Park School.

Staff appointments for the new junior school and infant school were now beginning to take shape with Mrs N Murfin electing to serve at the Junior School as a Clerical Assistant. Miss Kathleen Mary Stephens indicated that she was very glad to accept the appointment as headmistress of the Infant School and "that she will do her best for the children entrusted to her charges." She had been headmistress at Alvaston and Boulton Infants' School.

It was acknowledged that the existing body of managers would control both the Infants and Junior Schools after re-organisation. The managers recommended that the new school be named officially as Mickleover County Junior School and the old school be known as Mickleover County Infants' School. Agreeing with Mr Best's request the uniforms would conform to that introduced by him in 1950 which he described as "Ruby and Blue with a Silver outline for the badge".

No decision had been made on the siting of a new Secondary Modern School to serve Mickleover pupils.

The County Education Committee suggested that a third school should be built on the Etwall site, but this was strongly opposed by the South Derbyshire Divisional Executive Committee and the governors of Etwall John Port and Secondary School.

Roland Heath-Smith, the Divisional Education Officer, said "Mickleover is a much larger parish than Etwall and it is only reasonable that the school should be built there." He added: "To build a school on the Etwall site would spoil its beauty and would mean cramming too many children into a small area.

Two new groups were formed in the village in October. Mr and Mrs George Beavis of Brisbane Road became the leaders of the All Saints' Youth Group and it was agreed that meetings would be held in the Church Hall twice a month. The Vicarage Park Owners Residents' Association was inaugurated with the objects being to look after the interests of the householders living on the estate.

On October 2nd grandfather recorded that he walked around Vicarage Park. "There are yet some houses unoccupied. They are putting electric lamp standards in after having made up the streets."

A fortnight later he had walked to visit my mother at Brisbane Road and noticed that Wimpeys second phase was underway. "They have commenced building operations in the field by Nellie's", (Hamilton Close). On the following week he wrote: "They have almost driven the way for a new sewage pipe beneath the road, near to the [Bramble] brook."

It was the start of a busy week for him for on October 22nd he noted the "widening of road taking place on Burton Road, adjacent to Staker Lane junction."

On the afternoon he travelled to Tutbury with my cousin Tony, who has always been interested in railways. "We went out to have what may be our last ride on Tutbury 'Jinny'. They propose taking it off."

Jinny, or its original name Jenny, probably derived from the word engine and the train was used on the North Staffordshire Railway between Tutbury and Burton from 1848.

At the end of October grandfather went to Derby with Uncle Tom to purchase a new TV set. Tom settled for a Philco: combined TV, ITA and radio VHF. Very High Frequency radios were introduced in 1956.

Science and technology was moving forward at an increasing pace at this period. Jodrell Bank telescope, the largest radio telescope in the world, came into operation in October. However there were downturns, particularly with the fire at the atomic plant at Windscale in Cumbria, a serious accident in nuclear energy history.

"Announcement on the radio that the Russians had launched another satellite, this time with a dog in it," grandfather wrote on November 3rd. This was the second artificial earth satellite launched by the USSR. The first was launched in October and they called them Sputniks, "fellow travellers" (of Earth).

Modern technology was not helping Uncle Tom's new TV/radio reception. Although a new VHF aerial had been installed, "reception is interfered with by ambulance broadcasts from the station opposite. Dispatched card to Philco," wrote grandfather.

On November 12th an engineer from the Co-op called about the interference on the radio. "Made it worse. Sent notice about the interference to GPO." The General Post Office was the Government establishment who were responsible for reception under a Radio Interference Service.

With various "experts" visiting on a regular basis the situation was not improved until Spring 1958!

A 56 year old link with the Great Northern Hotel, held by the White family was broken in November. Mrs Harriet White, the 78 year-old licensee gave up the tenancy where she had lived all her married life. Mrs White's father-in-law first took over the hotel in 1901, and handed it down to his son Robert in 1909.

Harriet remembered the time when they opened at 6.00 am to supply rum and coffee to intending train travellers at Mickleover Station. She was fond of telling her customers how, when a girl in her teens, she was hoisted in a cradle to the top of the newly-built 100 feet high chimney of the brick works (adjacent to the station) where her father, Ernest Clarke lived.

There was still to be a family connection at the Great Northern as her nephew, Maurice Thornhill and his wife Kathy, from London, took over the house. Robert White, who served on the parish council, died in 1956.

At the November All Saints' PCC meeting, the Reverend Crockett said that after much work by Mr Ivy and Mr Draycott the organ was not improved. Owing to the weather Jim Land, Sexton, had not been able to do much to the Radford graves. However the Vicar said he would see that the broken cross was repaired.

Canon Boorman from Derby Diocese requested that if the tenants of Denton House, 145 Station Road, were to move he would like to see the house being adopted as a permanent benefice house. Previously owned by Miss Elizabeth Wild, it was left to the church in her will.

As the tenants were in fact moving out the church solicitors had the house valued at £2,500. Harry Rudkin, treasurer, proposed that if Denton House was sold the money should be put in a fund and then "if we can sell the present Vicarage we have some money towards building a new Vicarage."

At an Emergency Meeting of the PCC on December 10th Canon Boorman thought they should alter their decision and rent Denton House. Mr Rudkin explained to the Canon that it was Miss Wild's wish that the house should be sold and the proceeds go to the PCC and a portion to the Sunday School.

The estate agent had been told to withhold the sale for the time being but the PCC knew that the Trustees could let the house again. Mr Rudkin said that Allen and Farquhar had received an offer for Denton House. A member of the PCC was also interested in the property. It was sold in early 1958 for £2,650.

It was decided to accept the tender of Woodworm and Dry Rot Control Limited who proposed to start their treatment in January 1958. The Vicar said that at least on one Sunday the church would not be in use owing to the smell of timber fluid and the Church Hall would have to be used. The estimated cost for the work was £242 which would be paid for out of the Fabric and Furnishings Account.

Mrs Sarah Lingard asked the Vicar that as they now had a cemetery was it his responsibility to find a priest when people were buried. He replied that he had no control over the cemetery whatever but if there was a service in the parish church before the burial, then he would take it.

He explained later that as people were now being buried in the cemetery and Crematorium the Vicar's fees were affected. He asked if the council would, at a later date, go into the question of the Vicar's stipend, not only for himself but for the future incumbent who will not have the burial fees.

Mr T J Williams asked if the vaults that are falling owing to the growth of trees around them "could they be put right as they look so untidy." The Vicar said he would get free legal advice about the matter.

Planning permission had been requested for building a machine shop and workshop for W W Rushbrooke and Sons the new owners of Personal Service Garage at 11 Uttoxeter Road, opposite the County School. This was originally owned by Ossie Ashcroft.

A particular insurance company had agreed to insure all parish councillors. Rates were: 16 to 75 years of age, 4s.6d per year; 75 to 80 years 2s.3d per year.

After Sydney Clarke had raised the question of a village hall at the parish meeting, it was decided to write to the trustees of the Memorial Hut, asking them if they would be willing to lease it to the parish as a Village Hall. Mr Clarke said he thought it was time Mickleover had a village hall.

Grandfather notes on December 5th: "Mr E Nadin, a neighbour, died suddenly." Builder Ernest William Nadin had been running for a bus to visit his wife in hospital, when he had a heart attack. He had been a political partner of Tom Radford serving on both the parish council and Repton Rural District Council and he was also a keen member of the Arboretum Bowls Club in Derby.

Members of the parish council stood in silence in tribute to Mr Nadin at the December meeting. Ernest's final appearance at a council meeting had been on November 19th.

Cousin Tony left school in December but had "been unable to obtain job at RR. Tom had had further consultation with Co-op about VHF. They told him they had been in touch with Philco. Met a man on same errand."

Charlie Langley, landlord of the Masons Arms organised a concert in aid of

A dinner for Mickleover County Junior School was held at the Nag's Head Hotel on December 13th. Back row left to right: Mr Wright, Mr Kendall, Mr Williams, Gordon Parsons, Ron Fowler, Mrs Lindenberg, Mrs Hallsworth. Second row: Mr Peach, Mr & Mrs Bagguley, Mr & Mrs Johnson, Mrs Gaskill, Miss Ellis, Mrs Peach, Miss Beech, Mrs Yates, Mrs Dolby, Mrs Warner, Mrs Wright, Mrs Kendall, Mrs Williams, Pam Ratcliffe, Mr Gaskill. Seated, first row: Mr Warner, Mrs Best, Miss Stephens, Unknown, Unknown, Miss Wedd, Mr Barnes, Mr & Mrs Riley, Mabel Wibberley, Unknown, P Wibberley, Mr Ravensdale. Front row: Mr Brierley, Mrs Parkin, Mrs & Mr Ford, Unknown, Unknown, Unknown, Unknown, Olive Plumpton, Unknown. Right: Arthur G Ravensdale (chairman, School Managers, Miss Kathleen Stephens (headmistress, Mickleover County Infants School, Jimmy Best (headmaster, Mickleover County Junior School).

the widow of one of his customers. Her husband had died because of injuries received in an accident at the Havenbaulk Lane and Burton Road junction.

On the evening of December 20th a group of residents, headed by parish council chairman Tim Ford inspected the lighting and observed the speed of traffic coming down Pastures Hill. They intended to make representations to the RDC for immediate safety precautions "with a note of extreme urgency."

At the parish council, earlier in the week, some 20 angry parishioners protested about the junction and the lack of measures to make it safe.

Bad lighting and speed were suggested as "main contributing causes to the recent outbreak of accidents, fatal and otherwise which had occurred at the site."

Mr C E Stubbs of 85 Havenbaulk Lane wrote that a petition containing over 400 signatures had been sent to the Derbyshire County Council. Mr Ford explained that many of the improvements suggested by the residents had already been raised by the council.

He said that placing a pedestrian-crossing at the junction proved to be very dangerous on a de-restricted road, and the Ministry of Transport and Civil Aviation had refused to restrict the road.

Tim Ford also pointed out that a few years ago the council had set out to replace all the gas lamps in the parish, but because of prohibitive cost, it was unable to renew them all at the same time.

The keys to the new building for Mickleover County Junior School were handed over to the headmaster, Jimmy Best on December 6th. On December 11th they moved into the new building and the infants occupied the classrooms allocated after the vacation of the juniors.

Local events saw the opening of Borrowash by-pass and the Grand Theatre in Babington Lane, which had been disused since 1950, was being considered as a ballroom. The opening of a civil airport at Castle Donington was under discussion but the authorities were unwilling to talk about it. Air travel was now becoming a profitable business and an air service opened between London and Moscow just before Christmas.

CHAPTER FIVE
SECONDARY EDUCATION IN MICKLEOVER?
1958

Mickleover County Junior School opened on January 1st with 300 children on the roll. Miss Kathleen Mary Stephens took up her duties as headteacher at Mickleover County Infant School on January 6th. With 33 new admissions the number on the roll was 172. "Exactly 100 children staying to dinner."

Members of the 124th Derby (Mickleover) Troop Cub Pack held a New Year party at the Memorial Hut. Forty guests attended and it was organised by Mr Brown, Group Scoutmaster. Mickleover All Saints Church Cub Pack, had been formed in June 1957 and had made rapid strides under the leadership of Daisy N Rogers, Lady Cubmaster. On Monday, January 13th, the pack held its first open night in the Church Hall.

At the School Managers meeting on the same evening, Arthur Ravensdale took the chair with Harold W Brice, Joe Nadin and Arthur Riley present along with the heads, Jimmy Best and Kathleen Stephens. Arthur Riley was a railway man and he later told teacher Harry Gaskill that he voted for Miss Stephens at her interview because she was interested in trains.

Jimmy Best reported that the entry at the new school on December 11th had taken place smoothly. Mr J W Froxley, head of the schools division of the County Architects department, visited the school and gave a talk to more than 120 parents and staff about the construction and architecture of the new building.

Mr Best continued his strong discipline at the new school. Every morning he would stand where the children entered, watching for any misbehaviour.

Photo courtesy of the Derby Evening Telegraph

Mr Tom M Brown, Group Scoutmaster, hands the patrol trophy to David Petts, leader of "Mitchell" patrol, at a party and presentation awards held by the 124th (Derby) Mickleover Scout Troop at the Memorial Hut.

Photo courtesy of Mickleover Primary School

This air view of Mickleover County Junior School, taken in 1970, shows the playing fields, bottom left, with the old tennis courts; the corner of Watsons' the Corn Merchant, extreme right and the houses with the long gardens on Station Road (top left) which are described in Chapter One.

The pond was in front of his window, so on the first morning he told the children that there must be no running round the pond. David Purdy has some

MICKLEOVER COUNTY INFANTS' SCHOOL STAFF, JANUARY 1958
Headmistress: Miss K M Stephens

	Form
Mrs M E Henchliffe	Class 1
Miss M Wibberley	Class 2
Miss P Beech	Class 3
Miss K M Stephens	Class 4
Miss G Ravensdale	Class 5
Mrs D Lacey	Clerical Assistant
Mrs M Wall	Cook

recollection of accidentally stepping in the fishpond and "fearing possible ramifications from the strict headmaster!" Mr Best's deputy head, Harry Gaskill can recall that the only person to fall in the pond throughout his period at the school was a mother.

Harry Gaskill was still cycling to school but he eventually purchased a MG 11/4 litre saloon from Dodsley Motors on the corner of Stafford Street and Curzon Street. It once belonged to Joan Gee of builders, Gee Walker & Slater, but she only used it for golfing trips.

The Reverend Ben Crockett told All Saints' PCC that some Communion Wafers had been destroyed by mice, "although the workmen who carried out the deinfestation had said we would have no trouble with mice." He thanked Father Victor T McClaughry, of Pastures Hospital, "for letting us use their church while ours was being treated for woodworm." The deinfestation had been carried out and the bill came to £242.2s.0d. Mr Rudkin said he had sent a cheque for £240 as the workmen had broken two shades and bulbs.

An estimate of £24 had been received for the repair of three damaged graves (including Radfords'). It was agreed that the work should be done and payment would be made when the money from the Radford bequest became available.

Charges for the playing field facilities were announced in February. Tennis would be 2s.6d per hour; football 12s.6d per match; cricket 12s.6d per half day match, 18s.9d full day.

The Playing Fields Committee were looking into re-instating the putting green, with a charge of 4d per person per round. It was first suggested at a parish meeting in 1950 and opened to the public in March 1951 but it proved to be un-economic. It was agreed to re-open it by using the north side of the pavilion and alongside the main football pitch.

A committee was appointed at the parish council meeting to begin negotiations for the use of the Memorial Hut as a Village Hall. They were Sydney Clarke, Edward J Gothard and Arthur Ravensdale.

Les Miller, clerk, informed them that various considerations had to be discussed. Firstly, was it the intention of the parish council to acquire the property

Photo courtesy of the Derby Evening Telegraph

Snow down The Hollow photographed by the Derby Evening Telegraph *in January 1958.*

and administer it themselves, or secondly, were they just to act as a holding body and hand over the administration of it to a group composed of representatives of local organisations?

If they decided on the latter there were now so many organisations who could justifiably claim representation on a joint committee, that it would result in a committee of at least thirty persons, which would then be considered to be unwieldy.

However, the benefit of administering it themselves would provide for an amenity for a growing village that would result in a "home" for the parish council (ie council offices). A charge on the rates could be obviated by various bodies using the hall and organising regular efforts to raise funds.

Whatever conclusions they reached it would still depend on the respective attitudes of the parish council and the hut trustees.

"Heavy fall of snow over a wide area. Had to dig a way to gate and backyard door," grandfather wrote on February 25th. "Had to clear snow off hedge by garden path, it was bent right over."

On the following day he remarked that the "electric man called to change lamps. Current altered to 240 volts this morning." He continued: "TV rectified to new electric current and receipt of further new lamps.

A weekend of special efforts were held at the Methodist Church on February 22nd. A variety concert was given by the Men's Fellowship, when nearly 200 people attended a sausage and mash supper cooked and served by the men.

In the evening a programme of songs and sketches including a mock pantomime was produced by Don Fawcett. The Youth Drama Group presented a one-act play, *Spider Ring*, which was produced by Stella Green. The players were Peter Brown, Michael Green, Kenneth Guy, Peter and Rodney Hallam, Terrance Hutson, James Nixon and John Taylor. The group visited Allestree on March 8th to perform the play at the Youth Drama Festival.

A proposal by Arthur Morley from New House Farm, for the development of 28.4 acres of land for housing, north of Woodlands Hospital, was turned down by the RDC.

The reasons given were that the site was not within an area indicated for residential development; construction of access onto the main road would result in interference "with the free and safe flow of traffic and tend to cause dangerous conditions." After Arthur Morley lodged an appeal it became the subject of a hearing by the Minister of Housing and Local Government (see plan p85).

On March 20th grandfather took one of his favourite walks via Staker Lane, Burton Road and through Burnaston village to the main Uttoxeter Road. "Saw farmers chain harrowing with horses in pairs. A welcome sight."

At the March School Managers meeting Alec Eric Hannah of Darwin Road was appointed as clerk at a salary of £40 per annum. Jimmy Best reported that school signs had been erected at the junior school and a Police Cadet was constantly carrying out the duty of traffic warden. He also said that Miss Wedd had expressed her intention of retiring upon reaching the age of 65 later in the year.

His proposal that climbing equipment for physical education in the school hall would be carried out, and he had been assured that if he desired it, climbing equipment for use in the school grounds could be supplied. It was eventually installed in November.

Grandfather saw on April 8th a "new factory [Nestlés] beginning to look finished". They were the first and last commercial company to bring a production line factory to Mickleover. The company was beginning to interview candidates for the production of biscuits and sweets. A week later grandfather "spotted Sputnik 2 whizzing across the heavens about 7.50pm"

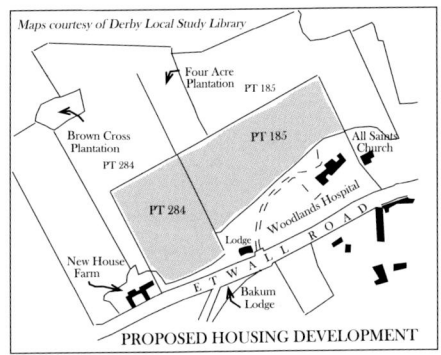

On April 21st "saw grandson Peter on the way home. He has acquired a motor bike." I bought my brother-in-law's James 125cc which I hoped would help me to arrive home for lunch during my working week at the *Derbyshire Advertiser*. I was able to park it on Derby Market Place (at a cost of course), but I never had to think about it being stolen or damaged during the day!

Eighty-four acres of "valuable grass keeping" was offered for auction by Richardson and Linnell on April 28th. The land, north of the hospital, was adjoining the Derby to Uttoxeter road, and was purchased at the auction of the Mickleover Manor Estate in 1937. The sale was commissioned by the Sheffield Regional Hospital Board as part of the removal of dairy farming at Pastures Hospital.

Stakerfield Farm and land, which belonged to the hospital, had been advertised as available for leasing. A sub-committee agreed to recommend the offer of Kenneth J Ashmole, 1 Gilling House Flat, Pastures Hospital, for the farm and land which extended to 38.013 acres.

The RDC Housing and Town Planning Committee received an application in April for the erection of two bungalow type shops with garages at the corner of Vicarage Road and Farneworth Road. They also proceeded to consider tenders for the construction of a footpath from Cavendish Way to Western Road. They accepted the tender of £67.13s.0d from Peter Robinson Ltd of Derby.

Photo courtesy of the Derby Evening Telegraph

Mickleover Womens' Institute 40th Birthday party

The Committee were informed later that five cottages at Alma Heights had been purchased. Only one family now needed to be re-housed. An application had been received and finally granted for the change of use of 74 Western Road for Walter W Upton. The ground floor was to become a retail grocery and greengrocery shop.

On May 7th a letter was received by the RDC Engineer and Surveyor from the Area Planning Officer regarding Mr J Mellor of Station Road. He wished to turn 16 The Square (Miss Shotton's old shop) into either a Fried Fish Shop or Decorating Materials.

Mr Lang, Engineer and Surveyor, stated "in view of the existing use as a shop, consent would not be required for the sale of decorating materials, although permission would be needed for use as a fried fish shop."

He concluded: "Although I should not normally favour the establishment of shops on the southerly side of the trunk road, I feel that in view of the existing use, little exception can be taken."

The application was deferred and the planning authority was informed that the likely acquisition of this property could be the extension of the Masons Arms. The RDC even thought of acquiring the property and adapting part of it for a public convenience.

At the School Managers meeting in May, headmaster, Jimmy Best said he had visited Litton Mill School Journey Centre and was "appalled at the filthy conditions of the building generally and the bad condition of the equipment." However, the school visited Litton Mill a few weeks later, at Whitsuntide, when he reported that there had been an improvement.

Harold Brice said he had not sought re-election to the parish council and this would be his last meeting of the School Managers.

Les Miller, clerk, Edward Gothard and Arthur Ravensdale met the Memorial Hut Trustees and Committee on May 29th, and after considerable discussion agreed to call an Extraordinary General Meeting. Two of the Trustees were Charles Ernest Ayre, and Donald Preston-Jones, the son of Alexander Preston-Jones, who donated the Hut to Mickleover. The purpose of the meeting would be to adopt a resolution which "would state the exact terms to which the Hut would be handed over to the parish council".

Mr F W Barnett, solicitor, later wrote to the council stating that Mrs Laura Slack, secretary of the Mickleover Memorial Hut, wished to inform them that the members were not in favour of making changes in the constitution of the Memorial Hut. It could, however, be raised at a later date.

The Area Planning Officer had supplied the parish council with a plan showing three alternative sites for a hall. Les Miller, clerk, explained that the Ministry of Housing and Local Government had informed him that the parish council were not empowered to build up funds to meet a debt. It would, therefore, be necessary to raise a loan to meet any capital cost.

The Village Hall Committee thought that as there was no immediate urgency for a village hall, the matter would be left until the development of the village had been completed.

Mickleover's Corn Merchant, William Hardy Watson, died suddenly at his home, "The Croft", on June 1st. He was seventy-seven years old. William was the South East Derbyshire area representative for the British Show Jumping Association and had been in business for more than forty years. He left a widow Florence, a son Donald and two daughters, Marjorie (Betty) and Nancy who had married John Flint and lived at Manor Farm on Vicarage Road.

A complaint was received by the parish council from a resident in Vicarage Road. A second pane of glass in his conservatory had been broken by children playing cricket against the chain-link fence on the playing fields.

The council's insurers wrote that they had not received a claim from the resident, although he had received an ex-gratia payment for an earlier incident. The

---

LOCAL ELECTIONS TOOK PLACE IN MAY 1958

PETER BEVRIC BEVERIDGE
(Representative)
HENRY RITCHIE BOWER
(Retired Local Government Officer),
JOHN MELLOR BOWER
(Retired Police Officer)
SYDNEY ARTHUR CLARKE
(Chartered Secretary)
WALTER HARRY COE
(Clerk)
HARRY BURTON CROSBY
(Retired Railway Official)
HENRY GIBSON (TIM) FORD
(Pharmacist)
EDWARD JAMES GOTHARD
(Company Director)
ALAN WILLIAM RATCLIFF
(Design Draughtsman)
ARTHUR GRANVILLE RAVENSDALE
(Schoolmaster)
PHILIP DONALD GEORGE SPILSBURY
(Training Officer)
THOMAS EDWARD WHITTINGHAM
(Schoolmaster)
ANTHONY SWAIN YEOMANS
(Tobacconist)

Photo courtesy of Geoff Guy

Harry Gaskill (deputy head) with Mickleover Junior School football team 1957/58 season. Back row left to right Tony Hall, Ian Pepper, Unknown, Geoff Guy, Greg Tomlin, ? Pether, Alan Melville. Seated: Brian Jennings. Front row: Alan Craig, Dave Hayton, Patrick Harkins, Jimmy Nealy, Gordon Severn.

letter ended by stating that they felt "that the playing fields are not really suitable for the playing of football and cricket, even in organised games."

An annoyed clerk, Les Miller, informed the company "that the insurance was taken out and given in all good faith" having been made aware of the additional risks arising from the development adjoining the playing fields.

Municipal Mutual Insurance Ltd wrote to apologise for the content of the letter. They said they were not attempting to evade their liabilities but wished to point out that the occupants of properties adjacent should be protected as much as possible from the risk of being injured "by flying cricket balls and so on." A week later a quotation of £3.17s.6d was received for a general Third Party policy, an increase from £2.13s.9d.

Grandfather wrote on June 30th, "they have put up a notice about making up Arundel Avenue at last." The avenue had always been an unadopted road, making it difficult for pedestrians and growing traffic to travel down a very bumpy, and at times, muddy road.

The parish council informed the County Surveyor that they "wished to ensure the preservation of the tree at the junction of East Avenue and Chestnut Avenue, if and when East Avenue is extended in an easterly direction." Councillor Yeomans requested that his dissent from this decision be recorded. The County Surveyor later replied that there was no intention to remove the elm tree.

Because of the increase in his duties arising from the growth of the parish since 1953, the clerk, Les Miller, received an increase to his fee from £146 per annum and £30 expenses to £190 per annum and £40 respectively. It was to come into effect on July 1st.

The end of June determined which school the children at the Junior School would attend at the next stage of their education. According to deputy headteacher, Harry Gaskill, the children always knew if they had passed the eleven-plus examinations as the envelope they received was thicker than those who failed. This was owing to the inclusion of a bus pass for travelling to Ashbourne Grammar School.

Children who lived east of Station Road and passed the eleven-plus went to Ashbourne Grammar School and those who failed to Littleover Secondary Modern School. West of Station Road the choice was John Port Grammar School for those who passed the eleven plus and Etwall Secondary School for the remainder.

The results of the Intelligence Tests determined the number of places. Coaching was not supposed to take place but every school knew that this was not being followed.

For the children on the border line it was officially left to the headmaster, who attended a tribunal to determine who would go to grammar school but Mr Best refused and told the panel to decide as he thought all of them should go to grammar school.

Miss Reece, Physical Education Organiser, visited the Infants' School to arrange for a site for apparatus to be installed in the playground.

On July 8th the Dedication of the Junior School took place with the Reverend F Raymond Stopard, Minister of Mickleover Methodist Church, leading the prayers and Ben Crockett, Vicar of All Saints', dedicating the school.

The Roman Catholic population in Mickleover was beginning to expand with the increased housing stock. An additional congregation was being transported by bus to take Mass at St Joseph's in Derby. This was causing something of an embarrassment, and an unnamed author wrote a poem about the antics on the bus. Father Key saw the need for a Mass Centre for the "Mickleover Mob"!

A meeting of the local Roman Catholic community took place at the Junior School hall on three evenings in July. The ladies would no doubt have been informed, by Jimmy Best, not to wear stilettoes in the hall. It was one of his first priorities to inform parents of the rule "to keep the school in a pristine condition."

A group had met at the Memorial Hut in June with the proposal of setting up

Photo courtesy of the Derby Evening Telegraph

Mickleover Royal British Legion Dinner and Dance.

Roman Catholic education facilities and ultimately the establishment of a Mass Centre at Mickleover. The first celebration of Mass was held at the Memorial Hut on June 15th.

Nestlé's were advertising for maintenance staff. "Electrician with experience of general factory maintenance; Fitter preferably with experience in wrapping and machinery; One General Maintenance Fitter with experience of installation of machinery and general Millwright's work."

Peter Sharratt was an early member of the workforce, having had previous experience producing biscuits at Joyces' factory in Derby. On leaving school he gained an apprenticeship as a millwright at Aitons'.

When Peter arrived at the factory the windows were still being glazed. As the brand new machinery, all British made, was in the process of being installed his skills in engineering were put to use in helping to get things ready for production. Although the RDC had expected the company to use the railway for the main traffic, with sidings built at Mickleover Station, this never transpired.

Not long after Nestlé's began commissioning their biscuit production, Gerald Hanson, from Mill Farm, bought all the waste biscuits and doughs as an animal feed, for his cattle and chickens.

Grandfather wrote of "alarming news from Arab countries," on July 15th. The monarchy in Iraq had been overthrown with King Faisal being assassinated. The establishment of a Republic was announced. A day later United States marines landed and this was followed by British troops being flown to Amman (Jordan), in response to King Hussein's appeal.

It had already been an eventful year in Britain. The London Planetarium had

Photo courtesy of Henry Gaskill

Mickleover Junior School Staff 1958. Back row, left to right: Ann Ellis, Lyn Kendall, Gordon Parsons, Pamela Ratcliffe. Front row, left to right: Harry Gaskill, Olive Plumpton, Jimmy Best, Edith Wedd, Stan Peach.

Photo courtesy of Henry Gaskill

Mr Gaskill's Junior School class 1958.

91

Junior School visit to Chester in June 1958.

been opened; the Clean Air Act had come into force in June, banning emissions of dark smoke, and motorists were facing yellow "no waiting" lines on roads. There had been a vacancy for a police sergeant in Mickleover since early June and at last Thomas A Shaw was appointed. He had been transferred from Chesterfield Town Police, and had joined the County Police in 1946. Detective Sergeant H Mackenzie, the previous sergeant, joined the Alfreton Division.

Grandfather had noticed that "the hedge at the old blacksmith's house [Station Road] next to roadway has been cut down." Tom Whitworth, blacksmith, had owned the four cottages called Elm Tree Terrace and had lived in the first (nearest Nat West Bank) with his wife, "Ginny".

The only daughter of Charles and Mabel Langley of the Masons Arms, Margaret Ann (Peggy) had been about to marry Thomas Robert (Jock) Goodwin in March.

He was serving on HMS Collingwood in Portsmouth during his National Service but while taking part in a football match in December, he suffered a multiple fracture of his right leg and was detained in hospital.

The wedding was hastily re-arranged for April 19th when he thought he would be fit. However, Peggy was informed that when the plaster was removed from Jock's leg, the bone had not set.

Another attempt was made to marry in June but this time Peggy's father was ill. They eventually married on August 16th.

At All Saints' PCC meeting in August the secretary was asked to write a letter of thanks to Christopher Dolchini and his helpers for all the work they had accomplished in the churchyard.

The Vicar had earlier suggested that, as it was an impossibility for the Sexton to keep all the grass cut, the leaders of the new Youth Group, formed in April, should be asked if members would help.

At the Annual General meeting of the choir it was decided that girls should be asked to leave, as boys and girls don't mix. Some young men took umbrage and left the choir.

Teacher, Miss Edith Wedd, retired after 21 years' service at Mickleover schools. With the exception of the period between 1924 and 1929, she had taught at schools in Derbyshire and Staffordshire for 44 years.

She lived at Tutbury travelling to Mickleover by bus and was proud of never being late for school.

On behalf of the pupils and friends she was presented with a gold watch! Gifts were also handed to Miss Pamela Ratcliffe who was leaving the teaching staff to take up an appointment in London.

Mrs Margaret Lowe from Peartree Junior Mixed School, and Miss Molly Watson of St Oswald's Church of England School, Ashbourne joined the staff on September 1st.

On September 16th, George Brown MP, said in Mickleover that a war with Communist China over the off-shore islands "would be the wrong war over the wrong issues, at the wrong time, in every sense of the word. It seems to me that we ought to be making that crystal clear to the Americans."

A bombardment by the Chinese on Quemoy (Formosa Strait) led the Americans to send more warships to join the Seventh Fleet. Following this action the Ambassadors of America and China were to meet in Warsaw for discussions.

The Conservative Prime Minister, Harold McMillan, had suggested that George Brown (Labour) should go to the United States on a diplomatic mission as Lord Attlee had when Prime Minister during the Korean War (1950), to use his influence "on the side of restraint, moderation and responsibility."

George Brown's speech, delivered from a loudspeaker van on the Devonshire Drive estate, was part of his summer campaign of outdoor meetings. A small group of people listened, but no questions were asked, although a few people spoke privately to the MP after the speech.

While he was speaking a young couple from a neighbouring road approached him and complained about the loudspeaker. "We have a young baby" they said.

The MP apologised about the loudspeaker when he ended his speech saying "we have come here to make friends, not to lose them." One hopes the same message of peace took place between the two ambassadors!

Under the Litter Act 1958 the parish council, together with the other local authorities, was able to institute a prosecution for the offence. Private individuals and the police were also empowered to institute proceedings. The parish council requested a larger litter bin to be placed in the Square and painted yellow to make it more conspicuous.

Those properties in Chestnut Avenue, at the time served by cesspools, "would now be connected to the main sewer."

Mr Edward F Speed of Chestnut Avenue had written to the parish council, asking if something could be done to prevent grass spreading from the public footpath to his property. The council informed him that they had recommended the closing of the path between Station Road and Chestnut Avenue (see map p61). The County Council had agreed to it in 1953 and had informed the RDC.

Mr Speed was told that he would need to make application to the Ministry of Transport for the closing of the footpath. He was also advised that certain formalities would have to be completed, including spending money on advertising.

An evening cricket knockout competition in aid of the Hughes Charity Cricket Cup involving Mickleover pub teams was held for a number of years in the 1950s on the playing fields. They were 20 overs games, which was fifty years before its time. Each player, apart from the wicketkeepers, had to bowl 2 overs and if a batsman reached a score of 30 he had to retire. The pubs that took part were the Nag's Head, The Vine, The Masons Arms, the Great Northern, a team from Wilson Close, near Pastures Hospital and the Royal British Legion. Although some were regular cricketers, anyone sitting at the pub bars would be persuaded to play, some still in their cycle clips or working overalls.

Throughout the summer of 1958 some of the matches were reported in the local press. In one match the Great Northern scored 76 and beat the Royal British Legion by 25 runs. The Vine Inn made 92 runs for 7 wickets with J Wilkinson scoring the maximum 30. This must have demoralised the Masons Arms team who were all out for 20. Their score was even worse against Wilson Close a month later, all out for 15. Wilson Close had opened the match with 97 with both Heaver and Ansty scoring 30. There is no newspaper report of the eventual winners of the cup.

A representative team from all the licensed houses played an invitation match against Dronfield Cricket Club, champions of the Sheffield Amateur League at the Royal British Legion Sports Field. The visitors declared for 139 for 7 but the home side were all out for 39. A collection tin in aid of the Hughes Charity Cup Fund raised £2.2s.6d.

Photo courtesy of the Derby Evening Telegraph

The Reverend F Raymond Stopard was to leave Mickleover Methodist Church and was presented with a cheque in appreciation of his ministry during the last six years. The cheque was handed over on behalf of the congregation by Mr Edmund King Wilkinson, secretary of the trustees at a meeting in the church hall following the evening service. The new Minister, Reverend Clifford Hawkins of Bristol took up his duties in September.

Mickleover Sports Club reported their highest aggregates for the 1957/58 football season since they were formed. The first team finished as runners-up in Section "B" of the Derbyshire Senior League. They would now compete in Section "A". The reserves were fourth in Section "E" and beaten cup finalists. This result, they thought, was unfortunate, as there were injuries prior to the final. Ken Guy was one of their new cricketers that season. He had also agreed to act as Match Secretary for the cricket team. Captain, Albert Wilkinson, had earlier requested two new bats and at least three new balls for the season.

Back in April a dance was held at the Trocadero Ballroom, Derby. However they were informed that before agreeing to another dance in 1959, the club must guarantee to sell 100 tickets. Dick Kenderdine said "surely it was not beyond the power of 25 members to sell four tickets each?" A written undertaking was made to the Trocadero along with a provisional date.

Mickleover Sports Club asked the parish council about the possibility of reimbursement of part of the fee paid by them for the cricket season because of the effect of the poor weather. Edward Gothard, seconded by Henry Bower, moved that "no refund be made in this respect to the club" and was carried. Gothard played for Derbyshire Cricket Club in the 1947 and 1948 seasons as a right-hand batsman and right-arm medium paced bowler. He was the man who bowled out the famous Australian, Donald Bradman, in their match against Derbyshire for 62 runs.

The Director of Education, Jack Longland, informed the parish council that he was prepared to attend an open meeting on November 18th to discuss the question of education facilities for Mickleover particularly in regard to secondary education.

This date, he said, would still leave time for the parish council to register objections following the publication of Public Notices at the end of October. The Education Committee proposed to provide future secondary education facilities for Mickleover at Etwall. This decision caused the largest public opposition in Mickleover in the 1950s.

The RDC Housing and Town Planning Committee gave further consideration in October to use the premises at The Square for the purpose of a bus shelter and public convenience. They felt a meeting on the site with the County Council and Ministry of Transport and Civil Aviation might prove useful. The applicant, [Mr J Mellor], who wished to use the premises for business, would be asked to agree to an extension of his application until a decision could be given.

An application for the development of a site for building a 1-form entry Roman Catholic Primary School was to be sent to the County Council. The Nottingham Diocesan Commission for Schools wished to include playing fields in their plan. The site was on the north side of Murray Road which the parish council had recommended as a playing field.

Nestlé's was granted permission to extend the building of their factory off Station Road. A management team had now been appointed, headed by Donald Cunliffe, the Factory Manager, who eventually lived at Kirk Langley. The team also included Len Appleby, Chief Engineer; Lawrence Martin, Production Manager; Colin Blakeman, Chemist; Mr Whibley, Chief Clerk. They all lived in company houses in Melbourne Close. Gladys Kirkham was the Personnel Manager.

On November 3rd grandfather walked to Chestnut Avenue. "This building estate growing apace." Later in the month, "work proceeding on making up the roadway on Arundel Avenue." He continued: "Building is almost complete in the hollow of the brook off Cavendish Way," (Hardwick Drive).

When the time arrived he made the point that "they considered 2-form and 3-form entry schools to be too small, and that a sufficient number of pupils at schools was required to merit the appointment of full-time specialist teachers."

Mr Longland continued, "it was thought desirable to make provision for pupils about the margin between the highest level of intelligence at secondary modern schools and the lowest level of intelligence at grammar schools." The opinion of the Education Committee thought their policy should provide larger units for secondary education.

They had informed the Minister of Education that Etwall "could provide secondary education, principally among children from six other parishes, including Mickleover, by enlarging the Etwall County Secondary School."

The minutes of the meeting record various questions raised by the parish council, objecting to the proposals.

The Council-in-Committee finally formed the opinion "that they could come to no effective decision in the matter, in view of the fact that the Education Act, 1944 as amended, does not appear to make the parish council, as a body, competent to submit objections to the Minister of Education with regard to the County Council's proposals.

"The Act provides specifically for objections to be lodged only by any ten or more local government electors for the area concerned, apart from specified education bodies.

"Notwithstanding this position, it was felt that a parish meeting should be called for the purposes of acquainting the parishioners as fully as possible with the County Council's proposals."

At the chairman's request all members of the council stood in silence as a tribute to the sudden death of Mr Harry Burton Crosby, their late fellow councillor.

The monthly meeting of the parish council reported that David Besley Rowen had consented to fill the casual vacancy.

The School Managers had earlier made a request to the parish council to consider the question of swimming facilities, particularly for school children.

After a $2\frac{1}{2}$ hour discussion on December 5th, over 100 people, who attended the parish meeting at the Junior School decided to take immediate steps to officially object to the proposed extension of Etwall County Secondary School to accommodate Mickleover children.

Councillor J B Hancock, vice chairman of Derbyshire Education Committee, and Mr C W Phillips, Assistant Director of Schools, answered questions and gave reasons for the proposals which in the end were unanimously rejected.

A sub-committee of 14 was elected to draft the final reasons for the objection to send to the Minister of Education.

When complete it required a minimum of ten signatures and it would be widely publicised in an effort to obtain the support and signatures of more people.

The sub-committee had little time to draft the objection as the proposals were advertised on November 8th, and they had just two months to send their objec-

Photo courtesy of the Derby Evening Telegraph

Mickleover Methodist Players presented Job for the Boy *in the church hall in November. The play was produced by Lorna Aitchison. Cast, Hilda Blades, Margaret Dommett, Donald Fawcett, William Bowley, Bob Roberts, John Horner and Jean Parry.*

tions to the Minister. Arthur Ravensdale, who was presiding, thought this was a good occasion to gain more information before deciding on their actions.

Councillor Hancock explained: "We [the committee] have a statutory responsibility and you have a parental responsibility. In the light of the experience we have gathered, it is incontestable that secondary modern education cannot be provided in schools of small numbers.

"At the end of the scale," he said, "there are children who had just failed the entrance examination for the grammar school, and at the bottom of the scale there were children who would not go that far. We had a responsibility towards both these groups, but in a smaller school these might only be two, three or four children.

"With groups this size you have not the staff or facilities to give each child a chance, but in the larger schools these might become 12, 13, or 15 and it is only in this way that you will achieve first-class secondary modern education which is our objective and the child's right."

Councillor Hancock said the second reason for building the school at Etwall was that it would offer a better standard of education in the immediate future, and provide for future proposals in the changing pattern of secondary education.

Answering questions he denied a suggestion that the proposals were the first step towards a comprehensive school. Some thought that this 'experimental' system would replace the present system "which had provided good education over many years."

Other views expressed the dangers in transporting a large number of children three miles to Etwall every day; the newly formed Parent-Teacher Association would suffer; a bus timetable would debar the children from extra activities at the school.

Owing to the vandalism of the Offertory Boxes in All Saints' it was suggested enquiries be made to Chubbs regarding their wall safes.

At All Saints' PCC meeting in December agreed that the Easter Sunday Offerings in 1959 and the sum of £15 per annum be given to the Vicar. The £15 would be allocated to cover telephone charges and office expenses.

Photo courtesy of Magic Attic Archive, Swadlincote
Councillor Sydney Arthur Clarke of 49 Western Road, chairman of Mickleover Parish Council and a member of Repton RDC, pictured with Miss Dorothy Teagle of Littleover after their wedding on November 22nd at St Peter's Church, Littleover.

As late teenagers, I, and a group of friends who had spent the last few years together, were finding other interests. Sport took precedence with some turning out weekly in summer playing cricket and football in winter.

The centre of Derby was offering more in the way of entertainment for younger people. Dance halls became popular with local bands such as Syd Arkell providing the popular tunes for dancing. We had been fortunate in receiving dance tuition at the Methodist Youth Club, saving us from embarrassment when dancing with the partner of our choice.

Healthy males between the ages of 18 and 26 were still having to think about compulsory National Service, if they had not already completed it. It remains the only period of peacetime conscription in the United Kingdom's history.

Our drama group was beginning to diminish, although we had been brave enough to attempt the comedy *The Happiest Days of Your Life*. Set in a private school for boys, the staff and pupils became overwhelmed by the arrival of a girls' school because of a ministerial blunder. I can find no confirmation of the play being performed, but I do recall reaching final stage rehearsals.

CHAPTER SIX
THE DRIEST SUMMER FOR 200 YEARS
1959

Grandfather's interest in science and sport continued when he began his 1959 diary with "News of Russian rocket on the radio, aimed at moon," followed by "Black news about the Test Match in Australia." His constant thirst for knowledge, particularly in sport and history, was certainly passed to me.

Planning applications continued to arrive at the Repton Rural District Council offices, some not bearing fruit.

Alterations to 21 North Avenue entailed the creation of two shops (ladies' hairdressing, Post Office and general store), combined with living accommodation. This was turned down as "an area of land on Devonshire Drive has been allocated for development as a small shopping centre in accordance with the Local Planning Authority's policy." This led the applicant to appeal and a public enquiry was held at Burton-on-Trent in the summer. His reason for his appeal was the "complete disgust and distrust of our local planning committee." He was not represented, but went on to state that during the course of his enquiries he had received little satisfaction.

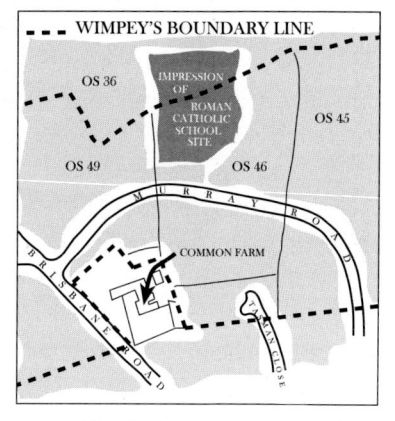

Objections were heard from many residents in North Avenue, plus a written objection bearing the signatures of twelve neighbours.

Outline planning application for the erection of a one-form entry Roman Catholic Primary School was granted, but with certain conditions imposed. Nottingham Diocesan Commission for Schools had commissioned Wimpeys to build it on the north side of Murray Road, complete with playing fields.

The main talking point in Mickleover at the beginning of 1959 continued to be the need for a Secondary Modern School and the formal objections were now to be sent to the Minister of Education (Rt Hon Geoffrey Lloyd).

The seven-point resistance plan was subscribed to by some 900 to 1,000 local electors. It emphasised that a site was already available at Mickleover which had received the approval of the Planning Authority. It was also included in the Development Plan.

Extensive housing development was stated to have expanded the child population of the village. The present Junior School was catering for 320 pupils and was now full, and a second Junior School was to be built in the near future so it was expected that a Secondary Modern School would subsequently accommodate over 450 pupils.

On the third point it was explained that by the period of 1968 to 1971 the school would provide at least a five form entry school with 30 pupils per form.

As the numbers of pupils involved would result in at least 600 by the end of a four year period, the Local Education's plan to provide for them in Etwall meant they would have to be transported there. "This would leave large numbers of children waiting by the side of busy roads and they would have to travel along a main road even if the projected by-pass materialises."

The health of the children also needed to be considered, having to wait in all weathers. This had already been experienced, the report commented, by children travelling to Ashbourne Grammar School.

It was pointed out in item six that the Education Authority representatives had refused to deny that some form of comprehensive education on the Etwall site was their ultimate aim. Mickleover residents felt that such education would be inferior to that provided already. This, the Minister was informed, was evident at a parish meeting. To enlarge Etwall to a seven form entry school would also prejudice the standard of education with a lack of personal contact between staff and pupils.

The final objection was the lack of out-of-class activity for the children which was "so valuable at the Secondary School stage." Also, the contact between parents and teachers, "so well established at Mickleover schools, would be severely restricted."

New members of staff at the Infants' School were Mrs Doris Maéné who was to take Class 4, and temporary teacher Mrs Emma Brierley, Class 5.

Grandfather found the miserable weather in the first weeks of the year quite depressing. "Perhaps the enforced rest of the last twelve days or so will not do me any harm, although I shall be glad to be able to go walking again."

As the sub-postmaster, Bert Davies, was granted immediate release from his appointment on medical grounds, the sub-Post Office at Western Road was closed in December 1958. The new owners of the shop were Tom and Edith Smith. They would be licensed to sell stamps, and hopefully, the parish council thought, the post box would remain at the premises.

When the new appointment was advertised, nearby building development was taken into consideration and it was decided that a Post Office would be opened in February at the new shopping precinct in Devonshire Drive. The successful applicant was Derek Butterworth.

The development of a partly residential Training College with playing fields, for approximately 400 mixed teachers, was being suggested at Mickleover. Part of Rough Heanor Farm was being considered on behalf of the Diocesan Training College. The owners of the land were still the Sheffield Regional Hospital Board and forty acres would be required for the college, on a total land area of 190 acres.

All Saints' PCC called an Emergency Meeting on February 1st, to be held after the evening service at 7.45pm. The Reverend Ben Crockett, chairman, opened the meeting and explained that he had written to the archdeacon to enquire about appointing a Stipendiary Reader. The Archdeacon replied that a part-time Assistant Priest would be most favourable. He suggested Father Ivan Joseph Harris, a retired Mechanical Engineer who had been ordained in August 1957, after being a lay reader for many years.

The Vicar had met Father Harris who had confirmed that he was willing to be transferred from Boulton St Mary's, Alvaston. He wished to continue his duties as Chaplain of the Manor Hospital but he would undertake all services and parish requirements in the Vicar's absence. He had not previously used vestments but was prepared to accept the wearing of them.

Father Harris' means of travel was a motor scooter and public transport but he was prepared to purchase a car. Until this was obtained his salary would be £175 per annum (£130 stipend and £45 expenses). The diocese were willing to grant £50 per annum towards an Assistant Priest's salary. The Bishop had said that a full-time offer of help was not yet called for but he was willing to transfer Father Harris as Mickleover had a greater need.

The Reverend Crockett said this was the first offer of help during his fourteen years' ministry at Mickleover. He continued to explain that the population was now 8,000 and would soon be in the region of 15,000.

Percy Pickering said the church could not afford a full-time Priest even if one were available, but explained that the £156 per annum interest on the sale of Denton House would more than meet an Assistant Priest's salary at the moment.

At the February meeting, Les Miller, clerk, was asked to remind the RDC that the provision of public conveniences in Mickleover, discussed over many years, had been raised by Mickleover Women's Institute. The council now required a "full indication of the present position in the matter."

The Divisional Education Officer, Roland Heath-Smith, informed the School Managers that the authority proposed a further two-form infants' school in the 1959/60 Building Programme. This would be followed by a correspondent junior school on the same site but yet to be programmed.

"When the new infants' school is in course of erection, the Managers would have to be consulted in defining suitable catchment areas for the two infants' schools."

He said it was doubtful if the authority would add any further building in the old school as it already contained classrooms surplus to required accommodation. These "could eventually be developed for the purpose for which the Managers had in mind." Junior School headteacher, Jimmy Best, thought they would have to make use of the Derwent Hut on the old school site when a further member of the teaching staff arrived in September.

However, the Managers thought additional accommodation should be provided on the Junior School site by the provision of temporary hut classrooms. This would mean the children would take part in the corporate life of their school.

Grandfather made note of houses being erected by H J Warner in between Hartington Way and Western Road (Portland Close). He went a walk to the end of Staker Lane. "In a chat with the road man he told me that work had begun on the by-pass road." He would have been referring to the Lichfield to Burton-on-Trent section.

Photo courtesy of the Derby Evening Telegraph
Horace Warner at the Derby and District Association of Building Trades Employers dinner.

Following a letter to the Divisional Commander further complaints had been made about the behaviour of members of the newly named British Voluntary Ambulance and Nursing Service who were hiring part of the Infants' School. The leader, Mr D Gutteridge, was asked to attend the next meeting of the School Managers.

He was told that the cadet unit could have the use of a room and the hall one evening during the school's Easter holiday, and then it would depend on the satisfactory behaviour of the cadets.

The County Council wrote to the parish council to say that if the decision to extend Etwall Secondary School was agreed then a provision would be made for a swimming pool as part of the facilities. However, if Mickleover was to have a new secondary school, a swimming pool would not be included because of the cost.

The parish council replied that the facility would be patronised by the village and should not relate to the question of whether or not a secondary school is to be built in Mickleover.

The Area Planning Officer made note of two basic provisions for open space north of Western Road. One on the green wedge from Devonshire Drive, extending east and the other a major playing field area on the northern periphery of the housing development.

He said the green wedge had been excluded from housing development and was agreed in principle by the parish council in April 1957. He thought in addition to a children's amenity, provision for tennis may also be possible.

The envisaged northern limit of housing "is very approximately about the line that runs from Station Road by the house 'Sunningdale' [Mill Lane] and the major playing field would be be between here and the railway."

He continued: "It is difficult to indicate a specific site at the moment, as the matter may well be affected by the question of siting a secondary school in this area. This question has yet to be resolved, though in any event, there should be an adequate area available for playing fields."

The long awaited statement by the Derbyshire Education Committee on their policy on the re-organisation of secondary education was made public in the last week of March. It named the abolition of the "eleven-plus" system of selection as an objective for the future; favoured comprehensive schools in principle; and declared an alternative system of junior and senior secondary schools.

From April 1st 1956 tenants of council houses became responsible for interior decoration and for some items which included renewal of tap washers, replacing broken or cracked squares of glass and repairs to hat and coat rails.

Reports on the workings of the scheme was explained at the RDC Housing and Town Planning and Plans Committee meeting.

Some items had to be reported to the council such as repairs to electrical and gas equipment, clearing sink, bath and lavatory basin wastepipes and blocked drains. The tenants were warned of the danger of inexperienced persons attempting to repair electrical and gas apparatus. Payments for lodgers had been introduced in 1950. These were generally parents of the tenant and his wife. There were cases of both parents living in council houses.

For the first time Custom clearance facilities came into operation at Derby Airport, Burnaston. Before then the planes flying to Jersey had to divert to Birmingham.

"There is only one way to keep Mickleover from becoming surburban, and it is to have a village hall," said Councillor David Rowen when the question was brought up once again at the April parish meeting.

Because of the lack of demand, Edward Gothard said he was against the idea. He added that if it was decided to put up a village hall "it would be a dead loss by the time the novelty had worn off."

Photo courtesy of the Derbyshire Advertiser

Pupils at Mickleover County Junior School who gained success at the Derby and Derbyshire Musical Festival. Top: The choir won a shield and first prize in a hymn singing class. They were also awarded an honours certificate and gained second place in another class. Above: Members of the recorder group, who gained second and third places.

Agreeing with Mr Gothard, Thomas Whittingham said: "Had there been demand, the Memorial Hut would have been developed and would not have been in the state it now was."

It was suggested by the chairman, Sydney Clarke, to leave the matter in abeyance and for the council to take no further action.

The chairman of the RDC Housing Committee reported that the sub-committee, with the chairman and representatives of the parish, investigated the possibility of further housing sites for the elderly in the parish.

Six were looked at, the first being the orchard belonging to Ivy Farm (from Limes Avenue to the Nag's Head Hotel), together with additional land to the rear, in the ownership of Charles Ayre. "This site lends itself to development for old peoples bungalow's and would accommodate approximately 14 units," said the report.

Site number two was the field behind the Methodist Church in Station Road, forming part of Donald Watson's farm.

"Access could be gained either from Park Road or probably via the large garden to the house adjacent to the church in Station Road," the report noted.

The sub-committee also thought that access could be gained if developed in conjunction with site three. This was adjacent to the above but near Warner Street and also forming part of Watson's farm. The two fields together would accommodate approximately 30 houses they thought.

The fourth site comprised the four houses and gardens of numbers 64-70 Station Road in the ownership of Joe Nadin, together with additional lands and an orchard also belonging to Mr Nadin.

"This site would be rather difficult to develop as the existing houses would have to be demolished to gain access to Station Road. In addition the orchard becomes waterlogged in wet weather." Approximately 12 old people's bungalows could be developed on this site.

A frontage site at Havenbaulk Lane of approximately 110 yards between numbers 49 and 73 was suggested for site five. Twelve houses could be accommodated here without site development works, announced the report. "Provision would have to be made for agricultural access at one end of the site."

The final site opposite the above would be a continuation of the existing council housing development on the south-western side of Havenbaulk Lane towards the junction with Staker Lane.

"It is not expected that planning consent will be given for this as it constitutes ribbon development." Plans for the sites were submitted to the County Planning Department and their observations were expected for the next meeting.

The sub-committee also inspected premises in Vicarage Road, consisting of a lock-up garage and extension, which might possibly be demolished to provide a site for a public convenience. A preliminary application was made to the County Planning Officer for an additional site where five cottages stood (numbers 6-10 Vicarage Road) which were subject to a Demolition Order. In the meantime the clerk to the RDC, Harry Bailey, was asked to negotiate with the brewery with a view to providing a convenience at the Masons Arms.

At the Annual Parochial Church Council Meeting the Reverend Ben Crockett said "we are making history at this annual meeting as it was the first at which an Assistant Priest had been present, and how fortunate we are in having such a valued friend on the staff."

On April 12th I went to see grandfather, the day before I was to leave for my National Service. I had attended a medical examination and went through the process of either taking an examination or an interview, memory fails me, to determine which service I would join.

The author's National Service Record!

I was sent the relevant paperwork to report to Cardington, the reception station for the RAF. Now completely resigned to carry out two years in an alien environment, I was hoping at some time to be sent to Germany where my work colleagues had served with some interesting experiences.

It was not to be. Having to attend a further medical on my second day of service I was informed by the Medical Officer that he had received a letter from my doctor in Mickleover, Doctor Charlton (Senior), explaining that I suffered from migraine. Within a very short time I was issued with only a train pass enabling me to return to Derby and nothing else. I had the company of another recruit from Birmingham, but it must have been my lucky day as I found a sixpenny coin on the station platform.

Although I was given a rank and number I was never issued with a uniform!

I arrived home without being able to inform my family about my discharge. No mobile phones then! Having no door key, my father opened the door and with little questioning announced my return. My mother, having accepted that it was true, shouted from the kitchen: "It can't be, his bedding hasn't been dried and aired."

National Service came to an end in December 1960, but my friend Jim Nixon was one of the unlucky ones, joining the RAF in July 1960. Ken Guy received notification that he would not be called up.

Following the recent survey, formal planning application was made to develop the two fields which formed part of Watson's Farm between the Methodist Church and Vicarage Road, and used for the building of old peoples' bungalows.

Mickleover Parish Council had reminded the RDC that they did not wish to

Photo courtesy of the Derby Evening Telegraph

Mickleover Amateur Dramatic Society performed The Chiltern Hundreds on April 18th. Back: Don Jackson, David Rowen, Donald Potter, Wendy Gardner, Ron Buchanan. Below: Edna Ford, Lois Dracup, Ann McCutcheon.

acquire the green wedge of Devonshire Drive and asked them to look again at their objections regarding dampness etc. The clerk asked whether the fields OS numbers 45 and 46 were still available (see map p100). This was the site suggested by them.

The Area Planning Officer replied by asking the parish council to revise their decision on the green wedge for open space. He said the fields they referred to have been the subject of planning consent for housing and a Roman Catholic primary school "with the undrainable part of the fields to be used as school playing fields."

On April 29th Uncle Tom went to Smith's Nursery in Station Road to purchase Sweet Peas for grandfather. "He brought me three dozen good plants, 3s. He only asked for two dozen!"

At the beginning of May grandfather "went a walk via Pastures Hospital. Saw a group of patients in the fields in the care of two nurses. One of them a bit intractable. Felt sorry for the women and admired the nurses for their vocational duty."

Recruits in Psychiatric Nursing received £335 per annum at the age of eighteen, increasing to £350 when they reached nineteen and £370 at the age of twenty.

Derbyshire Education Authority would not agree to the erection of temporary huts at the Junior School. The Divisional Education Officer was of the opinion that the school hall at the Infants' School could be used until the Infants' School now referred to as "off Devonshire Drive" was ready for occupation. He also informed the School Managers that this new school would be used for juniors and infants in the first instance.

Mrs Maggie A Simnett had become a new member of staff at the Infants' School on Uttoxeter Road, and the suggestion that Miss Wibberley be appointed Deputy headmistress was turned down by the Authority.

The RDC purchased the cottages 1-8 at Alma Heights together with gardens, being 552 yards. "There is now sufficient room, after the demolition, for the erection of one pair of houses."

Fred Bailey, RDC clerk, had written to the Executors of the late W H Watson stating that the District Valuer would negotiate in acquiring the cottages in Vicarage Road for public conveniences and car parking.

Conversion of the shop at 16 The Square into Fried Fish and Chip Shop was granted but, as with many applications, complications began to occur.

Residents in the Wimpey development had asked Trent about the provision of a bus service in the area. Trent requested a meeting with members of the parish council to discuss various proposals.

On May 16th grandfather walked to Black Wood. "Brook bridge has been repaired." However at the parish council meeting ten days later Les Miller, Parish Clerk, was asked to inform the County Surveyor that the bridge over the stream had collapsed further. "If it became necessary to replace the bridge, we hope the type of construction will be in keeping with the surroundings."

An investigation was required by the Medical Officer of the RDC after complaints that Bramble Brook was becoming a nuisance to the public health. Rats had been seen in the Sydney Close area and may have come from the vicinity of the brook. Unfortunately the Rodent Officer was unable to make a full inspection because it was overgrown with hawthorn and obstructed in parts with rubbish and building materials.

The Chief Public Health Inspector stated that "the general condition of Bramble Brook is unsatisfactory and it requires thorough cleansing," which he believed to be the responsibility of the riparian owners (bank of the brook).

Having spoken to the builders who had erected notices prohibiting the depositing of rubbish, the Inspector added that apart from the occasional misuse of surface water drains by residents discharging soapy water, there was no danger to public health.

In 1959 a good deal of the land belonging to Mill Farm was sold, eventually to

Courtesy of Barry Hanson

Mill Farm before it was demolished in the 1970s.

build Onslow Road. This meant that dairy farming could no longer continue as it was not practical to drive the dairy cows along Station Road to the remaining fields.

The monthly cheque received from the Milk Marketing Board was much healthier than it is today, so the Hanson family had now to rely on the sale of eggs, chickens and potatoes for their income. At the appropriate time of year plums and damsons were available.

Barry Hanson remembers his boyhood days on the farm when the sheaves of corn were removed from the barn and "thrashed", separating the stalks and chaff from wheat. "A farming contractor would be hired with their powerful, green Marshall tractors and thrashing and baling machines," he says.

All the labour, local farmers, worked for the meals provided but they expected the courtesy to be reciprocated when it was their turn.

Mickleover Royal British Legion requested the council to give consideration to having the name of Sgt L G Bentley added to the War Memorial. A wireless operator in the RAF, Sgt Bentley was killed in action on July 28th 1943 and his home address was "Grove Cottage", Vicarage Road. His parents however, had moved to Kirk Langley when the Roll of Honour was drawn up.

At the May parish council meeting the clerk, Les Miller, reported that John Smith and Company (Derby), had indicated that the name of Sgt L G Bentley could be inserted by a strip on the 1939/45 War Memorial plaque, but F Garratt and Son, who had fixed the plaque, had informed him that the removal for the work to be done and the subsequent re-fixing "presented almost insuperable difficulties in that it was secured with a self-locking device which would make it necessary to deface the War Memorial itself to carry out the work."

The Royal British Legion was informed that the council was unable to take any action in the matter. The Vicar was asked to include the words "and others who we may not know of," or similar, to be said at the Memorial Services.

Repton Rural District Council issued Public Notices in the local press stating that various public paths were being deleted as rights of way. In Mickleover the path from the north end of Chevin Avenue leading over the railway tunnel to Radbourne Lane was one. The other was the footpath which had been in discussion with Harry Petts off Station Road in 1954 (see Chapter One).

The Nestlé Company Ltd again running a recruitment campaign this time for were advertising for young men and women in the Spring 1959 "with an initial education to at least GCE passes at Ordinary Level and willing to undergo further training." Promotion was emphasised to those who would accept transfer to other parts of the country or possibly abroad. Vacancies were available in Accounting and Costing, Laboratory Control and Production and also Maintenance Engineering.

An industrial dispute affecting the whole of the printing trades developed into being the most serious industrial stoppage since the General Strike of 1926. By June 20th work had ceased throughout the greater part of the industry, the only major section not involved were the national newspapers covered by a separate employers' organisation.

My family was affected, Auntie Hilda Straw worked for Simpsons' the printers in Friar Gate, as did my friend Peter Hallam. Cousin Tony was an apprentice at Derby Printers, and was, like myself and Peter, not affected by the loss of work as we were apprentices. As weeks went by the stoppage had an ever-widening effect on industry and commerce.

Grandfather wrote: "Peter is at work by virtue of being an apprentice on the paper *Derbyshire Advertiser*. He and another apprentice are doing the necessary typography on a necessarily reduced paper."

The imposed pages were dispatched and printed at the Avian Press, a subsidiary of the *Derbyshire Advertiser* at Ashbourne, which was not involved in the strike. We apprentices went to help with the printing and packing.

The County Surveyor, Stanley Mehew, informed the parish council "that the bridge near Black Wood had suffered severe malicious damage" and arrangements were being made for the bridge to be patched up and re-erected.

Although he appreciated it should be in keeping with the surroundings, he felt that in view of the type of vandalism he did not feel any great expenditure could be justified in providing a new bridge.

The children's' play equipment at the playing fields had been re-sited to the north but the see-saw, which had been out of use since before 1948, was written off as scrap. Builders, A L Bradley, were given the job of providing an additional access to the fields at the north-east corner.

Miss Lizzie Everitt, Matron of Pastures Hospital for the past twenty years, retired. Miss Everitt began her nursing career in Birmingham in 1926 and spent 18 months at Derby City Hospital before going to Mickleover in 1930, nine years before being appointed matron. Miss Annie G Jeffreys, Assistant Matron, also retired. The new Matron was Mrs Vivian Auton.

On June 26th the Minister of Education approved Derbyshire County Council's proposal to enlarge Etwall Secondary School to take several hundred Mickleover children. A council deputation had met the Parliamentary Secretary in May following local objections to the scheme saying that the proposal "seemed a bit unreasonable." A spokesman for the Education Committee declined to comment on the Minister's decision other than to say it was in line with the committee's plans. It now meant that a secondary school would not be built in Mickleover.

An interested resident told the *Derby Evening Telegraph* that it was disappointing. "There should have been an enquiry so that people could express their views."

In early July the headmaster of the Junior School, Jimmy Best, gave a talk to parents of the children who were transferring from the Infants.

At the School Managers meeting the Divisional Education Officer, Roland Heath-Smith, considered that their estimated numbers on the register as over-optimistic. He said the existing accommodation, including the huts on the Infants' School site, and school halls, would have to be used to full capacity until the new school was ready for occupation which he thought would be September 1962.

He added that the Managers had no power to expend money on displaying notices in the village requesting parents to register the names of children who would require places at the Infants' School.

After discussion the School Managers agreed that the headteachers should display posters in shops in the village. These invited parents to inform them in writing. A notice was also published in the *Derby Evening Telegraph* at the Managers' expense.

All Saints' PCC were making headway into a Christian Giving Campaign to increase the churches contributions from £12.10s.0d per week to £29.

The Campaign Committee had decided to divide the parish into seven areas but unless enough helpers came forward it would probably be necessary to omit the Rykneld Road area.

Courtesy of G A Yeomans

On August 2nd 1959 the last excursion trains from Mickleover departed for Skegness and Dudley Zoo. When Godfrey Yeomans took this photograph in May 1959 the platform at the station was now becoming overgrown with grass and weeds.

Invitations to a free dinner were to go out to 450 families and it was hoped all of them would be represented at one of the five dinners which would be held in the Nag's Head Hotel. It would be there that the purpose of the campaign would be explained.

It was hoped to commence the campaign during the first week in September, continuing for eight weeks and ending on All Saints' Day when the Bishop of Derby would be present at Evensong.

The expenditure would have to be raised by cashing in investments, an overdraft, or by loans to be paid back within one year, free of interest. Arthur Morley offered a loan of £400. Father Ivan, on behalf of the council, thanked Mr Morley for his generous offer.

The summer of 1959 was described as the driest in 200 years and it was extremely hot for a number of weeks. This presented a problem for the production at Nestlé's factory as the chocolate on the biscuits would not set.

The main product lines were all chocolate coated; prize bars, chocolate fingers and animal shapes. Chocolate along with bulk milk, condensed milk and sugar was delivered by tankers and packaging was brought in, probably once a day, from Parcel Terrace in Derby.

The whole operation, including labelling, was carried out on the site. As they had an air conditioned warehouse the finished products were delivered weekly in their small fleet of vans.

In a perverse kind of way I was disappointed when the printing strike came to an end, as it was a period when I gained more skills in newspaper production, achieved by sheer persistence and imagination.

The Junior School opened after the midsummer holiday with 335 children. One class was housed in the Medway Hut on the Infants' School site, half-a-mile away from the main building. Changes in the staff included Miss Jean Bunting arriving straight from College, Carol Hammerton took charge of a second year group and Miss C Heywood replaced Margaret Lowe. Maggie Simnett became a new member of staff at the Infants' School.

Don Barnes, caretaker at the Junior School, was appointed as part-time groundsman in preference to a maintenance contract. At the Infants' School his father, William Barnes, retired as caretaker and was replaced by Mr Percy G Warner.

Two interesting notes recorded in grandfather's diary during early September began on the 9th: "There is water in the cattle trough down The Hollow and it is running from a pipe leading from a natural supply." Internationally, on the 13th: "The Russians announced that they had hit the moon with a missile [Lunik II] tonight." Britain had announced its own success two months earlier when the hovercraft made its first Channel crossing from Dover to Calais, in just over two hours, and a transatlantic record flight was set up by a Vickers "Vanguard" turbo-prop airliner covering 2,500 miles in $5\frac{1}{2}$ hours.

It was announced at the parish meeting that they had requested junior library facilities as the demand had become evident. The County Council Librarian had agreed that, although they were needed, he was not optimistic about their provision.

He said that Mickleover residents had brought up the subject some time ago, but nothing could be done because the accommodation at the Memorial Hut was far from satisfactory for the present facilities. It was indicated that the solution would be found in the building of the proposed new library, although no idea could be given as to when the work would commence.

The parish council was informed in October that provision had been made for a junior library in the 1960/61 spending. "Bookcases and books will be ordered as soon as possible." The council hoped it would not be too long before it was operating "even if it was on a temporary and somewhat inadequate basis."

The "Robin" in Devonshire Drive opened for the first time on Monday, September 11th. It was the eleventh Offilers house to be built since the Second World War. A sporting theme was chosen for the bar with novelty wallpaper depicting a golf course and another showing racing cars at speed. Even the beer handles sported a small figure playing golf.

Kenneth Howe was the first manager, and he had been assisting at a licensed hotel in Staffordshire. In October 1960 the licence was transferred to Ronald George Leach.

A village hall was again discussed at the September parish council meeting. Les Miller, Parish Clerk, explained that a 60 year loan at $5\frac{1}{2}$ per cent interest would cover half yearly payments on £12,000 capital cost. He added that it would not include running costs.

David Rowen said that building on a large scale would last for many, many years. "It is no use building a small village hall if the village was going to expand and expand."

Edward Gothard said that if they were to be taken as separate items it would cost more. "If we are going to do anything, we must tackle it as a whole," he added.

Mr Thomas O Topsham of Topsham Stores, Vicarage Road, informed the parish council that residents were talking about the need for a Post Office on the estate. The council thought the matter of a further Post Office should be deferred until development of the new estates had been completed.

Councillor Rowen resigned from the parish council because he was leaving Mickleover to take up an appointment in Bristol. William E (Bill) Hallam from Rykneld Road filled the casual vacancy.

Grandfather wrote in September that "buses have commenced running around Brisbane Road." However objections were made by the residents of Devonshire Drive for the use of their road by a new bus service. An organised petition was sent to the Ministry of Transport.

Councillor Spilsbury said that behaviour in the Devonshire Drive area "were worse than slums the way children are allowed to run the streets." He continued: "If parents would keep their children off the roads there would not be so much danger. There is a complete disregard for road safety."

The parish council decided to take no action but directed the clerk to request the Trent Company to arrange for the 8.35am service from Derby to proceed via the Darwin Road loop, in order to serve the needs of children going to the Infants' School on Uttoxeter Road.

On September 23rd grandfather noted that "the chimney at the old factory, now used as a builder's yard near the station, has been taken down." Uncle Tom commented about a new fruit shop being opened at 2 Station Road.

On October 8th the Infants' School was closed for the General Election. "We watched election results programme on TV. I soon saw the tendency of the complete results and so went to bed," commented grandfather. The Conservatives won easily with 365 seats, Labour 258 and Liberal 6. He observed on the 15th that a wall had been built at the front of the Memorial Hut.

Courtesy of G A Yeomans

This interesting photograph taken by Godfrey Yeomans shows not only Mickleover Station and the signal box but on the top left Nestlé's factory under construction and probably the last photograph of the chimney of the old brickworks. (See Book One).

Criticism of the use of classrooms at Mickleover Infants' School by pupils of the Junior School were voiced by parents at a meeting held at the Junior School on October 14th.

Concern had been felt by some parents as children in the Lower III form had to walk from one school to another for lessons.

Arthur Ravensdale had arranged the meeting so that Roland Heath-Smith, Divisional Education Officer, could attend and speak to the parents about the present and future accommodation difficulties. He explained that since the opening of the County Junior School there were two classrooms not in use in the Infants' School. It was those that were being used for the overflow. The School Managers were very concerned about the use of the hall for physical education as other activities needed the space.

The situation would only improve when the new school was built in 1961/62 on the east of the parish, said Mr Heath-Smith and pressure could not be brought on the Education Authority to bring forward the building until all the present available accommodation was in use.

At the annual dinner of Mickleover Golf Club on October 16th, club captain, Ernest Nix Gray, said that in spite of the scare about the new road cutting through the clubhouse, and the reported sale of the course for building land, "the latter, a rumour without foundation."

Overall the club had enjoyed a successful season. There had been record entries for the club competitions and the success of the junior members had been most gratifying, he added. Mr Gray was the manager at the Westminster Bank, Iron Gate, Derby.

Mickleover Sports Club informed the parish council that the Derby and District Football League were unhappy with the pavilion facilities at the playing fields.

The parish council had earlier decided to take no further action regarding the lighting of the pavilion by the East Midlands Electricity Board. The Board had said that it would cost about £20 to lay a point to the lavatories, leaving the extension from there to the pavilion to be provided by the council which would be £45 extra overhead, and £60 underground. The council authorised the purchase of not more than two pressure oil lamps for lighting the pavilion.

They wrote to the Sports Club saying that as sports and recreational facilities throughout the parish were under consideration, which may involve the provision of new pavilion facilities, they could not contemplate incurring expenditure on the present building.

Account for the Mickleover Sports Club Dance in April

On October 28th grandfather "saw on television the first showing of the Russian photographs of the dark side of the moon." The following day he was shown round the grounds outside the old Manor House, "now used as an annexe by the Pastures Hospital. The patients seem to be well cared for."

Two new wards had been opened at Pastures Hospital, named Walton, holding 16 patients for women and Melbourne a mens' ward. Mr A V Martin, Chairman of Sheffield Regional Hospital Board, said: "In four years time there will be very few wards in hospitals in the whole region that had not been modernised."

He added that a good example of the public's new attitude towards these hospitals was the high wall which surrounded the building had now been removed. the former small rooms with heavily barred windows were now wide and airy and the barred windows have disappeared and bigger areas of glass had been used.

The chapel at the hospital had been renovated and re-decorated in August. The building was shared by the Church of England and the Free Churches and the Anglican Church had appointed the Reverend Victor T McClaughry.

Arthur Waplington of Grey Street, Derby, had requested permission to turn the front room of 80 Western Road into a "Gentlemen's Hairdressing Salon", but this led to an appeal against Repton RDC and Derbyshire County Council.

This took place in November and Mr J Barr, representing Mr Waplington said it seemed that the whole crux of the matter was the distinction between a ladies' and gents' hairdresser's establishment.

He added: "What puzzles me is that the RDC, who represents the local people, have granted permission for a ladies' hairdresser's establishment in the same road."

Mr Waplington said he had been a gentlemen's hairdresser for 13 years and he wished to move because of his wife's health. Her doctor had told her she must get away from the centre to somewhere on the outskirts.

H Bailey, Derbyshire County Council Deputy Area Planning Officer, said "At Mickleover it is considered that the two new shopping groups at Vicarage Park and Devonshire Drive, together with the main concentration of older shops on Uttoxeter Road should adequately cater for the future needs of the village. The Minister decided in Mr Waplington's favour in April 1960.

Grandfather: "went out on bus – my first ride on a new bus with engine at the back. You definitely get the sensation of being pushed." Trent had purchased the new Leyland Atlantean buses each having 78 seats.

On taking a stroll along Station Road on November 27th grandfather found "the smell from Nestlé's factory was appetising."

The Parish Council-in-Committee in December reported on their meeting with Mr G L Larkin (Messrs T H Thorpe and Partners, Architects), for the inspection of sites for swimming facilities. The chairman presented an outline scheme for a proposed swimming pool and future community centre to be sited off Station Road, behind the Memorial Hut, "this being the most suitable site from the point of view of obtaining the necessary planning approvals, and other considerations."

It was also proposed that he should approach the owner of the site to ascertain whether or not he would be prepared to sell the land to the council.

Regarding the cattle grazing on the playing field at Havenbaulk Lane, the RDC had informed the council that permission had been granted in June 1951 for a period of ten years. The parish council informed them that they wished to consider purchasing the field for recreation purposes.

The clerk, Les Miller, presented a copy of the Sherwood Foresters' Cottage

Homes Charity which set out that proceeds of the sale of property in North Avenue had benefited non-commissioned officers and men of the Foresters. The regiment's badge can still be seen on the houses in North Avenue.

The Chief Public Health Inspector received a complaint that certain shops in Mickleover were not conforming to the hours of evening closing.

"Rapid urbanisation of the area tends to encourage shopkeepers to stay open later" he said, "and administration had always proved difficult." The closing hours for grocery provision were 8.00pm weekdays and 9.00pm Saturdays, whilst for the sale of table waters, sweets, sugar, confectionery etc the evening closing hours were 9.30pm weekdays and 10.00pm Saturdays.

Wimpeys sought the release of part of the land to the north of their present estate for further development, now that the site was no longer required for a Roman Catholic School.

The clerk stated that the views of the RDC had previously objected to further development on the grounds that this would encroach upon the open space between the residential area and Derby's Mackworth Estate and further difficulties would be experienced in the disposal of sewage and drainage.

The County Planning Authority supported the views of the RDC and had decided the present land could not be released as the site had been reserved for the school and should be used for educational, recreational or institutional purposes. These views would be expressed at any future appeal made by Wimpeys.

The Assistant Chief Constable recommended street lighting at the north end of Station Road for the benefit of the employees of Nestlés' factory who returned home towards Mackworth after dark.

Fewer than 250 people were employed at Nestlés, mainly on a dayshift system, although there was an evening wrapping operation and factory cleaning on night shift. The employees were recruited from Mickleover and Mackworth. Some came by bus from Tutbury as staff numbers had been cut at the Nesmilk factory. Others moved from Ashbourne to Mickleover.

"In the afternoon [Saturday, December 19th], Sheila and her dad called for me with the car and we went to Nellie's for Peter's 21st birthday party, and the celebration of 25 years of married life of Fred and Nellie. It was a very jolly party attended by old and new."

My circle of friends widened after attending college and meeting friends of friends since becoming employed. Most were in the printing trade or banking. One friend who attended my party was the now famous screen, stage and TV actress, Gwen Taylor.

CHAPTER SEVEN
PUBLIC SWIMMING POOL?
1960

The Reverend Ben Crockett told members of All Saints' PCC that part of the Vicarage garden was to be sold because of the widening of Uttoxeter Road and the wall would have to be demolished.

Early in January grandfather walked down Staker Lane and back. "Stimulating, had a chat with road man who gave me an onion in sound condition which he had picked up. This helped to make onion sauce for dinner."

The Secretary of the Royal British Legion Service Committee, had informed the council that the name of Sgt L G Bentley had now been added to the 1939-45 plaque on the Parish War Memorial in the churchyard. The parish council agreed to contribute £5.5s.0d to the work which was carried out by Batterby and Hefford of Derby.

The Infants' School had so many children staying to dinner that they were forced into having two sittings. The police had asked for the assistance of the school to find a suitable person for the school crossing and steps were also being taken to stop vehicles parking outside the school.

The School Managers told Jimmy Best, the Junior School headmaster, that the staff would be increased by two teachers from September. He outlined his proposals for improvising classrooms in the library and in the entrance hall. He was considering bringing back the detached class at the Infants' School to the main

Photo courtesy of Chris Brown

The garden at the old Vicarage.

Photo courtesy of the Derby Evening Telegraph
Mickleover Brownie Pack's annual party in the Church Hall, Limes Avenue.

school at half term and replacing it with the Upper II with teacher Ann Ellis. This would become the detached class.

Mickleover Parish Council-in-Committee discussed the proposed new swimming facilities and community centre having received a notice from the RDC granting permission to develop the 3.38 acres of land behind the Memorial Hut. This was on condition that no work should commence until detailed drawings of the proposal had received the approval of the Local Planning Committee.

However the full council were informed that planning approval had already been given for private housing development on this site. Former butcher, Arthur Platts, the owner of the land, had informed the RDC that he could not enter into any further negotiations. This didn't prevent the parish council's application being published in the *Derby Evening Telegraph* on February 2nd 1960.

The belief that Mickleover residents felt that the new facilities would be built behind the Memorial Hut is highlighted in the minutes of Mickleover Sports Club, football section on February 9th. It was suggested that "the Secretary write to the parish council enquiring about their plans for facilities at the playing fields, now that the swimming baths were to be situated behind the Memorial Hut."

The main object of the meeting was to assess the number of players in both

Photo courtesy of the Derbyshire Advertiser

On February 16th Grandfather wrote of traffic being directed down Station Road and Western Road "owing to mishap by the brook on Uttoxeter Road." The hedge at the junction of Uttoxeter Road and Cavendish Way saved the lorry from skidding off the road and dropping 20 feet into the field in one of several accidents caused by snow and ice. Right: In recent times new safety barriers have been erected where the accident took place.

the first and second eleven teams. "Players had been crying off somewhat regularly," said Football Manager, Dick Kenderdine.

He went on to say that there were still no official trainers for either side and he had only players to discuss selection of the second team.

Thirty two players had signed on but only 23 were playing on a regular basis and the Manager stated that the "players met very little off the field." Despite all this, the first team had reached the Semi-Final of the Divisional Cup which was to be played at home. Players were asked to sell tickets and although it was not possible to count the number of spectators, a third of the money taken went to the club. Those who were not able to play in matches were asked to return their shirts.

Les Miller, clerk, told the council that enquiries were still being made into supplying the allotments in Vicarage Road with running water. He said the esti-

Photos courtesy of Ann Ellis

The Junior School had to have a detached class at the Infants' School on Uttoxeter Road in 1960. The infants were replaced by Miss Ellis's Upper II Class after half-term.

mated cost would be about £60. A warning was given that rents would have to go up, "probably by about 2s.6d," if water was laid on.

On March 8th grandfather wrote: "The Vicarage wall is being taken down and some trees in the Vicarage garden. This is opening up the view towards the church," he wrote. A week later, "work is proceeding on corner against Vicarage. Tons of soil being moved."

The early meetings of the RDC Housing and Town Planning Committee continued to be busy with Mickleover business. They were informed that Arundel Avenue had now been adopted by the Derbyshire County Council as "a publicly repairable highway." An order for Compulsory Acquisition of 3.5 acres of land at Holly End, Vicarage Road, was made in readiness for the building of old people's bungalows.

Application was granted for the use of the bungalow/shop at 124 Vicarage Road as a fried fish and chip shop following an earlier refusal for a similar business at 20 Vicarage Road.

This led to a Public Inquiry which was held in Derby on March 9th. William (Bill) Varey, the applicant, was keen to convert an outbuilding into a shop at his premises, formerly Holly Bush Farm.

Mr F W Barnett, acting for Bill Varey, said that there had been various fish and chip shop businesses in the locality, one had been situated opposite Mr Varey's premises which had changed to a greengrocery business. Harry Thornhill had opened a chip shop just after the Second World War but he could not compete with Foster's at the corner of Warner Street and Meddings in Park Road.

"The fact that there was a need for a fish and chip business in the area was borne out by the fact that permission had been given for such a shop at The Square, next to the Masons Arms," he said.

From outside information he said he knew that the shop would not now be opened. Mr H Crossley, for Derbyshire County Council, told the Inspector that he had also heard the information.

The outcome of Miss Shotton's old shop was settled and Mr J D D'Arcy Clarke began to advertise "The Antique Shop, 16 The Square, Mickleover" on a regular basis in the *Derbyshire Advertiser* in September.

Mr Barnett went on to say that since Bill Varey had applied, permission had been granted for a similar shop on the Vicarage Park Estate and Mr Varey was to serve the whole of Mickleover and not just for the benefit of the estate.

Answering questions about parking, Bill Varey said there was no need for parking on the road if his shop was set back and he had a yard at the rear where customers could park.

Mr Crossley for the County Council said that if Mr Varey's proposal was approved, it would be likely to embarrass the Council in carrying out a policy designed to ensure the grouping of shops, and it was considered that if the sale of fish and chips was to be carried on in a residential suburb, it was essential that it should be located in a shopping group.

The appeal was turned down by the Minister at the end of April. He said "it would be detrimental to the visual and residential amenities and quietude of nearby dwelling houses, particularly at night."

Residents of the Vicarage Park Estate were to petition the RDC against the use of 124 Vicarage Road as a fish and chip shop and were informed that they were not required to advertise in the local press to object.

A school crossing patrol was now on duty on Uttoxeter Road and the School Managers were informed that the new school had now been included in the 1960/61 Major Building Programme.

As the contractors were still on the Junior School site it was decided to retain the Vicarage Road Playing Field for at least a further twelve months.

Councillor Phillip Spilsbury complained at the March parish council that the "wedge of land [Bramble Brook], originally planned as a public open space was being whittled down gradually." He was commenting on the proposal to build a branch library at one end of the wedge and a suggestion of a church should go at the other. "How do we know when it is going to stop?" he wondered.

Enquiries had also been received from the Federation of Independent Evangelical churches to build on Common Farm (Brisbane Road) where an application to develop the land for shops had been deferred.

Cleveland Petrol Co Ltd had also applied for the site at the corner of Devonshire Drive and Darwin Road as a petrol station.

The council thought the library proposed was a shock as it had hopes of building a community centre in another part of the village, with accommodation for a library.

"I don't think we will get two libraries," said Arthur Ravensdale.

They informed the County Librarian that the site was appropriately located at the Memorial Hut and his proposal would prejudice this and any facilities in due course.

Grandfather was disappointed with the Chancellor of the Exchequer's Budget on April 4th. "Nothing for Old Agers." Two days later Dr Richard Beeching was chosen to head the team to rationalise the rail network just after the last steam locomotive of British Railways had been named.

A committee was appointed comprising chairman Sydney Clarke, Tim Ford, Edward Gothard, Anthony Yeomans and Phillip Spilsbury. G L Larkin was also on the committee in an advisory capacity. The purpose was to discuss further the question of swimming facilities, a library, the community centre and the provision of open space in the parish.

Members of the RDC Housing Committee were concerned about Wimpeys activity in the fields to the north of the parish. Mr Lang, Area Planning Officer understood that only a comparatively small area of land in that area could be drained to the public sewer and it appeared little objection could be made to it being developed, "particularly as the Secondary Modern School will not now be built in this area."

A letter was sent to Wimpeys asking for details of their proposals and for a formal planning application to be submitted for their consideration.

The Reverend Ben Crockett said at All Saints' PCC April meeting that he was encouraged to find Mr and Mrs David Hufton were willing to be Leader and Assistant Leader of the Senior Youth Club.

Ken Taylor reported that they were not getting the £40 per week as hoped for in the Christian Giving Campaign. The offering had risen from £15 to £35 during the first quarter and there were 243 members of the scheme.

Photo courtesy of Geoff Guy

Derby & District Senior League Cup Final 1959-60 at the Baseball Ground. Mickleover Sports Club were the runners-up. Standing left to right: Local referee, Jim Mills, Brian Kenderdine, Brian Swindell, Phil Starkey, Mick Pickering, Alan Smith, Ken Orme, Dick Kenderdine (Manager). Kneeling: Frank Peake, John Raynes, Charlie Kenderdine, Eric Smith, Ken Guy.

Father Ivan Harris said there had been an improvement in attendance at Evensong and Matins, but he was disturbed at the small numbers attending the 9.15 am Service, "considering the amount of communicants there are in the parish."

Derby Corporation announced their proposals at the end of March, for extending the town to well over twice its size. Derby, they said, was in need of money to finance huge development schemes and they were applying to the Local Government Commission for England in the form of answers to a number of questions.

More than half of Mickleover, it was proposed, should go into Derby, namely 1,398 acres of the parishes 2,241 acres whilst 178 acres were proposed to be taken from Radbourne and 47 from the outlying portion of Findern.

In 1951 the areas proposed had a population of 55,246 but in 1959 this had grown to 74,100. The Corporation estimated that by 1978 the population it envisaged taking over would have grown to 114,000.

The Corporation's case, in a nutshell, was that the area it now claimed was the true Derby, containing a population that looked to Derby for its services and to the industries of the borough for jobs for the population.

On the evening of May 6th grandfather "watched TV film of Royal Wedding." Princess Margaret married Antony Armstrong-Jones in Westminster

Abbey. The Director of Education had said that the school would be closed to celebrate the occasion.

The RDC Chief Public Health Inspector described the deterioration of the eight cottages at the Heights of Alma because of damage by children. "I have taken the liberty of a further up-to-date estimate for the demolition of the properties." A quotation of £100 to demolish the cottages and clear the site was accepted.

On May 19th the boys at the Junior School won the football league championship organised by the Trent Valley Primary School Association.

Harry Gaskill, deputy headmaster, was the coach for the first and second teams in football and cricket. In later years Mr Goodman took care of the rest which usually led to over 30 boys taking part in two teams. The teachers were also responsible for blowing up and lacing the footballs.

Coaching the football team made the men teachers very popular with the boys. Holding this position entailed them spending time with them on a Saturday morning and in the evenings during the week. Mr Gaskill sometimes did not arrive home until 7.00pm, having taken the team to an away match. The headteacher, Jimmy Best, would be on the touchline during matches, not, apparently to support the team but to stop any booing, even by the opposition.

The parish council had informed the RDC on several occasions about the defacing of the bus shelter at Cavendish Way "with indecent writing and drawing." It was decided that the in-

Photos courtesy of Harry Gaskill
On May 26th 87 Second Year children from the Junior School visited the Peak District, accompanied by five teachers. Top: The Coffin Well at Tissington. Centre: Examining the stocks at Eyam. Bottom: Trying to answer questions at Treak.

side of the shelters should be heavily creosoted to provide a surface at least "not conducive to writing upon."

Sydney Clarke, chairman reported on the County Council meeting he had attended together with Alan Ratcliff, Phillip Spilsbury and the clerk, Les Miller. It explained the position concerning the Derby County Borough Council's proposals to take over the whole or parts of the rural parishes at present on or near the Borough boundary.

A committee comprising the chairman, vice-chairman, Bill Hallam, Alan Ratcliff and Anthony Yeomans, was to deal with the matter and to draft a statement for submission to the Local Government Commission.

Planning applications submitted to the RDC in May included the rebuilding of the headquarters of Mickleover 124th Boys Scouts Group on land north of Western Road. The scouts were given permission to use the hall at the Infants' School until Easter 1961. Eleven bungalows, south of North Close were to be built by Bolton Builders Ltd. The parish council discussed probable road names and finally decided upon Oak Drive, because of "a row of oak trees behind the road."

Grandfather noted that new electric lamp standards had been erected along the main Uttoxeter Road.

At the opening of the parish council meeting in June the chairman, Sydney Clarke, congratulated Arthur Ravensdale on being awarded the OBE in the Birthday Honours List. Peter Beveridge was having to resign from the council owing to his move to London and Albert Ellis Clarke of Farneworth Road was elected to fill the casual vacancy.

The Playing Fields Committee reported on their inspection of the strip of land adjoining Bramble Brook and it was decided to open negotiations for the acquisition of the land.

A number of residents petitioned the council, alleging "various nuisances arising from the land in its present state." They wished to acquire or lease parts of the land to obviate the problem. The matter was left until the land passed into the council's ownership.

"Old houses at The Alma now all taken down," wrote grandfather in early July. "Fence been created against Vicarage."

The Roman Catholic congregation and residents were becoming embarrassed and frustrated with the Memorial Hut being used for Mass. One of the distractions was the space being used by lively children who became very vocal. This annoyed the curate who bellowed "some of us are trying to damn well pray"!

Committees had been formed and much work was being done towards an

Photos courtesy of Harry Gaskill

Seventy-eight Fourth Year children at the County Junior School and six adults visited London on June 1st. Top: Boarding the boat on the Thames to the Tower of London. Centre: at The Tower. Below: Ready to board the train. Mr Best always carried a black umbrella on the London trips. Not to keep him dry, but to stop the traffic, allowing staff and children to cross the road.

Photo courtesy of Our Lady of Lourdes Archive

A barbecue held in Mickleover Lodge in support of the building fund for a new Roman Catholic Church.

eventual church. Doctor Michael McCahey and his wife Kathleen opened their garden at Mickleover Lodge to set up a barbecue for over a hundred guests.

A storm over education blew up at Mickleover Parish Council meeting on June 21st when a draft statement for submission to the Local Government Commission was debated. They were expressing views on Derby Corporation's boundary proposals.

Arthur Ravensdale commented on a view contained in the statement – drawn up by a sub-committee – that the County Council was making "reasonable provision" for primary education in the parish.

He said "the present junior school was an eight-form school but it would have 12 classes in the next school year. By the time a new infants' school was built it would be equally congested, and another junior school was not yet estimated.

"It is not reasonable provision for Mickleover," he said.

Edward Gothard pressed for the deletion of the word 'reasonable,' and pointed out that if it were included the County Council could later "come back" and say the council said there was reasonable provision in the parish.

With the deletion the draft statement, not yet made public, was approved and every member was handed a copy.

Mr Ravensdale attempted to delay the statement until the parishioners views on the "in or out of the borough" were received.

Sydney Clarke, chairman, said that if the Corporation proposals were allowed the provision for secondary education would not be remedied.

A ward of the borough would be "the replacement of 13 parish councillors, five rural district councillors and one county councillor by, say, two ward representatives." This would mean, they explained, "a drastic diminution in personal contact between the electors and the elected."

Mr Clarke also said that if the Corporation proposals were allowed, Repton Rural District would lose 51 per cent of its rateable value and this would involve an additional rate of 2s in the £.

"There has been no strong expression of opinion from residents of the affected area pressing to be absorbed in the borough; at least some of the new residents of Mickleover who came from Derby have indicated that they did so, among other reasons, to get out of town."

The land adjoining Bramble Brook was owned by a farmer in Allestree and amounted to 5.3 acres. It could be purchased for £4,000 together with costs by the District Valuer.

Parish Clerk, Les Miller, said that $6^{1}/_{4}$ per cent would be required on a £4,000 loan and this would mean a charge of £300 a year for 30 years, making the aggregate cost £8,900.

The District Valuer was also asked to open negotiations with the Exors of W H Watson for the acquisition by the parish council for the field to the south of Vicarage Road Playing Fields. This was with the view to building a swimming pool and future community centre. He also began talks with William Barnes for the land to the rear of Park Cottage, along the western boundary of the playing fields.

Reg Ratcliff was given permission to use the playing fields for organised cricket net practice. The facility would only be used to a limited extent in the year but more fully in 1961 when Mr Ratcliff would have arranged the laying of a proper practice pitch.

Reg was at the forefront of setting up a cricket club which was called The Revels. They had held their Supper and Social earlier in the year at the Memorial Hut when eleven members were presented with a "duck", one of the plastic birds which decorated the top of an iced cake, designed as a cricket pitch.

Dick Kenderdine, football team manager, of Mickleover Sports Club, reported at the July meeting that it had been a successful season with the First Eleven, becoming runners-up in the DFA Divisional Cup and the Section "A" League Cup. "There could be no grumbles about the results," he said. "One remembered two fine Semi-Finals and the Senior Cup match at South Normanton had been a highlight." He added that the club had obvious fighting qualities, but

Photo courtesy of Geoff Guy

On July 15th Mickleover Sports Club became the Butterley Cup Winners at British Railway Cricket Ground. Left to right, top row: Brian Cottington, Ken Guy, Gordon Smith, Maurice Johnson, Brian Kenderdine, John Dolby, Jim Mills. Bottom row: Eric Smith, Charlie Kenderdine, Albert Wilkinson, Phil Starkey, Ken Dolby. Mickleover gained a convincing victory over Chaddesden 2nd by 38 runs. Openers Ken Dolby and Phil Starkey put on 45 runs. In 16 eight-ball overs the total reached 96 for 6. Chaddesden were completely shattered by Gordon Smith's hostile bowling and his 6 wickets for 26 runs helped to confine them to 58 runs for 9 wickets.

injuries had been no help near the end. Charlie Kenderdine and Albert Wilkinson had been chosen to represent Derby Senior League.

The Second Eleven had fallen away, winning only three of the last 21 matches. Many changes had been enforced and deputy goalies were to be thanked. Ken Guy had made a good start in the higher grades he said. He had in fact scored a hat-trick in the 5-2 win over Allenton Athletic in the Derbyshire FA Divisional Cup (South). One can only speculate how many goals he would have scored had he not broken his specs during the game. Dick Kenderdine went on to praise others in the team and highlighted Alan Smith's "wet ground performances."

Robert Edwin Shuttlewood of Park Farm, Burnaston and Margaret Titterton of Bottom House Farm, Burnaston, were married at All Saints' Church, Mickleover on September 7th and on their return from honeymoon they opened their

Photo courtesy of Peter Arnold

The recognised bowlers at Mickleover Royal British Legion green are the parents of Peter Hallam, a friend of the author, Bessie, left, and Bill far right. Arthur Waplington, fourth left, who had just successfully been given planning permission to open his Gents' Hairdressing business in Western Road.

butcher's shop on Western Road which had been disputed by Ernie England, the butcher at Devonshire Drive in June.

Edward Gothard told the parish council that he had attended a meeting at the RDC offices in Burton on September 12th which discussed outline planning applications for residential development off Station Road by Wimpeys.

He stated that the development would take place and following the parish council's intention to acquire land for open space to the north east of the development, the clerk, Les Miller, was directed to obtain a full report on the position of the open spaces in the whole area concerned so they could proceed with the necessary acquisition of land.

The additional land beyond the existing western boundary of Havenbaulk Lane was to be acquired to extend the playing field so preliminary enquiries to the Reverend Ben Crockett would be made in view of the land in question being owned by the Ecclesiastical Commissioners.

Albert E Clarke raised the question of the condition of the pavilion and its facilities, following inspection which he carried out with a representative of the Sports Club.

Edward Gothard said he was aware of a wooden hut which could be purchased second-hand by the council and re-erected at the playing fields to provide pavilion and other facilities at a relatively low cost.

After protracted discussion and in view of the proposals to purchase other land adjoining the playing fields, Phillip Spilsbury moved "that no action be taken in the matter." The notion was not seconded. It was then moved, and seconded that steps be taken to purchase the hut. The approved committee was given the power to act in all aspects to purchase the hut and have it removed and re-erected subject to the total cost not exceeding £500.

On the evening of October 6th a special meeting was held at the South Derbyshire Divisional Education Offices. The managers and headteachers of the two Mickleover schools discussed the provision of school places with Mr Roland Heath-Smith, the Education Officer, in view of the rapid building development in the village.

A questionnaire to the major building contractors operating in the village had revealed that a further 260 houses and bungalows would be completed and ready for occupation in the twelve months ending on August 31st 1961.

Mr Heath-Smith said that owing to certain difficulties it seemed doubtful whether the new Infants' School on the Devonshire Drive site would be completed in time for the Authority to take possession in the middle of August 1961, as originally intended. It would therefore be necessary to use hired accommodation in the village from the beginning of the Autumn term 1961. The new school, he said, would provide places for 240 children in 6 classes and would in the first instance be used for both Juniors and Infants.

School Managers' chairman, Arthur Ravensdale, said that Mickleover parish council had purchased a hut (60' x 25') which was to be erected in the playing field. He thought this hut could be used as a temporary accommodation by the Junior School, provided the parish council was prepared to let it to the Authority.

At the beginning of the new school year in September there were 263 children registered at the Infants' School and Emma Brierley was called in as the number of classes had risen to seven.

Young families arriving in Mickleover were registering their children at the two County Schools. Teacher, Colin F White, and his wife Pat, moved from Leicester in September 1960 with their three young sons Andrew (8), Rodney (5) and Nicholas (1) to a newly-built house in Gisborne Close.

Rod would have found a contrast at the Victorian Infants' School on Uttoxeter Road. "Our class was a double classroom, separate from the main block," he recalls. This was the HORSA classroom which had been erected under an emergency building scheme in 1947 and still stands.

Photo courtesy of the Derby Evening Telegraph

Peter Arnold (right), a member of the 124th (Derby) Mickleover troop, receives his Queen's Scout badge from Mr E Page, Scout District Commissioner for Derby North. This was the sixth Queen's Scouts award gained by the troop. They were making a determined effort to raise funds towards building a new scout hut on the Royal British Legion Memorial Field at this time.

His teacher was Maggie Simnett who he describes as "an exotic teacher: Canadian, lots of hair, and long lacquered nails, which I had never seen before."

The playgrounds were shared with children from the Junior School. "I remember that there was a block of toilets in the middle of the playground: basically a wall with a screen," writes Rod. There were no indoor toilets.

His elder brother, Andrew however, saw the Junior School as a revelation against the old Board School building in Leicester, "more like a factory or warehouse in architecture and not much different in its mode of education. I was taught there in a class of 40 by a Mrs Moody – a well-named woman whom I remember with no affection at all."

He was one of the pupils who had most of their lessons in the hut at the Infants' School. "A few times a week we had to walk between sites, crocodile fashion, to do PE and attend assembly or music in the hall."

His teacher, Miss Ann Ellis, asked him to read aloud in class. At his former school he had been more used to speaking in a dull monotone where all that mattered was to pronounce the words without expression. However Miss Ellis stopped him after a few seconds and made him start again, having made her expectations clear. "I was completely mortified," recalls Andrew.

Ann Ellis had very high standards and soon after his first encounter she asked him to do a piece of writing.

"I produced the five or six lines that I was accustomed to write in half an hour or so, only to be told that this was completely inadequate and that I was to stop in at playtimes until I could produce something more substantial," writes Andrew.

He accepts that Miss Ellis put him under more educational pressure that Mrs Moody ever had. "No doubt it was good for me," he admits.

Miss J Franklin and Miss Audrey M Fearn had joined the staff, along with Miss Sue J Taylor who was a Training College leaver. She recalls her first weeks at the school when the dominance of Mr Best made her fearful of making the slightest mistake. She was not expecting the demand made of her, such as playing the piano. Her first error was to take a flask of tea into the classroom for a drink in mid afternoon when the staff never took a break. With no forewarning Jimmy Best walked into the classroom and admonished her in front of the pupils. Although she concedes that her time at the school was beneficial it was quite stressful.

Twenty-two members attended the first weekly meeting of the Mickleover's new Darby and Joan Club at the Memorial Hut.

The club was organised by Mrs Marjorie M Howarth and a surprise for members was the gift to each of a basket of fruit and flowers from All Saints' Church harvest festival.

The Parish Clerk, Les Miller, had asked the Area Planning Officer if any outline planning applications had been made in respect to Watson's land near the playing fields. He replied that his records revealed no such applications and he did not know if any were imminent. "The present Town Map makes no provision for housing development in the area and any such applications would be refused accordingly," he wrote.

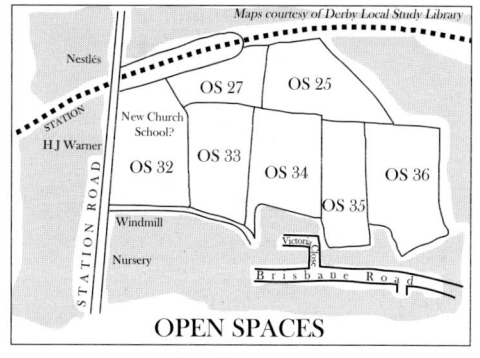

Mickleover Parish Council was told at the October meeting that the Derby Diocesan Education Officer had considered part of the land off Station Road as suitable for the site of a new Church of England Secondary School.

The site was shown on a plan which the Area Planning Officer had submitted to the council after they had requested information on land available for open spaces at the north end of Station Road, before the bridge.

A sketch plan indicated the layout proposals for the area with the site of the

Photo courtesy of the Derby Evening Telegraph

Described as Mickleover's first "American style supermarket", was opened by the famous Brooke Bond TV chimps on October 13th. Proprietor John Jacklin had extended his premises on the corner of Station Road and Park Road. He explained that shoppers would be able to obtain fresh frozen food, and all kinds of groceries, by self-service. Wines, spirits and confectionary, he said, would be obtained from normal counters. Six shop assistants were employed. Local businesses were involved with A L Bradley Ltd, builders of Park Road, the main contractors and the electrical work was carried out by H I Petts Ltd, Station Road. Left: Rosy, the chimp from Hints Zoo near Tamworth (now Twycross), entertains two-year-old Richard Thornhill.

proposed school shown in the angle formed by Station Road and the railway line east of it. To the immediate south of this site, the plan was the area suggested as public open space, comprising a number of fields to the east of the proposed school and housing sites.

Anthony Yeomans said he was in favour of open spaces, but wondered what the land would cost and asked if it could be used for building.

Mr Miller commented that part of the site would be used for housing development and the council instructed him to ascertain whether the open space site was suitable for housing or not, so the council could purchase it for existing use as they decided in April.

Vice-chairman, Arthur Ravensdale, pointed out to members of the public who attended the meeting that land which was suitable for housing, whether it was used or not, had to be bought at housing prices. The council was trying to secure land which was not suitable at a reasonable price, he added.

He went on to accuse the RDC of negligence over the parish council's 14 years old negotiations for public conveniences in the village. He said that if the RDC had "clinched" the matter when they had been asked, the village would have public toilets.

The clerk said that the District Valuer was being delayed in his negotiations for a site in Vicarage Road and it was decided to ask the RDC to look for another site if there was further delay. The yard at the Masons had at one-time been suggested.

Reporting on work on a pavilion for the playing fields, Edward Gothard said that a wooden asbestos-roofed hut had been bought for the pavilion and the foundations were ready to be laid. He said the work was going smoothly and no snags had been encountered, but could not say when it would be completed.

Donald Carr, captain of Derbyshire Cricket Club, was the principal guest at the annual dinner of Mickleover Sports Club at the Nag's Head Hotel on October 28th.

In proposing the toast he referred to its success in winning the Butterley Cup and retaining the Purcell Cup.

Mr C H Marshall, secretary of Derby and District Senior Football League spoke of Albert Wilkinson as "an outstanding personality in local football." He played throughout the season but missed two cup final games owing to injury.

The new sewage disposal works at Bunkers was opened on November 1st. Costing £60,000 they had taken two years to complete and constructed on the same site as the original works built in 1925.

These new works were enough to serve a population of 1,500 and were sufficient until privately developed estates began to appear away from the old village. They were now expected to cope with a population of 9,000.

The Minister of Transport's decision to make an order for the construction of the Mickleover by-pass and link road was reported on November 2nd to Derbyshire County Council.

It stated that the by-pass would run from the Derby to Uttoxeter Road near Huffen Heath to avoid Mickleover on the south, and the link road would join the Derby to Burton road west of Pastures Hill.

Although an Order under the Highway Act 1959 was now under consideration for a new by-pass, engineering details were not yet available. The Parish Clerk applied for detailed plans as soon as possible as they wished to have the opportunity to make observations, particularly with reference to the crossing at the Hollow.

Tributes were paid to Councillor Bower's keen and dedicated work during the time he had been a parish councillor. He had died since the October meeting. Mr Laurence Sydney Stevens was elected to fill the casual vacancy.

John Mellor Bower had been president of Mickleover Produce Association for eight years, a member of the Mickleover Conservative Association for 15 years and for the last six years served on the council.

He retired from the Derbyshire County Police Force in 1939 after being the personal assistant to the Chief Constable. He then became the security officer with the Midland Bank in Derby and took a great interest in the County Junior School, presenting a cup to the class obtaining most points in a bulb growing competition.

Sydney Clarke, chairman, was the representative of the council at a meeting with Trent Motor Traction Co Ltd. He was asked to raise various points regarding bus services beginning with a desirability for a service being provided up Brisbane Road as far as Victoria Close, at least.

The parish council would also be pleased to have the opportunity to comment on any proposals which might be formulated before they were submitted to the Traffic Commissioners. Trent replied that any future plans would be passed to them when they were formulated. They wished to be informed as to the future of East Avenue and the likelihood of it becoming a through road.

Having noted the proposed open space, housing development by Wimpeys and the Church of England Secondary School off the north end of Station Road,

The Derby Diocesan Training College, designed for 40 female students on New Uttoxeter Road, was to be enlarged to cater for 400 by 1962 at a cost quoted to be at least £392,000. The College was now admitting male students and was to offer to selected women students a specialist course in physical education. The management committee acquired 35 acres on "green belt" land off Chevin Avenue, giving enough room for blocks of lecture rooms, halls, gymnasia, offices and one medium sized hostel together with playing fields. Seventy-five per cent of the cost was to be borne by the Ministry of Education and the College found the remainder. It was hoped that when the new buildings were completed in the following September a member of the Royal Family may consent to perform the opening ceremony.

Photo courtesy of the Derbyshire Advertiser

the parish council indicated that when Wimpeys layout was received, access to the open space through the extension of Victoria Close would be safeguarded.

The future link between Buxton Drive and Brisbane Road was at present being prevented by the reluctance of the landowners concerned to sell the necessary land to the developers. However a pedestrian access from Clifton Drive to Gisborne Close would enable residents of the Devonshire Drive area to have reasonable access to the proposed open space.

The *Derbyshire Advertiser* reported on November 11th that John Dicken of Bonehill Farm, off Etwall Road, received compensation for seven heifers and bullocks which were killed by a night goods' train. They had strayed through a gate on to the line between Mickleover and Etwall, where the Meynell Hunt had been earlier.

Mrs C R Farquhar, the wife of Colonel Farquhar, Joint Master of the Hunt, said: "This was an absolute tragedy. We all feel so terrible about it. We have made enquiries and it seems there were some pony tracks around the gate in question and this leaves us to believe that a child might have been responsible, although we are not certain."

Mrs Farquhar added: "We always have a duty gate man to close the gates after the Hunt. This was done during the Hunt on Saturday [November 4th] to the gate we went through, but somebody went through the other gate and left it open." In all 33 beasts strayed on to the line which ran near Bonehill Farm.

Photo courtesy of the Derby Evening Telegraph
Arthur Granville Ravensdale received the insignia of the OBE from the Queen at Buckingham Palace on November 15th. Head of Hardwick Junior Boys' School. He was awarded the MBE in 1955 Birthday Honours List.

Mrs Kathleen Dicken, the wife of the farmer, said "It was just like a battlefield with the cows' bodies all over the place. It is a wonder more were not killed. My husband and I are all for the Meynell Hunt and this has not changed our minds. It could have been anyone who left the gate open, although the Hunt have agreed that we should be paid compensation."

Mr Roland Heath-Smith, the Divisional Education Officer, had approached the Trustees of the Methodist Church with a view to using the hall for teaching purposes. However, owing to many commitments they were not able to accommodate him.

As to the use of the hut at the playing fields, he thought the HM Inspector of

Schools should be approached as to the minimum requirements, particularly toilets, to enable this hut to be used. He thought the parish council would give sympathetic consideration to providing the necessary facilities.

Grandfather attended the Old Age Pensioners' tea and social at the Memorial Hut on December 3rd. "Won 1 cwt of coal in the lottery." On the 14th, "street lamps have been erected beyond the factory [Nestlés] to Mackworth Estate." Three days later he "went shopping at new shops on Fryers estate [Devonshire Drive]. Bought a new saucepan, $^1/_2$ gallon 12s.6d."

On December 19th the Reverend Ben Crockett welcomed the Bishop of Derby, the Reverend Geoffrey Allen, and the Archdeacon to the PCC meeting to seek their opinion on the possibility of a new church being built in Mickleover.

The Bishop said, "it was our duty to keep alive pastoral work in the new housing areas, therefore a place of worship should be within reasonable distance of the houses concerned."

The Archdeacon told the PCC that the Diocesan Pastoral Committee had met the Standing Committee at Mickleover Vicarage and a new site had been acquired opposite The Robin and on the corner of Devonshire Drive and Darwin Road.

"This project was a matter of urgency as the population of Mickleover was 8,500 at present, but in 10 years time would probably be 10,000," he said.

The first decision to be made, the Bishop said, was whether the new parish should be a Statutory District, "that is one that in time would be a separate parish with a consecrated building and a suitable house, or Daughter Church."

In the Bishop's opinion the former would be most suitable and there would be considerable grants from Diocesan sources, but All Saints' would have a share of the responsibility.

Mr Roche asked if one Incumbent and two Curates would not run a parish of 10,000 effectively. Apparently, according to the Archdeacon, a shortage and mobility of young Curates would make this difficult.

A discussion on the various types of churches followed and Ken Taylor asked if decisions were required at this meeting. The Bishop said that the things to be considered were whether the church should be a Statutory District or Daughter Church. The next step would be what type of building would be required and the choice of architect. They also needed to appoint representatives for an Advisory Committee.

The PCC were in favour of setting up a Statutory District with the Bishop pointing out that they would have to have the Church Commissioners response to this before the type of church could be provided.

It ended with agreement that the Vicar and one layman should meet Mr Gruffydd John Wynne Thomas of 2 East Avenue, a local architect.

Photos courtesy of Peter Sherratt

The first Chistmas party for children and staff at Nestlés was attended by more than 80 guests on December 31st. Entertainment was provided by Tommy Harris, magician and Santa Claus, Ivor Stevens.

The RDC Health and Public Works Committee began an investigation at Mickleover Station where bones and offal were being deposited. The open and disused cattle enclosure adjoining the platform was being used prior to dispatch by road to Crewe. From enquiries, Chemical Interests Company of Crewe was collecting the bones from Derby and its outskirts and when a sufficient quantity was accumulated at the station, transported to Crewe. The District Commercial Manager of British Railways, Derby, requested the firm to cease their activities immediately and vacate the yard.

The December meeting of the parish council followed the Bishop's visit to the PCC and they began by discussing the Area Planning Officer's plans regarding the development in Devonshire Drive.

It had been agreed with the Church Authorities that the site at the Darwin Road junction would be used for a combined church/church hall with car parking facilities. His letter indicated that the site at the western end of the land adjoining Bramble Brook would be a convenient position for the proposed filling station in the neighbourhood. The filling station, he wrote, would not provide repair or garage facilities, and would be backed by a reasonable fence or wall to conceal it from the public open space behind, to which access would be provided at the side of the filling station.

Finally, the letter indicated that the County Librarian had had further thoughts with regard to siting a branch library in the position now proposed for the petrol station. "The sub-centre at Devonshire Drive appears rather removed for the purpose and various sites nearer to the Station Road/Uttoxeter Road junction were suggested as more convenient for most of the residents.

The Local Planning Authority deferred the parish council's application to use Bramble Brook site as a public open space and was asked to consider the Area Planning Officer's proposal to site a Vicarage on land to the western end of Nelson Close. The council informed him that they had no objections to the proposal.

Mickleover's spread of developments was causing some difficulty for people finding new roads in the village according to the parish council. Even residents were no assistance as they did not know where the new roads were.

Tim Ford suggested that the council should adopt a street list, prepared by the clerk, naming all the streets alphabetically with explanations of how to reach them.

He pointed out the difficulty of siting a display map in the centre of the village even if the cost was borne by advertising revenue.

The last few months of 1960 saw changes in British life with the introduction of MoT tests and Traffic Wardens who were first seen in London. Farthings ceased to be legal tender and the call-up for National Service was abolished on the final day. On television, the first episode of *Coronation Street* was broadcast.

Vandalism was being reported regularly in some of Derby's suburbs and Rock 'n roll music was dominating youth culture.

In the meantime Harold Barker of Staker Flatt Farm enquired about the possibility of using the Havenbaulk Lane playing field for the grazing of his livestock. The council replied that they could not agree and the chairman commented that the council's insurers were against the playing equipment supports being used as rubbing posts by livestock.

CHAPTER EIGHT
RAVENSDALE REMEMBERED
1961

Despite all the changes in Britain and the world, including the election of John Kennedy as the President of the United States, Derby was trying to reach international recognition by sending an invitation to President Kennedy to attend the Derby Press Ball in March, as the guest of honour. It was known that he had family connections with the Duke and Duchess of Devonshire.

Life continued for my grandfather in much the same way as it had for the last thirty years. He was among many who continued to take his shoes to the local cobbler, Ernie Toon, for repair, engaging a local chimney sweep and having his bread delivered on a weekly basis.

He did concede to the conversion of his electricity meter, from coin operated, to a more modern method. He was growing tired of obtaining shillings and sixpences!

Street lighting was still limited to certain hours of the night. Mickleover Parish Council were approached by their Littleover counterparts to leave the light on at the bottom of King's Drive, between Jackson Avenue and Uttoxeter Road.

This was brought about after a nurse was accosted in the badly lit area on her way to work at the City Hospital. It was reported that she had been receiving a police escort since the incident.

Grandfather's first diary note on the happenings in Mickleover occurred on January 2nd. "Road full of cars [Station Road]. Funeral of Chief Clerk of County Council [Mr Edmund King Wilkinson] at chapel." Mr Wilkinson lived at 'Casita' Moorland Road.

Mr G J Thomas, architect, attended the Advisory Committee on new churches and was asked to prepare preliminary sketches of a church suitable for a particular district. This would probably become dedicated as Bishop Rawlinson Memorial Church, the Bishop of Derby from 1936 to 1959 who died in July 1960.

Miss Kathleen Stephens, headteacher, told the School Managers meeting on January 10th that a "letter box had been provided at the Infants' School at last but it was still not deep enough and letters were left protruding."

Mrs Pat Ellison joined the staff to take Class 5 in place of Mrs Emma Brierley who had had to leave. Mrs Seabridge came to take the Reception Class.

One of Mrs Ellison's pupils was Rod White, the son of Colin and Pat White, her neighbours in Gisborne Close. He remembers the mile long walk to and from the school. With Brisbane Road and Buxton Drive still cul de sacs he went various routes, no doubt with his mother, from the end of Clifton Drive. In winter he suffered from chapped knees, "short trousers rubbing large sores just above the knee."

He also recalls the free milk, "frozen in winter, warm in summer, revolting any time of year. Never liked milk at anytime of my life."

The Divisional Education Officer, Roland Heath-Smith, had discussed with the two Mickleover headteachers ways and means of determining which children should transfer to the new school later in the year.

Much information had been provided but the Managers were having difficulty making neatly-defined catchment areas when Jimmy Best, headteacher at the Junior School, produced a map he had had specially prepared.

They asked Mr Heath-Smith to keep the existing managing body, at least in the initial stages, to also serve the new schools when they were elected.

A request was made for him to arrange for temporary use from April 1961 of the pavilion being erected on the Vicarage Park playing field, and that every effort be made to keep the existing schools fully staffed so that there would be an adequate number of teachers to transfer with the children when the new school was ready for occupation.

Arthur Ravensdale pointed out at the parish council meeting that the council had undertaken to give access to the new school, now being built, for children from Brisbane Road and Devonshire Drive. This would require the development of a footpath before September when part of the school would hopefully be open.

Concern was building up in the Chevin Avenue and Hobart Close district as householders were becoming worried about the new Diocesan Teachers' Training College which was being built behind their houses.

Very few residents knew what was going on and whether the view from their kitchen windows would have less light because of the College.

Councillor Stevens said: "The residents are puzzled because large lumps of earth have suddenly appeared on the land." The council agreed to his request to allow them a sight of the plans at the Parish meeting in March.

Despite this, some residents were still worried. "The place looks like a battlefield," said one. "If it is going to darken my living room my electricity bills will soar," commented another.

To try the lessen the worry the *Derbyshire Advertiser* approached Captain Williamson-Jones, secretary to the Training College. He said: "We regret the residents' concern over the new college. The building will follow exactly the photographs which appeared in the press, ornamental gardens will be laid on the west side and there will be trees all around."

Of the actual buildings themselves, he said: "They will be virtually all two-storey buildings with nice colour toning and slightly sloping roofs. There is nothing to worry anyone about the height. They certainly will not be as high as the Technical College on Kedleston Road."

Regarding the land to the south of Vicarage Playing Fields, owned by the late W H Watson, John Flint, the tenant from Manor Farm, expressed a wish to sow crops in Spring 1961 and it had been agreed with the District Valuer that the council would not want the land before September 29th 1961.

The District Valuer had asked for an indication of the date the council would require possession of the land in regard to swimming facilities but he was told that nothing could be given with any certainty at that time.

The Ministry of Housing and Local Government were in the process of distributing an official publication dealing with the provision of swimming baths. The County Council considered it would be in the "best interest of all concerned to await receipt of the publication before calling a meeting of representatives of all district councils who were contemplating swimming facilities, or would do so if financial assistance were to be forthcoming from the County Council.

Land adjoining the playing field to the rear of Park Cottage was not available at a figure which could be recommended for the council's acceptance. The District Valuer offered to provide his report if they decided to proceed by means of Compulsory Purchase.

Councillors noted the contents of a letter dated January 23rd from the County Librarian stating that it was true that his committee was considering an alternative site for a branch library to that previously proposed in Devonshire Drive.

"Grandson Peter has acquired a car. Roomy and powerful engine, Morris." The author photographed with the Morris Six in the garden of 39 Brisbane Road. "For someone who had not long completed his apprenticeship and not a holder of a full driving licence, this purchase was not based on economics, neither was it the most reliable car on the road. It was the largest car built by Morris, then known as the British Motor Corporation. It was regularly being taken to Lol Bottomley at Park Road Garage for tweaks and adjustments. Nevertheless it took four or five young men to places they had never visited before."-author.

A site in Vicarage Road was being considered and had reached the stage where the County Architect had confirmed that the site would be suitable and the RDC had been consulted to see whether or not a library building could be agreed.

It was understood that they had a scheme already for the redevelopment of the site concerned for housing and public conveniences.

Sometime ago the council requested Trent to provide additional bus services in the East Avenue area. Although the proposal had not yet been accepted, they considered it impossible for a bus to pass a tree which stood at the junction of East Avenue and Chestnut Avenue. The council decided to await a letter from the District Surveyor, outlining the situation, before taking any action.

An invitation from the Principal of the Diocesan Training College, Miss Amy E G Sephton, was brought to the notice of the council. She kindly offered to show the councillors a model of the plans of the new buildings. The council unanimously agreed to accept.

Grandfather wrote of a "burglary with violence on Uttoxeter Road this morning [February 21st]. Old lady of 85 assaulted in her own home."

W C (Bill) Barker had commenced his duties as Sexton at All Saints' Church at the end of January, replacing Jim Land who had moved to an old peoples' home.

The Reverend Ben Crockett announced at the February PCC meeting that the parish boundary between Littleover and Mickleover would be adjusted along with the boundary between Mickleover and Radbourne. "The part of Radbourne which lies south of the railway line at present," he said, "would be transferred to the parish of Mickleover St John."

He went on to explain that the Church Members Scheme in 1960 had not yet met the required amount, being £30 down on the year.

There were several reasons for this, he said. "The disappearance of envelopes which were thought to contain at least £5; Christmas Day falling on a Sunday probably accounted for loss of about £20, and the main cause – quite a number of 1960 envelopes were still outstanding at the end of the year."

In his opinion he thought the parish had been inoculated against a further campaign for a number of years. The Church Members' Scheme Committee preferred to keep people informed by a monthly bulletin in the church magazine, by personal contact where possible and by public relation activities in general.

He concluded by saying that the new church in Mickleover would seriously affect the financial side of All Saints', temporarily at least. "We must remember that with all the romance of a new church, the old church must not fall by the wayside."

The Junior School headmaster's discipline was constant. Jimmy Best looked into every classroom during the day and unfortunately one boy was caught tipping a waste paper basket over another boy's head during a craft lesson. He received the instruction "Go to my room," which every boy feared, as they knew the outcome!

Pupil Andrew White recalls that it was sometime before he encountered the headmaster. "This imposing suntanned man in a well-cut grey suit strode to the front of assembly, and promptly sent me out. I was a pale-faced child, and apparently he thought I was about to faint."

On March 3rd grandfather took a "stroll around the building site behind the hut." Houses and bungalows in Portland Close were being built by H J Warner at that time. The following day he walked down Station Road towards Radbourne and stopped to watch a football match at Nestlés sports field.

There was an active sports and social club at Nestlés. The Sports Club belonged to the Sunday Football League (cricket was never played). However they mainly played friendly matches with local and works teams and young farmers.

They held a works football match every year between married and single members of the workforce. The married men always won apart from one occasion when the singles won 6-0. Denis Driscol, quite a good footballer, had transferred from the singles to the married men for the first time. Darts, table tennis and skittles would be included following the construction of a timber building. Annual day trips to the Burton breweries, Wedgwood at Stoke-on-Trent or the Players' cigarette factory at Nottingham were well supported with a full coach every year.

The Education Authority had agreed that the Managers would carry out their duties at the new school. The clerk, Alec Hannah, stated that he had been informed that the candidates for the headship of the school would be interviewed on May 1st. Arthur Ravensdale, Arthur Riley, Joe Nadin and Mrs Gordon would represent the Managers.

Mickleover Parish Council held their March meeting at the Junior School where Sydney Clarke, chairman, referred to the growth of the parish during the last 16 years with the erection of approximately 1,350 new dwellings.

Open space for public recreation was now being considered and subject to the necessary loan approvals, areas of land were to be acquired around Bramble Brook, Vicarage Road playing fields, west and south, and adjoining the railway line in the north east amounting to approximately 40 acres.

The original intention of the council was to borrow a sum not exceeding £20,000 repayable in not less than 80 years.

The decision was made after a voting result of 28 to 27 against, with an amendment that the matter was adjourned until the council had collected more information about the project.

Criticism in the press from correspondents had incited the councillors to make efforts to meet the needs of the parish, said Sydney Clarke.

"The council feel that if we are to have open fields, the acquisition of them must be considered with the utmost urgency," he added.

Mr G B Clements of Farneworth Road wrote to express regret for the breaking of a window in the new pavilion by his seven-year-old son and offered to pay the cost of the repair. His son's accompanying letter promised to "give his word of honour" that he would not do it again.

The chairman of the parish council, Sydney Clarke, remarked on the laudible action taken by Mr Clements, as the damage caused was only a minor part of the total damage to the pavilion by vandalism.

On April 13th grandfather wrote that the "Russians announced putting a man [Yuri Gargarin] into orbit around the earth. His journey lasted 108 minutes and he was landed apparently unhurt."

Britain saw the end of the old black and white £5 notes, the Graduated Pensions Scheme was introduced and the Factories Act consolidated the safety regulations in industry.

A new headquarters costing more than £400 for the 124th Derby (Mickleover) Scout Group was completed and opened on April 17th by Clive Bemrose, County Commissioner and owner of a large printing company.

The new structure on the Royal British Legion Memorial Field replaced a Nissan hut and was made up of two ex-Army huts placed end-to-end. It was the result of more than three years' effort by the parents' committee under the chairmanship of Reg Ratcliff.

As scout meetings had now ended in the Infants' School, agreement was reached between All Saints' Church and the Education Authority that the Church Hall could be used by the school between the hours of 9.00am to 3.30pm on school days during the Summer Term from April 17th to July 21st.

Patricia Beech moved her class into the Church Hall with Lyn Kendall going into her room with class 6. The school now had nine classes and the number on the roll was 351, including 54 new entrants.

The County Council paid the sum of £5 per week for the hall inclusive of lighting and cleaning services, plus the use of the piano and heating when required. They were responsible for any rates or water charges which became payable during their occupation and for the repair or reinstatement of any damage caused by the children.

The parish council again held their meeting in the Junior School where "by an overwhelming majority" the council was authorised to borrow a sum of £20,000 to acquire land to be developed for recreational purposes.

The land included Devonshire Drive to Brisbane Road which would cost £6,000 and another 34 acres made up of 8 fields in the north-east of the parish plus the land around Vicarage Road playing fields which would cost £14,000. The council was not yet sure if it could acquire all this land. However a start was made in June when Sheffield Regional Hospital Board sought the consent of the Ministry of Health to sell $6^1/_2$ acres to Mickleover Parish Council on land formerly farmed by Rough Heanor.

Answering parishioners' questions about the Bramble Brook area, clerk, Les Miller, said that the council would undertake to see that adjoining householders were not annoyed when the land became a recreation centre. The council, he said, would also discuss culverting and cleaning the brook if it was decided that it might be a danger to the children.

A complaint had been made about cyclists and motor cyclists using the footpath between Gisborne Close and Clifton Drive. It was suggested by the County Council that "No Cycling" notices be erected at both ends by the parish council.

"Such notices, though unofficial and not sufficient to support a prosecution, have been found to be effective."

"No cycling" signs between Gisborne Close and Clifton Drive, Edale Avenue and Western Road and Farneworth Road to West Drive were installed in September.

W J Warren, Headmaster of Ravensdale School.

The RDC recommended that the new development off Victoria Close be named Onslow Road from the junction with Brisbane Road.

This led to the renaming and renumbering of 1 and 2-8 Victoria Close, as 1 and 2-8 Onslow Road. The renumbering of the existing 3-15 and 16-25 Victoria Close as 1-13 and 2-14 respectively.

The School Managers met on May 9th and the chairman, Arthur Ravensdale welcomed W J (Wilf) Warren to the meeting. He had been appointed to the headship of Mickleover's new school after being formerly at Ashbourne Methodist Junior and Infants' School.

Kathleen Stephens, headmistress at the Infants' School, reported that from

April 1st her school was in Group 3 and would be entitled to appoint a deputy headteacher under the scheme of Special Allowances. She again recommended Mabel Wibberley for the post which was accepted.

At the Junior School Jimmy Best said that although the school had been occupied for nearly four years the playing field was still not in use. He was able to report later in the month that the grass had been cut several times and weed killer applied twice. He said that everything was being done to bring the field into proper condition.

Teaching staff for the three schools had been fixed as:- Junior School, headteacher plus 10 Assistants; Infants' School, headteacher plus 6 Assistants; New School, headteacher, plus 5 Assistants.

Wilf Warren doubted whether his establishment was adequate in view of the large number of infants expected in September. The Managers considered the situation should be left flexible in order that an application could be made for extra staff if necessary.

One member of staff would have to be transferred from the Junior School and Mr Best had discussed the matter with his staff

Photo courtesy of Miss Ann Ellis

A hundred Second Year children at the Junior School journeyed to Tissington, Ladybower and a tour of the Peak District on May 11th. They were accompanied by Miss Ellis, left, Mrs Hammerton, Miss Fearn and Mr Best. Ivy Well at Tissington (left) has an apt message!

but there was no volunteer. He therefore recommended that Sue Taylor, the last teacher appointed, should be the one to transfer. This was never carried out for Miss Taylor served at the school for four years, becoming Mrs Hartley in 1963.

It was agreed that the remaining post in the Junior Department of the new school should be filled by the appointment of a man. It was decided to discuss the naming of this new school at the next meeting.

Six candidates were interviewed for the post of Assistant Master at the new school when Mr L Jones was appointed. For the Assistant Mistresses, Miss P A Borton, Miss Patricia Beech and Miss J Richardson were successful followed by Mrs M J Baker. All the staff would begin their duties on September 1st. Miss Beech was on the staff of the Infants' School and it was agreed that Mrs E P Seabridge, a supply teacher be appointed on a permanent basis.

An upper room at The Robin, Devonshire Drive, was used by the Bishop's Church Extension Committee on May 18th. Bishop Allen convened the meeting where Gruffydd J W Thomas' sketches, which had been approved, were enthusiastically received.

The organist and choirmistress at the Methodist Church, Joyce Wardle, died on May 26th after being ill for more than three years. For the past five years she had been organist at Pastures Hospital.

Nurse Alice Marshall, who had served the village since April 1938, brought news to my grandfather on June 3rd that my sister Sheila had given birth to a baby boy, Mark. "This of course makes me a great grandad," he wrote.

John Ratcliff of Western Road, who had been Assistant Scoutmaster of the 124th Scout Group for the last two years was appointed Scoutmaster. He was presented with his warrant by Mr E Page, District Commissioner for Derby north. John was a founder member of the Mickleover troop and had been in the movement for the past thirteen years.

Lord Fisher of Lambeth, Archbishop of Canterbury, spoke of his 30 years' episcopate as "rounded off by training colleges" when he laid the foundation stone of Derby Training College's new building on June 15th.

MICKLEOVER PARISH COUNCIL ELECTION: SATURDAY, MAY 13th 1961

*	H G Ford	390
*	A G Ravensdale	379
*	S A Clarke	375
*	E J Gothard	328
*	A S Yeomans	318
*	L S Stevens	302
*	A W Ratcliff	298
	N Porter	298
*	H R Bower	295
	M G Harper	294
	G K Smith	290
*	P D G Spilsbury	271
*	A E Clarke	259
*	W E Hallam	251

Not elected D J Phillips 246, G Hayden 222, * W H Coe 209.

* Sitting member

This was one of the key parish council elections in the Repton District where representatives of the parish's new housing estates won seats on the increased council to 14 seats. The county council made an Order on February 21st.

The proposed Church of St John the Evangelist – Drawn by the Architect, Gruffydd John Wynne Thomas, MA, ARIBA.

The new parish of St John the Evangelist would include the new buildings of the Derby Training College.

The Bishop of Derby, Dr A E J Richardson, wrote in the *Derby Diocesan News* "that part of the cost must be raised by the people of the locality for they would only feel that their church and hall were their own if they themselves had helped to build it." There was not room for a Vicarage he said, but it was hoped that one would be provided not far away early in the new year.

With the building of a new church, the forthcoming opening of a new school, a public house, shops and a future petrol station, the nucleus of another village was developing in the north-eastern section of Mickleover.

Vehicles travelling along the private Chevin Avenue to get to the new site of the College were causing trouble to the residents, it was alleged at the June parish council meeting.

Sydney Clarke, chairman, said residents complained about the dust by vehicles travelling at high speeds and encroaching on verges "usually carefully tended."

He continued: "The development of the college will continue until 1963 and apparently the inconvenience will continue until then."

A County Council street works official, said the responsibility for the repair and maintenance of a private road was with the developers and then with the owner of property.

"The County Council has no jurisdiction over extraneous traffic using the road," adding that although Chevin Avenue was developed in 1933-35 no plans had been deposited with the local authority. The road had never been considered up to the appropriate standard the council required before adoption." He added, "The public have access to the road, but it is not repairable at public expense."

After an expected deputation from residents failed to arrive, the parish council decided they had no responsibility in the matter and could make no suggestion. The residents would have to take any action they wished.

The council were also told that the police did not have to be informed of house-to-house collections or have to approve them.

The summer of 1961 was seeing building changes agreed by the RDC and the County Council.

Nestlés were carrying out additions to their factory warehouse and plant room. The extension of 20,720 cu ft also included offices and process area. The temporary timber building consisting of a pavilion was now being constructed on their sports field.

A proposed site for a library and public convenience on Vicarage Road by the County Planning Officer was approved and in September demolition of the row of terraced cottages, 6 to 10 Vicarage Road was sought.

At All Saints' Parochial Church Council meeting on July 3rd Charles Kitchell said that the new church would in fact be a Daughter Church of the Diocese and Sister Church to All Saints'.

He continued that there would be no set financial target expected from All Saints'. Twenty three people were to assist in a survey to discover who in the new Parish would be interested in the church, and to enquire whether they wished their children to attend Sunday School which would commence in September in temporary premises.

Mrs Sarah Lingard said she thought a map of the new Parish should be exhibited in a prominent place. Mr Kitchell said that a map would soon be seen on a hoarding near the site of the new church.

Suggestions for naming the new school were discussed at the July parish meeting but it was School Manager, Joe Nadin, who said it should be called the "Arthur Ravensdale School" to which everyone concurred.

Arthur Ravensdale, according to the headmaster, Wilf Warren, was very honoured, but he would not agree to it being called the Arthur Ravensdale. "Call it Ravensdale if you like. Long after I've been forgotten it will still ripple off the tongue."

The recommendation was accepted by the Education Committee and the school was officially named "Ravensdale County Junior Mixed and Infants' School" in honour of the chairman of the managers, Mr A G Ravensdale OBE.

Grandfather wrote that the "hut at the old works near the station now gone. Roads being made to new building estate beyond the windmill."

Wimpeys were beginning the building of bungalows and houses north of their existing development which ended at the top of Brisbane Road and Victoria Close on the east. They needed to demolish two houses on the bend of Victoria Close to allow the construction of the entrance to Onslow Road (see plan on p146).

An ad hoc committee of the parish council had decided at the beginning of the year that an asbestos roof for the new pavilion would be unsatisfactory, increasing the cost. Provision was made for a verandah with roofing.

They asked Mickleover Sports Club to assist in "maintaining the well-being of the new pavilion" by requesting their members to keep a protective eye on it whenever they were in or near the playing fields.

The parish council agreed to the completion at the July meeting. Costing an estimated £1,463 it would include kitchen facilities, changing rooms, showers, toilets and main hall. The building would be electrically heated and an electric water supply installed, but users of the pavilion would have to pay for the electricity through slot meters.

A long discussion took place on proposals for the development of the Bramble Brook site. It was agreed that children's playground equipment should be bought, that the brook should be cleaned out from Brisbane Road to the pumping station and fences erected at danger spots.

Mr A N Hubble, administrative secretary of Mickleover Evangelical Fellowship, who had applied for land on the site for building a church on old Common Farm, was told that the application would be considered at a later date.

He told the *Derby Evening Telegraph* afterwards that the proposed building would be designed to seat 200. The aim of the Fellowship was to serve new estates. They had sufficient funds to buy land.

Grandfather wrote on July 21st: "Pipes Band marched from The Square to Royal British Legion this evening. This caused a show of excitement."

The pipe band gave a display of music and counter marching on the Memorial Field after starting at the Square at 7.30pm. Around 350 people attended the event. A collection was taken for the Memorial Field.

A circus came to the Manor Farm Field off Vicarage Road on July 27th and 28th. Grandfather wrote: "Visited circus ground with little Derek; saw the wild animals."

Two-and-a-half year old Derek Moore was a regular visitor to my grandfa-

Photo courtesy of the Derby Evening Telegraph

Above: The Pipe Band of the 51st Ordnance Field Park Unit TA outside the Royal British Legion. Below: Lewis and Tom Straw with Derek Moore, the son of their neighbours, sitting on the barrow Tom used on his window cleaning round. Right: Lewis helping Derek of 20 Station Road in the little cart he had made him.

Photos courtesy of Derek Moore

156

ther's home from the time he could walk, sometimes daily, he often shared breakfast with him. Derek grew to regard him as his "Grandad Straw". He was a constant companion on his walks around the village. As with all little boys he could sometimes misbehave and grandfather was left with no choice but to send him home.

On August 2nd he "went a walk along the new road off Station Road, below Windmill Farm and thence through the considerable new estate - was amazed with its development."

The following day he travelled to Derby "bus fare now 1s.5d return."

Wilf Warren spoke at his last speech day as headmaster of Ashbourne Methodist School.

He said: "I consider good music, speech and work in all departments, depend on the tone and atmosphere of the school, where consideration of other people is paramount and where manners matter most." He thanked the staff and all who had supported him during the four years plus he had been at the school.

All Saints' PCC considered at their August meeting that there was a public interest in the Memorial Chapel project and it was thought the time was opportune to make a start on the long-delayed project (the Reverend Ben Crockett, having first suggested it in 1951).

It was agreed to authorise the Vicar and Church Wardens to apply for a Faculty to establish a Chapel at the east end of the north aisle. A member of the council Herbert James (Jim) Stampfly promised to assist in the preparation of all necessary plans and drawings required.

Following the parish survey it was decided to periodically circulate a St John's Newsletter to each home, the first being issued on September 2nd 1961.

Application was made by Wimpeys to erect a two storey house for use as St John's Church Vicarage, at 7 Onslow Road.

A successful sale of farming stock and effects was conducted by W S Bagshaw and Sons at Ivy Farm, Limes Avenue, on August 31st. The farm had already been sold by William Radford and Son who had continued to farm there after the death of Tom Radford, the man who was most responsible for the running of the parish council since its outset in 1894. William, it is believed by the author, was the nephew of Tom. After his death his wife and son moved to Blackpool.

At the September meeting of the School Managers the National Union of Townswomen's Guilds were given permission to use the hall of Ravensdale School for a public meeting.

Wilf Warren, headmaster, said the number on the roll was 179, organised into two Junior classes and three infant classes.

The Managers thanked Mr Warren and all his staff at Ravensdale who had worked until 10.00pm on the night before opening on September 5th.

Three residents of Portland Close were concerned at the way in which their houses had been numbered, the parish council heard on September 19th.

In a letter to the council, dated August 3rd, Leslie A Sims of 2b Chesil House said he had received notification from the RDC that his house would be numbered 2c and the adjacent ones, which were built after the others, would have to be numbered 2a and 2b.

"I am astounded at the clerk [RDC] demanding that I should display the numbers within 14 days after I have been waiting months to have my house numbered," he said.

In a second letter, Mr Sims pointed out the confusion which would be caused by this inane system of numbering.

"My house number on hand written envelopes could easily be mistaken for a 20," he stated. Mr Sim's house was the first on the right hand side of Portland Close off Cavendish Way.

The parish council agreed that the clerk, Les Miller, should approach the residents of the house numbers 2, 2a, 2b and 2c and re-arrange them in a logical order, so that Mr Sims would be 2 and the three adjacent houses would follow as 2a, 2b and 2c.

MICKLEOVER COUNTY INFANTS' SCHOOL STAFF, SEPTEMBER 1961

Headmistress: Miss K M Stephens

Form	No in Class
Mrs M E Henchliffe	Class 1	36
Miss M Wibberley	Class 2	36
Mrs D Maéné	Class 3	36
Mrs Seabridge	Class 4	37
Miss G Ravensdale	Class 5	34
Mrs M A Simnett	Class 6	33
Number on Roll		212

In December the RDC recommended that the name "The Grove" be allocated to the three houses as suggested by the householders.

Charles Kitchell, Chairman and Organising Secretary of the St John's Committee applied for accommodation at the new school for Sunday School purposes. However, because of practical difficulties, the School Managers said it was difficult to accommodate them. Mr Kitchell was head of religious education at Bemrose School and in 1965 became lecturer in theology at Leeds College of Education.

The United Kingdom had applied to join the EEC but there were worrying developments with the USSR announcing the resumption of nuclear weapons testing and the USA retaliating by saying they would now continue underground nuclear weapons testing.

Bertrand Russell, the philosopher was imprisoned for protesting against such weapons and there was a large anti-nuclear bomb demonstration in London.

Photo courtesy of the Derby Evening Telegraph
Produce was brought by the children at Ravensdale School for the schools harvest festival.

Mickleover Parish Council were informed earlier in the year that Charles F Currey of 84 Station Road had been appointed Civil Defence Sector Warden to cover the area of Littleover, Mickleover and Willington. They were also advised that the Warden Service should be increased in membership to an effective strength which would be most helpful to the Section Officer to have the co-operation of the parish councils in his efforts to establish the service very firmly in the sector area.

A public meeting at Ravensdale School took place on Tuesday, October 10th to discuss the formation of a Townswomen's Guild and was well attended.

Mrs R S Goose presided, Mrs C Astle a member of Alvaston Guild outlined the activities of the movement. After discussion it was agreed that a Guild be formed.

Names and subscriptions were taken and Mrs Goose announced that of those present, 157 had become members. It was agreed to hold the meetings on the first Tuesday of the month at the school. They had been informed that there would be limited canteen facilities and priority would be given to school functions.

After complaints from council members that the gas lighting in the streets was inadequate, they decided to ask the RDC to replace all the gas lights with electric lights. The Engineer and Surveyor authorised to dispose of the gas columns

Photo courtesy of the Derby Evening Telegraph

The Derby Evening Telegraph published a full page of children starting their first day at Mickleover County Infants' School. Right: Miss Gladys Ravensdale greets twins Joan and Marion Short. Above: Julia Walmsley contemplating building bricks. Bottom right: Jonathan Skinner and John Charlton play with cut-out model animals. Left:: Simon Grudgings, Ann Forester and Carolyn Schofield enjoy a drawing lesson along with (below) Peter Clowes, Susan Curtis and Michael Young.

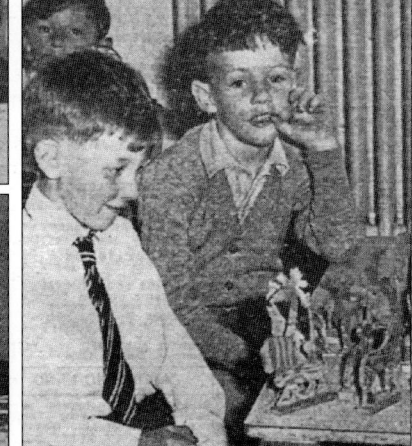

160

and lanterns on the best terms available and disconnection was completed in July 1964.

In a low poll an Independent candidate, George Hayden, of 15 Lea Drive won the by-election at Mickleover to fill the vacancy on the RDC. He secured 444 votes, against 374 cast for a Labour candidate, Henry Carter. The vacancy occurred by the resignation of Philip Spilsbury.

Mr F G Hulme, Chief Constable of Derby said he hoped there would be a new Roman Catholic Church at Mickleover in the not too distant future. He was speaking when he opened a bazaar which realised £160 at the Memorial Hut. A priest who was ordained in Rome in 1951, the Father Edward Byron, moved from St Hugh's College Tollerton, Nottinghamshire, to take charge of the new Roman Catholic parish of Mickleover. The parish had been created out of that of St Joseph's, Derby.

Mrs M J Baker was to leave Ravensdale School on December 31st with Mrs Jean Pickering joining the staff on January 1st 1962. The new school uniform for Ravensdale School was displayed to the Managers.

Application for the construction of a Cul-de-Sac, west of Station Road and south of West Drive, led to a meeting on the site by the County Council, parish representatives, and H J Warner the contractors, to discuss the question of surface water drainage.

Photo courtesy of the Derby Evening Telegraph
Jack Thornhill (right) handing the Thornhill Trophy to R E (Dick) Kenderdine who was voted 'Clubman of the Year' by Mickleover Sports Club. The presentation was at the Nag's Head and looking on is Jim Mills, chairman.

The small estate was to contain 26 properties on 3.5 acres of land. On November 13th Joe Nadin and George Hayden, RDC representatives, met with the authorities. They agreed that the watercourses would clear the neighbouring area. However a condition should be contained in the conveyances of the properties sold that it should be the responsibility of the new owners to maintain the watercourses.

In view of the complexity of the drainage position in this area it was considered that a survey should be made by Stanley Mehew, the County Surveyor, to ascertain the size of pipe necessary to deal not only with the existing and proposed development but also for any in the future. Approval was granted and the estate named Hope Avenue.

The petrol filling station application, east of Devonshire Drive and opposite the shopping precinct, this time by Shell-Mex and BP, was being discussed by the RDC. It was for a sales room, oil store and petrol pumps with tanks. The siting of a pole forecourt sign was agreed along with a wall built along the eastern boundary, 5 feet above ground level.

An architect's plan showing the proposed development of a piece of land adjoining Bramble Brook was submitted at the meeting.

The plan included provision for a children's playground and garden for old people. The council decided to hold a special meeting on Thursday December 7th to consider the plan.

On November 21st grandfather wrote that "old houses on Cattle Hill [6-10 Vicarage Road] are being demolished" and "work is proceeding on Personal Service Garage alterations".

William W Rushbrooke, who owned Personal Service Garage on the corner of Limes Avenue, was having a pump island and forecourt, along with petrol storage tanks, constructed. To add to the changes a store and part of the garage was being demolished.

"Looked at where they have been taking down old house and saw that electric place was damaged," grandfather wrote of November 25th. The 'electric place' he was referring to was the sub-station which still exists. "Wall cracked – a stone capital over the door had been propped up." In the following week he noted that, "work proceeding on damaged electric station in Vicarage Road."

The RDC admitted that during the demolition of the cottages, 6-10 Vicarage Road damage was caused to the brickwork of the adjoining electricity sub-station by the contractor's workmen.

On November 28th an Order of Her Majesty in Council was published in the *London Gazette* to the effect that the diocesan new parish be constituted "to be taken out of the parishes of Mickleover, Littleover and Saint Francis, Mackworth, thus altering the boundaries of the parishes of Mickleover, Littleover and Radbourne."

Bishop Allen had informed the St John's Project Committee that the Reverend Martin Pierce, BA, of Taddington and Chelmorton, had accepted the invitation to St John's Mickleover. He had previously been the Vicar of St Andrew's, Derby.

Grandfather's last note of local interest in his 1961 diary was the opening of Jacklin's chemist shop at the corner of Station Road and Park Road on December 5th.

At a special meeting of the council an approval was made, in principle, to the plans for the new recreation centre at Bramble Brook. Les Miller, clerk, said it was unlikely that anything could be done at the site until May.

It was decided not to discuss the detailed proposals at this stage but if the development was to be phased, priority should be given to the children's playground, cleaning the brook course, cutting the grass and providing the main path.

A Mental Health Act had brought about a change in peoples approach to mental illness said Mr A V Martin, Chairman of Sheffield Regional Hospital Board when he presided at the opening of a new nurses' training school at Pastures Hospital.

The pattern of psychiatric nursing had changed with the new acceptance of mental treatment. Emphasis was now laid on the care of the mentally ill in a community rather than a hospital.

"This means a reduction in the number of patients treated in hospital, and the increased effort to prevent illness will reduce the numbers in hospital care," he continued.

"There is still a grave shortage of staff, but the reduction in the number of patients will bring down the staff to patient ratio," declared Mr Martin.

The Marchioness of Lothian opened the training school and also presented the prizes and certificates, as the ceremony was combined with the hospital's annual prize-giving.

CHAPTER NINE
"GOODBYE GREEN FIELD"
1962

The new year began with snow on the ground and grandfather complaining on January 3rd: "I shall be glad when the snow has gone and I am able to resume my walking."

Because of a spell of severe weather a number of pipe bursts had been reported to Repton Rural District Council by tenants. "With the hard weather coming immediately after the holiday period it was found that quite a number of tenants had been away for Christmas and found on their return water pipes were frozen."

Two well-known Mickleover characters were in the news in 1962. Henry Ritchie Bower of 119 Western Road announced that he couldn't give his customary attention to the work of the parish council on which he had served since 1950.

Mr Bower was Clerk to the council from 1926 to 1946 and was largely instrumental in securing street lighting and the numbering of houses in the village.

He had been a member of the staff of Derbyshire County Council health department for 42 years and was with the Derby No 1 Hospital Management Committee when he retired in 1950. In addition he was Clerk to the managers of Mickleover County School. As a founder member of Mickleover Royal British Legion he was also mainly responsible for the Gymkhana, then regarded as one of the best events of its kind in the district.

Photo courtesy of the Derbyshire Advertiser
Henry Ritchie Bower.

When the parish council wanted somebody to keep bus shelters clear of litter in 1956, Joe Dakin was the man they employed. Once a week, at the age of 85, Joe started at 7.30am and took a three mile walk around the village, getting paid five shillings for it.

Joe told the *Derby Evening Telegraph* in 1959 that he couldn't remember the last time he visited the doctor, saying "It keeps me fit."

He took the paper he collected in a sack and burnt it in his greenhouse. Another job Joe voluntarily took on was to keep the village war memorial clean, tidy and supplied with flowers. A bachelor, he had been in turn a farm labourer, brickyard worker, and railway platelayer.

Joe lived with Mr and Mrs A Holloway in Moorland Road from the age of 25. When employed at the railway during the 1914-18 War he had been known to get up at 4.30am, walk to Radbourne, milk 50 cows at Potlocks Farm and report for duty by 7.00am at Mickleover Station, continuing after his day's work to help on a farm at Mickleover until dusk.

He was carrying out his duties on the Thursday before his death on January 14th 1962. He would have celebrated his 88th birthday on the following day.

As part of the possible improvements to the County Infants' School the managers suggested a request was made to the Divisional Education Officer that the Authority consider using the school as a Youth and Community Centre and in its place build a new Infants' School, possibly on a site behind All Saints' Church.

They were soon informed that the Ministry of Education would not entertain the use of the school for other purposes.

The tree at the centre of the road at the junction of East Avenue and Chestnut Avenue was discouraging the Trent Motor Traction Company from extending their bus services in Mickleover.

The council decided to take steps to have the tree removed and suggest to Trent that they amend their routes and submit proposals for new routes to the council.

Mr J C Clymo, Assistant Traffic Manager, told the parish council that it was hoped to start a route incorporating Western Road, Brisbane Road, Darwin Road, Devonshire Drive and East Avenue and down Station Road to the Railway Station.

He pointed out that if the company did decide to include the Wimpey estate it would probably mean that some buses now operating from The Square would cease. However the Tutbury service would cater for people wishing to catch buses at the Square.

The Reverend Martin Pierce and G J W Thomas, architect, attended a meeting of St John's Project Committee on February 9th. Under the chairmanship of Charles Kitchell the committee consisted of Frank Chesterman, Geoff Poolman, Harry Rudkin, Alan Saunders, Steve Thorley and Ken Taylor. He spoke for the rest by stating it was "a privilege and an honour to be selected to serve in this once in a lifetime opportunity to launch a New Parish of the Anglican Church."

They agreed to "raise within ten years the sum of £10,000, assuming a rate of interest of not more than three per cent."

The Vicar held the first "House Communion" at the Kitchells' home in Chestnut Avenue on the following day where 26 people were present.

Ravensdale had opened a School Bank and in February headmaster, Wilf Warren, informed parents that the savings were to be collected on Thursday mornings. "The items are entered in each child's personal savings book and the sum total is banked weekly in the School Savings Account with the Post Office."

He also informed them that "the Tootal fabric for school dresses is 6s.11d per yard and is available at school. This material is exclusive to this school within a radius of 20 miles."

One of the largest and most modern gymnasiums in the United Kingdom was completed and formerly handed over to the Derby Diocesan Training College on February 12th. It was the first building on the new Training College to be completed.

In the grounds, six netball courts, two basketball courts, a running track and all-weather hockey pitch had been built.

The Infants' School suffered damage to roofs caused by a gale and the misery continued for headmistress Kathleen Stephens when her study door lock broke and someone from Personal Service Garage had to go and release her.

The gale on February 16th was the worst in memory of most of the county's inhabitants. The winds blew fiercely over towns and villages of Derbyshire, damaging roofs and felling trees and interrupting telephone and electricity services. The towers at Pastures Hospital and Kingsway Hospital were severely damaged.

Grandfather noted the news on February 20th that the "USA flight of man in space, three orbits accomplished, man returned safely." The first flight attempted in January had been cancelled.

At All Saints' Annual Church Council Meeting on February 22nd the Reverend Ben Crockett, began by saying "that we are now facing what is probably the most critical and challenging time in our own church's history, as quite possibly before the next AGM, the new Church of St John the Evangelist would be built."

A very urgent matter to be considered was a new Church Centre comprising an Assembly Hall with platform stage, Council Chamber, Choir Room, Parish Office, well equipped kitchen, storage space and toilets, to be built if possible on part of the Vicarage garden, nearest the churchyard. It was later suggested that a new Vicarage could be built there with the old Vicarage converted into a Church Centre.

"We cannot delay much longer as the present Church Hall was totally inadequate. It would cost seven to eight thousand." All Saints' Fellowship would have an important role in organising money raising functions.

Members of the press and the public were excluded from a meeting at the February parish meeting for 25 minutes when the council received a report on the Bramble Brook land.

Plans drawn up by a member of the council Norman Porter, and a business colleague, were found to be satisfactory by the County Architect who praised various items, both in the children's playground and the old people's gardens.

Photo courtesy of the Derby Evening Telegraph

Pupils of Ravensdale School pictured at the Derby and Derbyshire Music Festival, where they competed for the first time in a choral verse speaking session at the Municipal Art Gallery, Derby. They came second in their section.

Laurence Stevens followed Henry Bower in offering his resignation from the council as he was moving from the district.

Mickleover children who were due for transfer to secondary education would be admitted to Etwall County Secondary School as the extensions there would be ready for occupation. This was agreed at a meeting in Derby by the South Derbyshire Divisional Education Executive, altering the approved catchment areas between Etwall and Littleover County Secondary School.

Roland Heath-Smith, Divisional Education Officer, reported that there was already evidence that Ravensdale School would be unable to accommodate all the children being admitted there during the next two or three years.

A comprehensive census had been taken in the area of children under school age, to demonstrate the need for an additional junior school on the Ravensdale site.

The Director of Education wrote to the School Managers saying that as Ravensdale Infants' School was anticipated to be a Group 3 it would be entitled to a deputy head. The appointment of Miss Borton would therefore be on a permanent basis and when re-organisation took place she would still remain as deputy head of the Infants' School. She had begun her duties on January 1st.

At the annual parish meeting on March 20th thirty-seven parishioners heard chairman, Sydney Clarke, ask the meeting to authorise the parish council to borrow a further sum in addition to the £1,900 already agreed for the development of the land adjoining Bramble Brook.

The sum of £4,100 had been borrowed to acquire the land but a further £2,900 was needed to purchase the land adjoining the southern boundary of Vicarage Road Playing Fields.

The position regarding the purchase of land for open space in the north-east of the parish was now doubtful but the loan repayment in respect of the £20,000 was already reflected in the 1962-63 rates made by the RDC.

Following discussion it was agreed the parish council would borrow £12,000 for the purpose of developing the land adjoining Bramble Brook.

Agreement was made at the meeting that the development of Bramble Brook land should proceed. This included clearing the brook and filling it in, planting trees, building an infants' and children's play centre, a running track, and a rest garden for old people.

Mr Clarke commented that the time may be ripe to divide Mickleover into two wards. This would enable us to get better representation on the RDC and eventually better representation on the County Council".

Since his last annual report he said the parish election had resulted in 14 councillors, "and introduced a slightly younger element on to the council", which he thought pleasing.

Mr Clarke welcomed two new members, Mr George Hayden and Mr Derek J Phillips.

Mr Larkins' drawings and plans showing his proposal for the new Choir Vestry for All Saints' Church, which would cost in the region of £850 were explained. There was unanimous agreement that the Standing Committee for the new Church Centre should consist of two churchwardens, the treasurer and Mr Morley.

Grandfather met Joe Evans "when I went to post office for pension" on April 12th. He told him that he was on duty again acting as a traffic warden for the children at the County Infants' School.

On April 26th 1,500 Rolls-Royce workers who lived in the Derby area lost their jobs. One man employed at Rolls-Royce for many years told the *Derbyshire Advertiser*. "I'm not surprised, this has been coming. We have all been living in a fool's paradise. There is just not enough work for the large labour force we have. Lots of little empires have been built up, but if we are to compete in the world's markets on equal terms we must cut out waste and streamline our industry. This is perhaps only the beginning but it is a very necessary one."

Advertiser news editor, George Corbishley, wrote: "one cannot help feeling that the happy face of prosperity with which Rolls-Royce has long faced the world, has changed somewhat in the past months!"

One young man who was soon to be looking for another job said "The party's over." There had been an increase in unemployment in the Derby area before this announcement.

At the beginning of May grandfather had seen men measuring and surveying on the field beyond his back garden. On the following day he noted "the field at the back was chain harvested today."

A layout for the development of land for housing in Vicarage Road had been forwarded to the County Planning Officer. It contained 20 two-bedroomed bungalows together with space for garages if required. To comply with the County Surveyor's requirements re visibility, "it would be necessary to acquire a further 0.130 acres of land which was in the ownership of Bill Varey, 20 Vicarage Road [ex Holly Bush Farm], who was willing to negotiate."

The School Managers lodged an application with the Ministry of Education for the inclusion of the new Junior School in next year's building programme. It was also reported that the Divisional Education Officer was pressing the Authority to provide two Terrapin Classrooms on the Ravensdale site from the beginning of the next Summer Term at the latest.

The official opening of Ravensdale School was a dedication Service on May 11th at 10.30am. The Vicar of St John's, the Reverend Martin Pierce and the Minister of the Methodist Church, the Reverend Clifford Hawkins, were jointly invited to take the Service.

Mr Colin F White

Arthur Ravensdale was elected chairman of the parish council at the annual meeting on May 22nd. He succeeded Sydney Clarke who had held the office for the last four years. Alan Ratcliff was elected vice-chairman.

A vacancy on the council occurred because of the resignation of Edward Gothard who could no longer serve owing to pressure of other work. The position was filled by Colin F White, deputy head at Etwall Secondary School.

The Local Government Commission's proposals to enlarge Derby to a town of 211,000 people was published at the end of August.

It explained: "The development areas immediately outside the county borough boundaries at Breadsall, Chaddesden, Spondon, Alvaston and Boulton, Chellaston, Sunnyhill, Littleover, Mickleover, Darley Abbey and Allestree (extending into Quarndon parish) are substantially continuations of the town area. They are wholly residential, and serve as dormitories for Derby. Their links with Derby are strong, and the Commission are satisfied that they should be included in the county borough.

"The village of Mackworth is separated from Derby and the Commission are not satisfied, bearing in mind the other extensions they propose, that the inclusion of land here is necessary to meet the future needs of Derby."

Arthur Ravensdale gave a parish council view in the *Derbyshire Advertiser*. "We took a plebiscite of the people some time ago and they were overwhelmingly opposed to inclusion in the borough. I believe the people of Mickleover should make the decision as to their own future."

The RDC spokesman Gordon Robotham said that "so far the boundary commission had only put forth these propositions and they were in no way decisive."

A complaint was received about galloping horses on the Bramble Brook land which the council had acquired. "There have been cases of young children playing on the land, who have nearly been run down by these horses," Mr Ravensdale said.

It was agreed that a "Horse Riding and Cycling Prohibited" notice should be erected on the land.

The Licensing of the Priest-in-Charge, the Reverend Martin Pierce at St John's Church, had taken place at Derby Cathedral and he had taken up residence in the new Vicarage on Onslow Road.

He attended his first public meeting in the parish which was extremely well attended. Martin and the Committee were encouraged and it was decided that a second survey was necessary. This time they hoped to recruit helpers for all activities which were likely to be part of parish life.

There had been little sign of action since building was approved on March 23rd on "a piece of waste land, full of puddles and pools on which the children used to play."

The South Derbyshire headteachers launched "Education Week" on June 1st and schools closed on the afternoon. This was to enable the public to see the work which schools were doing and George Brown, MP declared the week open at the Drill Hall, Beckett Street, Derby.

However on June 1st, in the presence of about 200 people, the first turf was lifted after each member of the Project Committee had made a cut in the turf. A cross of 2" x 2" rough timber had been erected on the site made by a member of the Young People's Group, Jonathan Kitchell. It is still in existence today and used on ceremonial occasions.

Photo courtesy of the Derby Evening Telegraph

Inset: *This model by architect G J W Thomas was shown to parishioners at the first public meeting organised by St John's Project Committee.* Above: *Looking on to the first turf being cut for the new church by Revd Martin Pierce are, from left: Harry Rudkin, Ken Taylor, Gruffydd Thomas and Charles Kitchell.*

Events were now happening at a pace when the first Parish Eucharist took place in an upper room at the Royal British Legion on Western Road on June 17th.

The parish council felt that golfers "double parking" their cars in Arundel Avenue whilst using the Mickleover Golf Course were causing "danger and inconvenience to passing motorists."

Members agreed at the June meeting that the clerk should write to the club asking them to look into the overcrowded parking.

Mr F Weaver, captain, said 1962 had been one of success and new records. The decision to have water laid over the whole course, coupled with the arrival of a new green keeper had shown "wonderful improvements".

Photo courtesy of the Derby Evening Telegraph
Two pictures published in the Derby Evening Telegraph *during "Education Week". Above: Country dancing by pupils at the County Junior School. Right: Pupils present a physical education excercise.*

There had been a steady influx of members throughout the year and the playing strength had reached such proportions that the admission of further playing members was receiving serious consideration by the club committee.

The clubhouse at that time was directly opposite Arundel Avenue and close to the main Uttoxeter Road. Fred and Cecile Hales who had built their new house on the site of the old "Plough Inn" opposite (see Chapter One), often found golf balls in their garden.

Mickleover Royal British Legion had formed a golfing section in May which was thought to be the only Royal British Legion golf club in the Midlands, if not the country. The 35 members played on the Mickleover course and to stimulate interest Reg Cooper presented a silver rose bowl for annual competition.

"[Auntie] Hilda and I took little Derek with us down to Black Wood. We saw a goods train go by." wrote grandfather on June 9th. Financial losses were piling up all over the railway system and although the Mickleover line was among thirteen other lines to be closed a few years earlier only economies continued.

July saw the dissolution of the St John's Church Project Committee before the first Parochial Church Council was formed on July 12th. The move was welcomed because the workload was fast becoming overwhelming and with the election of the PCC the load was spread further, formalising the parish structure.

Grandfather noted that, "Bussell, newsagent, is having a new shop built after demolition of the old premises which he has been occupying." This new building was on the western corner of The Square and The Hollow. It was last occupied by Forbuoys as a newsagents in the early 21st century.

He had been talking to the Sexton of All Saints', Bill Barker and asked him if he would be willing to help him cut the front hedge of his house at 22 Station Road.

Bill called on July 23rd. "He offered to do it for 10s. I told him I should give him more. He came in the afternoon and chopped the hedge and the tree – Sycamore. The cuttings were abundant. Tom and I set about about clearing the drive of lopped branches of the tree after dinner. I gave Bill 15s."

Arthur Ravensdale, chairman of the parish council opened a very special meeting which referred to the local Inquiry, held at Burton on July 12th.

George Wimpey had been refused planning permission to build on 49 acres of land north east of Onslow Road. They conceded that 20 acres on the site be put by for open spaces.

Wimpeys had stated that "we shall be happy to provide a local shopping parade to increase facilities in the area."

George Brown MP had been approached by parishioners to make representations at Ministerial level for the retention of the land to provide "some of the amenities which were lacking on the adjoining estate."

Strong opposition was also heard at the Inquiry from Mickleover Freeholder's Association and the County Council said that if the development was agreed their plan in the area would be frustrated.

A good number of parishioners present made statements and put questions about the financial implications and the estimated cost to be borne by the parish rate.

The clerk, Les Miller, presented the figures, indicating that about a 1s rate would be needed to meet the proposals. The figure included the provision for the

ST JOHN THE EVANGELIST FIRST CHURCH COUNCIL

Churchwardens	Frank Chesterman
	Harry Rudkin
Vice Chairman	Charles Kitchell
Secretary	Jean Brinklow
Treasurer	John Smith
Building Fund Treasurer	Bernard Wakelam
Committee Members	Alan Bland
	K Kendall
	Doris Kitchell
	Eric Mawby
	Ken Taylor
	Steve Thorley
Diocesan Representative.	Geoffrey Howarth
Ruridecanal Representatives	Ray Knibbs
	Doris Arnold

Photo courtesy of the Derby Evening Telegraph

Judges and stewards at Mickleover Gymkhana on the Royal British Legion Memorial Field. From left: Mr P Owen, Mr Frank Grimshaw, Mr Henry S Fitch, Arthur Morley, Mr E Smith, Mr R Toye and Mr W H Cheshire.

purchase of land in the north-east of the parish at an extremely high cost and no account had been made of possible grant-aid from other authorities.

South East Derbyshire Area Planning Officer said that the northern part of the area could not be drained by gravity to the pumping station at Bramble Brook which was to serve the majority of the new development east of Station Road.

"By far the greater part of Mickleover is drained by gravity or with assistance sewage pumping stations to the Bunkers disposal works which have been designed and largely rebuilt to accept only discharge from this part of the unit. The increased flow would eventually overload the plant."

With only two dissensions the meeting was of the opinion that the whole 49 acres should be used for open space, but not for housing.

The clerk was directed to convey the resolution to the Minister of Housing and Local Government, Dr Charles Hill.

Regarding the authorisation for the parish council to borrow the necessary sum for the acquisition of part of the Wimpey appeal site, it was resolved that the matter be deferred until the Minister's decision on the Wimpey appeal was known.

In the absence of the Deputy Director of Primary Education for the county – whose attendance had been expected – the chairman submitted a statement

Photo courtesy of Mr and Mrs Colin & Pat White

A group of prize-winners with Mrs V Gordon, school manager, who presented the awards at Ravensdale Schools' first Speech Day celebrations in July 1962. Back row, left to right: R Berry, Susan Underwood, Kathy Tuck, Mrs V Gordon, David Hoare, Heather Stewart, Tone Howard. Middle row: Jane Spencer, Paul Johnson, Chris Ellison, Rodney White, Andrew Blakeman, Colin Hutchinson, Stephanie Windle, John Bagguley, Selwyn Adams, Ann Dawson, Danny Lacey. Front row: Norma Garnett, Chris Warren, Tim Cook, Neil Giltrap, Keith Rodwell, Cheryl Rainford, Janet Walmsley.

concerning the position with regard to education facilities in the parish. He indicated, among other things, that figures were based on a census carried out by Roland Heath-Smith in March which had led to the Minister of Education advancing the building date for the junior school on the Ravensdale site, "which would now be in the 1963-64 programme".

The census figures showed that, even then, the accommodation for primary schooling would still be inadequate for the needs of the neighbourhood.

The meeting proceeded to discuss education facilities, including provision for secondary education, in so far as the parish generally was concerned, and the discussion ended with Arthur Ravensdale pointing out that it was hoped that future meetings between the parents immediately concerned and the Director of Education could be arranged for the purpose of discussing particular general education problems. A vote of thanks to the Rt Hon George Brown for all he had done and was doing in the above mentioned connections was moved by A C Holden, duly seconded and adopted with acclamation.

The Reverend Clifford Hawkins, Methodist Minister of Littleover and Mickleover churches for the last four years left the district in August to take up another ministry in Somerset. He had been appointed circuit superintendent at Glastonbury. the Reverend Alan O Barber, who had been serving in Doncaster, replaced him.

In 1961 Father Edward Byron had announced a new Roman Catholic parish to be dedicated to Our Lady of Lourdes. He celebrated Mass as the Mickleover Parish Priest for what is thought to be the first time in 400 years. At that time Father Byron was staying with the McCahey's at Mickleover Lodge.

The Nottingham Roman Catholic Diocese bought 127 Station Road for £2,700 where Father Byron set up home with an upper room being converted to a small chapel for weekday Mass.

More than 200 visitors attended what was becoming an annual barbecue at Mickleover Lodge, the home of Doctor Michael J and Mrs Kathleen McCahey. The event was in aid of the building fund for the proposed Catholic Church.

Staff changes were happening at all the parish schools ready for the new school year on September 1st. Maggie Simnett left the Infants' School to take up a post in Derby borough and Mrs Brayne replaced her. George Peter Edward Goodman joined the staff at the Junior School with Jean Bunting having left to get married. Miss Molly Watson of 152 Vicarage Road, also married in August, becoming Mrs Cavill. At Ravensdale School Mr L Jones resigned and Training College leaver, Jack P Skertchly was appointed to fill the vacancy.

The ban on the wearing of stiletto heels at the Junior School was continued at Ravensdale, but the headmaster, Wilf Warren, reported that members of the Townswomen's Guild were still wearing them on some occasions.

The new Derby Diocesan Training College building taking shape. It was planned to have many of the College departments in use by the beginning of the autumn term. This picture shows the progress on the central library section and the classroom and tutorial wing to the left. Right: The Principal's home was a Scandinavian style house situated in an unbroken view across the College playing fields towards Uttoxeter Road. Miss A E Sephton, Principal, had been in residence since March with her daschund Mitzi and her cat Nipper.
Photo courtesy of the Derby Evening Telegraph

Photo courtesy of the Derby Evening Telegraph

Mrs Gertrude Warner won the award for the best cook in the Derbyshire Education School Meals Service three times in a period of four years. The gap was in 1960, when she was placed second. She supervised the preparation of 250 meals every day at Mickleover County Junior School in Vicarage Road. The choice of dish for the competition was Russian fish pie. Picture shows Mrs Warner holding the cup and her helpers, Mrs K Morrison, Mrs F Sowter, Mrs J Wilson and Mrs H J Ashworth.

The Guild were now using the hall on a regular basis. The Drama Group on Mondays; The Choir and meetings Tuesdays; dancing every fortnight and Keep-Fit every week on Thursdays.

School Manager, Joe Nadin, was sent a letter congratulating him on becoming chairman of Repton Rural District Council. He and Mrs Nadin had attended the final assembly and prize giving at the Junior School.

On September 3rd grandfather wrote that I was now "in possession of another car – Vanguard." The Morris 6 had given up the ghost and my Grandmother Brown had loaned me the money to buy a Standard Vanguard from a farmer near Ashbourne. My Grandfather Brown had died in July.

I was to learn in very recent years that Grandson Peter was the only grandchild in the Brown family who was treated so generously. In actual fact, only a few weeks passed before grandmother told me not to continue repaying her, making it our secret!

We were very close. She was the manager of the Shaftesbury Restaurant in the Morledge, Derby, and I often spent my lunch hour with her while working at

Photo courtesy of the Derby Evening Telegraph

Above: The single girl's mounting an attack in the annual football match staged by Nestlés factory girls. Left: Former Derby County footballer, Ken Oliver refereed. With him are Miss Joyce Harrison, Mrs Kay Bailey and Harold Cooper who kicked-off. Below: The victors – the married women's XI.

178

the *Derbyshire Advertiser*. It was not unknown for her to treat me to a free lunch when funds were low!

In September the County Planning Authority approved the site for a Roman Catholic Church, at Ivy Farm, at the corner of Limes Avenue and Uttoxeter Road, the old farmhouse of Tom Radford's which was still standing. All Saints' Church Hall backed on to it.

The RDC however replied that they did not feel this to be an appropriate site for a church. Joe Nadin said "it could better be used as a shopping centre."

Following this was an application by builders H J Warner for the development of Radford's orchards which stretched to the Nag's Head. They wished to build shops, with living accommodation, garages, and service yards.

The RDC Housing and Town Planning Committee made arrangements to meet representatives of the County Council and expressed the view that the project was one which should not be considered in isolation, and that the whole centre of the village of Mickleover, together with land which in all probability would fail to be developed in the future, should also be considered. They were not against the siting of a Roman Catholic Church but considered it should be on an appropriate site.

Even though Wimpeys had lost their appeal to build on the north-east, members of the parish council were asked by the RDC for their observations on an-

Photo courtesy of the Derby Evening Telegraph

A group of competitors who took part in Mickleover Royal British Legion Bowls Clubs championship events, held at the club green.

other extensive residential development. They felt that Mickleover was big enough already without having further development and they decided to oppose a proposed 65 acre site off the west side of Vicarage Road and the west side of Vicarage Park Estate, extending to the railway line in the north west.

George Hayden commented that "schools are grossly overcrowded already and we just haven't the amenities to cater for more houses and people in the village." The council agreed that the matter should be discussed at a meeting to be held with representatives of the RDC.

Anthony Yeomans reported on a meeting with the RDC concerning a Meals on Wheels Service which was to operate in Mickleover and Etwall from October. "It isn't a charity, it is just a scheme to ensure that people who are incapacitated get a square meal twice a week." he said.

The service would be in the hands of the WVS at Mickleover who had held a meeting in September to welcome those who were willing to help in the service on Tuesday and Friday of each week. The council agreed to support the scheme.

After a discussion on the Local Government Commission the council thought an early meeting should be held with representatives of the RDC.

George Hayden said: "The County Council have decided to oppose it, the rural councils have decided to oppose it, and the parish council should fight it too."

October was an extremely busy month for the new parish of St John's. On the 6th a procession took place from Ravensdale School, led by a member of the original Project Committee who carried the 2"x2" timber processional cross. Visiting clergy and other official representatives followed. The occasion was the laying of the foundation stone for the new church by Mrs Mildred Rawlinson, wife of the late Bishop, to whom the church is a memorial.

On the following day children attended the first Sunday School classes in various homes.

By October 21st the Royal British Legion room was not large enough to hold the St John's congregation for services. The hall at Ravensdale School was offered for use on Sunday mornings for Eucharist and the problem was solved.

The Reverend Ben Crockett said All Saints' Church was very sorry to lose Ken Taylor and Frank Chesterman who were now on the Parochial Church Council of St John's. Mr Maurice Johnson had also attached himself to St John's although he was still a member of All Saints' PCC.

The October parish council meeting was delayed for half an hour. The councillors arriving at the County Infants' School found that the gates were locked and after making enquiries it was found that the caretaker had forgotten about the meeting and gone out for the evening for bingo. The meeting was resumed in the

Photo courtesy of Colin Haxell

Promotional Activities were happening in aid of St John's Church. In July an open air service in the car park at the Robin was held and then a round-the-parish walk was led by a scout band. On September 23rd an Open Air Rally, complete with bagpipes and the church banner was held as an exercise for the Sunday School.

Photo courtesy of the Derby Evening Telegraph

Mrs Rawlinson laying the foundation stone of St John the Evangelist Church accompanied by the Rev Martin Pierce, the Bishop of Derby, the Rt Rev Geoffrey Allen and Anthony Rawlinson, son of the late Bishop.

memorial hut and kept up the theme against the Commission's proposals about entering the borough.

A survey of some of the parishes on the fringe of Derby was undertaken by the *Derbyshire Advertiser* on the borough expansion in October.

Reporters interviewed residents and found a fair proportion in the new estates in favour, as better services would transpire, some thought the county centre at Matlock was out of touch. Many however objected as they saw an increase in rates. None of the quotes came from people in Mickleover.

If the proposals were to be carried out the County Council would have to decide under a County Review Order what should be done with what it was left under its control. Any representations on the proposals had to be made to the Commission by November 14th.

The proposed boundary would follow a line roughly north west to Radbourne parish crossing Burton Road near Highfield House leaving Pastures Hospital in the county, but taking in the developed part of Mickleover.

Crossing the main Derby to Uttoxeter road on the Derby side of New House Farm, it was proposed that the Borough would take in a few fields in Radbourne parish on the west of Mickleover Station, using the railway line as the boundary.

Grandfather wrote on October 23rd: "Very upsetting news from USA about threatened blockade of Cuba." The Soviet Union's installation of rocket bases caused the American action and acute international tension prevailed until the missiles were withdrawn on the 28th. The blockade ended on November 20th.

On November 7th grandfather walked to Black Wood. "Found much damage caused by irresponsible youths round about the brook. A shame that so pretty a spot can be treated in such a manner."

Two days later he reported, "This morning workmen brought a big digger to start work in making a road, ready to erect bungalows in the field at the back."

The tender of H J Warner Ltd in the sum of £35,560 was approved by the Ministry of Housing and Local Government. Consequently contract documents were prepared and the RDC hoped that an early commencement would be made to the 19 bungalows, roads and sewers, east of Vicarage Road, eventually named Hilton Close.

According to grandfather it was "goodbye green field and quiet open space, with a view towards open country of Radbourne, Bearwardcote and the uplands of Needwood. Progress!" His young neighbour, Derek Moore, however was excited about the arrival of the big digger.

Following the Ministry's consent for the purchase of additional 0.32 acres of land adjoining the site, three extra bungalows would be accommodated.

Warners were prepared to extend their present contract to include them at £1,475 each plus additional work, making a total of £4,554.15s.0d.

Following the laying of the foundation stone of St John's Church an all-out drive was launched to raise the £10,000 the parish had to find during the next three years. Mr Bernard Wakelam acted as treasurer of the newly formed building fund committee.

Norman Hayton asked at the All Saints' PCC meeting when plans of the Lady Chapel, in part of the existing Clergy Vestry, would be exhibited in the church porch. Legally, plans with the citation have to be on view for 10 days.

In his review of the magazine, Jim Stampfly said "a year ago circulation was approximately 725, and even then it was losing money. With the coming of St John's there had been a gradual loss of circulation which was now about 625, and they start their new magazine in the new year." He thought it would be difficult to maintain 500 but that was the number required for it to be economical."

An additional teacher was authorised for Ravensdale from the beginning of Spring 1963. Mrs P M Hobson was recommended.

The headmaster at the Junior School, Jimmy Best, was arranging a series of talks to parents and others interested in the school. They were entitled "Selection for Secondary Education" by R Heath-Smith, "Comprehensive Education" by Mr B Gledhill and "Education in the Sixties" by J L Longland, Director of Education.

Miss Kathleen Stephens, headmistress at the County Infants' School, made the practical request yet again for a staff toilet in the main building, or alternatively a covered way to connect the main building with the existing toilet block.

An Authority electrician had pointed out to her that it was dangerous to connect apparatus to electric light sockets. A request was made for 5-amp, 3-pin sockets to be provided in all classrooms.

The National Union of Townswomen's Guilds was looking into the possibility of forming other Guilds in Mickleover and requested the use of the hall at the County Junior School in January 1963 followed by monthly meetings in the event of a Guild being formed.

The managers felt this might be a repetition of the situation at Ravensdale and asked about any sort of preferential claims for lettings.

The meeting was told that Mickleover Labour Party held meetings on the first Wednesday in each month, monthly classes in Religious Education until St John's Church was ready, worship on Christmas Day and Good Friday 1963. The church already used the school for Worship on Sunday mornings.

Mickleover Evangelical Fellowship were rejected from using the hall at Ravensdale for a Sunday School Christmas Party as it would not be used for educational purposes, thus leaving the door wide open.

The provision of grammar school places for Mickleover children was discussed and it was resolved to send a letter to the Divisional Education Officer stating that John Port School was only a 2-form entry grammar school and was at present "bursting at the seams," that approximately thirty per cent of children in Mickleover got to grammar schools, and the managers feared that when the

Ravensdale School children leave that school in 1964 to enter secondary schools the John Port School would not have sufficient places to cope with all the children entitled to a grammar school education, and that the managers wished to know how the Authority proposed to cope with the matter.

The reasons for the Minister of Housing and Local Government turning down Wimpeys appeal to develop land in the north-east of the parish were explained at the November parish council meeting.

On the grounds that there was "a need to preserve the distinction between the two units development" led the council to feel the decision strengthened their statement to the Commission concerning the separateness from Derby borough.

Although there was no permanent library in Mickleover at that time representations pointed out that the County Librarian had recently indicated that the layout of a site had been agreed with the RDC and the Area Planning Officer. The scheme would provide Mickleover with permanent library facilities, and an administrative centre for all the County Library services in the southern part of the county.

"This good news loses much of its effect when coupled with the probability that the County Council are unlikely to proceed with the scheme, if the Commission's draft proposals are implemented" the council stated.

Grandfather wrote of "interesting news of bye-election results" on November 23rd. In the five bye-elections that had taken place throughout the country the Labour Party had gained the majority.

The *Derbyshire Advertiser*, staunch supporters of the Conservative Government, wrote "dragging on the Common Market negotiations has lost the government a lot of votes, simply because people are now tired of waiting for it. They expect results. "Today an upsurge of materialism has swept the country. It may be the price we have to pay for the loss of influence in other spheres throughout the world."

On the 24th grandfather wrote that he travelled to Birstall to visit my parents "and met Lewis and family and Peter and Ann – his sweetheart."

Reg Ratcliff died on December 3rd, aged 57. He was in business as a nurseryman at Mickleover and had a stall in Derby Market.

He was chairman of the Memorial Hut Trustees and chairman of the 124th Derby Mickleover Boy Scouts Parents' Association and his two sons, John and Bill, Scout Master and Assistant Scout Master respectively. A keen cricketer, Reg formed the Revels Cricket Club and regularly captained the team.

Robert (Bob) Hinton, Chief Male Nurse at Pastures Hospital said the overall staffing position showed a patient-nurse ratio of four to one which was "far above the national average, and one which is desirable to maintain."

Photos courtesy of Peter Sherratt

Nestlés Chistmas Party for children and staff.

He was speaking at the annual prizegiving and was followed by the Matron, Mrs Vivian Auton, who reported on the female nursing situation. Here too there was a slightly upward trend and "recruitment was satisfactory," she said.

She was leaving to take up a similar post at Lancaster Moor Mental Hospital having been at Pastures for the past three and a half years. Her successor was Miss Marjorie I Fowler, Deputy Matron of St Ebba's Hospital, Epsom.

The parish council decided that tenders should now be invited for the Bramble Brook development scheme.

After receiving complaints that people were tipping clay and other rubbish on the site, Alan Ratcliff reported to the parish council meeting that he had personally inspected the area and had seen a certain amount of rubbish had been left. The council decided that a "No Tipping" sign should be erected at the site.

Mr N Porter, who had represented the council on the scheme, said he would be leaving the district at the end of the month and this would mean he would have to resign from the parish council. Philip Spilsbury also said he would be spending a considerable time away from the district in future and it was decided to deal with the question declaring a casual vacancy at the next meeting on January 15th.

CHAPTER TEN
EVERYONE'S CONVENIENCE
1963

Building work on the old people's bungalows off Vicarage Road was delayed because of the appalling winter weather which affected all outside work. It continued to be at a standstill in March but at least agreement had been made that the new road be named Hilton Close as a tribute to a former vicar.

Mr R A Davoll, Cleansing Superintendent for Repton Rural District Council commented on the difficulties of the refuse collectors. "I would like to place on record the outstanding efforts of all the men who have carried out their work under the most arduous conditions."

The new Pakamatic 34 refuse vehicle had begun to operate in Mickleover with the crew being increased by one man to six (Pastures Hospital not included).

"This vehicle has greatly eased the work as it has the capacity of two and a half loads of a fore and aft tipper," said Mr Davoll.

The men had now been put on a bonus system of payment and "weather permitting every house now enjoys a weekly collection."

Courtesy of Colin Haxell

St John's Church gets underway. The first issue of St John's Parish Magazine was distributed in January 1963 and a model of the Cross (inset) was submitted to the PCC by Mr K J Wilkinson, the designer and maker. He explained that "the design was modified by varying the angle of the crosses and inclining them towards one another in order to achieve a free and interesting interplay of shapes."

Photo courtesy of Aerofilms
This photograph was taken by Aerofilms in 1963 when the factory was then trading as Keillers. The factory sports field is just visible on the right and builder, Horace Warner's house is on the left before the entrance to his yard, close to Mickleover station.

Mrs P M Hobson joined the teaching staff at Ravensdale School at the beginning of the year. At the School Managers meeting, headmaster, Wilf Warren, having seen the plans of the new Junior School to be built on the site, was asked to go to the County Offices to discuss them with the County Architect.

Fifty people attended a public meeting in Vicarage Road Junior School on January 16th to discuss the formation of an additional Townswomen's Guild to serve the estate residents. The Guild was to be held on the fourth Wednesday in each month and forty-five of the ladies present signed membership forms.

Mickleover Townswomen's Guild decided to include the word East in their title to distinguish the branch from the recently formed West Group.

Mr Don Cunliffe, the Factory Manager at Nestlés factory on Station Road, announced to the press on January 14th that "owing to an internal change of policy, they will now concentrate on producing confectionery for a subsidiary company James Keiller and Sons (Dundee)."

He added that Nestlés products would gradually be replaced by Keiller products although some would still be produced under the Nestlé label.

Mr Cunliffe said that most of the production at the factory was scheduled for export and if the increase in the volume of export trade continued he hoped to increase the total staff of the factory from about 250 to 400, "but that would be a gradual process."

The Nestlé Company was the fourth largest in the world, outside the USA and Russia. The firm of Crosse and Blackwell, famous for its jams and pickles going back to 1706, entered the group in 1960.

However Nestlés were going through a bad phase when the government announced the Selective Employment Tax, where tax was paid on every employee. This put Rolls-Royce into trouble, together with Crawfords Biscuits who closed down one of their factories.

The Vicar of All Saints' Church, Reverend Ben Crockett reviewed the year at the Annual Parochial Church Council on February 22nd.

"It had been one of consolidation following the formation of the new district of St John's. We have to make up our minds where we are going and the feeling of the council is that the next three years must be used to benefit the church and congregation," he said.

Arrangements were being made as speedily as possible to start work on building a new Choir Vestry adjacent to the church tower. The scheme would also include a Lady Chapel in part of the existing Clergy Vestry.

Grandfather writes in February of Harold Wilson being elected to the leadership of the Labour Party. The appointment was due to the death of Hugh Gaitskill who had followed Clement Attlee in 1955. Local MP George Brown lost the ballot by 31 votes but he continued to be the Deputy Leader of the party.

Photo courtesy of the Derby Evening Telegraph
Lord Wakehurst, Lord Prior of the Order of St John, invests Miss Elsie Ferguson Bell, of Ivy House, as a Dame of the Order at a ceremony at the Grand Priory Church, Clerkenwell, London.

The parish council had received the RDC's approval for a grant towards the acquisition and development of land adjoining Bramble Brook as a children's playing field. The county council also agreed to make a grant to the parish council towards the cost of the acquisition of land to extend the Vicarage Road playing field.

A tender for £9,135 was accepted by the parish council for the proposed development of new playing fields on the Bramble Brook land.

The work was to be carried out by H J Warner Ltd and the chairman of the council, Arthur Ravensdale, said he had received an assurance the scheme would be finished by the autumn.

Clerk, Les Miller, said he had received a letter from the County Librarian following the council's request for a branch library in Mickleover.

However they were not prepared to take any action over the matter until the question of the boundary proposals was settled. Councillor Hayden said he felt the County Council's view of holding back was not at all satisfactory.

Mickleover's bus service was causing much discussion in the *Derby Evening Telegraph's* correspondents pages.

The principal complaint, along with the varying intervals between buses, was the lack of display on buses routed along either Western or Darwin Roads. "It is frustrating when a bus carries on straight along Western Road instead of making the expected turn into Brisbane Road," wrote one complainant.

Wilf Warren, headmaster at Ravensdale School, had arranged to employ Mrs Elma M Dyke as a supply teacher owing to the resignation of Miss Borton, as she was about to marry. Mrs Kathleen L Cummings was interviewed for the ad-

Photo courtesy of the Derby Evening Telegraph

The Duchess of Gloucester visited the Womens' Voluntary Service North Region in April and it was among the young mothers and babies of Mickleover at the Memorial Hut when the informality of the tour reached its climax. The Mother and Baby Club was launched in March 1962 and had doubled its membership.

Courtesy of G A Yeomans

Fortunately Godfrey Yeomans was one of the few railway enthusiasts to take photographs on the Mickleover line. This steam goods train is just emerging from the tunnel.

ditional assistant teacher in February and she was to begin from April 25th. Mrs Pat Ellison would be appointed to the deputy headship on the same date.

Mrs E P Seabridge, assistant mistress at the Infants' School was to leave at Whitsuntide, Mrs Joan Patricia Larder replaced her. Mrs Emma Brierley was appointed as an additional teacher at the school during the Spring and Summer terms.

At the parish council meeting in March, Arthur Ravensdale, chairman, referred at length to the school accommodation in the parish and the attention being given to the matter by the School Managers with whom he and Anthony Yeomans served as representatives of the parish council.

"The building of a new junior school on the Ravensdale site could relieve congestion for infants and juniors for the time being, but there was a strong demand for nursery provision from intelligent parents who desire some form of pre-school socialisation for their children," continued Mr Ravensdale. The provision he said was barred at government level.

At the other end of the scale, there was such a demand for adult education "that it has become almost a source of embarrassment."

They were grateful to the public-spirited people in the village who were giving time and energy to satisfy this demand through voluntary organisations.

The Vicarage Park Estate playing field had been reorganised and further land to the south purchased for future development. Havenbaulk Lane Playing Fields became more fully under council control.

Lord Beeching's plan for streamlining the railways was reaching its conclusion and it was announced that Derbyshire only needed six stations and some closure of passenger services.

As an example he mentioned the line through Derby Friargate which included Mickleover would be required for freight traffic. "In this area", he said, "the business is coal."

Grandfather took his young neighbour, Derek Moore, a walk "proceeded to Black Wood where we spent quite a while watching the trains and throwing stones in the brook."

Other local news was the announcement that Castle Donington was to be developed into East Midlands Airport. This was under the joint consortium of four councils.

Derbyshire County Council agreed however to spend nearly £7,000 at Derby Airport (Burnaston), due they said to an ultimatum from HM Customs who were thought to be withdrawing customs facilities for the Easter holiday traffic if this was not done.

The Reverend Martin Pierce, Priest in Charge of the district of St John's, hoped the weather would be kind to him and the churchwardens on March 30th for on that day he would be seated in a wooden hut with a coke brazier for warmth at the site of the new church. He hoped people would bring donations to help raise the £10,000 needed in the cost of the building.

On April 18th grandfather wrote, "work has commenced on erecting public lavatories on the piece off Vicarage Road."

The parish council representative at the May meeting of the Local Government Commissions meeting held in Derby Town Council chamber, Les Miller, was also representing the parishes of Radbourne, Findern, Twyford and Stenson.

Called by the Commissioners, the meeting discussed their proposals for boundary alterations.

"If Derby Borough boundary is not extended there will be a rural council on its doorstep with a larger population than itself," declared the Town Clerk of Derby, Norman Fisher, "making administration increasingly difficult."

Fred Bailey, clerk to Repton RDC said there was a physical break between Mickleover and the town area, only a narrow strip of ribbon development joining the two, and the Commissioners did not always take the view that ribbon development was continuous development.

Mickleover was quite definitely a separate community and the Town Council had not erected any council houses in the parish he said. All those representing the parishes outside the Borough supported the opposition to the proposals.

The parish council made strong protests to the County Council concerning

Photos courtesy of Sid Sprinthall

Ravensdale School Infants, May 1963. In the top photograph Miss Pat Ellison is the teacher, below Mrs Kathleen Luvia Cummings.

their "inactivity" in connection with a number of schemes in the parish, because of the Boundary Commission's draft proposals.

At their annual meeting the council agreed to write to the County Council raising certain matters, and if satisfactory information was not obtained then they intended to refer the matter to George Brown MP.

Requests had been made to the clerk to the County Council to receive a deputation from the parish council over financial aid for open space development and this, along with other matters, had been ignored.

In a letter from the County Librarian, it was stated that he would investigate

Photo courtesy of Henry Gaskill
Jimmy Best, headmaster and Harry Gaskill, deputy head, inspect the playing fields at Mickleover Junior School, Vicarage Road.

Photo courtesy of Ann Ellis
Teacher, Miss Ann Ellis, enjoying her duties on a Junior School visit to Treak in Derbyshire.

the possibility of increasing the number of books available at the branch library, following representations made by the parish council.

H J Warner Ltd announced on May 31st that they had reached agreement with Page-Johnson Builders Ltd that the latter would acquire for cash the entire share capital of H J Warner Ltd and its wholly owned subsidiaries, Shipmans (Ashby) Ltd, Richard Kershaw Ltd and H Newbury and Son (Builders) Ltd. The transition was due for completion in early August.

Page-Johnson Builders Ltd was formed in 1960 to take over the building and property owning business started in the beginning of the century in Birmingham by the late Herbert Johnson. Horace Warner and R Kershaw agreed to remain managing

193

directors of their respective companies. The four companies combined to trade as Page Johnson (Contracts) Ltd at Warner House, Station Road on January 1st 1964.

On the same day of this announcement grandfather collected the first payment of his increased pension, £3.7s.6d.

The spacious new buildings of the Diocesan Training College drew a steady stream of visitors to its first open day on the last Saturday in May.

The Principal, Miss Amy E G Sephton, had an academic staff of over 40 members for 460 students who took three year training courses to teach in both primary and secondary schools.

As no official opening date had been decided she felt obliged to write to the *Derbyshire Advertiser*, correcting their report that the Queen or the Duke of Edinburgh would be visiting in 1964 to formally open the College as nothing had been finalised. The *Advertiser's* defence was that the report came directly from them.

Fluoridation in water was being advised more and more and Mr H E Gray, Senior Dental Officer, County Health Department at Matlock, said he was especially concerned with children under school age and said that "many parents do not appreciate the importance of the child's first set of teeth."

In his view the benefit to children and later on to the adult population would be enormous. The Minister of Health was preparing to approve local health authorities applications for the addition of fluoride to water supplies.

Normanton Barracks, the Derby depot of the Sherwood Foresters since 1877, closed. Many Mickleover men served in the Foresters in both World Wars. The last of the Foresters stationed there joined the Mercian Brigade Depot at Lichfield. The Sherwood Foresters' Regiment carried on and kept its own regimental associations, their Cottage Homes Charity had sold their property in North Avenue in 1959.

A motor accident occurred in Mickleover on June 24th. "We viewed the damage to Foster's shop [9 Uttoxeter Road] caused by wheels which broke away from an articulated lorry. Considerable," wrote grandfather. After the resounding crash of the double-wheel, complete with half-shaft, the police went to the scene.

"The trouble was we could not find the lorry," said a police spokesman. He said the twin wheels had apparently hit a lamp standard and travelled 50 yards before hitting Robert Foster's shop.

Lorry-driver, Norman Jones of Cheshire, had not realised until he reached Denby and he walked into the police station and announced, "I've lost two of the wheels off my lorry."

On the following day grandfather commented on the view from his bedroom window. "Builders have commenced putting on the roof timbers to the houses at the bottom of our garden. The landscape has vanished, only tops of trees visible.

Photo courtesy of Colin Haxell

June saw the first St John's Garden Party at the home of Dick and Doris Arnold at 169, Station Road. Later the first Advent Fair was held in the Hall. The parish's first confirmation service had been held at Ravensdale School.

This official vandalism puts paid to charm and beauty."

President Kennedy paid a surprise visit to Derbyshire at the end of June. He went to his sister's grave at Ednesor. She was married to the Duke of Devonshire's older brother, the Marquis of Hartington who was killed during the Second World War. Kathleen died later in an air crash.

At a football meeting of Mickleover Sports Club the secretary, Dick Kenderdine reported a very poor season. "There had been a lack of spirit amongst too many players, and far too few were helping to run the club," he said.

It was thought that new talent was needed from outside the village in order to maintain Section 'A' standards.

After arranging a further meeting, which was advertised in the press, 5 written (1 Mickleover); 3 personal (2 Mickleover) and another possible application were received which would produce 30 players if all re-signed.

Mickleover Cricket Club were beaten by Spondon in the semi-final of the Jackson Senior Cricket Cup competition. Spondon hit 98 for eight against Mickleover's 87 for seven. Charlie Kenderdine (34 not out) and Ken Guy (21) made brave efforts to win the game for Mickleover.

Wilf Warren, headmaster of Ravensdale School, had taken a party of swimming beginners to the baths at Derby. Unfortunately he was called on to jump into the water, fully clothed, to rescue an eight-year-old boy in difficulties. Luckily he was revived. Wilf recalls that he had recently purchased a DAKS suit for use at work from an outfitters at Buxton. Although the staff at the swimming baths attempted to wash and dry his suit in very quick time it shrunk dramatically.

He made an application to the Derbyshire Education Committee for an allowance and eventually £11.18s.0d was granted, a third of its cost. He was very grateful to the outfitters and DAKS who agreed to contribute the remaining cost.

Don Cunliffe, Factory Manager at Keillers, received notification from the Hull and Goole Port Health Authority that 55 cartons of confectionery had accidentally fallen into William Wright Dock.

It was part of a consignment being shipped to Copenhagen, containing fruit bon-bons. Following inspection by the Public Health Department the goods were voluntarily surrendered because of contamination and destroyed.

The factory was now concentrating on sweet production with the biscuit machinery being sold apart from two chocolate enrobing machines.

Barry Hanson, who lived at Mill Farm, began working at the factory in September 1962, the first grammar schoolboy to do so. He was sent to college for one day and two evenings a week.

He recalls that the one biscuit that made money was the animal shaped biscuit, and with Nestlés having a sale and return policy any biscuits returned were crumbled down to make a bar.

Barry says it was a very happy place to work with very good process control procedures that were ahead of their time. The main products, apart from bon-bons, were cream toffee, nougat and highland slab toffee in the soft boilings department. Fruit drops and buttered sweets with chocolate or fruit centres were made in the hard boilings department.

Williamsons of Mickleover had acquired Paramount Service Station on the junction of Uttoxeter Road and Station Road. They were Austin dealers for cars and commercial vehicles.

Arthur Ravensdale, chairman, said at the July meeting that the condition of overhanging trees in North Avenue was making it impossible to walk along. "It is useless lighting this road until the trees are cut down," he remarked.

The County Council would be asked to make a general report on all aspects of the road, including road sweeping and kerbing.

Following a meeting with the County Council on July 1st Mr Ravensdale told the council that he hoped there would be a little more co-operation in the future in helping with the normal development of the residential area of Mickleover.

Residents in North Avenue were alarmed at the prospect of losing the fine old trees on both sides of the road. Frederick Robinson, 1 North Avenue, enlisted the aid of other residents to organise a petition against the removal of the trees.

A copy of the protest letter, containing 111 signatures, was sent to the County Surveyor at Matlock and a further letter to the chairman of the parish council.

The residents realised that the trees needed to be pruned and the pavement required attention, but the cutting down of the trees would remove something "of irreplaceable beauty and character."

An order had been made increasing the parish council's size to 15 members in the combined rural and council elections in May 1964.

Visitors to the Great Northern Hotel enjoyed an added attraction, the Derbyshire Lounge, at the end of July 1963. Drinkers were already well acquainted with the fascinating collection of smokers pipes from many countries.

Photo courtesy of the Derbyshire Advertiser

Following protests, the trees in North Avenue were saved. A joint meeting of the parish council, the district council and the county council found it possible to site the street lamps in a position where it would not be necessary to fell the trees.

Licensee Maurice Thornhill believed the Great Northern was one of the few public houses with its own golfing society. The Great Northern Golfing Society had 65 members and the use of indoor practice nets. Maurice was the treasurer. He also conducted dog obedience training classes on Sunday mornings.

On August 2nd grandfather wrote "three huge tanks have been brought to Allsops Garage for use as a filling station. The old house [16 Station Road] has now been completely taken down."

Later in the month, August 19th, he was delighted to report that he "saw Peter who had become 'engaged' this weekend to Ann Parrell of Alvaston.

"Derek came running in at breakfast [August 21st] all excited about the business of putting the tanks in the hole prepared at garage above. We spent 2½ hours watching." On the same day he "tried out the new toilets very decent place."

The Tender of E J Taylor Limited of £1,900 had been accepted for constructing the public toilets in Vicarage Road and work had begun at Easter.

Work was delayed in May due to two deliveries of bricks which were found to be unacceptable. They were completed at the beginning of August but the RDC experienced difficulties in obtaining a cleaner. Following the appointment of Bill Barker, the Sexton at All Saints' Church, the building was opened on August 18th.

Derby Town Council announced the gradual end of Derby's 30-year-old trolley bus system. Ironically the decision came simultaneously with the departments annual report that showed that trolley buses made a profit in 1962 of £41,529 while motor buses lost £4,255.

Molly Cavill, assistant mistress at the Junior School left on August 31st and Mrs Evelyn Hind of Hartington Way replaced her but only to leave in December because of ill health. Other teaching appointments were Mrs H Evans at the Infants' School and Ron Brierley at Ravensdale School.

The final days of the public conveniences on Vicarage Road. Pulled down to make way for Mickleover's new Library, opened in May 2007.

Headmaster at Ravensdale, Wilf Warren, hoped Elma M Dyke would become a permanent member of his teaching staff.

As the children at the Infants' School lacked countryside knowledge, Kathleen Stephens, headmistress, considered hiring a coach to take a party on a visit to a farm. The Managers advised her to join the School Journeys' Association.

Plans were being discussed by the Ministry of Transport and the County Council for improving a section of the main road between Derby and Burton.

The proposed improvement over a four mile length between the Staffordshire border and Doles Lane, Findern. A further link would be the proposed Mick-

Photo courtesy of the Derby Evening Telegraph

Mickleover Royal British Legion Juniors who lost 2-5 to Nottingham Forest Juniors in a charity game at Mickleover. Back row, left to right: Ben Riley (vice-chairman and treasurer), J Mayhew, Joe Walker, Geoff Miller, B Cooper, N Foxon, Stuart Chapman (captain), Harold Jones. Seated: Ken Lax (trainer), Mick Riley, Ken Wilson, Alan Priestley, Ian Pepper and T Sharratt.

leover link joining the A38 and the A516 to the north. It had been hoped to make a start on the improvements this year but it was thought it would be in 1964.

Subscriber Trunk Dialling (STD) came to Derby in September 1963. This allowed people to dial direct to many of the principal cities and towns throughout the country instead of through telephone operator's switchboards at the Telephone Exchange.

Because of the rate at which spaces were being used on the consecrated part of Mickleover Cemetery the RDC General Purposes Committee decided to approach the Diocesan authorities for more land. It was stated that there were only 37 double spaces left in the cemetery.

An application to buy exclusive burial rights was deferred. Councillor D Prince said there was a danger that if purchases were allowed and families moved away from the district much needed grave space would be sterilised for all time.

The Regional Hospital Board reported that the towers at Kingsway Hospital were so badly damaged in the gales last year that they should come down.

At Pastures Hospital extensive repair work was estimated to cost £1,700. The Management Committee recommended that, rather than preserve the towers, which previously served as ventilators and flues, and now had no useful purpose, they should be demolished with the roof made good to avoid continuing maintenance expenditure.

"In addition their removal would improve the appearance of the hospital," the report stated. The Board were also asked to approve acceptance of the tender of Ford and Weston Limited, Derby, for £21,398 for the first phase of a scheme for replacement of patients' canteen, kitchen, and toilets at the Pastures.

On September 14th Charles Ernest Ayre JP, died, aged 86 years. Charles was the managing director of Masons Paints, the family firm which operated in Derby. He was a long time member of the parish council and Rural District Council. The Ayres lived at The Limes, adjacent to Tesco's.

Fred Bailey MBE, clerk to Repton Rural District Council, announced his retirement at the end of October. He was appointed **MBE** in 1945 for services in connection with evacuation.

"There are probably more books read in Mickleover than any other Derby suburbs," commented Councillor Colin F White.

He was referring to a letter received by the parish council from the County Librarian, stating that no action could be taken on their request for increased library facilities.

About £4,950 would be required to provide additional books and shelves he said, and it would mean the complete monopoly of the Memorial Hut.

Photo courtesy of the Derbyshire Advertiser
Mr R V Hawcroft (right) pictured with Fred Bailey, whom he succeeded as Clerk to Repton RDC in November 1963.

"The present library facilities are not good enough," said Colin F White. "Mickleover is starved of almost everything."

Archie S N Allison suggested the County Librarian should be asked for figures showing the amount of people using Mickleover library against those at Littleover.

It was also decided to discuss the future of the council's allotments sub-committee as Mr Allison announced that he wished to resign from it, because he felt it served no useful purpose.

He stated that since he joined the committee a year ago he had never been called to a meeting.

"It is farcical to have an allotments' sub-committee. We might just as well do the business in full council," he said.

Les Miller, clerk, explained that members were appointed as overseers of the allotments, rather than as a committee. "I deal with most of the business myself, and only call upon the committee when a serious opinion is needed," he stated.

Male superiority was humbled on September 20th when a team of women employees of Keiller's factory beat a men's eleven by 12 goals to 4 in the second comic football match at the work's sports ground.

It was a free for all game with referee Ivor Stevens keeping the peace. All the men sported skirts and blouses while the girls were attired in conventional football gear. Harold Cooper, outside right, played in a smart suit of pink pyjamas and Mick Blackwell, who helped organise the game sported a flower patterned skirt, and neat velour hat adorned with roses.

Acting on complaints from tenants of 26 and 28 Vicarage Road the RDC considered it uneconomical to bring the properties up to a reasonable standard.

Following their demolition the area was to be replaced by a further pair of old people's bungalows (numbers 1 and 3). This increased the development to 24.

On October 5th Mickleover's new church, designed by Gruffydd J W

The Bishop's procession heading to St John's Church. The petrol station in Devonshire Drive is just visible.

Right: The Bishop demands entrance! Below: The Consecration Service. Below: Rev Martin Pierce leads the choir from the church after the service.
Photo courtesy of the Derby Evening Telegraph

Breakfast in St John's Hall on the day following the Consecration.

Photos Courtesy of Colin Haxell

Thomas, a chartered architect, was Consecrated by the Lord Bishop of Derby, the Rt Reverend Geoffrey Allen.

The Bishop knocked three times on the door with his pastoral staff and he was admitted by Mr Thomas and presented with the keys of the church.

The procession entered a packed church with the service being relayed to the overflow congregation in the Church Hall.

In his sermon the Bishop referred to the first inhabitants of the church – two thrushes who built a nest and hatched out their young on a window sill, while the church was still being built.

The altar, standing on a dais at the south end of the church and designed in the form of an ordinary dining table, is of old English marble from Wirksworth.

It was the only church in Derbyshire where the Vicar conducts his service standing behind the altar.

The church was a memorial to Dr A E J Rawlinson, Bishop of Derby for 23 years and a letter from his wife was published in a special issue of the Parish Magazine. "It is such a joy to us that the first Vicar of St John's should be one of his closest friends among the priests in the Diocese of Derby," she wrote.

The culmination of a red letter month for the Reverend Martin Pierce was his induction by the Archbishop of Derby, in the new church on October 25th.

Mr Pierce became Vicar of St Andrew's Derby in 1952, moving to Taddington in 1956 and Chelmorton in 1962. He was educated at the University of Leeds and the College of Resurrection, Mirfield, Yorkshire.

"Although Mickleover has a population of over 9,000 it lacks any banking facilities and seems to have been completely overlooked," Colin F White told the parish council meeting in October.

"It is not always possible for people to get into Derby to do their banking and the Post Office discourages people from using the Post Office Savings Bank current account," he added.

George Hayden told the council that an application had been made for a bank in the area, but permission had been refused because of the unsuitability of the site.

Mrs Bessie Bew had applied for alterations to the living accommodation of her shop, and erection of a Bank or shop premises at 24 Uttoxeter Road at the junction with Station Road.

Supporting Mickleover's need for banking facilities in the parish the clerk reported that the Derby No 3 Hospital Management Committee of Pasture Hospital had written to the council expressing their wishes for a bank in the area.

With a staff of 700 the hospital was experiencing difficulty in persuading them to accept payment by cheque.

Colin F White added that several shopkeepers had complained to him that they were having to act as "unofficial bankers" for the district.

Grandfather complained on October 18th that "the political scenes among the Tory party is unworthy of honourable men."

He was referring to John Profumo, Secretary of State for War resigning after lying to Parliament about an affair with a call girl, who was involved with a Russian diplomat. This, and ill health forced Prime Minister Harold Macmillan to retire. He was succeeded by Sir Alec Douglas Home, formerly Lord Home on November 30th.

The clerk to the School Managers reported that it would not be necessary to use St John's Church Hall as had previously been requested as Mr Warren had had the assurance from the building contractors that part of the new school on the Ravensdale School site would be ready in time for an extra class after Easter 1964.

What was described as the negative attitude of Derbyshire County Council towards providing a satisfactory library service in Mickleover was criticised by George Hayden at the parish council meeting.

The clerk, Les Miller, read a letter from the County Librarian informing the parish council that they would try to persuade a better selection of books, but new facilities could not be found without considerable expenditure.

George Hayden continued: "At first we were promised a new library, and now we can't even have more books for our present one." A strong protest was sent to the County Council.

At least the School Library Service arrived at the Infants' School to demonstrate a new 'self-service' van.

The possibility of public swimming baths at either Etwall or Mickleover, and another to serve the southern part of the Repton Rural District was discussed at a meeting of the General Purposes Committee.

The committee decided that although it was in favour of the provision of swimming baths in the rural district, it would defer consideration of where they should be until they knew more about the County Council's intentions.

Mr R V Hawcroft, clerk of the council, said the Mickleover Parish Council had a suitable site for a baths and community centre (south of Vicarage playing fields).

The County Council were considering a scheme under which district councils might receive financial help for the provision of covered swimming facilities.

Councillor David Prince thought a baths at Etwall rather than Mickleover, which was very close to Derby, would be preferable. It would serve a wider part of the rural district and a large number of school children.

Councillor the Reverend L Tuckley disagreed. A baths at Mickleover would serve the big estate at Mackworth, the Littleover area, and the "truly rural" parts of the same neighbourhood. A possible site would be near Keiller's factory.

Supporting the suggestion that Mickleover be preferred to Etwall, Councillor Ratcliff said Mickleover had a 9,000 population. It would be only three miles for Etwall people to travel.

Mr Hawcroft reported that a pool 82ft x 42ft would cost about £150,000.

On November 22nd grandfather wrote: "There was a news flash about President Kennedy having been shot while visiting Dallas in Texas."

His words on the 25th aptly describe the feelings of most of us at the time: "I was filled with a strange combination of fear and sorrow, and felt the impact of the event poignantly even though a witness of it through the remote flatness of the television pictures."

Permission for the building of a Roman Catholic Church on the corner of Uttoxeter Road and Limes Avenue was granted by the RDC Housing and Town Planning Committee on December 5th.

The committee decided to pass the application on a recommendation of the Derbyshire County Council. The site on the late Tom Radford's Ivy Farm would include a church hall, presbytery and car parking facilities.

Permission was earlier refused to an application by H J Warner Ltd for the development of land near the proposed church, for shops. However the Local Planning Authority stated that "they would give further consideration to the application when the proposed Mickleover by-pass had been constructed. The County Council had turned it down earlier in the year as it would be likely to give rise to pedestrians crossing the trunk road and the parking of vehicles thereon to the detriment of traffic safety."

Horace Warner had now retired after 17 years as managing director. He was succeeded by David Hutchinson, formerly General Manager of Page-Johnson (Yorkshire) Ltd. The firm was founded by Mr Warner and his father, Harry Warner in 1932. It was made a limited company in 1945.

Harry Blow, chairman of Mickleover Royal British Legion, speaking at the annual meeting stressed the importance of recruiting more members.

"The British Legion is a closed shop, probably one of the first ever, because every member must have served some time in the Forces."

The Mickleover branch had nearly 300 members. During the year the club premises had been extended to include a billiard room for two tables, re-furnished and re-decorated throughout.

Dispelling fears that Pastures Hospital will be "thrown on the scrapheap in the foreseeable future," Dr S Shone, Senior Administrative Medical Officer to the Sheffield Regional Hospital Board, stated that £218,000 was to be spent on modernising wards in the near future.

Since the Health Service began in 1948, nearly half-a-million pounds had been spent on Pastures Hospital.

"More thought was being given to mental health services at the moment than to any other branch of the National Health Service," said Dr Shone.

CHAPTER ELEVEN
ROYAL VISITOR
1964

In the *Derbyshire Advertiser's* first issue of 1964 space was allocated to "Mickleover's New and Original Playground."

Nearing completion by H J Warner Ltd, now part of Page-Johnson (Contracts) Ltd, the editorial described it "as something out of the ordinary."

The scheme they produced for the sausage shaped area on the south side of Ravensdale School, designed by Grey, Goodman and Associates "was much more interesting and was intended to serve as a long term development plan, which would be realised in stages.

"Since part of the site is near the shopping centre the designers decided to make a playground for small children in a sunny corner with seats for mothers so that they can stay and perhaps watch over their friends' children while they do their shopping, or have a picnic lunch in the summer. Most of the tiny tots' playground is hard surfaced but part of it is raised six inches and planted with grass, trees and shrubs for hide and seek.

Photos courtesy of the Magic Attic Archive, Swadlincote

Mr Cyril Grace, Director General Manager of Dudley Zoo, presenting the Dudley Zoological Society's Perpetual Cup for the best school essay competition for entrants under 11 years to Anne Brown, Susan Lawrence, Robert Knight, Robert Bristow, Amanda Varley and Ian Munro, pupils at Mickleover County Junior School.

"The edge of this area makes a raised walk straight across the playground to the second pit. There will be a little see-saw and a swing here too, with a Wendy house (for playing shops), a toilet and a store – all part of the children's play house. The fence around the playground is only there to deter older children from coming in and getting in the way of the younger ones.

"The field on the other side of the stream will be laid out for older children with brick walls of various heights, including part which could be made into a theatre for plays in the summer for adding a temporary curtain. The walls are arranged so that there is a space in the middle which is partly hidden from the surrounding houses and a store will be built nearby. This area could be used by the children as an 'adventure playground' where they can dig holes, build wooden houses and generally make as much mess as they like.

"On the green around the brick walls and 'adventure playground' will be the mechanical equipment which is essential for every playground – arranged so that the children can go first to one thing, then see another further on, and so on around the ring. There is a hard play area at the top of the field which can be marked out for various games.

"There will be a ladder fixed to the side of the store so that children can climb on the roof and across the public path over a narrow bridge to the children's play

Photo courtesy of the Derby Evening Telegraph

1st Mickleover Girl Guides New Year Party at the Memorial Hut.

house and at the end of the play house there will be a slide down to the 'kick-about' area.

"A garden for older people has been included at the end, with flowering shrubs, paved walks, seats and a shelter.

"Last but not least important the hedges around the edge of the play park will be thickened where possible to protect the houses bordering the park and the stream will be opened up and cleaned out."

The County Council made a 20 year grant of £158.4s.2d per annum towards the cost of Mickleover Parish Council's new adventure playground, clerk, Les Miller, told the January meeting.

The grant would decrease to £65.9s.4d for a further 40 year period and the council hoped to get a similar grant from the RDC.

Chairman Arthur Ravensdale said that after reports about the slide on the playground had been made the makers agreed to add an extra four foot extension. The council members had decided that this was essential as children playing on the slide would otherwise hit their spines on the concrete base at the end of the slide.

Horace J Warner, former managing director of H J Warner Limited, died while on holiday at Las Palmas on January 15th, aged 59 years. His body was brought home on the *Monte Anaga* which docked at Liverpool on January 24th.

"The street lights went on the first time in the OAP road this morning, one of them is situated that it partially lights our back yard", wrote grandfather on January 16th. This led him to make a claim against his rate charges and he was granted a reduction of £10 per annum. Arthur and Ingebore Caborn were appointed Wardens for the Hilton Close bungalows from January 6th.

Grandfather suffered from poor sight from his teenage years and at the end of January remarked "I can't read much these days, my eyesight won't let me."

Candidates were interviewed for the appointment of headmistress of Ravensdale Infants' School by the School Managers.

In reply for information about the Ravensdale schools catchment area the Area Planning Officer stated that the only land which was likely to become available for housing in Mickleover within the next 12 months was some six acres at the northern end of Chestnut Avenue and east of Station Road (Rangemoor Nurseries), and that the figure of 50 houses quoted by the RDC was reasonable, "although the actual figure may turn out to be a little higher."

Miss Stephens, headmistress of the County Infants' School told the meeting on January 10th that "there had been an unlawful entry to her school, all teachers' table drawers had been forced and £1 dinner money, together with £1.1s.0d from a private fund had been taken but no apparatus had been damaged."

Ravensdale now had a fully-equipped football field and Mrs V Gordon, School Manager had presented a piano to the Infants' School. Mrs E W Matthews, clerical assistant, transferred to the new Ravensdale Junior School.

A special general meeting of the Mickleover Produce Association discussed whether it should be disbanded but decided that it should continue and the position reviewed in 12 months.

Walter Appleby, a committee member, spoke of the lack of interest shown in the affairs of the association and

Photo courtesy of the Derby Evening Telegraph

Nurse Marshall, who with 30 years' service as a midwife in Mickleover was presented with a retirement cheque for more than £120 at a special gathering in her honour by Mrs Anne Atkins (left) of Findern, who was the first baby Nurse Marshall brought into the world. Flowers were presented by Mrs M Carr, mother of the last baby she delivered. The money had been collected in her district and although she counted 750 as "her own" babies, she had been present at many more births. Many people in Mickleover had cause to remember her with grateful thanks for the help at all hours of the day throughout the years. Unfortunately bad luck had dogged her over the previous two years. First her husband died very suddenly and Nurse Marshall, mainly through overwork, collapsed under the strain forcing her to give up her duties.

Photo courtesy of the Derbyshire Advertiser

The latest Esso Service Station opened in Station Road after being "modernised and extended". The site was formerly Allsop's Garage and was bought by Esso eighteen months previously. A house, 16 Station Road, was pulled down to make room for a larger forecourt for cars and a salesroom and office were added. Mechanical and body repairs and car spraying was now available. The manager, Mr W D Webster, hoped to start a car sales service.

suggested that many members were only in it for what they could get in the way of cheap seeds and fertilisers. Mrs S M Hurd was appointed to take over the duties of secretary and treasurer.

The vacancy of treasurer had occurred due to the resignation of Mr E A Holland. Commenting on the lack of interest shown in the Association, at the annual meeting, Mr H G Stenson, former secretary, said "that many of the enthusiastic members were now too old, or had passed away, and the younger generation with their cars, motor cycles and TV had no time for gardening."

Derby and District Licensed Victuallers Association and John Jacklin, the licence holder at his store on Station Road, objected to an application by Derby Co-operative Society for a full off-licence for their shop at 139 Western Road.

Although Mr Singleton for the Licensed Victuallers said an application for a licence was refused two years previously, it was granted on this occasion due to the habits of the public having changed and there was a greater tendency to drink at home.

The headteachers of the three Mickleover schools spent the morning of February 5th at the Divisional Office with the Divisional Education Officer, Roland Heath-Smith, and the complete body of Managers.

Photos courtesy of Wilf Warren

Headmaster of Ravensdale Junior School, Mr W J Warren was the conductor of the schools three choirs. At the Derby and Derbyshire Music Festival in March the choirs between them won four awards. The accompanist was Mrs Jean Pickering.

The adventure playground had been officially taken over by the parish council and two caretakers had been appointed to supervise the children.

The council agreed that they should be issued with peak caps so they could easily be recognised by the children.

Mr Ravensdale said that cycling should be prohibited in the playground, except on the special "figure of eight" cycling track.

Anthony Yeomans said he thought the track would not be suitable for older children, but should be reserved for younger children on "fairy cycles."

However Alan Ratcliff remarked, "I've yet to see any youngsters playing on the track for they have their own part of the playground." It was agreed that they should wait and see what happened when the playground was in full use.

Alan Ratcliff's wife, Kathleen, was appointed as Clerical Assistant at Ravensdale Infants' School by Mrs Evelyn Fearnehough, the new headmistress having previously worked at Rolls-Royce as a shorthand typist. They had two small boys, Trevor and Peter, both of whom were attending the Ravensdale Schools. Peter was asked not to call her "mummy" whilst at school.

Evelyn Fearnehough had been a headteacher in Derby Borough and often relied on her husband, Harold's advice on school matters as he was an experienced head in the county. Her staff, all female, was Mrs Pat Ellison, Mrs Esme Turner, Mrs Jean Pickering, Mrs Joan Gibson and Mrs Marjorie Harper.

RAVENSDALE JUNIOR SCHOOL STAFF, APRIL 1964		
Headmaster: Mr Wilfred John Warren		
	Form	Pupils
Ronald Brierley	Class 1 (First year junior)	51
Jack P Skertchly	Class 2 (Second year junior)	50
Avril Owen	Class 3 (Third year junior)	46
Eric Amott	Class 4 (Fourth year junior)	42
Mrs E Matthews	Clerical Assistant	

Grandfather noted on February 14th that he "went to the Poetry Circle meeting in the evening . . . . had a chat with parson Crockett coming home on bus."

On March 15th grandfather reported that it was "snowing this morning. It must have snowed heavily in the night as it was thick on the ground. Reports of roads blocked and floods."

It must have deterred people from attending the parish meeting two days later as it began at 7.05pm with the chairman making his annual report and closing at 7.25pm.

However for the benefit of seven parishioners who arrived at the close of the subsequent meeting Arthur Ravensdale presented his report again and some informal discussion took place.

Further progress was made to the adventure playground when the re-fitting of a former pump house as a shelter for the two caretakers was approved.

Mr Ravensdale referred to the playground providing "an element of danger" for small children, who would slide down the clay banks very easily. "We have had cases already," he said.

He thought the only safe solution would be to "culvert the brook course for the length of the playing fields."

Colin F White referred to previous letters to the RDC asking for the introduction of a smokeless zone at Mickleover, which, he stated, had gone unanswered. "I think it is somewhat astonishing," he said, "that a matter which I took up two or three years ago, has seen no action.". When a reply was eventually received the RDC clerk said the matter had been deferred because of the lack of smokeless fuel.

Les Miller, clerk, reported that the Trent Bus Company had pointed out the difficulty for buses turning at the Square because of the number of parked cars. It was agreed to support the bus company's plea for the marking of a parking-free channel by white lines and the display of a notice at the Square drawing attention to the car park in Vicarage Road.

Peggy Goodwin recalls her father, Charlie Langley, the landlord at the Masons Arms sitting around the bar fire one afternoon in 1964 and thinking of something to do to liven up the village at Easter.

Photo courtesy of the Derby Evening Telegraph

Mickleover Royal British Legion beat Ley's and Ewarts Reserves 4-0 in the Derby and District Senior League, Section "E" Cup Final. From left to right: Mick Godkin, Brian Swindell (captain), Alan Priestley, Ken Wilson, John Potter, Ken Mensah. Front Ian Pepper, Ray White, Dave Warner, Ron Davies, Mick Riley.

Photo courtesy of the Derbyshire Advertiser

Members of the Mickleover Townswomens Guild (East) Choir pictured before their dinner at the Coppice Hotel on May 4th 1964.

He suddenly announced: "Well you are all builders, how about a wheelbarrow race?" Only two barrows competed in the event the first time it was held, but after that it really took off.

The race for two-man teams was round three public houses in the village – a round trip of about 600 yards. With one man in the barrow, each pair had to drink a pint of beer in the three public houses, The Masons, The Vine and the Nag's Head Hotel.

Hundreds of villagers watched as Arthur Brown and David Jackson, both from Havenbaulk Lane, came home winners in ten minutes. The prize was 20 cigarettes. "We shall get a cup and make it an annual competition" said Charlie Langley.

The opening of Ravensdale County Junior School took place on April 14th. Eric Amott became the deputy head at the Junior School and Pat Ellison at Ravensdale Infants' School.

Carol Hammerton had resigned as a full-time Assistant Teacher at the County Junior School and Mr A O Coleman was interviewed in connection with the vacancy to replace Mrs Hind.

The School Managers were now to deal with the four schools in Mickleover by dividing them into two groups in the new school year: (a) the County Junior and County Infants'; (b) Ravensdale Infants' and Ravensdale Junior. One meeting per term for each group would take place, but very urgent matters would receive attention at such meetings.

The 22 bungalows at Hilton Close had been completed and handed over on January 9th with Page-Johnson receiving a penalty for not completing the contract

Photos courtesy of Wilf Warren

Ravensdale Junior School's first organised three-day trip to London in June saw forty pupils set out. They were accompanied by four members of the teaching staff, the school secretary and the headmaster's wife.

on time. The two additional bungalows had been put out to tender as the price negotiated between the contractors and the council was felt to be rather high at £6,309.0s.0d. A tender of £4,109.7s.0d by A T Winfield (Chaddesden) Limited was accepted.

Nottingham Roman Catholic Diocesan Trustees informed the RDC that an opportunity had occurred to purchase Mickleover Lodge off the north side of Uttoxeter Road, as an alternative site to that already approved.

"After very careful consideration of both sides available the Diocesan Sites Commission has intimated preference for the site offered by The Lodge." They requested the council's approval.

Grandfather had noted that "a start has been made on taking down the three towers at Pastures Hospital." The work began on May 11th and it was expected to take six weeks to completely demolish each tower.

Linda (née Gibson) Lodge was a Ravensdale Junior School pupil in the party to London on June 11th and she has retained the full programme for the trip (cover above). Nothing was left to chance, right down to "a change of stockings" and pocket money, "ten shillings is quite sufficient."

Even the places of interest on the journey down were explained in full with Loughborough being described as the place for the casting of bells, (Taylor's Bell-foundry). "The great bell of St Paul's was cast here."

Travelling down by train they were met at St Pancras Station by a coach and taken to their hotel near Hyde Park.

Their day continued with seeing the sights of London and then to Windsor and finally London Airport. After "High tea" they went to "see a presentation at the London Planetarium."

The highlight of the second day no doubt was their visit to the BBC studios to see a recording of the *Ken Dodd Show* and the final day included a trip up the Thames.

The Duke of Edinburgh made a two day visit to the Derby area to perform the opening of various institutions. He arrived on May 15th on the Royal Train at Derby Midland station and made the short journey to the Loco Works followed by the formal opening of the British Railways Engineering Research Laboratories on London Road.

His next visit was the Diocesan Training College at Mickleover. Prince Phillip was introduced by the Bishop of Lichfield and Miss Amy E G Sephton, Principal, thanked him for opening the College. The Bishop of Derby, the Rt Reverend Geoffrey Allen, conducted a service in the College Hall before the opening ceremony.

On opening the college he spoke to the students and said that he did not know how anybody had the face to start training for teaching.

Photo courtesy of the Derbyshire Advertiser

Derby Mayoress, Mrs Brenda Barker meets the Duke at the Diocesan Training College.

Miss O Pettigrew shows the Duke the yacht she built at the College.

He felt that the essential qualities a teacher must possess were "the dedication of a saint, the patience of a bird watcher, the sympathy of a parent, and the leadership of a general."

The Duke said that teachers received no thanks for their leadership and added that people tended to pile extra chores on to them just because they were teachers. He apologised for causing them more work with his Award Scheme.

The crowds wait patiently in Devonshire Drive for the Duke's visit to St John's Church.

218

Photo courtesy of the Derby Evening Telegraph

A selection of photographs from the Duke of Edinburgh's visit to St John's Church.

He wished the students the best of luck in their careers, adding that they would need it, and he offered his sympathy to the staff.

All Mickleover Schools were closed for the afternoon and lined the streets for the Prince's visit. He left the College and was driven to the new St John's Church where he met several parishioners.

After the introductions by the Bishop of Derby the Duke paused to speak to Miss P Northend, captain of the 2nd Mickleover Girl Guides who were on parade with the 1st Mickleover Girl Guides.

He went inside the church and later inspected the adjacent hall. Before returning to his car Prince Phillip spoke to members of the church youth club and their leader Mr Peter Howarth and to District Scout Commissioner Mr Tom M Brown.

He asked members of the youth club about their activities in the Duke of Edinburgh Award Scheme. He was particularly interested in their work for the pursuits and public service sections of the scheme.

He also spoke to Guides and members of the three scout groups on parade including the 124th Derby (Mickleover) and 149th Derby (Mickleover Methodist).

"The unusual architectural design of the church drew the Duke's attention as he was leaving and he made comments to the Reverend Martin Pierce about this before waving a goodbye to the crowds pressing round his car," reported *The Derby Evening Telegraph*.

The Duke left the Church with Sir Ian Walker-Okeover, the Lord Lieutenant to spend the night at Okeover Hall before continuing his tour the next day. He officially opened the Derby and District College of Technology on Kedleston Road and in the afternoon travelled to Alfreton.

Following the Duke's visit correspondence began to appear in the local press regarding the condition of the road in Chevin Avenue. It was left to Miss Sephton, the principal, to explain why a temporary repair had been carried out for the Royal visit after residents had complained continuously since June 1961.

She said that the College had worked hard to have the road made up but it depended on the Ministry to sanction payment before the County Council could carry out the work. Long before the Duke's visit, she continued, "the Ministry had agreed that if there were delays caused in the permanent road works the college could undertake a temporary and superficial repair in the spring."

On June 13th grandfather wrote that "Hilda's watch, obtained with Green Shield Stamps came this morning." The stamps were very popular during the 1960s. Retail organisations purchased them from an American company and then gave them as bonuses with every purchase made, the more the customer spent, the more stamps they received. It was estimated that over 80 per cent of households collected the stamps in books to claim articles later from catalogues.

Grandfather was informed later in the month that my sister, Sheila, had given birth to a second son, Richard. Her first marriage had failed but all welcomed J W E (John) Harrison into the family.

Photo courtesy of Derby Museums and Art Gallery L9621

On June 11th Grandfather wrote that "the house and premises of deceased Tom Radford, once dubbed Mayor of Mickleover, is being demolished." He was referring to Radford's farmhouse on the left and all the outbuildings. This photograph was taken from Uttoxeter Road down Limes Avenue around the 1930s. This was the beginning of developments in this area.

The Boundaries Commission dropped its most controversial proposal to transfer Swadlincote and part of Repton Rural District Council to Leicestershire. However it stood by its suggested extension of the county borough of Derby in its final report for the area, addressed to the Minister of Housing and Local Government.

Objectors to the proposals, including local authorities, other public bodies and private people, now had until the end of October to make representations to the Minister. Public local inquiries were to be arranged during 1965 before decisions were taken on the various proposals.

The enlarged borough would have an area of 19,100 acres, a population of 215,000 and rateable value of £9,260,000.

All Saints' PCC said future fund raising for the Building Fund would include the provision of a new Church Centre. Mr G L Larkin, architect, said he would produce an estimated figure within a few days and it was agreed that it would be unwise to start on the appeal until that was known.

Mrs F D Beavis replaced Gladys Ravensdale at the County Infants' School. Elma Dyke and Miss Jennifer Dicken from Bonehill Farm, joined the staff at Ravensdale Junior School.

Jimmy Best, headmaster at the County Junior School had been making arrangements for the Managers, teaching staff, the primary schools and a number of parents to visit Fareham Comprehensive School, Clifton, Nottingham in readiness for the forthcoming announcement on a comprehensive school at Etwall. He said that in view of the numbers of replies it was possible to fill a forty-four seater coach.

The Managers were given permission to formerly open Ravensdale Junior School and could spend up to £10 on refreshments, decorations etc. The final cost was £15.11s.1d. Joe Nadin was asked to open the school.

A letter from the Area Youth Organiser was read at the May parish meeting stating that he hoped to form a youth organisation in the Mickleover area. He had obtained permission for the group to meet in the memorial hut twice a week, and he invited the parish council to send a representative to a meeting on June 2nd. The council agreed to send John Robert (Rob) Nield.

At a meeting of the RDC on June 25th it was agreed to oppose the final proposals to include part of the parish of Mickleover.

The scheme for road widening at Cattle Hill was proceeding "although very slowly," said the vice-chairman of the parish council, Alan Ratcliff, at the monthly parish meeting. Les Miller, clerk, said he had heard from Stanley Mehew, the County Surveyor, that work should start on the road, possibly next year.

Members asked if the County Surveyor could be asked if part of the bank (see

Photo courtesy of the Derby Evening Telegraph

Pupils of Mickleover County Junior School who attended the presentation at the school the day before the summer holiday.

No (3) map p271) could be removed as a temporary measure, to give both motorists and pedestrians more room.

All Saints' PCC agreed to go ahead with the Lady Chapel and Choir Vestry in January and by March the plans included re-siting the organ console at a cost of £42.

"In the Lady Chapel there is to be a silver cross made by a local craftsman at the School of Art and two candlesticks on the altar in place of a cross on the dosal curtain," said Percy Pickering.

The PCC were informed in June that the Vicarage would have to be inhabited for a further three to four years. This led to the Finance Committee agreeing that the Vicar be given central heating.

An estimated cost was £150 over three years which was hoped to be paid for by the Diocese with the PCC paying part of the running costs. The council would also be responsible for lagging the roof and work would be started as soon as possible.

The estimate for the Lady Chapel would be £1,100 and £3,590 for the Vestry, making a total of £4,690. The Diocesan Advisory Council had informed the council that "they were pleased with everything in connection with the project." The Form of Faculty was filled in and sent the day after the meeting.

It was announced that the last passenger trains from Nottingham Victoria to Derby Friargate would run on September 5th.

Pride in the Derby to Etwall line by the railway staff was rewarded when the stretch of line won the prize for the best kept length in the area, the last year in which such awards were made. Dr Beeching had now severed the last links of the old LNER for passenger travel.

Farewell gifts from parents, staff and pupils were presented to Miss Gladys Ravensdale in July. She retired after being a member of the teaching staff at the County Infants' School for 19 years.

Miss Pat Beech was to leave Ravensdale Infants' School at the end of August because of her forthcoming marriage. Esme Turner was appointed in her place. Sue Hartley also left the County Junior School.

A new sports trophy donated by the parents of the head boy and head girl was presented for the first time at the third annual speech day at Ravensdale Junior School.

Mr Warren gave a brief outline of the school progress during the year. He referred to the outstanding success of the school choir and the trophies that had been won which were on view.

Among the various changes to Mickleover Sports Club rules, heard at a General Committee Meeting in August, it was agreed that membership would be open to residents of "the Parish of Mickleover".

Photo courtesy of the Derby Evening Telegraph

Members of Mickleover WVS Mother and Baby Club pictured before setting off on an outing to Wickstead Park, Kettering.

A football section would be formed to be called the Mickleover Football Club and the cricket section Mickleover Cricket Club. Both would be confined to Mickleover Sports Club. Ken Guy, cricket secretary was voted "Clubman of the Year".

Complaints of air pollution caused by smoke in Mickleover were made at a meeting of the parish council when one member, Mrs Marjorie M Howarth declared: "It is far dirtier here than it is in the suburbs of London."

The council agreed once again to write to the RDC inviting representatives to meet them to discuss the possibility of the area becoming a smokeless zone.

Colin F White commented that he had made enquiries about Mickleover becoming a smokeless zone. "It looks as though we shall have to wait until we are in the Derby Borough," he said.

Taking the opposite view Joseph Charles Smith remarked: "I don't think there is any air pollution in Mickleover. If you have lived in a city then you will know what air pollution is." The RDC deferred a decision over taking action over smoke control for twelve months.

The burning of fuels which created smoke was prohibited in the Derby area beginning with Allestree in 1969. Others followed but Mickleover and part of Friar Gate was introduced in 1972 and Spondon to be the last in 1978.

Mr Donald Cunliffe took up his appointment as general manager of the Nestlé Company Limited at the Hayes, Middlesex factory.

Photo courtesy of the Derby Evening Telegraph
Donald Cunliffe, (seated), with the newly appointed general manager at James Keiller and Son Ltd, Stan F Hearn.

He was appointed site manager at the new Nestlé factory in October 1956 when building work at the Mickleover confectionery manufacturers, Station Road started and he was appointed general manager when the factory was completed.

His successor, Stan F Hearn succeeded him. He had been manager at the now named Keiller factory in Mickleover for a year. He had previously managed a Nestlés factory in Northern Ireland.

A meeting of the Primary and Secondary Education Sub-Committee was held at the County Offices, Matlock on October 6th.

The scheme for the amalgamation of Etwall John Port and Etwall County

Secondary School to form a Comprehensive School was approved. It had already been agreed with the Governors of the schools concerned.

Peter K Hall, headmaster of John Port was appointed headmaster and Mr Gledhill, the serving head of Etwall Secondary School was to become deputy head.

Mickleover heads were informed by Mr C W Phillips, Assistant Director of Education for Derbyshire at John Port Grammar School on October 21st that as from September 1965 the two schools would go out of existence.

Varying planning applications were being discussed by the RDC Housing and Planning Committee.

Permission had been refused to convert Horace Horner's hairdressers premises at 57 Station Road, because of the increased congestion of traffic. The applicant for converting 12 Uttoxeter Road (8) into office premises for a bank withdrew the application.

However applications for Barclays Bank premises at 3 Vicarage Road, (4) then a Post Office, and 24 Uttoxeter/Station Road junction (9) for National Provincial Bank were still in discussion.

At 1 The Square (6), the demolition of the existing property for the erection of 2 lock-up shops with flats over was being considered. The use of a vacant single room shop as a Betting Office at 10 Station Road (10) was to be advertised.

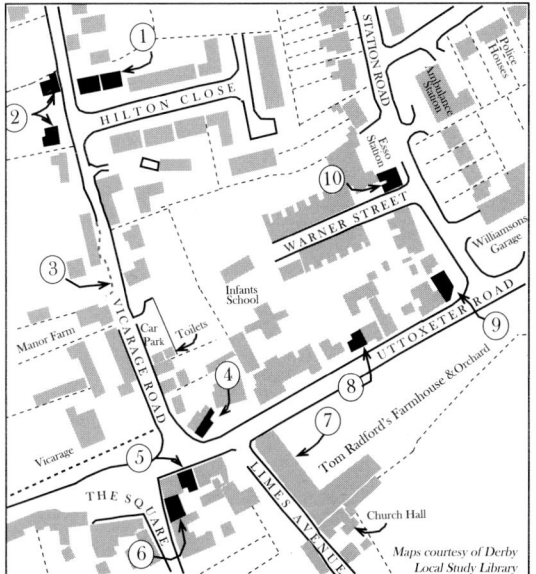

This plan shows some of the changes in property use applied for during 1964. The only exception is (5), the position of Bob Foster's shop which was damaged by lorry wheels in 1963.

Permission was granted on September 3rd to A Winfield Limited to build 4 detached houses and garages on the south side of Mill Lane, off Station Road and it was announced in the press that George Wimpey were to build 93 houses and garages in the Rangemoor estate.

Development of land for "residential purposes", between 25 and 29 Vicarage Road (2) was being considered. The applicants W R and N Millward were advised that "buildings now required a minimum distance of 8ft to be maintained between any windows of a room capable of use as a 'habitable room' and the plot and boundary where such windows occur on the side elevations. A 'habitable room' would normally include bedrooms, living rooms, dining rooms, studies and kitchens."

Despite the official view that a decision on library provision for Mickleover must await a settlement of the Derby boundary dispute, the parish council decided at the September meeting to press for a permanent library in the village, and insist that it should be proceeded with at once.

Arthur Ravensdale said there had originally been a scheme for a library on a South Derbyshire regional basis, with vehicle provision for a mobile library service, but this was now shelved.

Improvement of the present library facilities could not be included in the present budget, they had been told.

Les Miller, clerk, said that in the event of Mickleover being absorbed into Derby, a new library would simply pass to Derby ownership, along with the outstanding loan debt.

It was agreed to buy copies of the map accompanying the Derby proposals for members of the council at a cost of £1.18s.0d (see p227).

The council's request to the RDC for "local labour" to improve the grass verge in Havenbaulk Lane, by the recreation ground, brought a reply from George Hayden, who was also a member of the RDC. He said the matter had been discussed but there was a shortage of labour for work of this kind.

Told by the County Surveyor, Stanley Mehew, that funds would not provide for a pavement on Station Road, north of Moorland Road the council decided to press for this work to be done as soon as possible and for priority to be given to the provision of hard standing at bus stops.

The council approved the purchase price of £531.16s.0d for a piece of land adjoining western part of the playing fields and was told that a grant of £212 had been received from the RDC. A reply for a grant from the County Council was still awaited.

A service of Dedication was held at Ravensdale Junior School attended by about 200 parents and 80 invited guests. Reverend Martin Pierce led the prayers followed by a reading. Reverend Alan Barber, Methodist Church led the Dedication.

October: "Peter has acquired a bungalow [Gisborne Close] situated not far from where his mum and dad live."

The day before his 80th birthday, October 17th, he wrote that "we sat up until 1.30am watching election results on TV, exciting." Labour won with an overall majority of five and Harold Wilson became Prime Minister.

George Brown had an increased majority of nearly 2,000 and he was appointed First Secretary of State and Minister for Economic Affairs.

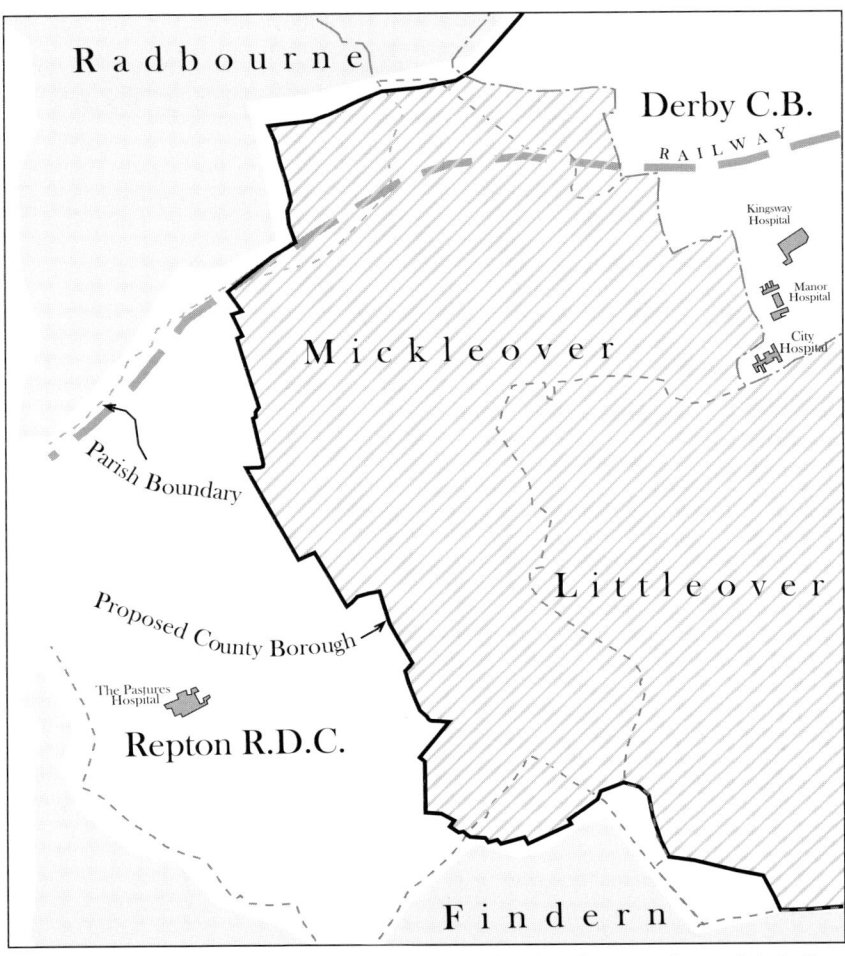

A large proportion of Mickleover Parish was to be taken into the county borough including the tips of Findern and Radbourne. Allestree, Alvaston & Boulton, Chaddesden, Chellaston, Darley Abbey, Littleover and Sinfin Moor were to see most of their parishes also included.

It was reported at the parish meeting that the teenagers known as "The Odd-Bods", who had been helping the old people of Mickleover to do their gardens, should be given lime, soil and grass by the RDC to help them in their job.

Arthur Ravensdale said "that they were helping to beautify the council's own property."

The council were having to pay back the sum of £50 to the County Infants' School, as they had paid rental for the playing fields when they had not used them. It had not been noticed for two years that they were using their own playing fields.

Grandfather was informed that he had won a place in the "A" short list for sonnets in the Shakespeare Centenary competition, promoted by the National Poetry Circle. Derbyshire's well known poet, Teresa Hooley, had written to congratulate him on being placed high on the "A" list and that in all there were 670 competitors. "I feel on top of the world'" he wrote.

Two public spirited Mickleover residents had approached the National Blood Transfusion Service in Sheffield with the proposal that a Blood Donor Session might be organised in Mickleover.

House-to-house distribution of enrolment forms and other publicity material was included at an exhibition, including film shows, held in the Memorial Hut on Saturday November 14th. It was hoped to encourage a response to the actual session which had been arranged for November 29th at All Saints' Church Hall in Limes Avenue.

The parish council had received a letter from the RDC regarding the road widening in Vicarage Road stating that work would be carried out at the earliest possible date.

The scheme was being held up because the District Valuer had not yet come to any agreement with the shop owner, greengrocer Sid Thornhill, about the value of his property. This would have to be knocked down and he was not prepared to let this happen until another house had been built on his land at the back of the present premises.

The District Surveyor had suggested that the scheme could be speeded up, if the owner would be prepared to move into temporary accommodation.

On November 18th grandfather wrote that "two old houses at the entry of the old age pensioners' bungalows on Vicarage Road had been taken down." (Map p271). He experienced the vacuum chimney sweep for the first time at a cost of 7s.6d.

Joe Nadin was elected as chairman of the School Managers as Arthur Ravensdale was having to retire from the post because of ill health.

November 27th saw the official opening of the first Crypton-Heenan "rolling road" in Derbyshire.

The rolling road, which simulated road testing conditions, was installed at Williamson's Garage on Uttoxeter Road and opened by radio and TV personality Ted Moult.

It was also the first garage in the area to install a Crypton tuner which they would now use in conjunction with the rolling road. Veteran cars and a traction engine show, plus the latest Austin cars, were on display over the two days.

Edward Gothard said how pleased he was to see so many members present at the annual meeting of the Mickleover Produce Association, especially after the very difficult year the Association had experienced when a special meeting was called with a view to winding up their affairs owing to a lack of interest.

The parents of members of the 149th Derby (Mickleover Methodist) Scout Group made a request to the parish council for a site on the land on the southern boundary of the playing fields, for the group's proposed headquarters.

They explained that there were many names on the waiting list to join the movement and the parents felt that if the group was able to have its own headquarters, the activities could be spread over five evenings a week, instead of the present two evenings. The group consisted of cubs, scouts and senior scouts with a ranger group for the future.

The group had accumulated their own equipment but were not able to use it to its full. It was estimated that the cost of the building would be in the region of £4,000 and a pre-fabricated building which could be extended had been proposed. Members of the council agreed with the plan in principle.

Grandfather had made his "booze order at the Co-op" for Christmas: 1 dozen Double Diamond 16s.6d, $\frac{1}{2}$ dozen Woodpecker Cider 7s.6d, $\frac{1}{2}$ bottle Johnny Walker 11s.6d, 1 bottle Landross Sherry 14s.6d. Total £2.10s.5d.

He went to the OAP tea and social at The Hut. "There was a goodly number present. The tea was excellent and the entertainment provided was enjoyable. We each of us present had a bag of sweets from Keiller's factory and I won a packet of tobacco.

"Visited Nellie [December 21st]. On arriving I observed a post set up at the front advertising the house [39 Brisbane Road] for sale. They have prospects of a bungalow nearer Mountsorrel where Fred works." He was presented with a diary, "a present from Peter and Ann."

1964 had been an eventful year highlighted perhaps by a second reading in the Commons of the Bill abolishing capital punishment. The first British space flight, the "Blue Streak' rocket, was launched from Woomera in Australia and 12 men were found guilty of taking part in the Great Train Robbery. Economically Britain received a £500 million loan from the IMF under the new Labour Government. On the fashion front three women in London were found guilty of indecency for wearing the fashionable topless dressess

CHAPTER TWELVE
THE NO! CAMPAIGN
1965

The School Managers announced teaching staff appointments at their January meeting. All of them concerned the Ravensdale Schools. Joan Larder began a part-time appointment, on a temporary basis at the Junior School until the end of the Summer Term. She was responsible for three groups of children for basic work. Mrs E A Jackson was to begin a full-time appointment in the Infants' School and Mrs Dorothy P McSwiggan and Mrs E A (Trindy) Swales took on half-time appointments until the end of the Summer Term.

A decision, subject to the approval of both the Minister of Education and a parish meeting, to lease a piece of land at the southern end of the Vicarage Road playing field to the 149th Derby (Mickleover Methodist) Scout Group was agreed.

The proposed piece of land, not to exceed half-an-acre, adjoined the two-acre site which was within that purchased and earmarked for the swimming pool and community centre. The lease was to be for not less than a period of 21 years.

Photos courtesy of Wilf Warren

The teaching staff at Ravensdale Junior School. Left to right, standing: Ron Brierley, Eric Amott, Wilf Warren (headmaster), Jack Skertchly. Seated: Mrs Elma Dyke, Miss Jennifer Dicken, Mrs Avril Owen.

230

Bob Foster, the greengrocer in the village, experienced another piece of misfortune when his lorry was badly damaged. "Fortunately he was still able to get about with it," wrote grandfather. Bob's shop was badly damaged by lorry wheels two years previously.

On January 24th grandfather reported that "on putting on the wireless about 8.45am I heard the announcement of the death of Winston Spencer Churchill."

This was the year when Mary Quant invented the mini skirt which became a symbol for the permissiveness of the sixties; the first long-distance footpath in Britain, the Pennine Way, was opened and the boxer Freddie Mills was found shot dead in his car.

Councillor George Hayden told Repton RDC on February 11th that he thought the council should use an advertising campaign in its fight to prevent Mickleover being taken into the County Borough of Derby.

"After reading a report in the local papers about the publicity which South East Derbyshire RDC was using in its fight to prevent a large portion being absorbed into Derby, and the £5,000 they have allocated to this fight, I thought we should start a similar campaign," he said.

The General Purposes Committee adopted the suggestion that the council give Mickleover every moral support to stay in the Rural District.

Councillor Reverend L Tuckley said that with Mickleover's population of 10,000 making up a quarter of the total population of the rural district "we should give them every support both morally and financially." He suggested £500 should be inserted for the New Year estimates.

Photos courtesy of the Magic Attic Archive, Swadlincote

The committee decided that as £1,000 had already been allowed for the Boundary Commission inquiry Mickleover Parish Council might fund extra money from this.

"I'm very much against any proposal to spend ratepayers' money on this fight – which I think is wrong."

Although this was stated by Councillor Colin F White at the monthly meeting of the parish council it was decided to issue leaflets and posters advertising the annual parish meeting in the hope that many of the parishioners would not only attend, but also show their willingness to "fight" the new boundary proposals.

Chairman, Arthur Ravensdale, stated that in a plebiscite three years ago, it was found that 90 per cent of the residents did not wish to go into the Borough of Derby.

Les Miller, clerk, suggested that when Mickleover wished to call a witness at the public inquiry it should be the chairman instead of the clerk who had originally been nominated. The council agreed with this advice and Mr Ravensdale should be the witness.

Mr Roland Heath-Smith, South Derbyshire Divisional Education Officer since the Divisional Executives were established in 1946, was to retire at the end of April.

In the Normandy landings, in 1944, he commandeered 102 Beach Sub-Area, which was responsible for landing the 3rd Canadian regiment on the beaches. His last teaching post was as science master in 1927 at King Edward Grammar School, Five Ways, Birmingham.

Mrs Doris Arnold of 169 Station Road, complained to the parish council about the muddy state of the east side of Station Road, where horses had churned up the grass verge. She pointed out that three bus stops and a County Council nursery were on the same side of the road.

Photo courtesy of the Derbyshire Advertiser
Roland Heath-Smith

The clerk, Les Miller, said there was no proposal for building a pavement and Arthur Ravensdale, chairman, said the only thing was to ask the horse riders for a sense of neighbourliness and good manners.

Margaret Salt of Huffen Heath Farm, Uttoxeter Road, appealed against the refusal by S E Derbyshire RDC to the installation of an egg-vending machine and the display of advertisements at the entrance to her farm.

At an inquiry HM Inspector heard the objections that the machine, which was installed in 1962, "was situated on a generally undeveloped stretch of the southern side of the trunk road." Because buying eggs from the machine would include pedestrians constantly crossing the road, and cars stopping for eggs, the council thought that this would give rise to danger.

The Derby branch secretary of the NFU, appearing for Mrs Salt, said however, that the machine had been there for some time and no traffic problems had arisen.

He continued to state that the farm was actually in the parish of Littleover, consisting of 166 acres and although the main production line was milk, there was a pig unit and also a poultry unit of about 30 hens, which yielded a production of about 200 eggs a day.

He added that eggs sold from the farm, both from the machine and the farmhouse, amounted to about 120 dozen in very good weeks.

Mrs Salt had not realised that planning permission was needed and her representative estimated that about three or four motorists stopped each day and about a dozen pedestrians came daily for eggs, plus members of the Golf Club nearby. Her objections proved to be successful as it was decided that the machine and the signs would not create a traffic hazard.

Most of the 250 residents who attended the annual parish meeting on March 16th backed the parish council to the full in their fight against the Boundary Commission proposals.

However one councillor, Colin F White spoke in favour of the proposals. He said the parish council had never been unanimous on the question since he had arrived and he thought the postal vote showing 90 per cent in staying out of the Borough was now valueless, as many more people had come to live in Mickleover during that time.

"You in fact are getting county borough services and paying county rates for them," said Mr White. He added that Mickleover was a village which depended absolutely on Derby for bus services, work and shops.

He said that Derby had spread outside its original boundaries and that they had to accept at some time or other that the boundaries would have to be altered. "Good government demands this."

"In a rapidly developing community, the provision of adequate educational facilities is of vital importance," said Mr Ravensdale. He added that because of the co-operation of both parents and staff, it had been possible to ascertain the requirements of school accommodation some five years ahead.

"A striking feature of Mickleover is the vast amount of voluntary work which is being done," he said, and added that besides the WI, Townswomen's Guild and Old Age Pensioners' Group were many organisations connected with the churches.

He concluded by saying that "arrangements are in full swing for a 'Friends and Neighbours' scheme with the idea for the old people of Mickleover to display cards in their windows showing that they needed help."

The meeting discussed several other matters and causes for complaint concerning the parish. These included the publishing of a parish magazine and cal-

Photos courtesy of Wilf Warren

Lower Junior Ravensdale Choir March 1965 at Derby & District Festival.

endar, the fouling of public places by dogs, the land in the north-east of the parish, the culverting of Bramble Brook, refuse collection and the bus service and highway matters. The chairman indicated that these matters would receive appropriate attention from the parish council.

After a vote of thanks from Tim Ford to the chairman and clerk the meeting closed with applause.

Photo courtesy of the Derby Evening Telegraph

Mickleover County Junior School choir, who were runners up in the under 10 years junior choir's section.

Percy Pickering told All Saints' PCC that three tenders had been received regarding the Choir Vestry and Lady Chapel and Mr G I Larkin, architect, would attend the meeting on March 30th.

Stanyon and Holmes, Burton-on-Trent, would complete the work in 26 weeks at a cost of £5,435; Dennis Moore, Ashbourne - 20 weeks £4,544; T W Draycott, Allestree - 32 weeks for £5,360. Mr Pickering proposed Draycott's tender be accepted which was carried and a formal contract would be sought.

Mr C F England, chairman, presided at the annual meeting of the 124th Derby (Mickleover) Scout Group in the Scout Headquarters.

In his report he told parents that the present headquarters would have to be moved to another site on the Royal British Legion Memorial Field. "If the group was to be efficient and able to cope with the needs of a fast growing community, a larger building was necessary," he stated. Mr T Brown, GSM, outlining the work of the group said that there were 80 members comprising 36 cubs, 30 juniors, seven seniors and seven scouters. He thanked Kathy Staff (Akala of the cub pack), who was retiring owing to ill health.

The Royal British Legion were proposing to start a cricket section and it was hoped that a series of friendly matches would be arranged on Sunday afternoons.

After a six month's absence the inadequate library facilities in the village were brought up again at the April parish council meeting. Councillors agreed that many people were using the library facilities of Littleover and Derby.

"I am positive that it is the same books all the time," said Mr Joseph C Smith, adding "that everybody must have already read them."

"Mickleover has a highly literate population, I should think the most highly literate in the district," said Colin F White.

He added that the library was no more than a shack which was open for a couple of afternoons during the week. "The county is failing to meet the demand here," he added. The council sent another letter to the County Library Committee, stating that they were completely dissatisfied with the library facilities.

The District Valuer was given instructions to negotiate for the acquisition of land at 12 Vicarage Road as the site for a new library.

A letter from the Chief Constable of Derbyshire in reply to the parking on Station Road said that it was regularly patrolled by police cars and action would be taken if cars were found parked in a bad position.

Colin F White, deputy head at Etwall Secondary School, pointed out that when school children were picked up just round the corner with Western Road, there were no less than three buses there and if a car was parked on the opposite side of the road there was no room for other vehicles to pass.

Photos courtesy of E Fletcher

Mrs Florence Spencer was a wartime recruit and was posted to Mickleover signalbox in 1942 and after serving for four years returned in 1961. Her sister was also employed on the Mickleover line. She is pictured here greeting the crew of "Black Five" at Mickleover in 1965.

He said that one morning a lorry had tried to pass between the buses and parked car and the lorry had gone through the side of the bus. As deputy head he was responsible for school buses and the discipline of the children, the girls taking the top deck and the boys the lower.

The council said it was a matter of regret that the police were taking so little notice of the problem which was becoming worse daily. In the following month it was agreed to move the bus stop about 50 yards towards the Memorial Hut.

Alterations to existing property and a ground floor extension to form a branch bank with car park was being considered by the RDC Housing and Planning Committee at 24 Uttoxeter Road for the National Provincial Bank.

Grandfather had drawn his increased pension of £4 per week at the beginning of April and he had observed repairs being done to the railway line on one of his walks. On April 23rd "Peter and Sheila turned up with the electric stove I am buying from Sheila. Peter brought it in his shooting brake [Morris 1100 Traveller]. He backed right up the drive, so that we had only to lift the stove a few yards." Sheila and family were moving into 39 Brisbane Road after the departure of my parents to Birstall, Leicestershire.

In 1963 George Brown, MP, led a deputation to the Ministry of Agriculture in protest against their refusal to allow Derbyshire County Council extend their smallholding scheme in the county.

The scheme, under various Agricultural Acts, was to provide suitable land and holdings for young men "desirous of setting up farming on their own," after qualifying.

Having inspected land at Pastures Hospital, which was part of the old hospital farm, the County Council were willing to buy back the 64 acres, which included two houses, to develop as smallholdings.

The Minister refused but in 1964, the County Smallholdings Committee asked the Finance Committee to approve the purchase of the land at a cost of £13,000. They would only agree to purchase Stakerfield Farm containing about 38 acres for £3,500.

Under a new Labour Government the County Council was still interested in buying the land and in early 1965 they planned to send a deputation to the Ministries of Health and Agriculture.

Opposition group leader asked why the Smallholdings Committee, having once "burned its fingers, was having another go."

Labour group leader said there had been no change in the council's views on the subject. "Young people should be given the opportunity in agriculture with a chance of getting farms on their own," he said.

Trevor Park, MP, for South-East Derbyshire, led a five members delegation to the Minister of Agriculture, Fred Peart, on April 8th.

In the course of the 40 minute meeting it was explained to Mr Peart that an answer was needed as the land, now owned by the Ministry of Health, was to be sold by auction on April 23rd.

The Minister was told that the council could not risk bidding in that auction with the certain knowledge that they could use the land for their original purpose.

A decision "within the near future" was promised.

In a separate issue regarding the Ministry's second review on farming activities, agreement was revealed between Sheffield Regional Hospital Board and the Derby No 3 Hospital Management Committee about 187 acres of land at Pastures Hospital. The Board's Planning Committee recommended to the Ministry that the land was surplus to requirements and consent to its disposal was sought. They also suggested that when disposing of the land adjoining the new southern boundary, a covenant be included at the time of sale to ensure the future use of the land for agriculture purposes only.

It was also recommended that approximately 51 acres be retained for any possible future development and leased for farming purposes in the meantime.

These pieces of land were not the ones which the County Council were seeking to acquire as smallholdings.

In a letter to Trevor Park, the Minister refused to consent to the plan to buy land to develop as two smallholdings under Section 50 of the Agriculture Act, 1947, and the land was sold to a private bidder. The 63 acres of grassland and two semi-detached cottages, 1-2 Laurel Cottages, Grassy Lane, were sold for £17,150, £4,150 above the District's Valuer's estimates. Bushby Cottage, Grassy Lane, sold for £2,625.

"With the changes that have taken place in agriculture since 1945 we must take a hard look at the future of smallholdings." He was awaiting a report later in the year.

Children of the third and fourth years at Ravensdale Junior School presented the pantomime *Aladdin in the Underworld* on May 20th and 21st in the New College Hall, Chevin Avenue. Much of the rehearsal and preparation was done by the children and staff during the Easter Holidays. Between 50 and 60 costumes were made by lady members of staff with the help of a few parents.

A new school was to be considered off Chain Lane and negotiations were proceeding for the site.

Most preparatory work was completed at All Saints' Church. However work was now held up awaiting cut stone. Some electric work and heating was also done and a new toolshed was in position.

The Reverend Crockett had said that the architect had put forward a scheme to provide the removal of two pews at the west end of the north aisle and the long pew at the back of the north block of Nave seating. The whole area could be paved with Granwood blocks.

The Vicar said a new Faculty would be required and entrusted that the Building Committee would make a final decision on their behalf.

Meeting with St John's Standing Committee was an excellent idea and it was hoped for the first meeting in the new future.

The Archdeacon of Derby and the Chairman and Surveyor of Repton RDC had requested that the PCC consider the whole question of a churchyard extension and taking over the administration of the cemetery.

Derby Corporation was challenged at the boundary extension inquiry on May 6th to produce "The slightest piece of evidence" to support the Local Government Commission's view that it would cause serious harm to the borough to remain in its present boundaries.

Mr Hugh Forbes, QC, for Repton RDC said the Commission's view ignored the problem of what was to happen to the rural district when its most populous parish was taken away.

He turned to over 5,000 cards being issued in September 1960 when about $4^1/_2$ thousand were returned. "Nearly 95 per cent were against inclusion in Derby borough," said counsel. "Mickleover was a self-contained community, wholly separate from the county borough itself.

"This view had been greatly strengthened by a recent planned decision of the Minister, who had refused to allow the gap between Mickleover housing and the Mackworth estate to be narrowed by further development," he added.

Mickleover, he said would be threatened by housing development if they fell "into the clutches" of Derby, and it would be a considerable loss to the rural district to take away its population of some nine or ten thousand.

The attitude of the Local Government Commission to suburban developments, said Mr Forbes, appeared to be that such houses "should go into the 'urbs' to which they are 'subs'.

Joe Nadin of Station Road, chairman of the Housing and Town Planning Committee of the RDC, said that Mickleover had its own churches and organisations, no less than 57 shops, meeting places and its own recreation grounds.

The RDC had plans for a swimming bath, possibly jointly with South East Derbyshire, to serve Mickleover and to serve generally that part of the rural district lying north of the rivers Dove and Trent.

He maintained that the RDC was able to deal with municipal housing needs of the area and referred to the bungalows recently built for the elderly. "It would be expected that more would be built in the not very distant future," he said.

The fact that many Mickleover people looked to Derby for their employment was not a sufficient reason for inclusion in Derby," he concluded.

Sir George Curtis, the Ministry of Housing Inspector, who was conducting the inquiry adjourned the meeting until the following week.

He chaired a meeting on Wednesday, May 12th at the Memorial Hut. He was welcomed by Councillor E H Wright, chairman of Repton RDC and thanked by Arthur Ravensdale, chairman of Mickleover Parish Council.

More than 200 people attended to protest against the proposed transfer of the parish. Representatives were there from Etwall, Findern, Hartshorne, Radbourne, Repton and Willington.

"The only reason why the Borough of Derby wants to take us in is to help their debts, by raising our rates," said Harold Wood of 64 Western Road. He said he had lived in Mickleover for 36 years and seen it grow. "This was because of the RDC and Derby had done nothing for them."

Councillor Albert Clark of Farnborough Road said that Mickleover had everything it needed for shopping and entertainment and read out a very long list of Mickleover's facilities. Mr J Barker of Western Road, a resident for 26 years, said that thanks to the RDC they had street lighting, playing fields and every facility a community could wish for. He added that if one wanted good entertainment, Derby was not the place to go, but Nottingham.

Geoff Larder thought that Mickleover should stand on its own feet, but agreed this might be difficult. "However they must persevere."

A resident from Fenton Road, Mr John E Hall, believed that at the moment Derby wanted Mickleover, then it would be Etwall and then Hatton. "Derby was going to build a ring-road 20 years ago, now they were still building it in small sections," he said.

A Mickleover parishioner spoke for going into the Borough of Derby. He said he expected the reaction from the old people of the village: "for maybe they could still see the old village life, but as a new member, he could see none." He told the meeting that if they were taken over by Derby they would still have the things they had now. When he said that it was reported that one got a much better standard of efficiency from a larger community there were great cries of Oh!

At the end of the meeting Sir George Curtis commented "As far as I am concerned it has been a valuable evening."

The *Derbyshire Advertiser* continued the publicity by including Mickleover in their series on other villages involved in the fight.

Included was an interview with Cecil F Storer *(featured in Books One & Two):* "If you ask anyone who built Mickleover they are very likely to direct you to Mr Cecil Storer of 83 Uttoxeter Road. As far as the older houses are concerned this is quite true of a large group of them."

Photo courtesy of the Derbyshire Advertiser
Cecil Storer with his grandson, Michael Veveris.

He first came to Mickleover in 1894 when Western Road was called Poke Lane and there were about eight houses and a farm on it.

"My father, brothers and myself built a few houses down Western Road," he said. "We always gravitated towards Mickleover because my father and grandfather were born here."

He married in 1902 and built the house he then lived in. He was asked if he had any idea how many bricks he had laid. "A few million I suppose," he laughed.

With his son he had laid all the bricks in the 90 houses he had built in Mickleover.

He was still building in 1965 having just completed a brick built garage. His daughter, Mrs Marie Veveris complained that he would not stop.

He had no strong feelings about the houses that had sprung up where open green fields used to be. "People have got to live somewhere," he said. A house behind his own home was scheduled for building. "I couldn't say much anyway, could I. After all, I was one of the people who began it."

May 22nd: "Grandson Peter gets married," grandfather continued his notes with "Rather nice day with sunshine and cloud. The ceremony [at St Michael's Church, Alvaston] was choicely performed before a large company. I went into the vestry and Ann [née Parrell] warmly greeted me, and we kissed each other." Our married life began, and continues in Gisborne Close. Mickleover friends Jim and Pat Nixon and Peter and Pam Hallam had married in 1964.

In the following week the parish clerk, Les Miller, reported that negotiations were being carried out with the RDC, for the purchase of land for the building of a library.

The County Council wrote to say that a site had been agreed and the County Architect had already been approached.

The author's third home in Mickleover, Gisborne Close. The Morris Traveller, left, is referred to in the text.

June began with grandfather noting that "work is proceeding at [Bessie] Bew's [shop] for the erection of Bank premises." He was referring to the Station Road, Uttoxeter Road junction where the Nat West Bank is situated.

Five-year-olds had begun to receive their first lesson in movement at the Hughes School of Dance and Drama, held in St John's Church Hall.

In the St John's Youth Club report it was agreed that a change in the constitution to have compulsory attendance at church be removed.

Peter Howarth, leader, stated that "very little change had been seen as a result of this, apart from the fact that Evensong is not disturbed quite so much by conversations from the back row."

Mr Howarth came to the question of what the Youth Club meant to the church. "Was it to be just a convenient labour force within the church or a service to the young people of the parish?"

He went on to state that in the two years of its existence the Youth Club had not received a single penny from the church. "We are sadly lacking in equipment, the sum total being one three-quarter-size table tennis table, which was privately donated, and one record player – of sorts – the parts for which were collected or bought by the club members themselves."

Out of a long list he had submitted to the Management Committee to consider as most urgent were a full-size table tennis table and a proper record player. "Before you throw your hands up in horror, said Peter Howard, may I mention that both could be equally needed by the Youth Church Group."

He ended by saying that he had received very warm support from so many people and how much he enjoyed running the Youth Club.

The Council agreed to explore the secondhand market for a table but the purchase of a record player would be deferred until they knew what the expenditure would be.

New ideas for school visits were begun at Ravensdale Junior School with a visit to Castle Donington Airport which had just opened and a farm at Egginton. Ninety First Year Juniors visited the Riber Nature Reserve at Matlock. In all cases the children contributed 1s towards the cost of the bus with school funds paying the balance.

Jimmy Best was away from the County Junior School on medical grounds and Harry Gaskill took over the headship until the opening of the new school year. A Fourth Year visit was arranged to the John Port and Etwall Schools.

The Reverend Crockett and the Churchwardens made an application for a Faculty covering the removal of the pews.

After ten years Arthur Parker was leaving to be Organist at St Werburgh's Church, Derby. The PCC passed on their good wishes to which Mr Parker replied by saying he was going with mixed feelings. There had only been one applicant to replace him, David Anthony Cooper, aged 16 and he was appointed as from July 28th 1965.

The Vicar had asked the Royal School of Church Music how they could help and encourage a young organist. They suggested a Summer School Course at St Elphin's School, Darley Dale.

The PCC hoped the new organist "would avail himself of the suggested Course, or a comparable one." They were to pay 50% of the fee and he was asked if he preferred the remaining 50% to be deducted from his first year's salary which was £78 per annum. David attended the course.

A letter was published in the local press about rats infesting Bramble Brook but Alan Ratcliff, vice-chairman of the parish council, said the complaint was completely out of proportion.

The Public Health Officer of the RDC had informed him that, along with a rodent operator, he had visited the brook. They had found some footprints in the soft bank and on questioning the residents only one person could say that he had seen a rat in the area. The Health Officer further stated that there was no rubbish in the brook, in fact nothing at all to encourage rats.

He continued to state that the brook area provided an excellent playground for the local children. "Therefore the question of baiting the areas with poison could not be considered."

Referring to the programme on BBC Midlands News broadcast on Whit Monday, which gave the impression that the Bramble Brook area was highly infested with rats, a councillor said that this was the wrong impression and that the BBC did not seem to have checked up at all.

It was decided to write to the Chief Public Health Officer and state that the parish council was doing all that was possible to get to the bottom of this story about the rats.

A National Blood Transfusion Service session was held at Ravensdale Junior School on July 4th. A total of 120 people attended.

The RDC Housing and Planning Committee received a letter from the County Council enquiring whether it would be possible to allocate the tenancy of one of the bungalows at present in construction in Hilton Close. They wished to place greengrocer, Sid Thornhill of 17 Vicarage Road, as his property had to be demolished for the proposed road widening scheme.

Mr Thornhill was in business at Mickleover for many years and was a familiar figure in the village which he toured daily by horse and cart making deliveries. His ponies Polly and Tommy gave pleasure to many children who loved to feed them.

The RDC replied that the owner was not on their waiting list. However they would be prepared to re-house him as and when a vacancy occurred.

Grandfather wrote in July that "The 'Mans' Shop near the Co-op [The Square] has closed down." It re-opened in September as the Oyster Coffee Bar.

He had a disturbed night on July 17th. "Sat up to watch the pictures from Mars sent to earth by the USA Satellite. A marvellous achievement."

The First Eleven of Mickleover FC had been relegated to Section "B" in the Derbyshire Senior League at the end of the 1964-65 season. They had played 26 matches and won only 6, 19 were lost. The Second Eleven fared little better losing 16 from 26 matches. Football Secretary John Baxter said at the Mickleover Sports Club meeting in August that 25 players had signed on for the two leagues.

Stuart Buchan obtained 100 wickets during the cricket season and the ball

The Derby Evening Telegraph *published two pages of pictures relating to Bramble Brook playing field. The caption read:* "If a Mickleover mother should happen to wonder at the late arrival home of her children after school finished for the day she usually reassures herself with the thought that they had stopped to play in Bramble Brook Playground, Devonshire Drive. For this new style recreation ground, an adventure playground with a difference, has all the equipment necessary to encourage a child's natural propensity for climbing and developing an adventurous spirit. It is a never ending source of delight to the youngsters of Mickleover. Equipped with natural and man made climbing obstacles and a track for young cyclists and children with scooters, the playground here has the additional attraction of the brook – for what boy or girl can resist the life of a natural watercourse."

Photo courtesy of the Derby Evening Telegraph

which took the 100th was mounted and inscribed and presented to him at the club's dinner.

There had been a wait of three months for the delivery of stone at All Saints' Church, but work would continue after the companies annual two weeks holiday.

Phase two envisaged by the PCC was to be the "provision of a modern Vicarage to take the place of the old house which is in constant need of very expensive repair and is inconvenient to a degree."

This would provide for phase three, "to provide a complete and up to date Community Centre to cater for all the foreseeable needs of our rapidly growing community." Work on phase one was hoped to be completed by Christmas 1965 with phase two in two to three years' time and the most complex phase three by early 1970.

The death occurred on Wednesday, August 11th of Mr Joseph Nadin, aged 63. He was the proprietor of E W Nadin and Son, builders, of 58 Station Road.

He had been a member of the Repton RDC for 16 years and was its chairman from 1961-63. Keenly interested in local government, Joe had been a member of Mickleover Parish Council for many years and was chairman of the School Managers.

During the war, from 1938 to 1944, he was area organiser for Civil Defence in North Derbyshire. He was survived by a widow, Mazie Elizabeth, a son, William, in the family business and a married daughter, June.

Photo courtesy of Harry Gaskill
Joe Nadin, watched by headmaster, Jimmy Best at a previous prizegiving ceremony at the County Junior School, Vicarage Road when he was chairman of Repton RDC.

Those present at the School Managers meeting in September stood in silence in memory of Joe Nadin. Arthur Ravensdale accepted the appointment as chairman for the next 12 months.

Alec Hannah, resigned as clerk to the managers after serving for eight years. James Aitken of Onslow Road was appointed.

An application for the erection of a Vic Hallam building for use as a temporary church was being considered for Nottingham Catholic Diocesan Trustees at The Lodge, Uttoxeter Road. The site had been purchased from Dr and Mrs McCahey.

"Car parking shall be provided at the time of development sufficient to accommodate all cars likely to call at the premises at any one time."

The parish council decided against the idea of culverting Bramble Brook for the time being because of the cost - £11,000. Mr W Spilman, engineer and surveyor of Repton RDC said that even to culvert the part of the brook which ran near the playing field area would cost £4,000. A suggestion that the area could be fenced at a lower point was also rejected on the grounds that fences, no matter how provided, were a challenge to children.

The RDC asked the parish church for their observations on a plan for the proposed residential development north-west of Station Road.

They replied that if planning permission was granted then due regard should be given to the provision of shops, banks, swimming pools, library and school facilities.

Many representatives of local organisations were present at an informal meeting in the Memorial Hut on September 14th to foster the formation of a "Good Neighbours" scheme.

Arranged by Arthur Ravensdale, chairman of the parish council, Miss M J Ewell, a County Council Welfare Officer, outlined the type of help available through official sources, but stressed the need for outside help which a "Good Neighbours" scheme would allow.

At the end of the meeting Mr Ravensdale was approached by two young ladies calling themselves the Odd Bods who explained they were going to college and had a small amount of money accumulated from gifts given in appreciation of doing odd jobs which they would pass on.

Peter Howarth, the Youth Club Leader at St John's Church, had taken over as Choir Master on condition of being relieved of the responsibility for the youth club. The chairman of the PCC was pleased that Brian Holland, who had previous youth club experience agreed to take over the position. Peter Howarth offered to purchase a table tennis table as soon as possible with an agreed price of £20 - £25.

Vic Evans reported on the large cracks on the east and west walls, loose windows to church, resulting in leakage of water and cracked floor tiles around the church door.

It was agreed by the PCC to approach the architect about these matters plus the leak around the bell rope and the faulty roof flashing.

The building fund was still outstanding £4,025 but it was agreed that a "Penny-a-Day" scheme was providing valuable income. The architect wrote later reporting that the leakage of water around the bell rope sleeve had been cured by Mr Evans with the aid of some plastic tubing and mastic.

The council decided to draw the attention of Fryers, the builders, to the "pre-

Photos courtesy of Victor Evans

Above: Vic Evans, inspects the 'TT' Triang 2 rail layout gauge at the first Model Railway Exhibition at St John's church hall in September 1965. Left: Churchwarden, Frank Chesterman, watering part of his own lawn on Jack Turner's layout.

mature appearance of faults in the church buildings."

The first model railway exhibition was held in St John's Church Hall on September 18th. It had been organised by a small group of people from the church.

Five working layouts were supplied, four by church members and although the *Derby Evening Telegraph* reported that over 1,000 people attended the show, the actual figures were 455 adults and 567 children, the latter providing a continuous audience.

Light refreshments were on sale and the visitors were offered a mixture of slides and films free of charge. There was a sundry sales stand of jigsaws, postcards and photos with Festiniog Railway Society having a stand to sell souvenirs. The whole event raised £45 for the church building fund.

Grandfather paid a brief visit to All Saints' Church on September 20th. "A Chapel is being built on the north side of the tower."

Mr Ravensdale referred to the recent death of Joe Nadin at the parish council meeting and asked the councillors to stand in tribute. He pointed out that Mr Nadin and his father had helped in the building of Mickleover as it was known at that time.

Mrs Marjorie Howarth was congratulated on her recent election to Repton RDC, her husband Geoffrey was the County Council Registrar and her son Peter Choir Master at St John's Church. She was the only candidate and stood as a non-party candidate for the vacancy caused by the death of Joe Nadin.

Councillors also extended their best wishes to Rob Nield, the youngest member of the parish council, on his marriage to Mary McDowell at All Saints' Church the previous Saturday, in the midst of the building work for the Lady Chapel. Rob and Mary remain great servants of All Saints' Church.

At the beginning of October the Reverend Ben Crockett told All Saints' Parochial Church Council that work was a month behind schedule on the project. This was mainly due to the stonework taken from the west wall for re-use being found unsuitable.

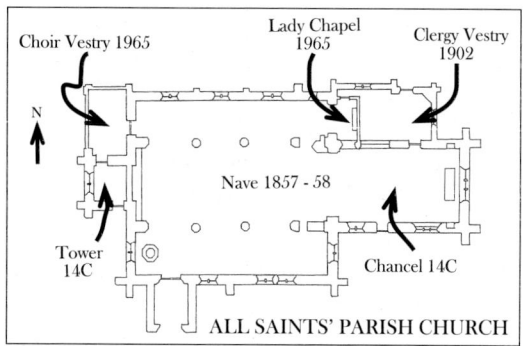

Derby Advisory Committee had rejected the Altar Frontal as they felt it was unsuitable for installation in a medieval church.

He went on to say that the Vestry roof was now complete apart from the guttering and the Lady Chapel wall was near completion.

Grandfather wrote on October 20th "the new Chapel looks complete."

The application for a Vic Hallam type four timber building as headquarters for 124th Scout Troop off Western Road was being considered, plus the erection of a Spooners (Hull) Ltd 'D' Standard Army Cadet Force Hut.

Mickleover Parish Council asked the RDC to defer consideration of planning permission for a bank and shops on Uttoxeter Road until the village was by-passed.

If it was decided to approve planning permission to Page-Johnson Construction, the council thought that adequate provision should be made for off-street parking and for the safety of pedestrians.

Les Miller, clerk, said he had seen a copy of the application. He explained that it proposed two alternatives, one for a bank and shops and the other for a bank on its own.

George Hayden explained that residents in the area were opposed to the development because of the danger from traffic on the main road.

Marjorie Howarth said "I am absolutely opposed to development on that side of the road. The rest of Mickleover is on the other side and this development would encourage people to cross the main road."

Chairman, Arthur Ravensdale, pointed out that when the main road was diverted the village would be isolated from heavy traffic and the danger would not then exist.

Mrs Howarth said she had received complaints about misbehaviour in The Square since the coffee bar, (attached to the Masons Arms) had been opened.

Arthur Ravensdale suggested that it would be a good idea for the re-surfacing of the tennis courts at Vicarage Road playing fields before winter as it would protect the courts against the frost. Les Miller, clerk, wrote to various firms for advice and tenders and an estimate of £720 was approved by the council.

An Emergency Meeting of the All Saints' PCC had been called for November 8th and it was agreed that a loan of £3,000 at $6^{1}/_{2}$% over three years be taken out instead of cashing in the church's capital. This was in regard to the expenditure of the Vestry and Lady Chapel.

Jim Stampfly suggested that people be asked for interest free loans in units of either £5 or £10, repayable in ten years. "An article in the *Derby Evening Telegraph* might interest other people outside our particular sphere."

Reverend Crockett said the church "must look at every possible form of charity organisation. Unless we do something like this it would be many years before projects two and three could be started."

As the tenant at 9 Limes Avenue, adjoining the Church Hall had now left, the question arose as to whether the house should be let again. "We could not afford repairs at this time," said Reverend Crockett. Several members inspected the property and repairs costing about £50 were carried out for the new tenants in 1966 paying a rent of 30 shillings a week.

The Reverend Martin Pierce vacated the chair at St John's Church PCC meeting in November while the question of a car allowance was discussed.

Robert Varley proposed that the Vicar should be paid £75 per annum from 1st October 1965 and this was agreed.

Wilf Warren, headmaster at Ravensdale Junior School wrote in his report to the School Managers about the proposed development of the area between West Drive and the railway. "This belongs to the Carlton Development Company. It is understood that an application has been made for permission to build houses in this area. If there is 90 acres to be developed at 10 houses per acre, this means 900 houses.

"Calculating at the rate of 1.5 children of school age per household, this means 1350 children. Of these it is likely a third or more will be primary school age. There is only one junior school in this area and this has been overfull for many years. There is no secondary school of any kind in this area."

At the County Infants' School, teacher, Doris Maéné was unable to work due to illness. Dorothy McSwiggan took her class in the mornings and Mrs Green in the afternoons.

Stella Mary Green was a supply teacher who was able to take her three-year old son Nick with her to school and thus began his early education. Her eldest son Geoffrey was at Vicarage Road School.

Stella later became a full-time teacher at the school and remained in education throughout her working life, eventually working for Ofsted. She was the person responsible for inspiring the Youth Drama Group at the Methodist Church which is referred to in Chapter Four.

Mickleover WI agreed to place a seat at Hilton Close to commemorate their Golden Jubilee. Provision had been made in a niche in the splay wall at the entrance to the estate. This was acceptable to the WI and a seat was ordered with a commemorative plaque placed on it.

On the question of charges for the sports amenities in the parish the council decided that the charge for tennis should be raised from 2s.6d to 3s per hour; football and cricket raised from £1 per match to £1.5s.0d and evening cricket matches from 12s.6d to 15s.

Arthur Ravensdale, chairman, reported on the death of a former councillor, George Holloway of Western Road. The council observed a minutes silence.

CHAPTER THIRTEEN
PASTURES HOSPITAL MODERNISED
1966

With the formal opening of the British Railways Engineering Laboratories by the Duke of Edinburgh in 1964, attentions were turned to providing some permanent test facilities close to Derby.

Activities were directed to a stretch of the 'down' line between Mickleover and Etwall. Improving freight vehicles was the aim along with the design of high-speed freight vehicles (HSFV'S).

On a half-mile stretch near the old gasworks sidings in Heage Lane "a series of short stretches of continuous welded rail into which various deliberate irregularities could be introduced," was explained by J C Berry in his series of articles for the *Link*, a magazine distributed by Mickleover churches.

The test trains, stabled at Friargate in Derby, ran between the existing freight services during the week and on Sundays. This work continued in 1966.

An application to demolish the existing property of 10 Uttoxeter Road and erect shops with car park at rear was made by Peakdown Investments Limited. (See (5) on map p252) and a copy of the plans had been forwarded to the parish council for their observations, by Repton RDC Housing and Planning Committee.

The parish council decided at their January meeting that although they were not prepared to stand in the way of the development, "they would like to draw the RDC's attention to the probable dangers for the school which adjoins the site."

"It is not desirable, but what can we do?" asked Councillor Archie Allison.

Marjorie Howarth said "I do not think shops should be installed at this point because of the danger to children crossing the road from school."

An Outline Planning Application to change the use of a house into a shop at

Photo courtesy of the Derby Evening Telegraph
Womens' Voluntary Service Mother and Baby Club New Year party.

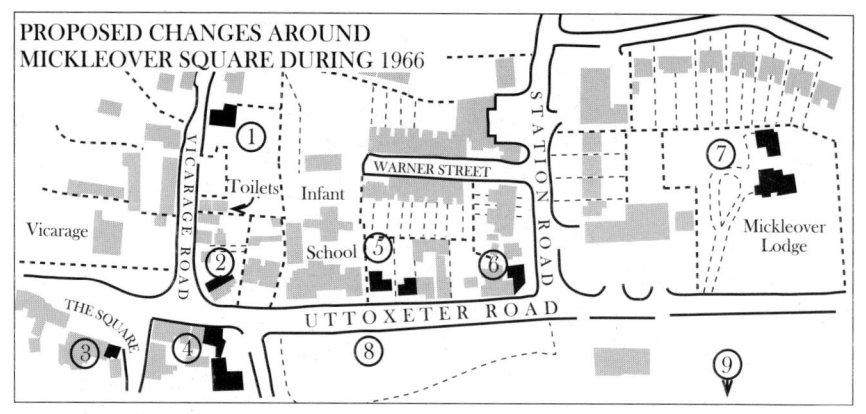

PROPOSED CHANGES AROUND MICKLEOVER SQUARE DURING 1966

(1) 12 Vicarage Road was proposed for new library. (2) 3 Vicarage Road to become a Barclays Bank branch. (3) 10 The Square. Do-it-yourself shop. (4) Changes to Personal Service Garage. (5) 10 Uttoxeter Road. Site for shops and car park. (6) Alterations to Bews shop for branch of bank. (7) Site of new Roman Catholic Church. (8) Ivy Farm, site for bank and shops. (9) Development of houses south of the Nag's Head Hotel.

12 Uttoxeter Road had been refused in November 1964 and the same conclusion was reached on this development a few weeks later. The Derbyshire County Council thought there was no satisfactory arrangements and it would result in "causing danger, obstruction or inconvenience."

Grandfather wrote "the small shop in The Square is being re-opened as a Do-it-Yourself affair." See (3) above. Tony Warner's family had traded as grocers in these same premises for a number of years but he was diverting into something different.

Grandfather complained that the post was going astray. "Everyone being delivered the mail for the house next door on one occasion and then wrongly delivered, although correctly addressed to houses further afield. One to Western Road."

The headmaster at Ravensdale Junior School informed the School Managers that the authority had still not granted permission for trimming and layering the hedges bordering the Ravensdale Schools.

RAVENSDALE INFANT SCHOOL STAFF, JANUARY 1966
Headmistress: Evelyn Fearnehough
Mrs Pat Ellison   Deputy Head
Mrs Marjorie Harper
Mrs Jean Pickering
Mrs E A (Trindy) Swales
Mrs Esmie Turner
Mrs E A Jackson
Mrs Kath Ratcliff Clerk
Miss Ann Bird   Welfare Assistant

Evelyn Fearnehough at Ravensdale Infants' School had released teacher Mrs E A Jackson as her husband had obtained a position in Glasgow. After asking to be considered, Dorothy P M McSwiggan from Vicarage Road Junior School, filled the vacancy.

Mr Brinklow gave a short report on the Sunday School at St John's Church

Photo courtesy of the Derbyshire Advertiser

Two months after opening a branch at Littleover, Barclays Bank, which claimed to be the biggest of Britain's "Big Five", opened its door of a new branch at Mickleover on March 1st. It adjoined the post office at 3 Vicarage Road and is now a branch of Scarsdale Veterinary Hospital.

Parochial Church Council meeting. It was divided into three sections: Under fives (37 children), with Miss Ruth Kitchell and three assistants; Infants (94 children) under Mrs Enid Glen and ten assistants; Juniors (120 children) with eleven teachers. There was an average attendance of 190 out of 250.

Representatives of Mickleover Albion FC were invited to meet members of the parish council to discuss the question of dressing room accommodation at Havenbaulk Lane playing fields.

This was decided at the February meeting of the council. "The ball is now in their court, it is up to them to reply," said chairman Arthur Ravensdale. No written evidence survives of the outcome.

The playing fields had been used by the football club for several months with the permission of the parish council. Before allowing them dressing room accommodation the council decided to see how the football club progressed.

On his walks around the village in March grandfather noted: "new wall is being built in front of the school on the main road;" "a high hedge in front of Mickleover Lodge down;" "alterations have been made to one of the farm houses [at Pastures Hospital]." This is reported later in the chapter.

All the boundary walls were being re-built at the County Infants' School. The retaining wall at the front of the school had been in danger of falling onto the pavement. A lorry delivering bricks to the school cracked the gate pillar just as the children were going home at lunchtime.

At St John's PCC meeting in March, Youth Club leader Brian Holland reported: "Included in the visiting membership are the rather noisier elements on motor scooters, whom I will now refer to as the outside element.

"When I took over the youth club in September 1965 this outside element was present in small numbers, but due to my own inexperience in handling them, their numbers gradually increased."

Mr Holland and his assistant Mrs J Shields attempted to encourage this group to stay and become full members of the club and church, however any attempt to run an organised programme resulted in them walking out.

This disturbing factor led to the "solid core of the club" feeling unhappy. Trying to encourage the outside element more made them worse and many felt it would be better if they left.

Discussing things openly at a committee meeting in December 1965 resulted in the club rules being revised and rigidly enforced leading to the outside element being virtually non-existent.

He ended his report by stating that the club still needed a record player and pleaded for £4 to purchase materials to build another full sized table tennis top. "We have in the way of sports equipment – 1 full sized table tennis table and one quarter sized billiard table."

The headteachers informed the School Managers that on the known population, with the exception of the County Infants' School, they were over capacity and that, by January 1967 the number of classrooms at the Ravensdale Schools would be insufficient for the number of pupils then in the schools. In view of the serious situation the Divisional Education Officer was requested to meet the Managers.

Regarding the proposed development between West Drive and the railway, Jimmy Best informed the Authority that: "It must be stressed that if and when this scheme is started, not a single child can be accommodated in this school." He was referring to the County Junior School on Vicarage Road.

"Furthermore", he continued, "temporary classrooms on this site will not answer the demand for places; only another junior school of a similar size to this with an infant school of appropriate size will answer the situation."

Medical and dental inspections had been carried out at the County Junior School with nearly half those examined needing treatment.

Miss Marriott, Welfare Assistant, was proving to be very useful. "There is a marked decrease in numbers of soiled pants now that children don't get taken home to Mum!" said Mr Best.

Photo courtesy of the Derby Evening Telegraph

Members of Mickleover Park Townswomen's Guild Choir with the Kenneth Allsopp trophy they won at the Derby Festival, Mrs G Lewis is holding the shield.

The County Planning Officer outlined the proposal to establish a primary school on approximately 4 acres of land south of the Derby to Uttoxeter Road and between Jackson Avenue and Chain Lane. There were no planning objections as this site of allotments had been zoned for the purpose.

The eventual entrance to this school, known as Wren Park School, is in the Mickleover Parish and close to where the first bomb in the Derby area was dropped in the Second World War. (See full story in *Mickleover Born & Bred - Book Two).*

Councillor Marjorie Howarth had received a letter of complaint about the proposed new 'bus service, leading to the Rangemore Estate and Farneworth Road area. A parishioner thought Derby Corporation had applied to operate jointly with Trent buses and Arthur C Holden of Onslow Road told the meeting that residents living in the area had signed a petition against the proposal, on the grounds that some of the roads on the proposed routing of the buses were far too narrow to accommodate them.

He said that the residents agreed that a service was needed in the area but "putting an 8-foot public service vehicle on this road seems a very strange thing."

During the next few weeks they agreed to the joint services for a trial period and accepted the routings with certain reservations.

The only objector was Archie Allison who said that his experience of the corporation bus service was that they were never on time. Clerk, Les Miller, also pointed out that buses turning on some routes would present a road hazard.

Acting chairman, Alan Ratcliff, said "that due to lessening demand for allotments, the council had decided to allow non-residents of Mickleover parish to have their names placed on the waiting list.

Of all the proposals for the development of the parish submitted by the RDC, Mr Ratcliff said the large acreage off the west-side of Station Road had been a major concern. A parish council committee had decided to ask the County Planning Officer to survey the land and see what trees should be retained.

As the original application had been withdrawn by the architects a request for a private housing estate had now been made by George Wimpey with the same area and dimensions and Alan Ratcliff said "due regard should be given to the provision of shops, a library and above all, schools."

Particular mention was made of health amenities, especially for the need of the sewage disposal to be self-sufficient, so as to place no burden on the existing facilities in the parish which were already fully extended. The RDC Town and Planning Committee thought the development might solve the housing problem for British Railways. Scientists and technical experts would be moving into the Derby area when the new railway laboratories became fully operational.

William W Rushbrooke, at Personal Service Garage, Uttoxeter Road, was given permission to build a paint spray shop and lubrication bay on the corner of Limes Avenue. This was granted for a limited period only, expiring on December 31st 1976. (See (4) on Map p252).

"On or before which date, the buildings shall be removed and the site reinstated to its former condition unless a prior application has been submitted and approved by the Local Planning Authority." The long-term proposals envisaged the existing properties in that location would be serviced from roads at the rear.

Similar restrictions were issued to the applicants who wished to build a house or bungalow on the north side of The Green, and behind the Co-op store in The Square (now Romac Motor Factors).

They were advised that the Local Authority plans for the area "envisage provision of a rear service road to shops facing The Square" and "the rear boundary of the plot may ultimately be required for such a purpose."

On April 1st grandfather wrote that "we sat up until 1.30am watching and listening to election results. They were most interesting and entertaining." The Labour Party were returned with an overall majority of 97.

The *Derbyshire Advertiser's* Leader writer was not a supporter of the Labour Party and even less of the Prime Minister, Harold Wilson. "If there are any cards upsleeves, Wilson will produce them and it will be as well for everyone to be on their toes before the new socialism really gets under way."

Reverend Pierce reported at St John's PCC on April 13th that the joint service in Holy Week, intended for all Christians in Mickleover, "was a great step forward in our efforts at local unity."

Photo courtesy of the Derby Evening Telegraph

(1) The second Easter wheelbarrow race organised by Charles Langley, the landlord of the Mason's Arms (holding the starting bell). (2) Off to an early start. (3) Keith Brocklehurst in the left barrow, pushed by his brother Garth. Right barrow Jim Bradley with "Jock" Goodwin, 1965 winners. It was Mr Langley's daughter, Peggy Goodwin, who retained these photographs from his collection.

(4) In come the runners-up. Top left corner is the old orchard of farmer Tom Radford which was soon to be developed as a bank and shops. (5) the winners in six minutes, Edward Ellis and Philip Hunt.

257

The Memorial Hut was full, with many standing at the back, along with the congregations of All Saints', St John's, Methodist and Roman Catholic churches and others wishing to attend.

After the latter had purchased Mickleover Lodge from Doctor Michael McCahey and his wife Kathleen, the house served as a presbytery, a chapel and a parish room. The McCahey's moved to Whittaker Road, Derby. However the orchard had now given way to a building erected as a temporary church and Mass was celebrated for the first time on Maundy Thursday 1966 and an end to services in the Memorial Hut.

The Minister of Transport, Barbara Castle, authorised Derbyshire County Council, the Ministry's agents for the trunk road to accept the tender of £1,236,000 submitted by A Monk and Co Ltd for the improvement of the Burton to Derby A38 road.

Delayed by restrictions on public spending the northern end of the Burton bypass at Clay Mills and Doles Lane, Findern, was to be put in hand and it was hoped to finish it within the next two years.

On May 12th grandfather took a familiar walk and noted: "They are widening the road down Staker. This means more heavy traffic, and therefore goodbye to its comparative quiet."

The Ministry said it hoped to publish proposals for a link road between the A38 and the A516 at Mickleover later in the year.

Grocer, Sid Thornhill, had died aged 69 in March, and an application was submitted to develop the land on the site of his property, 17 Vicarage Road for the erection of three detached houses or bungalows. Sid was a keen sportsman and at one time secretary of an early Mickleover Football Club. He served in the Somerset Light Infantry during the First World War.

A direct appeal to all parishes was made by the Provost of Derby Cathedral as £200,000 was needed for repairs and extensions at the east end of the Cathedral and the rebuilding of St Michael's House for Diocesan offices.

Various objections to the scheme were made public, mainly concerning the manner of presentation. St John's was in support and donated £25.

The Reverend Crockett arranged a "Cathedral Evening" to be held in All Saints' Church Hall on December 10th and it was decided to make it a "Cathedral Weekend" with offerings taken on the following day in envelopes provided.

Arthur Ravensdale sent apologies for his absence at the School Managers meeting in May, along with a note of his intention to retire both as a School Manager and a member of the parish council due to his ill health and serious ill-health of his wife.

Photos courtesy of Peggy Goodwin

Charles Langley, licensee of the Mason's Arms, organised a charity football event at the Royal British Legion field on May 29th with teams representing the Derbyshire Yeoman and the Mason's Arms. More than 300 spectators saw football league rules ignored by players and referee alike during this crazy football match. The Derbyshire Yeoman team were the winners with a score of "three goals to five tries to nil". The proceeds went to the Derby Fund for the Blind.

At the annual parish council meeting members were told of Mr Ravensdale's resignation. He had been a member of the parish council since 1946.

Several members paid tribute to Mr and Mrs Ravensdale for their service to the village. For most of his life he had been devoted to the savings movement. Before his retirement in 1962 he had been headmaster of Hardwick Junior Boys' School since 1940. In the Birthday Honours list of 1955 Mr Ravensdale was made an **MBE** and in 1960 an **OBE**.

The two Mickleover political giants from the beginning of the twentieth century were Tom Radford and Arthur Ravensdale. Both have been remembered in different ways. Vicarage Road playing fields were originally named "Radford's Pleasance", many believing that he donated the land. This was not so, it was purchased by the parish council from the Mickleover Manor Estate. However his name was given due to his dedicated service in seeing the project fulfilled.

Arthur Ravensdale's name lives on with the dedication of two schools even though he was a reluctant participant.

Alan Ratcliff, a senior contracts engineer at Rolls Royce, was elected chairman and George Hayden vice-chairman. Douglas H Binyon, a former member of the council and a School Manager, was co-opted as a casual member.

After the "Procession of Witness" had been so successful in May Jim Stampfly thought it should become an annual event, taking different routes. The general opinion at the All Saints' PCC meeting in June was "that it had done good," even if only for onlookers to see the various churches meeting together.

As Mr Harrison had resigned as leader of the Youth Club Jim and Theo Stampfly took his place on a temporary basis.

Tim Ward, Manager of Derby County Football Club, opened the annual garden party of All Saints' in the Vicarage ground. A competition for the most aptly dressed Derby County supporter was judged by Reg Matthews, the Rams goalkeeper. The event was organised by Arthur Tipper, chairman of the Social Fellowship Committee.

Simon Byworth reported at St John's PCC meeting that over fifty per cent of Mickleover was now covered by operating agents in the Good Neighbours Scheme, identified by the "Winged Hand" symbol in their windows.

Divided into ten sections a network of Agents were calling on householders publicising the scheme. People in need were able to contact the nearest agent who would put them in touch with the organisation best qualified to assist.

Mrs Margaret M Holmes of Onslow Road, with her husband, was the organising secretary. She explained that "the help we can give will really be for emergency periods, perhaps of two to three weeks."

The kind of help offered included transport if someone had to visit hospital; assistance with children if a mother had to visit hospital; shopping or reading for elderly or the sick.

Mrs Holmes also said "the main advantage is that there will be a central list of organisations which can offer not only practical help, but friendship too." Involved in the scheme were the four Christian churches, plus the Royal British Legion, Women's Institute, Townswomen's Guild and Women's Voluntary Service.

Vic Evans reported on nine items to be completed on the fabric of St John's Church, such as wall cracks and the hall painting. "The toilet door posts are now completely adrift, and the stage sets are not yet built. The heater switch was faulty, and the Emergency Exit signs, wrongly wired, have now been corrected. The biggest job on hand is repointing the church walls which would appear to be a job for a professional."

Peter Howarth the leader of St John's Church Choir expressed his appreciation of the hard work and sacrifice which the choir members were putting into music. It consisted of 7 sopranos, 4 altos, 2 tenors, and 3 basses. Besides the normal service coverage, works had been performed with the Derby Philharmonic Orchestra and also more recent experiments with modern services.

Photo courtesy of Colin Haxell

Peter Howarth leads St John's Church Choir. Note the water stains running down the wall!

A Mickleover parishioner who turned up at the June parish council meeting to bring a complaint had not been there for more than a few minutes when he found himself elected as a new member of the council, replacing Councillor Colin F White.

The new member, Albert E L Olphin of 60 Brisbane Road, was proposed by George Hayden. He was invited to take a seat at the meeting and take up his duties from there.

Wilf Dutson was appointed chairman of the School Managers and Archie Allison was welcomed as a Manager.

Jimmy Best, headmaster of the County Junior School was asked to convey the congratulations of the Managers to the children who had done so well in the Amateur Swimming Association's Life Saving Certificate Tests. Teacher, Miss Allcock left the school and Miss Katherine Skinner replaced her.

Kathleen Stephens, headmistress, said in her report that "the new Traffic Warden, Percy Warner, began his duties on July 4th. Praise be! The staff lavatory is now installed and is very much appreciated."

On July 27th grandfather wrote: "They have finished widening the road [Staker Lane]. I expected some heavy traffic on it, there was none."

Two days later he and Uncle Tom, along with the majority of the population, watched the World Cup Final football match. England won 4-2 by scoring two goals in the second half of extra time.

Permission was granted to Page-Johnson for a proposed bank and shops at the corner of Uttoxeter Road/Limes Avenue, once Ivy Farm.

As the County Council Library Committee no longer wished to acquire any part of 12 Vicarage Road the RDC recommended that the property be demolished, the site cleared and further consideration as to its future to be discussed (See (1) on map p252).

British Railways London Midland Region had informed the RDC that the Railways Board proposed to sell their non-essential houses and enquired whether they would be interested in purchasing them. Mickleover Station was among them and the District Valuer was asked to carry out provisional negotiations.

An application was made to use the waiting room and ancillary buildings for tyre sales and service depot by Elmbridge Tyre Services Limited of Swadlincote. This never materialised as they developed their business at Hearthcote Road in Swadlincote where they still trade.

Following a long discussion, members of the parish council decided that the matter of having bars fixed to the footbridge on the Bramble Brook playing fields should be looked into to prevent children from crawling into the culvert. They also decided that the question of extending the pedestrian barriers against the brook course at the culvert end should also be considered.

Councillor George Harry Gordon told the council that residents in Vicarage Road were complaining about rubbish which was constantly being thrown into their gardens from the nearby toilets.

After eight years the alterations to the whole of the original Pastures Hospital, built in 1851, including 12 wards, the main entrance hall, and the main kitchen, were completed at a cost of £228,467.

Because of the necessity of displacing patients, the project had to be done in six phases, the first of which was the modernisation of two wards, completed in 1958 and two more wards the following year.

The third phase dealt with the modernisation and enlargement of the main kitchen being completed in 1961. The fourth phase, with the alteration of four more wards was also completed in the same year. Modernisation of the main entrance hall which was completed in 1963 and the final phase was the alteration of four further wards. Pastures Hospital catered for about 1,000 patients and was staffed by 750 personnel, 400 of which were nursing staff.

The new wards were described as light and pleasantly large, with only 29 beds being the highest number in one ward, and 16 beds the lowest. This was a large

Photos courtesy of the Magic Attic Archive, Swadlincote

The exterior of one of the new wards at Pastures Hospital opened by George Brown. Right: The most up-to-date sleeping accommodation with built in wardrobes for each patient.

improvement on the dismal days of locked doors and dark corridors.

To commemorate the opening of these up-graded wards, the Rt Hon George Brown, MP, First Secretary and Minister for Economic Affairs unveiled a plaque in the new lobby of the main entrance on July 23rd.

It was hoped to modernise ten more wards in the future. The three annexes to the main hospital were the departments for occupational therapy, x-rays, chiropody, dental physiotherapy and male and female hairdressers.

Among other facilities were games facilities, and a nine-hole golf course which was already under creation for staff and patients.

Four boys, three aged 14 and one 15 admitted at Derby County Juvenile Court to damaging a bus shelter in The Square. They had cut through four portions of a seat with a hacksaw, which one of them admitted stealing from a building contractor working at All Saints Church.

They caused damage worth £1.15s.0d to the shelter belonging to the RDC. The boy who stole the hacksaw was sent to an approved school. The three other boys were each fined £1 for damaging the shelter and were ordered to pay 10 shillings restitution and one guinea advocation fee.

August began with an announcement that the long discussed boundary claims of Derby would be settled by the Boundaries Commission. It came down in favour of the Derby Corporation with sweeping acceptance of their claims.

It was understandable that the County Council, Rural District Councils and Parish Councils were voicing disappointment as they now had to rely on the final conclusions of the government to trim some of what they saw as drastic changes.

The *Derbyshire Advertiser* gave its view. "To claim that Mickleover, Littleover, Darley Abbey and Allestree are villages is nonsense and it is good to see that at last this masquerade is over. They are, whether they like it or not, suburbs of Derby and should take part in its government."

The Reverend Ben Crockett told the August meeting of All Saints' PCC that it had become apparent that there was no possibility of a new Vicarage for two to five years because of the development of the new by-pass and he had been advised to obtain a valuation of part of the garden and house of the Vicarage.

Richardson and Linnell, Estate Agents and Auctioneers, said it was only legally possible to build a Church Centre if the PCC purchased a plot of land not required from the Incumbent in an open market and £10,000 would be required to do this as no Diocesan help would be forthcoming.

Due to the Circuits being re-organised, the Reverend Alan Barber had now ceased to be responsible for the Methodist Church in Mickleover. He was the first non-Anglican to preach at St John's. The Reverend John Hope and his wife and family moved from the Mackworth Estate to Brisbane Road to take up his new duties at the church.

Wilf Warren, headmaster at Ravensdale Junior School, told the School Managers that "our choir have been asked to make a series of recordings of new publications by Messrs Chappell and Co Ltd."

Mr Machin from the County Architect's Department visited the school to arrange the siting of a further block of two temporary classrooms. It was decided that the most suitable site would be on the ground lying between the two schools.

Changes in teaching staff saw the arrival of Joan Larder at the County Infants' School and Ruth Beckford at Ravensdale Infants' School along with Mrs J Lee who was appointed as Welfare Assistant.

Councillor Allison was annoyed at a questionnaire received by the parish

Photos courtesy of Peggy Goodwin

The Vicarage photographed from the Masons Arms. In the foreground is the bus shelter which was vandalised by four boys.

council from the Ministry of Land and Natural Resources. It asked for information concerning allotments belonging to parish councils.

He described the lengthy document as "a most appalling thing. I would not try to answer it. You want a couple of blokes sitting at this for at least a week. Somebody is trying to build an empire which is not necessary."

He said later that all the Ministry needed to know was the number of allotments the council possessed, were they sufficient, and did they need any more?

The chairman, Alan Ratcliff, said that the clerk, Les Miller, "was far too busy to tackle this thing."

It was decided to return the document regretting that they could not complete the form, but the covering letter should give as much information as possible concerning the present position of the allotments.

George Hayden said that if the plan of a residential development by Page-Johnson on $12^1/_2$ acres of land on the southern side of Uttoxeter Road was approved there would be at least 100 houses on the site. "We have not got adequate facilities for schools and libraries. I am against development of that sort until we have facilities for the present population." (see (9) on map p252).

After Councillor Douglas H Binyon had said at least two schools were "bursting at the seams," it was decided to stress this point to the RDC.

In November the application, at the rear of the Nag's Head Hotel, was refused. The main reasons given were that property development was taking place north of Uttoxeter Road and if begun on the south it would interfere with the proposed Mickleover by-pass construction.

Burnaston Airport and Burnaston House were debated at a Derby Town Council meeting. In 1935 they had contemplated the purchase of a site adjoining Radbourne Lane to establish a Municipal Aerodrome. This involved compulsory purchase of land in the parishes of Radbourne, Mackworth and Mickleover. (For full story see *Mickleover Born & Bred* Book One).

After much protest and further discussion it was decided that the Radbourne site would not be large enough and Derby Town Council purchased the estate at Burnaston which belonged to Colonel Godfrey Mosley.

With the opening of Castle Donington Airport it was now agreed that Air School Limited be given a 21-year lease for land and buildings at Burnaston at a rent of £9,400 a year. Burnaston House, including the gardens, grounds, outbuildings and cottages were to be sold for £9,000.

There were difficulties for the council in putting the airfield on the open market as the County Council were not prepared to grant them permission to develop the site.

The Railway Exhibition was organised for a second time in St John's Church Hall. It was extended to cover two days in September and in addition to the smaller gauge layouts there was a larger and more complex unit on the stage. "O" gauge was further represented by a track running the full length of the hall, with controlled signalling.

At St John's PCC September meeting an offer was received from "The Silhouettes" beat group to run three dances for the building fund. In return they asked the committee to provide facilities for rehearsal twice a week.

After much discussion a trial run of rehearsals was agreed as long as they could be terminated "if good relations with near neighbours were likely to be impaired." A letting fee of 5s per hour was suggested. A dance was arranged for November 26th and this was followed by "The Silhouettes" continuing their rehearsals towards another dance, the last raised £10.8s.0d.

The clock face on All Saints' Church fell from the tower on October 16th. In spite of its forty foot fall to the ground there was little comparative damage to the 120-year-old dial. Decay in the stonework was thought to have been the contributing factor.

Photo courtesy of the Derby Evening Telegraph

Examining the damaged dial at All Saints' Church are John Locke; right, sales manager at John Smith and Sons Limited and Michael Seaman another of the firm's employees. Right Sexton Bill Barker and Rev Ben Crockett join the staff from John Smith's below the gaping hole in the tower.

John Smith and Sons Limited, Derby's famous clockmakers, carried out the repairs. They had installed the clock movement in 1895 but it was eventually replaced in 1986.

Grandfather visited his youngest granddaughter, Kathleen, on her engagement to Nick Merry in October and on the 25th: "Derek went with me on an errand to grocers and on his request afterwards we went to the church to look at the hole in the Tower from which the clock face fell recently."

Repton RDC informed the parish council that the Trent Motor Traction Company Limited had applied for a revision of bus fares between Derby and Mickleover.

Les Miller, clerk, said the notification did not state whether the fares would be going up or down. "They seemed to depend on one man running the bus and vary from 11d to 1s.3d," said Archie Allison. The council asked for more details.

"Gayware", in Devonshire Drive, an inappropriate title in the 21st century, had been offering a wide range of products for the previous six years.

However, in October 1966, Patrick Mooney and his wife Mary took over the business specialising in goods for the handyman and gardener, with Mary taking charge of the fancy goods side of the shop.

Patrick was a member of the well-known turf accountant family but always wanted to branch out into business on his own. He had trained as an interior decorator. The couple lived just round the corner in Chestnut Avenue.

Derbyshire Education Committee appointed a teacher from January 1967 for a unit at Pastures Hospital set up for maladjusted children aged between 5 to 12 which they were to administer. Grange House was being converted to accommodate the children by F W Kinsey Limited, Derby, costing £5,386.

Major F C Nicklin, chairman, and J E Aldred, secretary of Derby Senior Football League, were the principal guests at Mickleover Sports Club annual dinner and dance. It was attended by 150 guests at the Derbyshire Yeoman. Albert Wilkinson was presented with the "Clubman of the Year" trophy and Charlie Kenderdine received the cricketing trophy for his score of 141 not out in a match against International Combustion.

The cricket team had a fairly good season, beginning when Phil Starkey and Charlie Kenderdine plundered 23 runs in the fourteenth over against Rolls Royce. This took them to a five wicket victory in the Jackson Cup with a total of 115-5.

Charlie Kenderdine made headline sports news with his 141 not out against International Combustion. His total included 19 fours and 2 sixes, a new club record. Also a record was the final score, 236-4 declared, with batsmen Ken Guy (35) and Stuart Buchan (32) not out being the other top scorers. Gordon Smith's accurate bowling of 6-28 made sure Combustion were dismissed for 155.

The Ministry of Transport issued detailed information to the local press on the proposed Mickleover by-pass. Divisional Road Engineer for the Ministry explained that the entire scheme had reached only the draft Order stage and anybody objecting to it should write to the Ministry not later than January 28th.

It was hoped to go ahead with construction work following the completion of the current A38 (Burton) improvement. The scheme he said "should finish about April 1968, certainly by early 1969 and will provide a dual carriageway approaching motorway standards from the end of the Burton by-pass now under construction to Doles Lane, Findern.

Plans for this progress would mean the demolition of four bungalows, numbers 51, 53, 55 and 57 Havenbaulk Lane, which had been built a few years earlier. The Road Engineer, Mr F J S Best, told the *Telegraph*: "We have got to cross Havenbaulk Lane somewhere".

He continued, "Under an old trunk road scheme prepared several years ago, Havenbaulk Lane would have been crossed much nearer Rykneld Road." However on re-examination the scheme was found to be unsatisfactory and had to be modified.

"The new line was engineered to achieve balance between 'cut' and 'fill' during earth removal operations, and the new crossing point was the best choice from an engineering standpoint," he said.

A Derbyshire County Council spokesman said earlier that some properties in the Havenbaulk Lane area were bought some time ago by the Ministry as they came on the market.

Six premises on Uttoxeter Road were also included, but the planners had stated that "all reasonable efforts have been made to minimise such destruction." The spokesman for the County Council had commented: "Other affected properties have not been available for purchase and their acquisition, by negotiation or compulsory has still to be achieved."

Work had been progressing from Clay Mills during the year and by August the bridge support at the junction of Castle Way, Willington, and the road to Hilton had been constructed.

The parish council wrote to the Ministry of Transport informing them that they approved a draft order for a Mickleover by-pass and link road.

School Manager, Arthur Riley, died in October 1966. He was at one time an umpire in local cricket leagues of his native Staffordshire, coming to Derby 14 years previously, on his retirement from British Rail at Stoke where he was employed in the District Manager's office.

The chairman of the School Managers, Wilf Dutson, spoke of Mr Riley's work for the schools of Mickleover at the November meeting.

Due to the resignation of Mrs Beavis at the County Infants' School, Stella Green was interviewed for the teaching post from January 1st 1967. Mrs King was appointed as an additional teacher at Ravensdale Infants' School.

Don Barnes was serving as the full-time caretaker at the County Junior School but had also been asked to act as part-time groundsman during the winter months. Jimmy Best, headmaster at the school, commented on how well Mr Barnes had carried out both duties. However, he was concerned about the danger of children at Cattle Hill, opposite the late Sid Thornhill's shop. "The road at this point is very narrow and there is a very narrow pavement on one side of the road." The clerk was asked to write to the County Surveyor requesting an improvement. (see (3) on map p252).

Les Miller, clerk to the parish council, told the monthly meeting that he had received a letter from the Good Neighbours' organisation requesting grant aid to help them in their work.

Alan Ratcliff, chairman, revealed that he had recently become chairman of the Good Neighbours, but as he had only attended one meeting he could not give the parish council any information on the work.

"It is for the good of the people of Mickleover," said Marjorie Howarth. She continued to say that the group had been underway for just over a year and did a lot of work giving immediate help in emergencies. A month later the organisation was informed that it would receive a grant of £20 and an annual contribution of one guinea, starting April 1st 1967.

Douglas H Binyon gave a report on the site meeting at The Square, to discuss the problem of buses turning in a dangerous manner.

He said Inspector Brown who represented Trent buses reported that it was proposed to send all Mickleover buses down to Pastures Hospital in May 1967.

Jimmy Best reported that Harry Gaskill, deputy head at the County Junior School, would attend a one-year supplementary course in English, commencing in September 1967. The Managers recommended the Divisional Executive to agree to Mr Gaskill's absence on full salary.

On December 12th grandfather walked "as far as the station and saw a steam goods train."

With the initial period of the birth of St John's Church being over, an invitation had been sent to Father Adrian of the Franciscan Community at Cerne Abbas in Dorset. He was invited to live and worship among the community for a weekend.

He found parish worship "simple and beautiful" and felt that there was a strong core of people ready to lead any new venture. Father Adrian commended a form of group instruction, preferably given at house meetings, which would by discussion and reading take them through the Faith and other vital subjects.

The final meeting of the parish council in 1966 heard a discussion about the siting of a sub-station for the Bramble Brook area of the parish. A planning engineer for Derby and Burton area of the East Midlands Electricity Board told the council that the demand for electricity in Derby was reaching such a stage that the Board would have to buy houses for use as sub-stations.

The council accepted a suggestion that the new sub-station would be sited at a point near the rose garden on the playing fields.

The Derbyshire Association of Parish Councils gave evidence to the Royal Commission on Local Government in England.

The association stated that if necessary existing county boundaries should be superseded and existing councils absorbed into a new structure. Their existing entities they said should become of historical interest only.

Among their many complaints about what they deemed inevitable changes were, "a parish losing councillors, known to most inhabitants personally, and have in its place one ward member, who due to political requirements may not even live in the ex-parish."

Another: "the ex-parish requirements will be subordinated to a very low priority in what is considered by the council to be the required order of events, which may or may not be of benefit to inhabitants."

The Local Government Act of 1958 included provisions to review the areas of counties and county boroughs and to consider claims of extensions. A selection of five big provincial conurbations in England were selected for special review and by the beginning of 1966 the Commission had issued nine final reports, which included the Derby Borough Corporation.

When Labour's Richard Crossman came to office in 1964 there were hopes of a radical rethinking of Local Government beyond those of his predecessors.

Mr Crossman however said there was no chance of any sweeping reform for at least ten years, but he condemned present patterns. He went as far as to say that county and borough councils were archaic and that the Local Government Commission could not do the job that needed to be done.

In 1966 the Government decided to be bold and appointed two Royal Commissions to review and to revise Local Government in England and Scotland. They were expected to take two years to produce a finished plan. A third year would be needed to debate legislation so that by 1970 there should be a new structure for a "modern Britain."

The existing Local Government Commission was to be disbanded but the abundance of gathered facts on the management and staffing of Local Government was thought to be helpful in reaching a final conclusion. The order for the extension of Derby, which affected Mickleover was expected to be announced on April 1st 1968.

CHAPTER FOURTEEN
SUPERMARKET IN BRISBANE ROAD?
1967

One of the important projects being tackled by the Electrical Division of the Railway Technical Centre was establishing a control and communications link between signal boxes, stations, control centres and moving trains. An experiment called the 'wiggly-wire' system used a pair of of insulated wires between the rails and receiving coils beneath the train. This system was tested on the chosen site between Derby Friargate and Etwall in late 1966 and eventually covered the whole of the 6½ miles between Derby and Etwall.

"The Ministerial Order for the extension of Derby's boundaries was unlikely to be placed before Parliament before the Autumn, and may not be issued until early 1968," stated a press release in January 1967.

"There would be a 40-day period for objections to the Order following its publication," it continued. The enlarged borough with its included dormitories was thought to have at least three constituencies.

The local authorities now seemed resigned to the fact about the new changes. Sydney Clarke, chairman of Repton RDC and one of Mickleover's representatives, thought the new rates the rural

Photo courtesy of Mark Higginson

Mark Higginson took this photograph looking west at Mickleover shortly after the 'wiggly-wire' system was installed.

district were announcing would not be matched by the Derby Borough Council. However the Divisional Education Officer thought new schools would be built in the suburbs once the borough was increased.

Wilf Warren, headmaster at Ravensdale Junior School, told the School Managers that he had received a letter from the Divisional Education Officer stating that if the drainage difficulties could be overcome Wimpeys were likely to build 100 houses per annum for three years on the land west of the Station. "If the full

88 acres were developed there would be need for an additional two form entry Primary School," said Mr Warren.

Work was continuing on a golf course at Pastures Hospital on a do-it-yourself basis and aimed to convert 30 acres of parkland into a nine hole course for patients and staff.

The land was formerly part of the hospital's extensive farm, which, on Ministerial instruction was mostly being offered for sale on the open market.

It was called an amenity project which the organisers, Derby No 3 Hospital Management Committee were undertaking to improve recreational and therapeutic activities at the hospital.

Mr J R Priestley, the committee's secretary explained. "The course which is planned will measure just over 2,300 yards and the longest hole will be 350 yards."

A golf architect was consulted but "as far as possible the hospital staff are tackling the construction work themselves, aided by some patients for whom the construction work and outdoor activity is interesting and beneficial."

Simultaneously it was hoped to provide a pleasant conveniently adjacent wooded area where non golfers can walk "and take the air," said Mr Priestley.

The Staff Sports' Association regularly arranged activities, most of which the patients were encouraged to join.

"It is difficult to say precisely when the course will be available for play or how much it will cost," continued Mr Priestley.

"Total expenditure should not exceed a few hundred pounds.

"Whatever the outlay the cost will not be met by a Hospital Service Grant. Pastures Hospital receives on a bed basis a share of non-Exchequer raised by a central endowment fund and this revenue, intended partly for providing staff amenities, will largely finance the course project."

Staff members who play the course were expected to bring their own golf clubs and balls but some playing equipment would be provided for patients who "fancy a round."

DERBY No. 3 HOSPITAL MANAGEMENT COMMITTEE

Official opening of the new

GOLF COURSE

at the

PASTURES HOSPITAL MICKLEOVER, DERBY

by

ALDERMAN S. P. KING, O.B.E., J.P.
Chairman, Sheffield Regional Hospital Board

on

FRIDAY, 3rd OCTOBER, 1969

at

2-15 p.m.

Photo courtesy of ????? ??????

Mens' Foursome Exhibition Match following the opening when the 1951 Open Golf Champion Max Faulkner drove off.

Mr Priestley added: "Any gifts towards such equipment will be gratefully received. Members of the public would not be able to use the course, but guests would play in occasional competitions."

Doris Arnold told St John's PCC that hall lettings in 1966 had achieved £212, mostly from Mrs Hughes School of Dancing. One disturbing feature, she said, was the occurrence of damage in the hall and the council felt that locking the inner hall door could prevent much of this.

Derby Concert Orchestra conducted by Mr C Daly Atkinson visited Mickleover Methodist Hall in January to give a concert in support of the Methodist Church Organ Fund.

The Traffic Commissioners consented to an application by Derby Corporation Omnibus Department to operate buses on routes in Allestree and Mickleover and provide a joint service with Trent.

Members of Repton RDC heard from the clerk, Mr R V Hawcroft, that the swimming pool at the John Port School, Etwall, should be open to the public. The County Council were considering this suggestion, and in agreement over the provision of swimming facilities for the area.

Television was taking away cinema audiences in the 1960s resulting in the closing of cinemas in Derby. After one of its best box office weeks and after showing films for 51 years the Odeon Cinema in St Peter's Street closed its doors on May 1st 1966. It was sold to British Home Stores for development.

Against this trend the Superama opened in Colyear Street, Derby on February 9th. This brand new cinema was able to seat 650 people and the proprietors, Compton Group hoped "to give Derby a chance of enjoying modern cinema in the most modern surroundings." *Khartoum,* the spectacular epic starring Charlton Heston and Laurence Olivier was the first film to be shown on a screen with stereophonic wrap around sound. Sadly it had a short life and the site became a casino.

On February 14th grandfather "went a walk down Stakers this afternoon as far as Burton Road. New road signs going up."

Headmaster, Wilf Warren, told the School Managers that he was interested in the possibility of producing an operetta at Ravensdale Junior School titled *Flax into Gold* published by Chappell and he had been provided with vocal and instrumental scores to the value of about £10, free of charge. "If we do produce the operetta they would like to come and record it."

A team of children at the school were winners in a competition with Etwall County Primary School involving questions on History, Geography, Spelling, Science and Literature.

Mrs Pat White, wife of former parish councillor, Colin, carried out a period of observation at the school with a view to returning to teaching. She then acted as a supply teacher at both Ravensdale Schools.

Ravensdale Infant School was entitled to another teacher after Easter due to the increase of children on the roll. Mrs Val Shenton was recommended to the Divisional Executive.

The new Terrapin Classrooms, erected before Christmas were completed but the power had not been connected which left teacher Jennifer Dicken's class still using the Library.

Jimmy Best and Kathleen Stephens had attended a meeting of the Divisional Office. They reported that arrangements would now be that Ravensdale County Junior would accommodate its own surplus and the County Junior School the children from 300 houses to be built on land to the west of Station Road. It was proposed that eventually a new primary school would be built if more than 300 houses were built.

Children in the area east of the junction of Western Road and Uttoxeter Road would go to the new school in Jackson Avenue and a letter would be sent to parents living in Havenbaulk Lane asking them to send their children to this school.

Miss Stephens expressed concern at these changes, which was likely to reduce the number of children in her school still further.

Members of the parish council were asked at the February meeting to approve the erection of the sub-station at Sydney Close, Bramble Brook, extending an adjoining shelter.

The lease would be over a 21-year period and a nominal sum of £5 per annum rental was offered. In a letter to the council the Minister asked for assurance that there would be no opposition to the scheme.

They agreed that the sub-station was essential to the Central Electricity Generating Board's services to the district, Albert Olphn's request that the Board should paint the new structure every third year was accepted.

The proposed development of land along Uttoxeter Road from the Nag's Head to Limes Avenue included the erection of 12 shops, a supermarket, 24 garages, a car park and a four storey block of flats met with criticism and was dubbed "potential slums."

Marjorie Howarth considered this was not a good site for shops, and said that the area facing the new development was well served at present.

George Hayden said he objected because it meant bringing more people and children into the area, when already the school was "disgustingly overcrowded."

He said that an application of the Roman Catholic Church to build on the land had been refused. The Roman Catholic Diocesan Trustees had actually withdrawn their application in 1964.

Mr Olphin said that "the standard design in respect of both developments was not in keeping with the landscape of the district. There was inadequate car-parking facilities and the entrances to the proposed car park led out into a busy crossing which was already congested with a garage and hotel car park. The whole area from Cavendish Way to Limes Avenue should be dealt with as a single unit, not submitted for their approval piecemeal," he said. All these remarks were in reply to the RDC who were seeking council consent.

J H Fryer Limited tendered £357.10s.0d for the final ten pews at St John's Church, promising delivery in six weeks from receipt of order. The PCC agreed to proceed with the order.

Brian Holland reported that the youth club was now down to six regular members meeting in houses to retain the communal spirit. Many on the council thought there was no apparent need for the club but some thought that the increasing number of young people in the district would show where this club's future lay.

The parish council continued to carry out its normal duties despite the discussions about the Borough Extension. They faced a petition signed by 150 mothers calling for the widening of the path at Cattle Hill leading to the County Infants' School.

The County Surveyor had informed the School Managers some weeks earlier that improvements would soon be made and that land negotiations were well advanced.

Highlights of the chairman's report at this annual parish meeting concerned development, transport and highways.

Alan Ratcliff said a 34½ acre site off Station Road, the first phase of the 86½ acre scheme, had been submitted for approval. It was understood if this was so all the necessary estate facilities should be made available.

> Although no Mickleover Parish Council election was necessary in 1967, the nominations were:
> ARCHIBALD S N ALLISON
> VIOLET IDA ATHEL ALLSOPP
> DOUGLAS HARLOCK BINYON
> ELEANOR MAUD BREESE
> ALBERT ELLIS CLARKE
> GEORGE HARRY GORDON
> *MARJORIE MAY HOWARTH
> WILLIAM HALL
> *GEORGE HAYDEN
> JOHN ROBERT NIELD
> *ALAN WILLIAM RATCLIFF
> GEORGE KENNETH SMITH
> JOSEPH CHARLES SMITH
> *ANTHONY SWAIN YEOMANS
> *Also included in the nominations for Repton RDC along with Sydney Arthur Clarke and Frank Mosely Griffen.

Turning to the Mickleover bypass Mr Ratcliff considered the completion date would be 1969/70.

Referring to transport, he said a joint service had been arranged between Derby Corporation and Trent buses, but the council reserved the right to withdraw or amend the route through West Drive from its junction with Station Road to its junction with Farneworth Road, if safety conditions worsened. Turning of buses at the Onslow Road/Brisbane Road junction had been opposed.

Highways had shown some improvement, the ghost island at the junction of Rykneld Road and Havenbaulk Lane reduced traffic hazards. Improved road safety measures were being pressed home at The Square and after May 1967, buses would probably cease to turn at this point, continuing instead straight on to Hospital Lane.

The council later sent a protest to the Traffic Commissioners pointing out that for a man, his wife and two children travelling from Mickleover to Derby return fares would by 8s.

A meeting of the RDC Town Planning Committee met a few days later to discuss Wimpeys application for building 372 houses at Silverhill. There were calls for secondary education facilities in Mickleover with RDC Councillor Michael Clark saying that already there were a number of special buses taking Mickleover children to Etwall Comprehensive School.

An increase in the population could mean 500 school children when the houses were built. "This would require at least 10 extra double deck buses travelling to Etwall everyday," he said.

Mr W Spilman, Engineer and Surveyor for the RDC said that the parish council had pointed out that a composite plan of the area should be made showing provision for open spaces, recreation, primary education and civic centre.

People were continuing to take interest in amateur musical entertainment in Mickleover. *The Avagoose*, a local concert party under the direction of Mrs J Cook gave a concert at the Keiller clubhouse on Station Road.

On March 24th grandfather "went with Derek to look at where they are knocking down Thornhill's old house and shop on Cattle Hill." Four days later he wrote "it was now down."

Photos courtesy of the Derby Evening Telegraph
Mickleover County Junior School finalists for the Ben Robshaw trophy. Back row, from left: D Parker, C Sage, S Grudgings, J Green, S Mann, D Harrison, M Hancock, J Bishop. Front: S Holden, P Clowes, W Murfin, I Tucker, S Cunningham.

Photos courtesy of the Derby Evening Telegraph

The Mickleover Royal British Legion Pipe Band pictured with tutor Charles Craig, seated, third from left..

"A boy scout troop came round gathering stuff for their rummage sale. I gave them old gramophone records and the old HMV radio set dating from 1936", grandfather wrote at the beginning of April. He had also noted that "Wimpeys have commenced operating on new housing estate off Station Road."

The Mickleover Royal British Legion Pipe Band was formed in 1966 from former Derby Piping Society and had grown from its original five pipes to 14 pipers and five drummers.

They were frequently heard in the vicinity of the club when the band practiced in an outbuilding. Mr Charles Craig, an authority on the pipes, was the tutor instructor.

A mystery surrounding the cope which was accepted for St John's Church was explained at the PCC annual meeting. It was apparently among the vestments available to Bishop Rawlinson upon his arrival in Derby.

The Reverend Pierce read a letter from Mrs Rawlinson in which she reflected on the connection the cope had with British Honduras, and in a lighter vein she wrote of the swastika which unfortunately adorned it in the late 1930s. The swastika was an ancient cosmic or religious symbol but became the emblem of Nazi Germany in 1935.

Two Assistant Teachers were appointed at Ravensdale Junior School. They were David W Barton from Middlesborough and Mr D Kennedy from Etwall.

In the belief that a training college leaver had been allocated to the school, it transpired that none had been appointed which led to Miss C Rainbow from Burton-upon-Trent filling the third vacancy.

Arrangements were made to visit Nottingham Schools for staff from Ravensdale Infants' School to observe 'vertical planning' teaching methods.

Resignations had been received by Mrs M E Henchliffe and Katherine Skinner, teachers at the County Infants' and County Junior Schools respectively from August 31st. Katherine Skinner emigrated to Canada to teach at Estevan, Saskatchewan. She was keen to gain experience of all types of teaching and compare educational systems.

Three posts at the County Junior School were taken by Mrs Jean M Reavley, Bristol, Mrs Heather Tingay, Melbourne Close, Mickleover and Mr Alan Entwistle at the beginning of September. They joined Mr Herbert Edward Charles Weston from Burton-upon-Trent who was appointed Deputy Head Teacher.

Bishop Ellis, the Roman Catholic Bishop of Nottingham made his first Visitation and Confirmation at Our Lady of Lourdes on April 17th. Father Edward Byron welcomed the 200 people present. Sadly he died in 1972 and did not see the new church completed in 1982.

The need to maintain a healthy financial balance to establish equity on entering Derby Borough was emphasised by the clerk, Les Miller, at the April parish council meeting. He said the balance at the year end had shown an increase of over 30%.

One item under discussion was the offer of the New Opera Company of

Photo courtesy of Our Lady of Lourdes Archive

The first Mickleover Roman Catholic Church in the grounds of Mickleover Lodge.

Photos courtesy of Colin Haxell

The annual St John's Church Garden Party at 169 Station Road was opened in 1967 by Mrs Geoffrey Allen the wife of the Bishop of Derby.

Derby to provide a concert in Mickleover, but some members considered that the village offered no such facilities for such a body.

Councillor George Kenneth Smith said the matter should not be swept under the table without discussion after hearing the RDC had made a grant to the company.

He said "other possible channels ought to be explored and we should seek ways of bringing them here. Most opera and similar companies would prefer to play to a full but smaller hall than to find themselves in one of the grandest halls with only a few front stalls occupied by concert lovers." It was decided to ask the opera company what facilities they required for a performance.

St John's PCC had purchased 1,000 cards for balloon races at the annual gar-

Photos courtesy of the Magic Attic Archive, Swadlincote

Views from Clay Mills, Burton-upon-Trent, junction of the new A38 dual carriageway looking towards Findern.

den party in the interests of economy for this and future years. The use of golf balls for breaking china was noted as a hazard and it was hoped wooden balls could be sought instead.

Mrs Geoffrey Allen, opening the garden party, said it was hoped the £900 still required to clear the building fund debt would be realised by the end of the year.

However attention was drawn, after the event, to an incident arising from still using golf balls for smashing china. The Vicar, Martin Pierce, had received a a return from the balloon race from France.

The Rt Reverend Thomas Richard Parfitt, Assistant Bishop of Derby Diocese, consecrated the new Lady Chapel in the North Aisle and blessed the new Choir Vestry at All Saints Church.

Lord Hives opened the annual garden party at All Saints' Church in the vicarage grounds. Pupils of the County Junior School gave a display of country dancing arranged by teacher Olive Plumpton.

"After the dualling of the A38 trunk road from Clay Mills to Findern is completed early next year, there will inevitably be a delay before the work starts on the next stage of Mickleover by-pass," Mr Stephen Swingler, Joint Parliamentary Secretary at the Ministry of Transport told the *Derbyshire Advertiser* reporter after opening the five miles, £2^{1}/$_{2}$ million Burton-upon-Trent by-pass.

Mr Swingler explained that this followed objections to the published order indication line of the link road. "The delay is unfortunate," he said, "but we shall press ahead as soon as we can."

Photos courtesy of Harry Gaskill

George Brown, now Foreign Secretary, welcomed the party of 100 children and 4 teachers from Mickleover County Junior School to the Palace of Westminster. Mr Brown had to leave the party to rejoin a committee discussing the Common Market application, but his brother R W Brown, (MP for Shoreditch and Finsbury) and two other MPs showed them round.

Road pricing to cut traffic build-up in big cities and towns was being considered by the Minister of Transport, Barbara Castle. A study found that a charge of 6s a day for cars and 3s for motorcycles to enter central London was being recommended.

Brian Clough was ready to begin his appointment as manager of Derby County at the end of May. Chairman, Sam Longson had said "this is a new era for Derby. Our supporters are starved of success. He added: " I stand to sink or swim by this appointment. I've not had a good night's sleep for 14 days."

An application had been made to the RDC for the proposed development of a supermarket with a car park on the site of Common Farm on Brisbane Road, but the parish council decided in May to "object strongly".

It was felt that this would constitute a "piecemeal development" on the estate and would "lower the amenities of the adjacent houses. This would be the wrong place for an isolated development of this kind and the site was not big enough to develop a proper shopping centre."

Members also felt that those living in the vicinity would not welcome the idea of a supermarket, but if the site was going to be developed at all, they suggested that a doctors' surgery, group practice or a dentists surgery would be more suitable. (See map p100). They were to hear later in the year that permission had been granted to develop a small scheme of houses.

The County Planning Officer reported applications by Page-Johnson Limited in June 1967. The erection of four-storey blocks of flats and garages in Limes Avenue, plus the erection of shops and a supermarket on Ivy Farm site at the junction of Uttoxeter Road and Limes Avenue.

These were for the approval of details that had already received outline permission. The RDC however still considered they should be refused until the proposed link road had been constructed. The committee were advised there was no power to refuse the application for this reason in the terms of the outline consents.

An attempt by the Mickleover representatives to have pre-war council houses included in the RDC's first phase for electrical re-wiring so that they would be completed before Mickleover was incorporated in Derby Borough, failed when Sydney A Clarke's proposition was lost by 4 votes to 19.

Mr Clarke said: "If we don't get it done before we go into the borough it will be a very long time before it gets done."

Although the committee approved the first two phases of the re-wiring scheme, in neither case was Mickleover listed. The Housing Maintenance Officer said that it usually cost about £60 per house.

The clerk also reported at the June parish council meeting that the Ministry of Housing and Local Government had raised no objection to the council leasing 2,400 square yards of the southern extension of the Vicarage Road Playing Fields to the 149th (Methodist) Boy Scout Group for use as a site for a headquarters building for £10 a year. He added that provided that they obtained the necessary planning permission, they could now proceed.

The Bramble Brook culvert extension had been completed at a cost of £215, reported the clerk. The quotation from builders C F Wetton and Sons of Station Road had been accepted as they could complete the work within two weeks.

The new cricket pitch recently prepared by the Royal British Legion Club on the Memorial Field was officially opened when the Legion XI played a match against the Chairman's XI.

This was shortly followed by Mr Clive Bemrose, County Commissioner and High Sheriff of Derby, opening a new headquarters for the 124th Derby Mickleover Scout Group on the Royal British Legion Memorial Field. It replaced the ex army hut which had served as a meeting place for the past six years.

At the Royal British Legion AGM, chairman Arthur Waplington paid trib-

Photos courtesy of Harry Gaskill
Gifts were presented by Gillian Handie and David Harrison on behalf of the County Junior School to Deputy Headteacher Harry Gaskill, above, and Peter Goodman who were leaving the school.

ute to the Legion stalwarts who in 1946 had the courage and foresight to purchase land adjacent to the club premises now known as the Memorial Sports Field. He hoped those men, "some of them still living in Mickleover," would feel their efforts had not been wasted.

More than twenty schools competed at the Trent Valley School Athletics Meeting at the Municipal Sports Ground. The County Junior School took the overall championship, the boys' events championship and shared the girls' events championship with Shelton Lock Junior School. Harry Gaskill as chairman of the Association, presented a shield and two cups to the school.

Harry Gaskill left the school to attend a year's course in English at the Diocesan College, re-named Bishop Lonsdale College of Education, and Peter Goodman took a roll of Special Responsibility at the new Wren Park School in Jackson Avenue. Mr A Coleman had terminated his service at the school at the Easter Holiday.

It was reported that Derbyshire Education Committee were discussing the provision of milk to schools in cartons instead of bottles.

Grandfather wrote on July 10th: "Notices have gone up on Radford's old orchard about shopping and housing development. A fair which is being held in Flint's field [Manor Farm] is making outrageous noises with loud speakers."

Two days later: "I came back by way of Cattle Hill and noted that the hedge adjoining the narrow path to the church had been uprooted and the water bit behind the old house had been filled up. A start has apparently been made to widen the road."

Before Sid Thornhill ran his grocery shop at 17 Vicarage Road the property was owned by wheelwright/undertaker, John Watson. It was then called Ivy Leigh Cottage. John was the grandfather of Nancy (née Watson) Flint, who still lives in the adjoining Manor Farm. (See Book One).

Grandfather made further note in July that "Wimpeys have taken a house down where they are developing a new estate off Station Road." He was obviously referring to the entrance to Ladybank Road.

Discussions took place at St John's Church PCC meeting regarding the Building Fund.

As it was hoped to close the fund later in the year it was thought it was better to wait before making further appeals. "Our image would suffer if we continued the calls for money after describing last autumn's urgings as a final appeal," said Robert Varley.

It was agreed that following the winding up of the fund, future income should go to previously specified outside causes. As a result of an Advent Fair at the end of the year the target of £10,000 building fund was reached after opening five years previously.

The Derby Postal area was to be the first in the Midlands to be placed on the Postal Coding System. "The new codes, which should be written underneath the existing addresses, are now in the process of being sent to everyone in the area."

Henry Gibson (Tim) Ford MPS was appointed to fill the vacancy as a School Manager, the position created by the death of Arthur Riley.

Tim Ford was also on the Derby No 3 Hospital Management Committee and very much involved in the modernising of Pastures Hospital.

Mrs P M Campbell of Etwall Road was appointed as part-time Welfare Assistant at the County Infant School from a shortlist of 73 applicants.

Ravensdale Junior School gained 2 first, 4 second and 3 third prizes at Mat-

---

RAVENSDALE SCHOOLS STAFF AT THE BEGINNING OF THE NEW SCHOOL YEAR

JUNIORS

	Pupils
Mrs Dyke	43
Mrs Skipper (1st year)	42
Miss Dicken (1st/2nd year)	33
Miss Featherstone (2nd year)	44
Mr Barton (2nd year)	44
Mrs Larder (3rd year)	40
Mr Skertchly (3rd year)	42
Mr Brierley (3rd/4th year)	27
Mr Amott (4th year)	38
Mr Kennedy (4th year)	38

INFANTS

3T Mrs Turner	40
3B Mrs Beckford	36
3P Mrs Pickering	38
3H Mrs Harper	36
2E Mrs Ellison	33
2M Mrs McSwiggan	32
1S Mrs Swales (Reception)	22
1K Mrs King (Reception)	23
Cook: Mrs Rainford	

lock Bath Festival, plus a total of 6 honours, 5 distinctions and 5 merit certificates.

Headmaster, Wilf Warren, was asked to write an article on the music at the school for the *Times Educational Supplement*.

The County Infants' School re-opened after the summer holiday with the number on the roll down to 139 as so many children had gone to the new Wren Park School. Headteacher: Miss Stephens. Teachers: Miss Wibberley, Mrs Maéné, Mrs Brayne, Mrs Evans, Mrs Green.

The last trolley bus wended its way through the streets of Derby for the last time on September 9th. "They accelerated too quickly and then travelled too slowly. They took a great deal too much road at a corner when the vehicle had to negotiate an acute angle it was not uncommon for the poles to come off the wires" said a *Derbyshire Advertiser* reporter. The poles which held the wires were used to carry street lights.

On September 12th grandfather wrote: "The three storey farm house on Cattle Hill is being demolished." (See (1) map p252).

A forestry assistant had been called in to treat the Elm tree at the junction of East Avenue and Chestnut Avenue. It had been reported that there was fungus on the tree.

The parish council agreed at their September meeting to the revised 18 ward plan for the extended Derby as the lesser of two evils.

Previously the chairman read parts of a letter sent in "desperation" in a private capacity to the Queen by council member Marjorie Howarth requesting intervention in the general boundary proposals for Derby.

He said a reply written on behalf of the Queen was received four days later stating that Mrs Howarth's letter had been forwarded to the Minister of Housing and Local Government.

At a special Town Council meeting in March, to discuss the division of Derby, the press and public were removed. The reason given was "the confidential nature of the business to be transacted," a woman in the gallery shouted "Little Hitlers." The scheme in fact had to be submitted to the Home Secretary by the end of April 1967.

The Town Council Borough Extension Committee were then in favour of a 16 ward administration, even though an 18 ward plan was generally supported.

The Conservative Agent later explained to the *Derbyshire Advertiser* that a 16 ward scheme was "likely to arouse strong local resentment is that between the new Mickleover and Littleover wards which run for a long distance along Uttoxeter Road, and actually divided the old village centre of Mickleover.

"The communities of Mickleover and Littleover are naturally divided by a green area which is to be crossed in the next few years by a new trunk road, and it would seem natural for the ward boundary to keep approximately to this line."

Under the proposals Mickleover Hollow and the streets leading from it, and the Nag's Head public house would be in the Littleover ward.

An inquiry was closed within two hours in August due to the Town Council approving an 18 ward scheme. The officer conducting the inquiry, barrister Q T Edwards, had to adjourn the hearing to September 24th.

On re-opening the inquiry Ald M Lowe, chief witness for the Corporation was asked what led him to change his mind in regard to the number of wards from 16 to 18.

He said there was a considerable consensus of opinion among the people involved in coming to the decision that the 16 wards would not meet the situation.

It was conducted by Quentin Edwards, the barrister on behalf of the Home Office as Commissioner, and since some of the original objectors (councils and individuals) favoured an 18-ward scheme, there were fewer representations on this occasion.

An application for permission to go ahead with the second phase of the huge housing development off Station Road which the RDC Housing and Town Planning Committee had been told would include various public facilities had been withdrawn.

Councillor Alan Ratcliff proposed that the Area Planning Officer should be called in for further details, as these public facilities were regarded as necessary in view of the size of the first phase.

The area of land which was to be developed by Wimpeys in the second phase was 51.9 acres. They sent a letter withdrawing it on September 5th while it was still being considered by the County Planning Committee.

The RDC Committee told the County Council that they were concerned about an application being considered by the Area Planning Office for the erection of offices and use of land for light storage in Mill Lane.

Councillor Ratcliff said that Mill Lane was primarily a residential area, and this kind of development could upset nearby householders. Planning permission was very quickly rejected.

Grandfather witnessed the final demolition of the three-storey farm house on Cattle Hill. "Two bungalows are being erected on Thornhill's old piece [17 Vicarage Road]" and "the housing estate off Station Road is well advanced."

On his 83rd birthday he took a walk down Staker Lane. "The lane is now much used by heavy traffic taking material to where they are making the new dual-carriage way."

Photo, left, courtesy of Nancy Flint

The photograph above was taken from the north window at Manor Farm with the cattle grazing in the fields now mostly occupied by Catterick Drive. From the same window some years later are the bungalows referred to in the chapter.

Doris Arnold had told St John's PCC in September that a working party involved on the new Ecumenical Magazine in the village decided that it would more likely be published in July 1968, even though the previous April was thought to be most advantageous.

Secular as well as church news would be carried in the magazine with the suggested title of *Witness*. However many now thought "Mickleover" should appear in the title.

Each church was to bear equal financial liability although by October All Saints' PCC showed a reluctance, due to their financial commitments, to begin the publication before January 1969. It was suggested that St John's take on All Saints' share of the original outlay and possible loss for 1968 or that the other three churches each underwrite one third of the cost and loss.

In the event of the project being delayed for a further year it was agreed that St John's own magazine board should be strengthened by the addition of Catholic and Methodist points of view.

The Reverend Pierce was offered an American organ for St John's Church and it was inspected by the choirmaster Peter Howarth. The PCC Standing Committee accepted it and thanks were extended to the donor. Arrangements were made to transport it.

The problem in developing the new Silverhill Estate in All Saints' Parish plus the prospect of development behind the Nag's Head Hotel would have a great effect on the local clergy.

St John's PCC thought it was desirable to offer assistance for financial support for a clergy house or centre for worship, stipend etc.

Following the annual All Saints' harvest festival evensong, goodbyes were said to David Cooper, who had been choirmaster and organist for the past two years. Mr Cooper went to Lincoln College, Oxford as an organist scholar. He was succeeded by a former chorister at All Saints', Terence W Bennett.

Mickleover lost one of its recognisable sites in August when the station platforms and nameboards were removed by contractors to save maintenance costs. The siding in the goods yard were also removed and sold for scrap. In contrast a

Photo courtesy of the Derby Evening Telegraph

Mickleover Sports Club Dinner. Back row: Gordon Smith, Pat Mills, Jim Mills, unknown, unknown. Middle Row: Eric Smith, Margaret Smith. Seated: Mr Buchan, Mrs Buchan, Edward Gothard.

Photos courtesy of Mark Higginson

Mark Higginson, author of The Friargate Line, *photographed the battery-electric research vehicle about to enter the shed at Mickleover in 1980.*

railcar with a battery charging plant, in connection with the 'wiggly' wire research, made its first trip under its own power through Mickleover towards Egginton on November 12th 1967. A special battery charging plant from Aberdeen had been installed at Friargate.

Wilf Warren, headmaster at Ravensdale Junior School, told the School Managers that he had received communication regarding accommodation at both Ravensdale Schools from September 1968.

He had been assured that the County Authority would provide an additional terrapin on the site and that if the Borough Extension took place the terrapin would still be provided by the County Authority and the Borough Council would bear the cost.

The County Junior School having opened with four new members of staff Jimmy Best, headmaster, reported that things "had now settled down with fewer teething troubles than I expected." He continued: "Nevertheless, this year is bound to be a strain until every member of staff has experienced all the demands and activities of the school.

"The games and swimming have certainly got off to an earlier start than previous years. Mr Weston and Miss Mogridge are in charge of the football and netball, respectively. Swimming has fallen to Miss Mogridge and myself, mainly. The music section of the school has never been stronger, as far as the number of teachers capable of teaching this subject is concerned."

Gertrude Warner, the Cook Supervisor, retired after 22 years service to Mickleover Schools. She had been responsible for the production of approximately 1,000,000 meals for the Primary children of Mickleover. On four occasions she was the winner of the cooking and baking competition.

At the end of November grandfather commented about a BBC television programme. "Lively discussion on *Panorama* about [French President] De Gaulle's speech on England's application to join the Common Market."

On November 29th he "went a walk in the afternoon down Stakers as far as Burton Road. Entrance to farms spoiled with disinfected straw layer on account of Foot and Mouth epidemic." It had been reported in the local press that the disease had hit the whole county affecting business and social life and talked of it being the worst ever.

In early December grandfather had thoughts of going across the golf links, "but as these are closed on account of the dreaded epidemic", he was thwarted.

Alderman Mrs Gladys Buxton, chairman of the Derby No3 Hospital Management Committee spoke of the great need to fight against the institutionalism idea of mental hospitals.

She was formally accepting responsibility for the new shopping precinct at Pasture Hospital.

Since the commencement of the upgrading scheme in 1956 almost a million pounds had been spent on bringing the hospital up to standard although all the wards still had to be extended. Only two could be dealt with at one time in order to provide alternative accommodation for the patients.

The precinct included a pleasantly furnished library, a large shop which sold both food and clothing and hairdressing and beauty salons.

The scheme provided services for both the patients and staff. Regarding the library Alderman Buxton commented that "gone are the days when old, discontinued and worn out books are good enough for mental patients."

In formally opening the shopping precinct Lady Walker-Okeover said, "it must be a tremendous incentive to the patients to learn to gain confidence in their own capabilities and to learn to do the simple things in life.

"The lot of the patients is a hard one indeed," she said, and added that it was of the utmost importance that "we should alleviate the dullness of their everyday life."

A proposed scheme for a plot of land near the old All Saints' Church Hall in Limes Avenue for residential purposes was agreed to be quite appropriate the parish council agreed.

Following discussions with the County Council concerning litter in the village the parish council thought the main source of complaints was the large amount of paper wrappings dropped outside the shops.

Many councillors thought that the public should be educated rather than the provision of a scavenger [street cleaner] to clear up after them.

It was agreed that the council should accept the advice of the County Council concerning their request to make Orchard Street a one-way street. The County Council however had consulted the police and had reviewed the situation.

As they found traffic to be fairly light along Orchard Street, and there had been no record of any accidents there, they decided changing it to a one-way street would only add to the difficulties.

CHAPTER FIFTEEN
PARISH COUNCIL'S FAREWELL
1968

1967 ended with Britain's entry into the European Economic Community being vetoed by France and the pound being devalued with the prime minister, Harold Wilson making his famous "pound in your pocket" speech!

In his eighty-fourth year grandfather began 1968 by taking his "first walk of the New Year" - for two hours. He recorded a few days of "vile weather, snow began sliding off the roof."

A constant watch was kept each evening for two weeks by all male members of staff and several parents at Ravensdale Junior School after a break-in. Wilf Warren, headmaster, was on duty when the offender was caught "red handed", and the matter put in the hands of the police.

The Elm tree in the middle of the road at the junction of East Avenue and Chestnut Avenue had been reported as being in an advanced state of decay. The council confirmed their action in recommending that the tree should be removed but they had also asked the County Council to plant a semi-mature tree in the same position.

For some twenty years the tree had been the subject of discussion but it was reported it had been infected by fungus and although it could be restored it would be very expensive.

It was "with reluctance" that the council decided that the tree should come down, although not actually stated, it was very convenient as a new bus route was being required.

They did however agree to re-consider the matter at this January meeting due to the clerk, Les Miller, having received a petition asking for the tree to be replaced. "Earlier this month a contractor started to fell it and was almost lynched by the residents," remarked Mr Miller.

Some of the parishioners had offered to donate a tree and Derby Civic Society were willing to donate a Beech tree from their tree plant at Spondon.

Photo courtesy of the Derby Evening Telegraph
The damaged Elm tree on East Avenue.

Photo courtesy of the Derbyshire Advertiser

Mickleover Square where parked lorries were causing congestion outside The Oyster Snack Bar.

Mr Miller pointed out that he had received a letter praising the council for the tree's removal. The author "had spent 13 years dodging it and would be glad to see it go."

Archie Allison said the tree was the "finest piece of road safety on this stretch of road", but Councillor Gordon replied that young trees were "frequently being pulled down by gangs of vandals. If this tree is uprooted who replaces it?" he asked.

A resident in East Avenue wrote that the "tree gives the area character and beauty and attracted many of the householders in East Avenue and Chestnut Avenue to live there."

A complaint by residents that long distance lorries were blocking The Square whilst the drivers went into the Oyster Snack Bar was passed to the police.

A letter pointed out that residents were unable to park whilst they shopped in the village. If they did manage to park, their cars would be hemmed in for some time.

At the end of the month grandfather went "on business" to Derby. "I had a walk round and noted the upheaval being caused by the construction of a new inner ring road. This much in evidence including [recently] demolished St Alkmund's Church and Bridge Gate."

Any hopes of an early return to normal conditions from foot and mouth disease were shattered with fresh outbreaks and Derbyshire the main area of infection.

Two recently announced were close neighbours of Mickleover, Bupton Farm at Longford and Moorway Farm, Littleover. One case of infected sheep followed at Kirk Langley in February. The all clear came a month later.

Mickleover Produce Association, which came into being during the "Dig for Victory" campaign of the 1939-45, war was wound up.

Fifteen members attended the annual general meeting at the Nag's Head Hotel. Chairman, local teacher Harry Gaskill, said it was because of lack of support for the activities of the association. No nominations had been received for the secretary and treasurer or additional committee members prepared to give extra support.

"It would seem," Mr Gaskill said, "that members only wanted the association for the cheap seeds they were able to obtain."

A letter in the *Derby Evening Telegraph* from Mr J E Hickling of Station Road reflected many peoples feelings over the Borough extension.

"Judging from press reports of the meetings of authorities concerned, and the compiling of lists of prospective candidates for election to represent the newly-drawn wards, it would seem to be taken for granted that the Derby Borough extension is a foregone conclusion.

"Parliamentary sanction has not yet been given for the extensions. Why, then, is it being taken for granted in certain quarters?

"The overwhelming vote of the areas concerned was against being taken in. Apart from the merits or otherwise of the proposals, for what does the wish of the people count if such is to be overridden in this manner?"

Derbyshire MPs, with the exception of the Foreign Secretary, George Brown, supported a motion in the House of Commons on February 14th for the annulment of the Ministerial Order widening the boundaries of the Borough of Derby.

The motion was lost by 176 votes to 41, a government majority of 176. The order extending the Borough was in consequence now approved.

George Brown was in dispute with the prime minister over decision making in the government and resigned on March 14th. He took up a position with Courtaulds in 1968 but was defeated at the 1970 General Election. He died in 1985.

Lord Champion's House of Lords petition to annul the order for the extension was heard on February 26th.

He said that the Order was to transfer 11,000 acres of the Rural Districts of Belper, Repton and South East Derbyshire from the administrative area of Derbyshire to the County Borough of Derby. The object of the Order was to provide land inside Derby for re-housing.

Photo courtesy of the Derby Evening Telegraph

Under the guidance of their headmaster, Jimmy Best, these seven pupils of the County Junior School attained their gold award for proficiency in personal survival at Queen Street Baths. From left: Lynne Middleton, Kathy Jinks, Janet Haynes, Robert Randall, Gary Hartley, Andrea Holmes, Jonathan Cunningham. The test included undressing in the water, making a float from clothing and using it to float for five minutes without the use of arms or legs; and swimming 1,000 yards, surface diving during the swim 12 times head first and 12 times feet first through a hoop.

Lord Champion said he was firmly of the opinion that the Order was ill-conceived and ill-timed. "It would affect the services which had to be provided by Derbyshire County Council. He went on to say that if people had been suffering as the result of administrative inefficiency caused by the existing boundary then eight years since the first move towards this Order had been much too long.

"But if it was the case on both sides of the boundary they had managed very well there seemed to be not the slightest justification for pushing this Order through at this stage."

Lord Gainsborough asked why the Order should be rushed through now instead of waiting to get the report of the Royal Commission this coming autumn.

Lord Kennett in reply said there were individual pragmatic decisions and although difficult the Derby issue was urgent enough to be proceeded with even in view of the impending report.

Nobody disputed that most of the rural district inhabitants were against the Derby Order and Lord Kennett added: "Nothing I say will probably change their minds, but those familiar with Local Government changes know that the wishes of the inhabitants can be only one of the factors to take into account."

He said those people to be transferred under the Order to Derby would be cushioned against a sharp increase in rates. "The transfer of ratepayers over to the full rate would be phased over two or three years."

The adjournment of the debate on the petition caused a day of uncertainty and meant the postponement of the "greater Derby" election from March 21st to March 28th.

When the debate came up again on the following day the motion to annul the Order was formally withdrawn, by Lord Champion, he gave his reason.

He said he did not want to see the matter of statutory Orders becoming a constitutional issue between the House of Lords and the House of Commons even though he thought the objectors outnumbered others.

On March 9th grandfather noted that the "dual carriageway finished as far as Atkins Garage. (Now NYK Logistics). Two days later he posted his application for rates rebates to Derby Corporation.

Mickleover Parish Council held its final meeting on Tuesday, March 26th when it was addressed by the chairman, Alan Ratcliff.

"We have fought and fought well but we have lost," he said, and stressed to members that "we shall be living in the Borough and it is up to all of us to make Derby the town or city nearer the one we hope it would be."

Over the years, he commented, the parish council had been responsible for a large number of improve-

Photos courtesy of the Magic Attic Archive, Swadlincote

Further Views from Clay Mills, Burton-upon-Trent, junction of the new A38 dual carriageway looking towards Findern. The Willington power station towers can be seen in the background.

297

ments in the village, and although many were rather "mundane", there were such projects as the Bramble Brook Playing Fields, "which had turned out to be one of the most successful ventures."

Mr Ratcliff reminded members that this was one of the earliest efforts in the area to provide more of an adventure playground.

He also referred to the expansion of Vicarage Road Playing Fields but one of his greatest regrets was that they had been unable to provide the much desired swimming facilities in the parish. "Many others had not materialised and their requests had been turned down because of the boundary extension.

"The council, which was formed as long ago as 1894, had only three clerks during that time," he told members, and went on to pay tribute to Mr L J Miller who had been the clerk for the past twenty years. Les had been an RAF Instructor at Burnaston Airport during the war. He later took up an appointment at Belper Rural District Council.

A vote of thanks to Mr Ratcliff for the services he had given to the council was proposed by George Hayden, the vice chairman, and seconded by Marjorie Howarth.

In reply Les Miller commented that it had been a great pleasure to serve the council and assured members that he had many pleasant memories. He told members he had missed one council meeting because he was in hospital and even then he wrote the minutes up in the ward.

They received two "farewell letters," one from the Derbyshire Association of Parish Councils and one from Mr R V Hawcroft, the clerk to Repton RDC, who referred to the "painstaking efforts made by them to provide services to the parish."

In the last business to be conducted the council decided to donate 10 guineas

Photos courtesy of the Derbyshire Advertiser
Conservative Candidates for the Derby Borough Elections: Left, T D Barlow. Centre, R Greene. Right, J A Hobson.

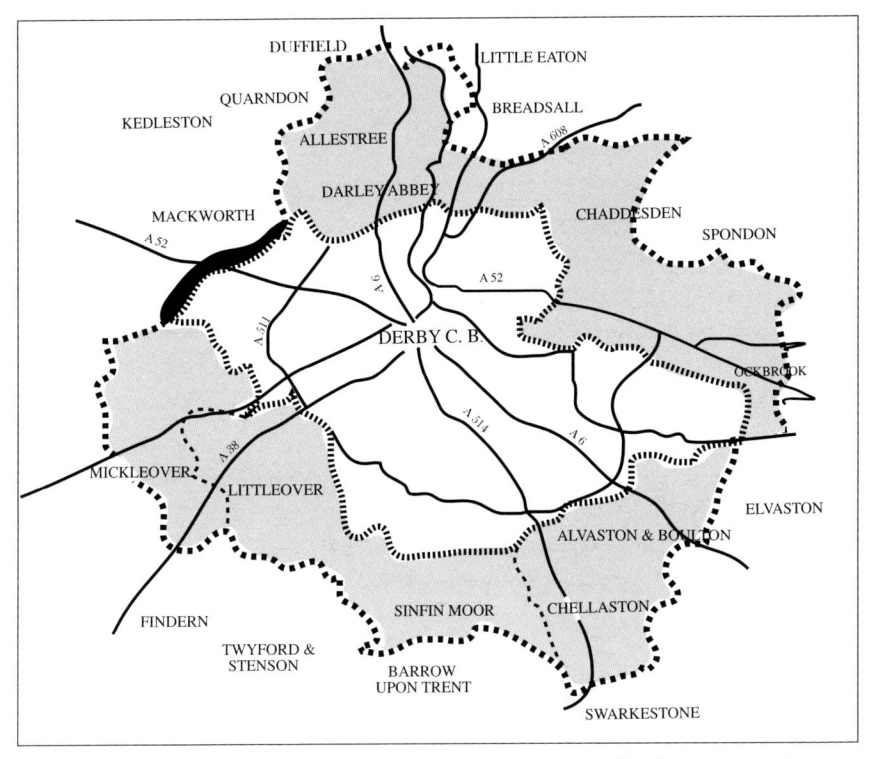

The above map shows Derby's new boundaries. The thick panel indicates an area lost to Derby.

DERBY BOROUGH ELECTIONS MARCH 28TH

R Greene (Con), company director, Chain Lane, Littleover   3,243
J A Hobson (Con), draughtsman, Station Road, Mickleover   3,240
T D Barlow (Con), quantity surveyor, Little Eaton   3,134
Not Elected:
A E Clarke (Lab), retired, Allestree   722
C Lowe (Lab), pattern and model maker, Farneworth Road   628
T Pendry, trade union officer, Derby   545
By-election caused by the appointment of aldermen.
Mrs S L A O'Brien (Con), widow, Kedleston Road   1,723
A E Smith (Liberal), technical author, Tasman Close   580

to the Derby Civic Society "for their recent services in planting a number of trees in the parish." Six were planted at the northern end of Station Road.

Grandfather and Auntie Hilda went to vote on March 28th. "Our first time as voters in the Derby Borough elections."

On April 1st 1968 the County Borough of Derby achieved by far the largest boundary extension in its history. With the approval of both Houses of Parliament parts of Belper, Repton and South East Derbyshire were added to the county borough. The Local Government Commission for England was abolished and the Derby Order was one of the last orders made as

299

Photo courtesy of the Derbyshire Advertiser
The former Great Northern line at Mickleover from the bridge on Station Road

a result of its recommendations. The government appointed a Royal Commission of Local Government to review the whole structure of local government throughout the country.

The borough council were now able to administer an area of 19,000 acres a population of some 217,183, compared with 128,430 in the old borough. It could now plan the location of new housing, new schools, new recreational areas and other public developments within its own area.

The new administration, with a Mayor at its head, was authorised in the Charter of 1682 to wear the black tricorne hat and black and gold robe.

Derby's first Charter was granted by Henry II in 1154 when Mickleover was paying tithes to Burton Abbey, and over the years only depended on Derby on market days. As a dormitory village it had its own roots in the railway age in a small way but it didn't fully develop until some time after the coming of the motor car.

Mickleover's station wasn't built until the 1870s and lay some distance from the village centre and it never attracted much in the way of commuter traffic. Derby lost its 90 year old rail link when the last train to pass through Mickleover was an enthusiasts' special from Birmingham in the late afternoon of May 4th at the beginning of May 1968 when the last freight trains ran on the line through Friar Gate station. Passenger services were withdrawn in 1964.

The line between Friargate and Egginton then became the responsibility of the Electrical Division of British Railways Research Department.

The Highways Committee of Derby Town Council said the rail tracks were clearly not practicable for incorporation in the inner ring road scheme, "But overall possibilities of the route from Kingsway inwards might be worth looking into."

Mickleover's population now depended on the town council for its welfare and health, most of whom were patients of Doctors McCahey and Charlton on Station Road and Doctor Harkins a few yards to the north.

The County Council still retained the Mickleover ambulance station to serve a wide county area but some borough vehicles were based there by arrangement.

"We are confident that householders will not notice any difference," said Mr C V Roberts, Director of Public Cleansing and Transport Manager. "Certainly, every service they have been getting will be continued without any interruption.

An interesting observation is his statement: "at the present time, and for some three months past, the department has no labour shortage." The first time this had occurred in his nine years as Director.

The schools ceased to be administered by Derbyshire County Authority and became part of the County Borough of Derby.

> Dear Mr. Best,
>
> Now that the Derby Boundary Order has been approved I am writing to you in a less formal way than in my letter of 4th March, which was necessarily concerned with the administrative arrangements for the transfer.
>
> May I, on behalf of the Chairman and members of the Education Committee, thank you and each individual member of your staff, both teaching and non-teaching, most sincerely for your loyalty and co-operation, and place on record our warmest appreciation for all you have done in the service of education in Derbyshire. My colleagues in the office and I would like to be associated with this expression of thanks to you all.
>
> We hope that you will find that service with your new Authority will be as enjoyable as it has been in Derbyshire, and we send you all our best wishes for the continued success of your work for the children in your schools.
>
> Yours sincerely,
>
> Acting Director of Education
>
> J. W. Best, Esq.,
> Headteacher,
> Mickleover C. J. M. School,
> Vicarage Road,
> Mickleover,
> DERBY.

The final letter to the headmaster of the County Junior School, Jimmy Best.

Mr C Middleton, Director of Education said: "there will be no sudden violent change, and our aim has been for an easy and painless takeover.

"It is quite clear that for some time all sorts of county procedures will continue unchanged." The county's John Port comprehensive school at Etwall continued to serve Mickleover.

Church schools continued to play a large part in Derby education. The Derby Diocesan authority expressed interest in the possibility of a church secondary school in the area, hinting "that this may materialise in the Mickleover district, which, alone of the absorbed parishes, has no secondary school at present."

*Photos courtesy of
Derby Museums and Art Gallery L3336 (above) and L5575 (left).*

A photograph believed to be taken in the early 1970s looking up Limes Avenue. The old cottages had survived. The steps to the block of flats built by Page-Johnson can just be seen on the right. Left: The Lodge to The Limes still survived and the gateposts at the beginning of the drive.

Only days after the extension Derby West police division announced that it was taking delivery of its Panda cars, Morris Minor saloons in light blue with the distinctive Panda stripe and clear police signs.

They were to be used to cover the west side of Derby which included Mickleover. A car was allocated to each area to operate 24 hours a day, "driven by a constable who will be equipped with a personal radio set." A detective officer was also attached to each area.

The area constable was described as being the "man on the ground". In most cases he resided within his beat area and worked on the beat and nowhere else. Three were allocated at Mickleover, Constables Slater, Baldwin and Fraser.

Grandfather had noted "the old tree in the centre of East Avenue has been removed and a sapling put in its place." On April 10th: "saw for the first time the sign of the borough boundary near the corner of Hospital Lane."

Members of All Saints' choir travelled to Lincoln, by invitation, at the end of April to join the Cathedral choir to take part in evensong.

Reporting on the fabric and ornaments at the church annual meeting, the Reverend Crockett spoke of things already done, including the reinstatement of the south clock face.

Referring to things that ought to be done, Mr Crockett listed the provision of toilets, the overhauling of the organ and the moving of the console to the south arcade of the nave and as a "long-term" project the clearance of the west end of the nave and the resiting of the font in a central position.

The new sub-branch of Normanton Road branch of the Midland Bank in Derby was to be opened on the junction of Limes Avenue on Whit Saturday, June 1st. The keys of the premises were formally handed over by the contractors, Page Johnson Construction, in mid-May. This was the first phase in changing the south side of Uttoxeter Road, opposite what is now the Community Centre.

"Learned from the Sexton [Bill Barker] that Manor farm is to be bought for council houses," wrote grandfather. Mickleover Parish Council had envisaged the land south of Vicarage Road Playing Field would be used as a community centre and public swimming pool.

This never materialised and in its place the Borough Council rented allotments and built the two-storey Holly Court flats for the elderly.

Grandfather's diary continued on May 11th, "they are putting the roof on the flats at the back of the bank. [Limes Avenue]"

Heavy rain caused St John's Church garden party to move to the church hall which was opened by Mr C Middleton, Director of Education for Derby Borough. He had lived in the area since 1938 and was a member of All Saints' Church.

Reverend Martin Pierce told the gathering that the two Anglican churches had joined forces to purchase a house on the Silverhill estate, to house an assistant priest to help in their ministry.

The Mayor of Derby, Alderman Enid Wood, paid her first official visit to Mickleover ward when she attended a ceremony at All Saints' on May 28th to witness the laying up of the old standard of Mickleover Royal British Legion and the dedication of a new one. The church was filled to capacity and arrangements were made to relay the service outside the church for those unable to gain admission.

Part of Mickleover parish, not included in Derby Borough, was added to the parish of Burnaston. With no shops, no pub, no church and no post office Burnaston formed its first parish council.

The modernised A38 approaching Derby petered out near Findern. Within minutes of leaving the dual carriage way the traffic would return to the old A38 towards Pastures Hill and reach the bottleneck at Chain Lane.

If the intention was to travel north in the Sheffield direction there was no alternative but to enter Derby town centre with the growing army of heavy lorries causing congestion.

The three-day public inquiry into the proposed Mickleover by-pass began on June 11th and Harold Marnham QC for the Ministry of Transport opened the proceedings by reading the Minister's statement of policy.

The Minister had recognised the need for an improved route between Nottingham, Derby and Stoke-on-Trent but a decision had not been reached. Whatever the outcome he would continue with the improvement of the trunk road through Mickleover village.

Mr Marnham went on to explain that the link would by-pass the built-up area of Mickleover and avoid the long steep gradient of Pastures Hill on the A38.

Several property owners were objecting to alternative routes proposed by the Minister, among them Jimmy Best headmaster at the County Junior School who lived at 277 Uttoxeter Road.

Outlining the history Mr Marnham said there had been an early scheme going back to the last days of the first world war and the early post-war period (1939-45) when the whole question was under consideration.

One of the matters in which everybody would be interested he said, was the effect it would have on individual properties. "It was much to be regretted that some of the effect would result in personal hardship, destruction of property, and some interference with amenity was possible.

"The Ministry's scheme fitted in well with Derby Corporation's proposals for the future, including construction of an inner ring road."

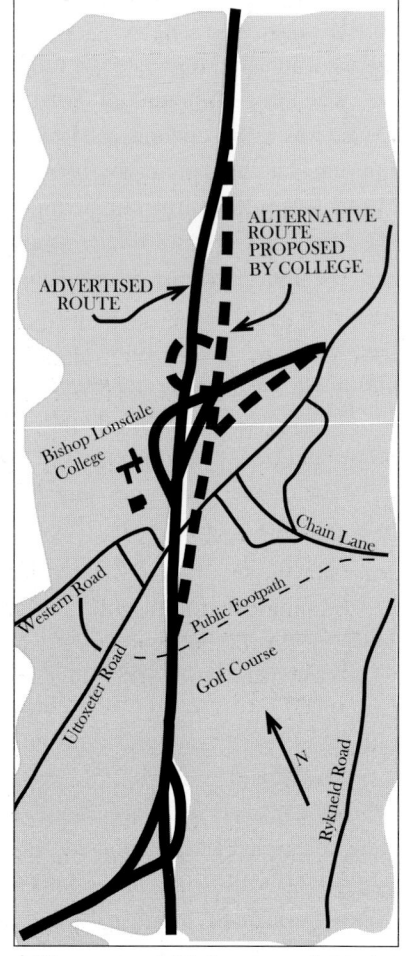

The proposed Ministry route, in black with the dotted line showing the College's alternative.

Principal objectors were Bishop Lonsdale College (formerly the Diocesan Training College), Mickleover Golf Club, the Sheffield Regional Hospital Board, Rough Heanor Allotments Society and the owners of a Service Station at the beginning of the new road.

Wednesday morning was devoted to objections of the Mickleover Golf Club and in the afternoon the inspector, Mr A Tildesley and other representatives travelled the length of the proposed route and visited the golf course and College sites.

Peter Frank Linnell, a chartered surveyor and witness for the golf club, said in evidence that an objection was served in 1960 to the proposed siting of the start of the link road at the end nearest Derby.

In 1966 and 1968 a modified plan was issued showing an entirely different position "which cut the golf course in half," said Mr Linnell.

Whilst the Mickleover Golf Club did not wish to obstruct the carrying out of the trunk road as proposed, they asked for assurances that the Minister of Transport would, at no cost to the club, provide adequate additional land for the reinstatement of the 18 hole golf course, erect a new clubhouse and ancillary buildings with services and construct a car park on a new site along with other requests.

Mr Marnham QC for the Ministry pointed out there was no schedule to say the Ministry should provide additional land and "has however less power to grant planning permission." At this stage there had been no response from landowners regarding the sale of land to the golf club.

Summing up for the golf club Mr Smedley said "consultation had to be given to the validity of the arguments put forward for the road."

In the opinion of the College Governors, the Ministry of Transport's proposals involved permanent impairment of the educational work of the College, whose life is envisaged in terms of a hundred years or more, and for nearly £500,000 of public and charitable money was invested.

"It would therefore be a very serious reduction of teaching efficiency to destroy these playing fields and put them somewhere else," said Mr Vaughan-Neil as counsel for the College.

The College proposed an alternative route, further east and "Stylites" in "Across the Market Place" in the *Derbyshire Advertiser* thought "it is a pity that College and Ministry could not have shortened matters by reaching an agreed solution. No doubt we shall hear why."

All objections and evidence would be the subject of a report by the inspector to the Minister, who would make the decision.

Grandfather wrote on June 18th: "I took a walk over the golf links. This is the first time this year. The footpath and links were closed during the foot and mouth

Photo courtesy of Sylvia Phillips

The staff of Ravensdale Infants' School 1969. Standing, left to right: Miss Pat Beech, June Towers, Trindy Swales, Pat Holwill, Sylvia Phillips (Welfare Assistant). Seated: Kath Ratcliff (Secretary), Joan Gibson, Evelyn Fearnehough, Jean Pickering, Ruth Beckford.

Photo courtesy of Pat White

The staff of Ravensdale Junior School 1972. Standing, left to right: Jack Skertchly, Joy Dunn, Chris Astill, Marilyn Jeffreys, Ron Brierley, Iris Barker (Secretary), Ken Simpson. Seated: Betty Bailey (Welfare Assistant), Danny Malachowska, Pat White, Elma Dyke, Wilf Warren, David Backhouse, Margaret Featherstone, Hilda Harris.

Photo courtesy of the Derby Evening Telegraph

Williamsons of Mickleover (E B Williamson) became a self-service filling station in August which was opened by Patricia Phoenix, the actress who was well known as "Coronation Street's" Elsie Tanner. One of the great attractions on its opening was the issuing of quadruple (20) Green Shield stamps on every gallon of petrol. Gone are the showroom with workshops and the canopied used car section.

epidemic. It is sad to think this fair field path with pleasant and extending views will be spoiled by the making of the motor by-pass road."

All Saints' Church suffered the same fate as St John's a month earlier for on June 22nd, owing to the weather, their garden fete was held in the Vicarage and was opened by the *Derbyshire Advertiser* columnist, Miss Rosemary Meynell.

In her "Derbyshire Woman's Diary" she wrote: "Poor Mickleover has had rainy days for the last four church fetes. Saturday was no exception but brave supporters rallied round and the stalls were moved into the Vicarage. I was interested to see the house which I remember in the days of **Mr Bindley**, Vicar for over 60 years. It was built in 1821 in the solid late Georgian manner."

From midnight June 25th the whole of England and Wales was freed from infected area restrictions for the first time since October 25th 1967. It was the worst outbreak of foot and mouth disease in our history. Derbyshire fell victim in November and was not finally cleared until the Spring.

Ravensdale Junior School annual speech day was held for the first time in the evening. Owing to limited accommodation only fourth year pupils and all parents were able to attend.

Mr Wilf Warren, headmaster, said it was a distressing thought that after years of agitation by teachers for smaller classes a class of thirty was still considered small in the primary school.

He continued, "a further mobile classroom was to be erected" and he thanked the managers for their vigilance and foresight which had ensured adequate accommodation throughout the life of the school.

On August 1st the chairman of Derby Town Council's Education Committee, Alderman J Tillett, said that the 11-plus examinations would be continued in the Borough for the rest of the year.

"The children of Mickleover," he commented, "would still be sent to John Port when they reached the age of 11, but children whose parents wished them to take the 11-plus, would be allowed to do so."

This was due to Mickleover being the only area "feeding" into a comprehensive school at the time.

"There would be those who wanted their children to go to a denominational school, which if they passed the 11-plus they could do with a grant. There would also be parents who because of the father's job, were forced to move around the country and might find themselves in a town which did not have a comprehensive system.

Derby and District model railway enthusiasts had the opportunity of seeing some realistic working layouts in early September when Mickleover St John's Railway Group staged its fourth annual exhibition in the Church Hall, Devonshire Drive.

The St John's Group was joined by friends from Mickleover Methodist Church.

"I went along Station Road and a little way up towards Radbourne. Railway beginning to look neglected," wrote grandfather.

Two days later on September 23rd he recorded "a fatal accident occurred on the main road near Arthur Morley's farm. An Etwall school teacher was killed."

Phillip John Starkey, physical education teacher at John Port School, was driving to school when the car he was driving was in collision with a lorry on Etwall Road and he died before reaching hospital.

Father of three children, Phil, a member of Mickleover Sports Club, was the opening batsman for Mickleover Cricket Club and formally played for Mickleover at football.

After extensive modernisation Mickleover Methodist Church was re-opened. New furnishings, including a font, communion rail, hymn board, two flower pedestals and a cross were dedicated.

Reverend Albert Hearn, the retired minister at the church performed the opening. The original building was erected during the 1914-18 War and soon after a small hall was added. The minister, Reverend John L Hope, thanked all who had made the modernisation possible. He said it had cost nearly £6,000 of which £4,800 had been raised.

The library facilities in Mickleover still consisted of three evenings a week at the

Photo courtesy of the Derby Evening Telegraph

This photograph, taken by the Derby Evening Telegraph *in October 1968 explains some of the changes taking place in Vicarage Road. The group are standing outside the old Holly Bush Farm which were then the premises of Bill Varey. It was Bill who applied to convert his outbuildings into a fish and chip shop (see p123). On the right is the side entrance to Mickleover Infants' School on Uttoxeter Road. From the left, Mrs T Broome, president of Mickleover Conservatives, Jimmy Best, head of the Junior School, Councillor John Hobson, John Godfrey (Traffic Engineer), and Arthur G Ravensdale, former chairman of the parish council and chairman of the School Managers. They are holding a traffic survey made by children of the junior school on the road dangers on the narrow section known as Cattle Hill.*

Memorial Hut. This was supplemented to include a further two evenings a week when a branch was opened at Ravensdale School.

At the beginning of November Councillor R Longdon, chairman of Derby Town Council Omnibus Committee explained the problems affecting any extension of Corporation bus services into the village and new estates in Mickleover at the weekly meeting of the Old Age Pensions Association.

He was introduced by Councillor Roydon Greene, a Mickleover representative on the Town Council, who discussed with members several problems concerning the community in general and with particular reference to the older citizens.

Over a long period concern was expressed about additional buses using Darwin Road, Brisbane Road and Onslow Road if Trent and Derby Corporation operated joint services through the village. It had even been suggested that buses should be operated along West Drive for a trial period of three to six months.

309

Posters in many parts of the village were promoting a new magazine sponsored by the four churches entitled "Vision".

It was to be published in January 1969 and was intended to reflect the interests of Mickleover combined with religious knowledge and information. Its aim was to encourage local news items and stories. The editorial board was headed by editor John Sanders.

Grandfather noted, "the new aspect to the landscape caused by the new housing estate off Station Road and viewed from Radbourne Lane."

Semi-detached houses were being offered by Wimpeys for £3,795 and houses had been completed in the first phase.

Accompanied by Ransome and Marles Band of Newark, 33 members of the choir of Ravensdale Junior School sang a version of *Jerusalem* to mark the unveiling of a war memorial at the Arboretum.

This was in fact a portable plaster one, and the solemn occasion a sequence for the D H Lawrence film, *Women in Love* which was on location in Derbyshire.

The children, who were fitted out with costumes of the 1920s, were selected because Ravensdale School choir was noted locally for its high standard.

The two main actors in the scene were Alan Bates and Jennie Linden, but a large number of local extras also took part as villagers watching the "unveiling" of the memorial dedication to men from the village of Beldover who died in the 1914-18 War.

Behind the scenes negotiations were taking place about the closure of Keiller's factory in Station Road by Christmas 1968. Not only was this to be a loss of employment in the area but the end of a reputation of a factory being a happy place to work in a very good atmosphere.

There were canteen facilities with full meals at a small price. At Christmas all the employees were served with a three course Christmas dinner and the employee's children were given a Christmas party.

The factory was always ahead of its time. Everything was made in batch form in sweet making but they also invested in new machinery for a continuous process which was quite complicated. Towards the end there was one girl looking after five machines.

Kath Ratcliff had enjoyed her part-time job as secretary to the manager of the factory, Stan Hearn. It tied in well with her working at Ravensdale Infants' School.

In the summer of 1968 Mr Wibberley, chief clerk, had asked Mrs Ratcliff to work during the summer holidays. On occasion her two boys of school age accompanied her to the factory.

Barry Hanson had worked at the factory since 1962 when it was still pro-

Photos courtesy of Peter Sherratt

A group of happy workers at the Keiller factory. From the left: Glenis Davis, Elaine Crosby, Diane Holden, Glynis Press and Dorothy O'Brien. Right: Nancy Bednall, Nora Foley, Linda Crosby, Gwen Holden and Christine Simpson.

ducing biscuits. He had been employed in every department and able to work all the equipment on the process side. In his final two years he had worked in the laboratory doing development work on new sweets and improving the quality.

After Keillers left, Rolls-Royce took on the site for training purposes, employing most of the administration staff.

The prohibition of burning fuels which created smoke were announced for the Derby area. Allestree was to be the first in 1969 followed by others soon after. Mickleover and part of Friar Gate in 1972 with Spondon the last in 1978.

Grandfather took a walk down "Stakers" as far as Burton Road. "Traffic seems to have increased in Staker Lane." He followed this with a "saunter down The Hollow and along the farm lane towards Brook Field Farm. Very pleasant."

The Bishop of Repton, the Rt Reverend Warren Hunt stated in early December that the proposed trunk road would "take away part of the present playing fields and be close to the College for comfort." He was speaking at the annual speech day at Bishop Lonsdale College.

He added that now the decision on the road had been made, compensation would be forthcoming and the playing fields they had lost would be made elsewhere, but the whole co-ordinated plan of the gymnasium, changing rooms and playing fields would go by the board. One of the greatest problems he thought would be that of the noise.

"The College had moved to its site, having fully consulted the Ministry of Education and had been assured that they could develop the ground. But then in stepped the Ministry of Transport with new road plans threatening the playing fields," exclaimed the Bishop of Lichfield, the Rt Reverend A S Reeve, chairman of the College Council.

"My own view is that now we've probably reached a sensible compromise, as the thing would have been disastrous with the link road right next to the main buildings, and we managed to have that improved. I fully realise the importance of expanding the A38," he commented.

"We, of course, ask for land as compensation, not only for the fields but for the expansion of the buildings."

Judith Wood of Ladybank Road wrote to the *Derby Evening Telegraph* complaining that the road nameplates on the Silverhill Estate had not been erected and she was constantly being asked for the directions to new roads "even a policeman asked me once," she said. "Already serious delays in the arrival of midwives, doctors and ambulances have been occasioned by their absence." She also stated that there was a lack of street lighting and a convenient public post box.

Norman Fisher, Town Clerk of Derby, replied that permanent nameplates had been on order and would be erected as soon as they arrive.

"It is usual on a private development for the Corporation to provide lamp standards but it is understood that they have made other arrangements," he said.

The Derby Headpostmaster said "the provision of a letter box on the Silverhill Estate is under consideration but one was unlikely to be provided until housing development is more advanced."

Mickleover Royal British Legion honoured Harry Blow at their annual meeting in appreciation of his long service to the branch since its foundation in 1931 and his work as branch chairman from 1949 to 1966.

Harry was an active member of numerous committees at national and area level and he said that "there was need for service, particularly when so many famous county regiments were being disbanded."

Grandfather's diary in December 1968 brings this book almost to its close.

December 1st: "Went a walk around the new Wimpey Estate, was not thoroughly impressed. A swarm of countryside is being turned into a morass of bricks and mortar."

December 12th: "Work is proceeding on the lower half of the field at the back [Hilton Close extension]; some sort of building operations."

December 21st: Saw the picture on TV of the launching of the American Moon trip. A marvellous and dramatic sight."

December 24th: Found a note from Sheila telling me that Ann, Peter's wife, had given birth to a son at 12.10am today. Peter called a bit later and confirmed the news. They have given him the name Simon Peter. Great news this." Simon was to have a sister, Julia Ann in November 1971 and it is to the children of her and her husband Arran these books have been dedicated.

December 27th: "Tom and I witnessed the details of the arrival in the Pacific Ocean of the three Astronauts from their journey round the moon. Amazing, inspiring, fulfiling. A deep feeling of marriage to God and man."

I can only hope that it is these final words and thoughts that will penetrate to my grandchildren and not those of military conflict that began my life and look likely to continue when it comes to an end. Mickleover of course is much smaller than the whole, but interestingly reached the hall of fame by becoming the largest suburb in Europe in the 1970s.

CHAPTER SIXTEEN
CONCLUSION
ONWARDS

With the aid of some interesting photographs this chapter helps to define some of the changes after the period of this book.

In 1970 David Milner arrived as the curate at both All Saints and St John's Church and following the departure of Martin Pierce in 1971 he was inducted as vicar in October.

All Saints' PCC sold the site in Limes Avenue which included a cottage and the Church Hall which led to the planning stage of a new centre close to the church. It became a priority when the PCC purchased a strip of land on the Woodlands Hospital site from the Sheffield Regional Hospital Board. A building of temporary construction arrived from Rolls Royce and opened in 1975. It still remains having been given various alterations and time spent on maintenance.

A new Vicarage followed, built nearer the church. The old building was offered for sale in early 1975 as a "most attractive Georgian residence suitable for private occupation" by Richardson and Linnell.

"Alternative planning permission in principle has been granted for erection of 29 aged peoples flats," continued the advertisement.

Photo courtesy of Mrs Pat Crockett
Ground clearance at All Saints grounds in 1974 in readiness for the Church Hall.

Photos courtesy of Colin Haxell
Above: The scaffolding round the old St John's Church and right the ground being prepared for the new church.

A newsworthy event occurred at All Saints' Church in 1989. The Verger, Bill Barker fell, uninjured, into an unknown crypt when a slab covering its entrance broke in two. He called church warden Don Baker, and after investigation the pair discovered numerous coffins belonging to the Newton family, the past owners of the manor. Don reported that the coffins were in good condition with the remains of wreaths on top. In the interests of safety the opening was quickly bricked in.

St John's Church faced more dramatic changes. The decision to close the 12-year-old church was taken by the Reverend David Milner, church warden Arthur Gibson, the Archdeacon of Derby and the diocesan architect and building engineer in June 1976 when it was discovered that parts of the building were in danger of falling down. The hall was thought fit to continue but the process to demolish the church was begun immediately and the present pyramid roofed church was consecrated in December 1978.

The first Mass in Our Lady of Lourdes Catholic Church was on the evening of July 30th 1982 followed by the Mass of Dedication on October 7th. In 2000/2001 members of the Methodist Church held services in the church while their new church was being built. With the exception of the 1956 School Hall, the buildings were demolished and the new Methodist Church was opened in 2001.

Doctor McCahey's wife Kathleen died in 1968 and he had retired before the opening of the Mickleover Medical Centre in Vicarage Road in January 1987. Four partners were initially involved in the Mickleover Medical Centre, Doctor Charlton senior, Doctor Doris, Doctor Charlton junior and Doctor Booth.

Our Lady of Lourdes Catholic Church which was dedicated in 1982.

Photo courtesy of Our Lady of Lourdes Archive

The other medical practice was at 110 Station Road under the guidance of Doctor Denis Harkins from 1948 to 1970. After he retired Doctor Pearson followed and the practice later moved to Cavendish Way in February 1984. Doctor Harkins died in 1975 aged 65 years.

Miss Ann Ellis was appointed Deputy Head at Mickleover County Junior School and some time later received promotion to the headship of Silverhill Primary School in 1971.

Secondary education arrived in September 1975 when Mickleover School, as it was then called, opened in temporary accommodation on Bishop Lonsdale College land. Their new building in Murray Road was opened a year later and this incorporated a Community Centre and a Sports Hall.

General reorganisation saw further building in 1989 and the school was renamed Murray Park Community School taking some children from Mackworth in addition to those at Mickleover. Some Mickleover children still attend John Port School at Etwall.

Brookfield Primary School was the last school to be built and this opened in 1985. The old County Infants' School on the main Uttoxeter Road was closed and eventually converted into Mickleover Community Centre. Vicarage Road School became Mickleover Primary School.

From the end of 1971 British Railways Research Department decided to discontinue the use of the railway line between Derby and Mickleover and concentrate on the test facilities in new buildings on the Mickleover Station site.

Photos courtesy of Dave Coxon

The Station Road bridge photographed by Dave Coxon in 1982. He also took the sign at the Great Northern in 1975. The footbridge, below, was finally removed around 2005.

The cutting and the filling in of the tunnel occurred in 1982 and the test track continued until July 1990. It remained abandoned until the line was converted to a cycle track in 2000 and now forms part of

Photo courtesy of Mark Higginson

The Mickleover end of the tunnel in 1978 before it was buried by tipping.

Photos courtesy of Peggy Goodwin

This photograph was taken by "Jock" Goodwin, landlord at the Masons Arms from the crane that was working on the demolition of the old Vicarage in the summer of 1978. It clearly shows the former school playground, the parade shops with Fine Fare and the development of Hillards supermarket with the constructors cabins on the road verge.

Photos courtesy of Mrs Pat Crockett

Above: The old Vicarage photographed from Vicarage Road.
Left: The Vicarage became dilapidated after the Reverend Crockett and his family moved

Photo courtesy of Derby Museums and Art Gallery L5800

the National Cycle Track network.
Throughout the 1970s the face of Mickleover was changing at a rapid pace. The old Vicarage had been demolished in 1978 and work began later to build the sheltered accommodation at Curzon Court, and this opened in 1980. Ironically it was named after the Reverend Frederick Curzon, a former Vicar and the builder of the Vicarage in 1821. He was a rather colourful character who more than once relied on his mother to pay his gambling debts (see Book One).

Other apartments for the elderly began to be built for both the public and private sector. Devonshire Court replaced the petrol filling station on Devonshire Drive and the coal merchants house and yard in Park Road were demolished with The Dovedales opening in 1986. Derby Borough Council's first venture into building homes for the elderly since the borough extension was Holly Court, west of Vicarage Road.

Work was still in progress at the eastern end of the shopping precinct on Ut-

Photos courtesy of Mrs Pat Crockett
Above: Reverend Ben and Pat Crockett stand in the footings of the new Vicarage. Below the new house is blessed by the Bishop of Derby.

toxeter Road. At the beginning of 1979 Hillards Supermarket (now Tescos) announced their opening on March 13th.

A week later the large crane, used on the building site at the old Vicarage was taken down. House building was now taking place throughout Mickleover.

Grandfather wrote of "the new development below the Nag's Head" in October 1979 and he was "delighted to see the old railway cutting has grown into a really beautiful tree-lined gorge", on October 15th.

A month later Rowditch Furnishers moved into the shop vacated by Fine Fare.

Mickleover by-pass was opened in 1975 and the wedge of land at the southern end of Ladybank Road was developed for Mickleover Court Hotel in the early 1990s.

It appears that 1975 was a very busy year of change for Mickleover. The Burton and Derby Co-op closed their store in The Square, much to the annoyance of my grandfather. There was an attempt to open it as a Radio and TV outlet but this never materialised. They did retain the store in Western Road. Woodford

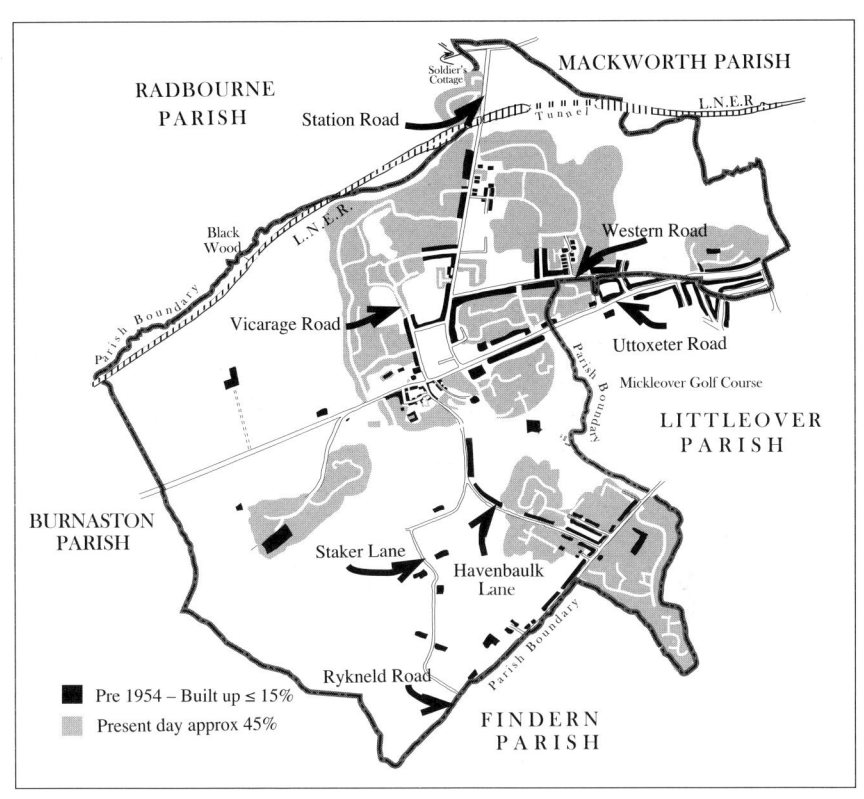

This map of Mickleover Parish gives an artistic impression of building expansion from 1954 to the present date. The parish boundary differs from the postal boundary which many of us are familiar with. This is the reason it was explained at the Huffen Heath Inquiry (see pages 234-235).

Garage took over the Personal Service Garage and later brought the sale of Mazda and Saab to the village.

Doctor McCahey's second wife, Pamela along with the former headmaster of Ravensdale Junior School, David Cooper, were among those heavily involved in securing the future of the old Mickleover Manor House when it was threatened with demolition in 1988.

The authorities of Woodland Hospital took over the site in 1956 but it was now reaching the end of its useful life. The campaign was successful after much hard work and with files reaching eight inches thick, albiet that they had to give way to just over 2 acres for house building. The site was re-developed in 1994 into executive homes on a private estate.

Pastures Hospital closed on December 31st 1993 fifty years after more effective drugs had led to a huge investment to improve the hospital's facilities. The

A final photograph of part of Derby University in Chevin Avenue before its demolition in 2008. It was formerly the Diocesan Training College, described within this book.

government introduced community care which made custodial care unnecessary. Developers moved in and transformed the buildings into luxury apartments. Another piece of Mickleover's history disappeared but we should never forget the dedication of the staff at Pastures who fulfiled a vital role for 142 years.

A final mention must be made of the Mickleover Sports Club. A meeting was held in July 1948 to form Mickleover Old Boys' Sports Club to "organise and encourage football and any other sports for which reasonable demand is made." A year later it was agreed that cricket was included and they combined with Mickleover Cricket Club who once played on a pitch on Asylum Lane (Pastures Hospital).

In 1987 the club embarked on a campaign to develop its own facilities by moving away from the local authority playing fields to a 9-acre site located at the north end of Station Road. The club merged with two local football clubs, Mickleover Sunday FC, and Whitecross Rangers FC to maximize the use of the site and improve fund-raising.

A 28-year lease was agreed and the formal opening was announced on October 9th 1992.

REFERENCES

(Documents held at the Derbyshire County Record Office, Matlock)

Derbyshire County Council (Minute Book): D919/1/1/10; (Education) D919C/1/17/44; (General Purposes Committee) D919C/1/3/4; (Libraries) D919C/1/57/1; (Planning) D919C/1/49/5; (Smallholdings Committee) D919C/1/14/5.

Electoral Registers (Belper Parliamentary Division): 1953, 1954, 1955, 1956.

Mickleover Methodist Account Book (1940-1957): D4137/1/2, D4137/3/2.

Mickleover Parish Church Council Meetings (1923-1966): D3288/14/2-3, D3288/21/1, D3288/22/3-4, D3288/29/1; (Faculty) D3288/8/9.

Mickleover Parish Council Minutes (1957-1961): D4531/2/8.

Mickleover Primary School (1940-1958): D1458/26/1.

Mickleover School Managers: D1458/26/2-3.

Pastures Hospital Land (1918-1967): D5549/6/20/1-2.

Ravensdale Junior School Log Book: D5309.

Repton Rural District Council: (General Purposes Committee) D1272/6/20; (Health & Public Works Committee) D1272/5/18-19-20; (Housing & Town Planning Committee) D1272/6/14-15-16-17-18-19; (Road Safety Committee) D1272/12/1.

Sheffield Regional Hospital Board: D4556/1/6-7-8-9-10-15-17-20.

Sheriff's Tourn Court, Morleston and Litchurch Hundred, 1606-1609: D6386

Derby Local Studies Library have kindly allowed me to refer to Ordnance Survey Maps 1882, 1901, 1914, 1919, 1938, 1957.

Mickleover Parish Church: Church Magazines 1945-1957: On loan from Mrs Pat Crockett.

Mickleover Sports Club Minute Books.

St John's Parish Church PCC: D3332/16/1; (Youth Club Report) D3332/16/1/1-2; St John's Church History: Supplied by Mr Colin Haxell.

The Magic Attic Archive, Swadlincote: *Derbyshire Advertiser 1954-1968; Derby Evening Telegraph 1954-1968, 1975, 1976, 1979, 1980; Repton RDC Valuation List (June 1956)*.

SELECT BIBLIOGRAPHY

20th Century British Political Facts 1900-2000 – David Butler & Gareth Butler 2000.
Churches of Derbyshire (Volume 3) – Dr J C Cox.
Derby, An Illustrated History – Maxwell Craven 1988.
Derbyshire Country House, The: 1 – Maxwell Craven & Michael Stanley 2001
Derby Trams & Buses (Vol 1 & 2) – Alan G Doig & Maxwell Craven
Friargate Line, The – Mark Higginson.
Illustrated History of Derby's Suburbs, The – Maxwell Craven 1996
Mickleover & Littleover a History – Susan Watson 1993.
Mickleover Story, The – H G Ford & A G Ravensdale 1969.
Modern British History, 1900-1999 – Michael Lynch 2000
Portrait of a Village, Mickleover – Margaret Welling 1997.
Story of Mickleover and its Church, The – V H Brix 1948.
Vision – The Mickleover Magazine – Mickleover Station by John Berry (No 58 & 59) 1973.

INDEX

Covering mainly Mickleover residents and major employers.

Italics refer to photographs or illustrations.

Adams, Selwyn *175*.
Aitchison, Lorna 74, *98*.
Aitken, James 245.
Allison (Coun) Archibald S N 200, 251, 255, 261, 264, 268, (panel 276), 294.
Allsop, Garage *210;* Marshall Eric 6, *7;* Rita *iv;* Ted *xi.*
Allsopp, Gillian *xvi, 11;* Roger *xvi;* (Coun) Violet Ida Athel (panel 276).
Appleby, Len 96; Walter 210.
Arnold, Doris (panel 173); 232, 274, 288; Ernest Richard (Dick) xii; Home *195, 280;* Peter xii, *xiv, 11, 59, 135.*
Ashford, Ossie iv, *iv.* 78; Tom iv.
Ashmole, Kenneth J 85.
Ashworth H J Mrs *177.*
Athill, Valerie *xvi, 11.*
Auton, Vivian Mrs 112, 185.
Ayre, (Coun) Charles Ernest iii, 16, (RDC) (panel 27), 87, 105, 200.
Bagguley, John *175.*
Bailey, Fred MBE (RDC clerk) 14, *15,* 19, 26, 27, 32, 37, 55, 57, 61, 63, 74, 106, 109, 191, 200, *200,* Kay *178.*
Baker, Don 315.
Bakewell, Ann 14, *73.*
Baldwin, (Police Constable) 302.
Ball, Deanna *xvi, 11.*
Barber, Reverend, Alan O 176, 226, 264.
Barker, George Henry xiv; Harriet Ann xiv; Harold 14, 143; J *239;* W C (Bill) xiv, 147, 173, 198, *267,* 303, 315; Sons xiv.
Barlow, (Coun) T D *298,* (panel *299*).
Barnes, Birdie 68 (Don & William see teachers/staff).
Baxter, John 243.
Beavis, Francis *59,* 76; George *59,* 76.
Bednall, Nancy *311.*
Beech, Ernie J 24.
Bell, Elsie Ferguson *188.*
Bennet, Terence W 32, *59,* 289.
Bentley, Sgt L G 110, 120.
Berry, R *175.*
Best, Brenda 45, *79* (Jimmy, see teachers).
Beveridge, Peter Bevric (panel 87), 128.
Bew, Bessie Mrs 204, 241.
Bindley, Reverend Reginald Canning 307.
Binyon, (Coun) Douglas Harlock 259, 266, 270, (panel 276).
Bird, David *x.*
Bishop, J *277.*
Blades, Hilda *98.*
Blackham, Richard *xv;* Roger *xv.*
Blakeman, Andrew *175;* Colin 96.
Blackwell, Mick 201.
Bland, Alan (panel 173).
Blood Tony *xiii.*
Blow, Harry 72, 206, 312.
Bonsall, Mavis *11.*
Booth, Doctor 316.

Bowden, Michael *xii, 15,* 59.
Bower, (Coun) Henry Richie 18, (panel 27), 37, 40, (panel 87), *95,* (panel 152), 164, *164,* 167; John Mellor (panel 27), (panel 87), 139.
Bowley, William *98.*
Bradley, A Les 112; Jim *257.*
Bradshaw, Allan 9, 36.
Breese, (Coun) Eleanor Maud (panel 276).
Brice, (Coun & School Manager) Harold W (panel 27), 30, 81, 86.
Brierley, Ann *xvi, 11;* Ron (see teachers).
Brinklow, Jean (panel 173); Ken 252.
Bristow, Robert *207.*
Brocklehurst, Garth *257;* Keith *257.*
Brook, Anne 73, 74.
Broom, T Mrs *309.*
Brown, Anne *207;* Arthur 214; Chris *xvi, 11;* George MP 12, 31, 47, 49, *53,* 170, 173, *175,* 188, 192, 226, 236, 263, *282, 295;* Pauline *11;* Tom M *81,* 219; Sam iv, *iv.*
Buchan, Stuart 243, 268; Mr *289;* Mrs *289.*
Buchanan, Ron *108.*
Bull ?John *xvi.*
Bullars, Alan *x.*
Burns, Pat *xiii.*
Burton ? *xii.*
Bussell, Anna *xvi.*
Butterworth, Derek Frank 101.
Byron, Father Edward 161, 176, 279.
Byworth, Simon 260.
Caborn, Arthur 209; Ingebore 209; Jim iii, *iv, v.*
Carnell, Billy *xiii.*
Carter, Henry 161.
Chambers, Joan *xvi, 11.*
Chapman, Stuart *199.*
Charlton, Doctor Jack 107, 301, 316; Doctor John *160,* 316.
Charnley, Frank 14, *53.*
Chegwidden, Edward & Ruby 68.
Cheshire, W H *174.*
Chesterman, Frank 165, (panel 173), 180, *247.*
Clarke, (Coun) Albert Ellis 128, 133, (panel 152), 239, (panel 276) (panel *299*); Dorothy (née Teagle) *99;* Ernest 77; (Parish & RDC Coun) Sydney Arthur 27, (panel 276), 78, 83, (panel 87), *99,* 105, 125, 128, 131, 139, 148, 149, (panel 152), 153, 167-169, 272, (panel 276), 283.
Clayton, Albert 42.
Craddock Dave *x.*
Clements, G B 149.
Clowes, Peter *160, 277.*
Coe, Walter Harry (panel 87), (panel 152).
Cook, Tim *175.*
Cooper, B *199;* David Anthony 242, 289; Harold *178,* 201; Reg 172; Sam *xi.*
Cottington, Brian *132;* Sheila *x.*
Cottrell, Patricia *x.*
Craig, Alan *88;* Charles 278, *278.*

324

Crockett, Ann 12; Reverend Benjamin *x, xii,* 4, 12, *15,* 27, 31, 42, 44-46, *59,* 67-69, 71, 77, 82, 89, 93, 99, 102, 106, 120, 125, 133, 141, 147, 157, 180, 188, 212, 222, 238, 242, 248, 249, 258, 264, 303, *320;* Elizabeth 12; Fenella *xvi, 11,* 12; Patricia *x,* 12, *59,* 67, *320.*
Crosby, Elaine *311;* (Coun) Harry Burton (panel 87), 97; Linda *311.*
Cunliffe, Donald 96, 187, 188, 196, 224, *224.*
Cunningham, Jonathan *296;* S *277.*
Currey, Charles F 159.
Curtis, Susan *160.*
Curzon, Reverend Frederick 319.
D'Arcy Clark, J D 124.
Daker, Ann *59;* Mrs *59.*
Davies, Bert 101; Glenis *311;* Ron *213.*
Dawson, Ann *175.*
Daykin, Joe 164.
Dickens' 34; John 140; Jennifer (see teachers); Kathleen 140.
Dolby, John *132;* Ken *132;* Edith Mrs *79.*
Dolchini, Christopher 93.
Dommett, Cyril 65; Margaret *98;* Michael *11.*
Doris, Doctor 316.
Dracup Lois *108.*
Driscol, Denis 148.
Dutson, John *11;* (School Manager) Wilf 30, 261, 269.
Eastap, Fred 71; ?Pearl *xvi.*
Ellis, Edward *257.*
Ellison, Chris *175.*
England, C F 235; Ernie 133.
Edwards, Janet *xvi, 11.*
Etches, 34; Charles 37, 38; John 37, 38.
Evans, Joe 168; Victor 246, *247,* 260.
Everitt, (Matron) Lizzie Miss 112.
Fawcett, Donald 65, 84, *98.*
Finney, George *xi.*
Fitch, Fay 53; Henry S 53, *174;* Ursula 53; Barry 53.
Flint, John 21, 87, 146; Nancy 21, 87.
Foley, Nora *311.*
Follows, Ann *xvi, 11.*
Ford, Edna *79, 108;* Hugh *11;* (Coun) Henry Gibson (Tim) 19, 21 (panel 27), 29, 32, 47, *55,* 56, 58, 71, 74, 79, *79,* 80, (panel 87) 125, 143, (panel 152), 234, 285.
Forester, Ann *160.*
Foster(s) 124; Robert 194, 231.
Fowler, Marjorie Iris Miss 185; Ron *79.*
Foxon, N *199.*
Fraser, (Police Constable) 302.
Frost, David *xvi, 11.*
Gardner, Wendy *108.*
Garnett, Norma *175.*
Gascoigne, David 71.
Gibson, Arthur 315.
Giltrap, Neil *175.*
Glen Enid, Mrs 253.
Godkin, Mick *213.*
Goodman, Peter *xii.*
Goodwin, Peggy xviii, (née Langley) 213; Thomas Robert (Jock) 92, *257.*
Goose, R S Mrs 159.

Gordon, (Coun) George Harry, 262, (panel 276), 294; (School Manager) V Mrs, 30, 148, *175,* 210.
Gothard, (Coun) Edward James (panel 27), 29, 83, 86, (panel 87), *95,* 104, 105, 115, *125,* 130, 133, 138, (panel 152), 228, *289.*
Graves, Paul *x.*
Gray, Ernest Nix 116, 117.
Green, Geoffrey 250; J *277;* Michael 52, 53, 84; Nick 250; Stella Mary (née Nichols) 52, 53, 62, 65 (panel 65), 69, *73,* 74, 84, (see also teachers).
Greene (Coun) Roydon *298,* (panel 299), 309.
Greenbury, Eric *59;* Joyce *59.*
Gibbs, William H J *xii.*
Griffen (RDC Coun) Frank Mosely (panel 276).
Grimshaw, Frank *xi, 174.*
Grudgings, Simon *160, 277.*
Gunn, Neil *xvi.*
Guy, Geoff *88;* Ken *ix,* 14, 26, 38, *50,* (panel 65) 71, *73,* 74, 84, *95,* 107, *126, 132,* 196, 224, 268.
Hackett, David *xvi.*
Hall, John Edward 240; Tony *88;* (Coun) William (panel 276).
Hallam, Bessie *133;* Bill *133;* Pam (née Riley) 241; Peter 14, (panel 65), *74,* 84, 111, 241; Rodney *11,* 84; (Coun) William E (Bill) 115, 128, (panel 152).
Hallsworth, Mrs *79.*
Hammond, Peter *xvi.*
Hancock, M *277.*
Handie, Gillian *284.*
Hannah, Alec Eric 50, 85, 148, 245; Gillian *xvi,* 14, *50.*
Hanson, Arthur *34;* Barry *xiii,* 34, *34,* 35, 110, 196, 310; Dorothy 33, 34; Gerald 33, 34, 42, 90.
Harkins, Doctor Denis 301, 316; Michael *x;* Patrick *88.*
Harper, (Coun) M G (panel 152).
Harries, May Irene 25.
Harris, Father Ivan Joseph 102, 113, *126;* Richard *xii.*
Harrison, David *277, 284;* Joyce Miss *178.*
Hartley, Gary *296.*
Hawcroft, (RDC clerk) R V *200,* 205, 274, *298.*
Hayden, (Coun) George (panel 152), 161, 168, 180, 189, 204, 226, 231, 249, 259, 261, *265,* 275, (panel 276), *298.*
Hawksworth, (née Purdy) Elaine 37 *45.*
Hayles, Cecile 12, *172;* Fred 12, *13, 172.*
Haynes, Janet *296.*
Hayton, David *88;* Norman 67, 183.
Hearn, Reverend Albert 308; Stan F 224, *224,* 310.
Heathcote, Rosemary *xvi, 11.*
Hemsworth, Mary 31; (Station Porter/Clerk) Stephen 31.
Henderson, Brian *xii,* 56.
Hickling, J E 295.
Hill, Peter *xiii, 11.*
Hinton, Margaret *xvi, 11;* Robert (Bob) K 184.
Hirst, Harry O 23, 42.
Hoare, David *175.*
Hobson, (Coun) John A *298,* (panel 299), *309.*
Hodgson, Charles *xvi.*
Hodgkinson, Linda *xvi.*
Holden, Arthur Colin *255;* Diane *311;* Gwen *311;* S *277.*
Holland, Brian 246, 276; E A 211, 254.

325

Holloway, A 164; (Coun) Jim 6, 18; (Coun) George (panel 27), 57, 250.
Holmes, Andrea *296;* Margaret Mary, Mrs 260.
Hope, Reverend John 264, 308.
Horner, Horace 225; John *98.*
Horobin, ? iv, *iv.*
Horton, Molly (née Peake) v, vii.
Howard, Tone *175.*
Howarth, Geoffrey (panel 173), 248; (Coun) Marjorie Mary 136, 224, 248, 249, 255, 270, 275, (panel 276), 286; Peter 219, 241, 246, 251, 260, *261,* 289.
Howe, Kennth 114.
Hubble, A N 155.
Hufton, David 125; Mrs 125.
Hughes, Bill *xi.*
Hulland, Graham *xiii, 11.*
Hunt, Philip *257.*
Hurd, S M Mrs 211.
Hutchinson, Colin *175.*
Hutson, Terrance (panel 65), 74, 84.
Jacklin(s), *137,* 162; John 211.
Jackson, David *xiii,* 214; Don *108.*
James, J Mrs 31.
Jeffreys, Annie G Miss 112; Jean *xvi,* Mary *11.*
Jennings, Brian *88.*
Jinks, Kathy *296.*
Johnson, Arthur *xii;* Maurice *132,* 180; Mr & Mrs *79;* Paul *175;* Roy *xvi.*
Jones, Harold *199.*
Judson, ?Philip *11.*
Keiller, James and Son (Dundee) 187, *187,* 188, 196, 201, 205, 224, 229, 310, 311.
Kendall, K (panel 173); (Lyn see teachers); Mr *79.*
Kenderdine, Brian *126, 132;* Edward 31, 32; Peter (Charlie) 67, *126, 132,* 196, 269; R E (Dick) 71, *95,* 122, *126,* 131, 132, *161,* 195.
Key, Father 89.
Kirby, Jim 67.
Kirkham, Gladys 96.
Kitchell, Doris (panel 173); Charles 154, 158, 165, *171,* (panel 173); Johnathan 170; Ruth Miss 253.
Knibbs, Ray (panel 173).
Knight, Robert *207.*
Kniveton, Janice *xvi, 11.*
Lacey, Danny *175.*
Lamb, Charlie *16.*
Land, Jim 67, 69, 77, 147.
Lane, Maxine *11.*
Langley, Charlie xviii, 78, 92, 213, 214, *257;* Mabel xviii, 92; Margaret Ann (Peggy) 92.
Larder, Geoff 240 (Joan see teachers).
Larkin, G L 118, 125, 168, 221, 235.
Lawrence, Susan *207.*
Lax, Ken *199.*
Leach, George 115.
Lee, W G 19, 26, 30.
Lemmon, Edna *xvi,* 14.
Lewis, G Mrs *255.*
Lichfield, Charlie *xi.*
Lindenberg, Gladys Mrs *79.*
Lingard, Sarah 78, 154.

Littlefield, ?Ashley *11.*
Lodge, Linda (née Gibson) 215.
Lowe, C (panel 299).
Mackenzie, (Detective Sergeant) H 92.
Mann, Stephen *277.*
Maps and Plans: xvii, *5,* 13, 26, 28, 61, *85,* 100, 136, 225, 227, 248, 252, 299, 304, 321.
Mark, Colin (panel 65), *73,* 74.
Marshall, Alice (Nurse) 152, *210.*
Martin, Lawrence 96.
Mawby, Eric (panel 173).
Mayhew, J *199.*
McCahey, Doctor Michael 130, 176, 245, 258, 301, 316; Kathleen 130, 176, 245, 258, 316, 321; Pamela 321.
McClaughry, Reverend Victor Thomas 82, 118.
McCutcheon, Ann *108.*
Meddings 124.
Mensah, Ken *213.*
Mellor, J 86, 96.
Melville, Allan *88.*
Mickleover Farms;
   Avenue Farm 26.
   Bonehill 34, 140, 221.
   Brook Field 34, 37, *38,* 311.
   Common Farm 24, 125, 282.
   Holly Bush 123, 169, *309.*
   Huffen Heath (Littleover Parish) 138, 232.
   Ivy Farm 105, 157, 179, *220,* 283.
   Manor Farm 21, 34, 52, 87, 146, 155, 284, *288.*
   Meadows Farm 39.
   Mill Farm 33, 34, *34,* 42, 90, 109, *110, 157,* 196.
   New House 14, 34, 68, 84, 182.
   Rough Heanor 24, 34, 41, 42, *53, 54,* 102, 150.
   Stakerfield 85, 237.
   Staker Flatt 143.
   The Oaks 24.
   Watson's Farm 105-107.
Mickleover Public Houses:
   Great Northern Hotel 59, 77, 94, 197, *317.*
   Masons Arms xvii, 62, 78, 86, 92, 94, 106, 124, 138, 214, 249, *257, 259.*
   Nag's Head Hotel 7, *8,* 12, 19, 28, 33, *59,* 74, 94, 105, 113, 138, 179, 214, 266, 275, 287, 289, 295.
   The Plough 12, *13.*
   The Robin 26, 114, 141, 152.
   The Vine *46,* 94, 214.
Mickleover Schools Teachers/Staff/Administration:
   Adams, Sheila *vii.*
   Allcock, Miss 261.
   Amott, Eric (panel 212), *230,* (panel 285).
   Astill, Chris *306.*
   Backhouse, David *306.*
   Bagguley, Ronald *vii* 37, 39, *79;* Mrs *79.*
   Bailey, Betty (Welfare Assistant) *306.*
   Baker, M J Mrs 152, 161.
   Barker, Iris (Secretary) *306.*
   Barnes, (caretakers) Don 68, 114, 269; William 68, *79,* 114, 131.
   Barton, David W 278, (panel 285).
   Beavis, F D Mrs 221, 269.
   Beckford, Ruth Miss 264, (panel 285), *306.*

Beech, Patricia Miss 71, *79*, (panel 82), 149, 223, *306*.
Best, J W (Jimmy) (Head) xi, 7-9, 45-47, 52, 61-63, 67, 69, *70*, 74, 75, *79*, 80-82, 85, 86, 89, *91*, 103, 112, 120, 127, 136, 145, 148, 151, *151*, *193*, 221, 242, 254, 261, 269, 270, 275, 290, 304, *309*.
Bird, Ann Miss (Welfare Assistant) (panel 252).
Borton, P A Miss 152, 167, 189.
Brayne, P Mrs 176, 286.
Brierley, Emma Mrs 45, 101, 134, 144, 190; Ron *79*, 198, (panel 212), *230*, (panel 285), *306*.
Brown J G Miss 30.
Bunting, Jean Miss 114.
Campbell, (Welfare Assistant) P M Mrs 285.
Cavill, Molly (née Watson), 93, 176, 198.
Charlton, J N xvii.
Coleman, A O 214, 284.
Cooper, David 321.
Cummings, Kathleen Luvia Mrs 189, *192*.
Dicken, Jennifer Miss 221, *230*, 275, (panel 285).
Dunn, Joy *306*.
Dyke, Elma M Mrs 189, 198, 221, *230*, (panel 285), *306*.
Ellis P A (Ann) Miss 52, 63, *70*, *79*, *91*, 121, 135, 136, *151*, *193*, 316.
Ellison, Pat Mrs 144, 190, *192*, 212, 214, (panel 252), (panel 285).
Entwistle, Alan 279.
Evans, H Mrs 198, 286.
Fearn, Audrey M Miss 136, *151*.
Fearnehough, Evelyn Mrs 212, 252, (panel 252), *306*; Harold 212.
Featherstone, Margaret Miss (panel 285), *306*.
Franklin, J Miss 136.
Gaskill, Avis xiv, *79*, *91*; Harry Matthew (Deputy Head) xiii, xiv, 39, 45, 47, 62, *70*, *79*, 81, 82, *88*, 89, *91*, 127, *193*, 242, 270, 284, *284*, 295.
Gibson, Joan Mrs 212, *306*.
Goodman, George Peter Edward 127, 176, 284.
Green Stella Mary (née Nichols) 250, 286 (see also Green).
Hammerton, Carol Mrs 114, *151*, 214.
Hancock, J B (Derbyshire Education Committee) 97.
Harper, Marjorie Mrs 212, (panel 252), (panel 285).
Harris, Hilda *306*.
Hartley, Susan J (Sue) (née Taylor) 136, 152, 223.
Heath-Smith, Roland (Divisional Education Officer) 48, 75, 102, 112, 116, 134, 138, 145, 167, 175, 183, 211, 232, *232*.
Henchliffe, Mrs M E *vii*, (panel 17), *70*, (panel 82), (panel 158), 279.
Hewitt, Thomas iii.
Heywood, C Miss 114.
Hind, Evelyn Mrs 198, 214.
Hobson, P M Mrs 183, 187.
Holwill, Pat *306*.
Jackson E A Mrs 230, 252, (panel 252).
Jacquest, John Walter *vii*; Mrs Mary J *vii*.
Jeffreys, Marilyn *306*.
Jones, L 152, 176.
Kendall, Lyn Mrs 65, *70*, *79*, *91*, 149.
Kennedy, D 278, (panel 285).

King, Mrs 269, (panel 285).
Lacey, D Mrs (clerical assistant), (panel 82).
Larder, Joan Patricia Mrs 190, 230, 264, (panel 285).
Lee, J Mrs (Welfare Assistant) 264.
Longland, Jack (Director of Education, County) 49, 53, 96, 183.
Lowe, Margaret Mrs 93 114.
Maéné, Doris 101 (panel 158), 250, 286.
Malachowska, Danny *306*.
Marriott, Miss (welfare assistant) 254.
Matthews, (Clerical Assistant) E W Mrs. 210 (panel 212).
McSwiggan, Dorothy, 250, 252, (panel 285).
Middleton, C (Director of Education, Derby) 301, 303.
Mogridge, Miss 291.
Morrison, K Mrs (Cook) *177*.
Murfin, N Mrs (Clerical Assistant) 75.
Owen, Avril Mrs (panel 212), *230*.
Parkin, Ken *vii*; Mrs Nancy E (panel 17), *70*, 71, *79*.
Parsons, Gordon 71, *79*, *91*.
Peach, Stan E xvii, (panel 17), 30, *70*, *79*, *91*.
Phillips. C W (Assistant Director of Schools) 97, 329; Sylvia, Mrs (Welfare Assistant) *306*.
Pickering, Jean Mrs 161, *211*, 212, (panel 252), (panel 285), *306*.
Plumpton, Olive Mary Miss *vii*, xvii, (panel 17), 67, 69, *70*, *79*, *91*, 281.
Rainbow C Miss 279.
Rainford (Cook) Mrs (panel 285).
Ratcliff, (Clerical Assistant) Kathleen 212, (panel 252), *306*, 310.
Ratcliffe, Pamela M Miss 52, *70*, *79*, *91*, 93.93.
Ravensdale, Gladys Miss *vii*, (panel 17), *70*, (panel 82), (panel 158), *160*, 221, 223.
Reavley, Jean M Mrs 279.
Richardson, J Miss 152.
Roscoe Joseph Peter (panel 17), 49.
Seabridge, E P Mrs 152, (panel 158), 190.
Shenton, Val Mrs 275.
Simnett, Maggie A Mrs 109, 114, 135, (panel 158), 176.
Simpson, Ken *306*.
Skertchly, Jack P 176, (panel 212), *230*, (panel 285), *306*.
Skinner, Katherine Miss 261, 279.
Skipper, Mrs (panel 285).
Sowter, F Mrs (Cook) *177*.
Stephens, Kathleen Mary Miss (Head) 75, *79*, 81, (panel 82), 144, 150, 166, 183, 198 209, 261, 275, 286.
Swales E A (Trindy) 230, (panel 252), (panel 285), *306*.
Tingay, Heather Mrs 279.
Towers, June Mrs *306*
Turner, Esme 212, 223, (panel 252), (panel 285).
Walker Robert Charles *vii*, viii, ix.
Wall, H Mrs (Cook) (panel 82).
Warner, (Cook) Gertrude E 45, *79*, *177*, 291; Percy George (caretaker) *79*, 114, 261.
Warren, Wilf J (Head) xv, 150, *150*, 151, 154, 157,

158, 165, 176, 187, 189, 196, 198, 204, *211*, (panel 212), 223, *230*, 249, 264, 272-274, 286, 290, 293, *306*, 307.
Wedd, Edith M Miss vi, *vii*, (panel 17), 52, 63, 65, 67, *70, 79, 85, 91,* 93.
Weston, (Deputy Head) Herbert Edward Charles 279, 291.
White, Pat Mrs 134, 144, 274, *306*.
Wibberley, Mabel Miss *vii*, xvii, (panel 17), 36, 37, *70, 79,* (panel 82), 109, (panel 158), 286.
Williams, Mrs *70*.
Wright Mrs 65.
Middleton, Lynne *296*.
Miller, Geoff *199,* Les (Parish Clerk) 18, 22,-26, 37, 53, 55, 58, 63, 64, 83, 86-89, 102, 109, 110, 115, 118, 122, 128, 131, 133, 136, 137, 150, 158, 163, 173, 189, 191, 201, 204, 209, 213, 221, 226, 232, 241, 249, *255,* 265, 268, 270, 279, 293, 294, 298.
Mills, Jim 67, 71, *126, 132, 161, 289;* Pat *289.*
Millward, Janet *11,* N 225, Sid 68, W R 225.
Milner, Reverebd David 314, 315; Ian *60,* 68.
Mitten, Elizabeth *59.*
Morley, Arthur 14, 15, 34, 42, 68, 84, 113, *174,* 308; Arthur (2) 42; Frank 3, Fred, *3;* Joe 3, *3;* John 3, *3;* Nellie 3; Peter *xii;* Richard *xii.*
Mooney, Mary 268; Patrick 268.
Moore, Derek 155, *156,* 157, 172, 182, 191, 198, 267, 277.
Moseley, Chris *xii;* Glyn *xvi, 11;* Mr & Mrs *59.*
Munro, Ian *207.*
Murfin, W *277.*
Nadin, (Parish & RDC Coun) Ernest William iii, (panel 27), 57, 78, 245; (Parish & RDC Coun) (school manager) Joe 12, 16, (panel 27), 30, 57, 62, 81, 106, 148, 154, 161, 177, 179, 221, 228, 239, 245, *245,* 248; Mazie Elizabeth 245; June *xii,* 245; William 245.
Nealy, Jimmy 88.
Nestlé Ltd 32, 53, 59, 60, 70, 85, 90, 96, 111, 113, 118, 119, 148, 154, *185, 187,* (refer to Keiller's).
Newton, Frances Emily Miss 27, Isaac 27.
Nield, (Coun) John Robert (Rob) 221, 248, (panel 276); Mary (née McDowell) 248.
Nixon, Chris xvii, xviii, 9, 37, 45, 63, 67, Jim xvii, 1, 2, 14, 50, (panel 65), *73,* 74, 84, 107, 241; Pat (née Edwards) 241.
Nordemann, Mick xii, *xiii,* 8, 30, *31,* 36, 63.
Northend, P Miss 219.
Nuttall, Gordon *x.*
O'Brien, Dorothy *311;* (Coun) S L A Mrs (panel 299).
Olphin, (Coun) Albert Edward Laurence 261, 275, 276.
Orme, Ken *126;* John 35.
Owen, P *174.*
Page-Johnson Builders Ltd 194, 207, 214, 248, 262, 265, 283, 303.
Parker, Arthur 32, 47, *59,* 71, 72, 242; D *277.*
Parkinson, C H (panel 27).
Parnell, Reg 18,
Parry, Frank *xiii;* Jean *x, 98.*
Pastures Hospital: iii, xvii, 9, 10, 14, 16, *16,* 23, 39, 41, *41,* 42, 53-55, 64, 71, 82, 85, 94, 108, 112, 117, 185,
186, 199, 200, 206, 215, 237, 253, 262, 263, *263,* 270, 273, *273,* 285, 321, 322.
Peake, A H 33; Edwin Charles v, vii, *xi*; Frank vii, *126;* Ken Edwin v,*v,* vi.
Pearson, Doctor 316.
Pendry, Tom (panel 299).
Pepper, Ian *88, 199, 213.*
Perry, Cynthia (panel 65), *73,* 74.
Pether, ? *88.*
Petts, Harry 5, 6, 111.
Phillips, Derek John (Panel 152), 168.
Pierce, Reverend Martin 162, 165, 169, 170, *171, 181,* 191, *202,* 203, *218, 219,* 219, 226, 249, *256,* 278, *280,* 281, 289, 303, 314.
Pickering, Mick *126,* Percy 68, 102, 222, 235.
Platts, Arthur 14, 24, 121, Peter 24.
Poolman, Geoff 165.
Porter, (Coun) Norman (panel 152), 185.
Potter, Donald *108,* John *213.*
Press, Glynis *311.*
Preston-Jones, Alexander 35; Donald 35, 87; Isabelle Mary 35.
Priestley, Alan *199, 213.*
Purcell, Cynthia ('Pat') *xii;* Vi *xii.*
Purdy, David xiii, 63, 82.
Randall, Robert *296.*
Radford, George 71; Lydia Mary 68, 69, 83; Tom iii, 68, 69, 77, 78, 157, 179, *259;* William 157.
Rainford, Cheryl *175.*
Ratcliff, (Coun) Alan William (panel 87), 128, (panel 152), 169, 185, 205, 212, 221, 242, 256, *259,* 265, 270, 276, (panel 276), 287, 297, 298; John x, *59,* 71, 152 184; Peter 212; Reg 131, 149, 184; Trevor 212; William (Bill) 184.
Ravensdale, (Coun. & School Manager) Arthur Granville MBE, OBE, 12, 22, (panel 27), 30, 32, 40, 61, 63, 69, *79,* 81, 83, 86, (panel 87), 98, 116, 125, 128, 130, 134, 138, *140,* 145, 148, 150, (panel 152), 154, 169, 170, 173, 175, 189,190, 196, 197, 209, 212, 213, 226, 227, 228, 232, 233, 239, 245, 246, 248-250, 253, 258, 259, *309,* Florence 10, *10;* Gladys (see teachers); Kathleen 12.
Raynes, John *126.*
Riley, (School Manager) Arthur 30, 69, *79,* 81, 148, 269; Ben *199;* Mick *199, 213;* Mrs *79.*
Roberts, Bob *98.*
Robinson, Audrey *xii;* Frederick 197; Sid *16.*
Rodgers, Alan *x.*
Rogers, Daisy Nellie Mrs 81.
Rodwell, Keith *175.*
Roome, brothers 71,
Rowen, (Coun) David Besley 97, 104, *108,* 115.
Rudkin, Harry 15, 18, *59,* 67, 69, 77, 83, 165, *171,* (panel 173).
Rushbrooke, William Wylie & Sons 78, 162, 256.
Sage, Chris *277.*
Salt, Betty *11,* Margaret 232, 233.
Samuel, David *xvi;* Linda *34.*
Sanders, Jean, Miss (panel 65); John 310.
Saunders, Alan 165.
Schofield, Carolyn *160.*

Seddon, Guy *11*.
Sephton, Amy E G Miss 147, 194, 216, 219, 220.
Severn, Gordon *88*.
Sharp, Eva *iv, v*.
Sharpe, Walter *xi*.
Sharratt, Peter 90; T *199*.
Shaw, Sandra *xvi, 11*; (Police Sergeant) Thomas A 92.
Sherrat, Mrs 67.
Shields, J Mrs 254.
Short, Joan and Marion *160*.
Shotton, May 62, 86, 124.
Shuttlewood, Margaret (née Titterton) 53, *54*, 132; Rob 53, 132.
Simpson, Christine *311*.
Sims, Leslie Arthur 158.
Skinner, Johnathan *160*.
Slack, Laura 87.
Slater, (Police Constable) 302.
Smith(s), A E (panel 299); Alan *126*; Edith 101; Eric *126, 132; 289*; E *174*; Gordon*132*, 268, *289*, (Coun) George Kenneth (panel 152), (panel 276), 280; John (panel 173), (Coun) Joseph Charles 224, 235, (panel 276); Margaret *289*; Nursery 108; P T 28; Tom 101.
Speed, Edward Fitroy 94.
Spencer, Florence *236*, Jane *175*.
Spilsbury, (Coun) Philip Donald George (panel 87), 115, 124, 125, 128, 134, (panel 152), 161, 185.
Staff, Kathy Mrs 235.
Stampfly, Herbert James (Jim) 157, 183, 249, 260; Theo 260.
Starkey, Capt J G 23; Phillip John *126, 132*, 269, 308.
Stenson, H G 211.
Stevens, Ivor 201; (Coun) Laurence Sydney 139, 145, (panel 152), 167; Pamela (panel 65).
Stewart, Heather *175*.
Stiles, Harry *xi*.
Stopard, F Raymond Reverend 89, *95*.
Storer, Cecil 240, *240*.; Joyce *xii*.
Stubbs, C E 80, Edgar *xi*.
Sutton, Julia *x*.
Swindell, Brian *126, 213*.
Tate, George *16*.
Tatford, Pamela *xii*.
Taylor, Alan *16*; Eric *x, xii, 59*, 71; Helen *xvi, 11*; Ken 125, 141, 165, *171*, (panel 173), 180; Paul *16*.
Teat, T G 6.
Thomas, Gruffydd John Wynne 141, 152 165, *171*, 201, 203.
Thomson, Charlie *16*.
Thorley, Steve 165, (panel 173).
Thornhill, Arthur *xi*, Harry 124; Jack *161*; Kath 77, 197; Maurice 77, 197; Sid 228, 243, 258, 269, 277, 285, 287.
Titterton, Hilda 24; Horace 47; Muriel 24; Tom 24, *24*, 26, 34.
Toon, Ernie 144.
Toye R *174*.
Tipper, Arthur 260.
Tomlin, Greg *88*.
Tomlinson, Jennifer *xvi. 11*.
Topsham, Thomas Oswald 115.

Tuck, Kathy *175*.
Tucker, I *277*.
Turner, Barry *xii*; Ernest *xiii*.
Underwood, Susan *175*.
Upton, Walter William 86.
Varey, William (Bill) 123, 124, 169.
Varley, Amanda *207*. Robert 249, 285.
Veveris, Marie Mrs 241; Michael *240*.
Wain, Albert *16*.
Wakelam, Bernard (panel 173).
Walker, Doctor E J vii, viii, ix; Joe *199*; Mrs viii.
Walkerdine, Harold John 59, 60.
Walklate, Alf 36; Lillie 36.
Wall, Brian *xiii*; Frank *xi*.
Walmsley, Janet *175*; Julia *160*.
Walters, Alice *iv*.
Waplington, Arthur 118, *133*, 283.
Ward, Eric *x*, 71.
Wardle, Joyce Miss 152.
Warner, Archie 36; Dave *213*; (Gertrude, see teachers/staff); H J 19, 26, 66, 103, *103*, 148, 161, 179, 182, 189, 193, (see Page-Johnson); (Percy, see teacehrs/staff) Tony 252.
Warren, Chris *175*; Irene xiv.
Watson, Donald 87, 105-107; Florence 87; John 285; Marjorie (Betty) 87; Nancy (née Watson) Flint 87; William Hardy 5, *52*, 87, 109, 146.
Weaver, F 171.
Webster, Graham *xvi, 11*.
Wetton, C F & Sons 283.
Whelan, Janet (panel 65).
Whibley, Mr 96.
White, Andrew 134, 135, 148; Colin, *xii, 15*; Colin F 134, 144, 169, *169*, 200, 204, 205, 213, 224; 231, 233, 235, 261, 274, Mr *59*, Harriet 77, Nicholas 134, Pat (see teachers); Rodney 134, 135, 144, *175*, (Coun) Robert 77; Ray *213*.
Whittingham, (Coun) Thomas Edward (Jim) 21, (panel 27) 51 (panel 87) 105.
Whitworth, "Ginny" 92, Tom 92.
Wibberley, Mr 310.
Wild, Elizabeth 77.
Wilkinson, Albert 71, *95*, *132*, 268; 138; Edmund King *95*, *95*, 144.
Williams, T W 32, 67, 78, *79*; Walter (panel 27).
Williamson of Mickleover 196, 228, *307*.
Willis, Anne *xvi, 11*; Geoffrey *xvi*; Iris 41.
Wilson, John 24; J Mrs *177*; Ken *199, 213*.
Windle, Stephanie *175*.
Winspear, John T 74.
Wood, Harold 239; Judith 312.
Woodlands, Hospital xvii, 53, 60, 84, 314, 321.
Woolley, Ted *iv, iv*.
Wright, Mr & Mrs *79*.
Yates, Mrs *79*; Sandra *xvi*; Thomas Henry 24.
Yeomans (Coun) Anthony Swain 25, (panel 27), 31, (panel 87), 88, 125, 128, 137, (panel 152), 180, 190, 212, (panel 276).
Young, George *xi*; Michael *160*.